Born in Vienna and educated in Darjeeling and Kolkata, Ashis Ray is an award-winning broadcaster and print journalist, who became a test match commentator on cricket on All India Radio at the age of 24. As a member of *BBC's Test Match Special* team, he covered the 1979 and 1983 World Cups, including commentating on the final of the latter event. He has also broadcast ball-by-ball or as a summariser on Doordarshan, the Australian Broadcasting Corporation and the Caribbean Media Corporation. Australia's *Sun-Herald* newspaper hailed him as 'Voice of India'. Trevor Bailey, former England all-rounder and a co-commentator, highlighted his commentaries as being in 'precise classical English'.

Ray has written on cricket for almost every major paper in Britain and India. His 1987 video, 'Great Moments of Indian Cricket: 1932–86' became an international bestseller.

A foreign correspondent in London since 1977, Ray became CNN's first South Asia bureau chief in 1992, before being appointed its consultant editor. He has extensively penned his thoughts on political affairs in British and Indian media, and has occasionally lectured on South Asian matters to students at Oxford University and the London School of Economics.

This is his first book.

ONE-DAY CRICKET
The Indian Challenge

Ashis Ray

HarperCollins *Publishers* India
a joint venture with

New Delhi

First published in India in 2007 by
HarperCollins *Publishers* India
a joint venture with
The India Today Group

Copyright © Ashis Ray 2007

Ashis Ray asserts the moral
right to be identified as the author of this work.

ISBN 13: 97881722 36670
ISBN 10: 81-7223-667-0

HarperCollins *Publishers*
1A Hamilton House, Connaught Place, New Delhi 110001, India
77-85 Fulham Palace Road, London W6 8JB, United Kingdom
Hazelton Lanes, 55 Avenue Road, Suite 2900, Toronto, Ontario M5R 3L2
and 1995 Markham Road, Scarborough, Ontario M1B 5M8, Canada
25 Ryde Road, Pymble, Sydney, NSW 2073, Australia
31 View Road, Glenfield, Auckland 10, New Zealand
10 East 53rd Street, New York NY 10022, USA

Typeset in 11.5/14.5 Weiss
Nikita Overseas Pvt. Ltd.

Printed and bound at
Thomson Press (India) Ltd.

To my parents, Sachis and Roma for their abundant affection.
To my wife, Pritha for a precious partnership.
To my sister, Pia for her steadfast support.
And to my children, Debika and Agnish with plentiful love.

I have known Ashis Ray for many years and have found him outstanding in his work in the media, and I'm sure this book will be interesting and informative, particularly as I was at Lord's in 1963 when the first one-day Final was televised by BBC. I hope the book is a great success.

Richie Benaud

Contents

Foreword

It seems like it was only yesterday that the first limited-overs international cricket match was played in Melbourne. Yet, when you pause to reflect on how the one-day game has rapidly evolved, 5 January 1971 can also appear to be so far away. Coloured clothing, white cricket ball, black sight screens, day-night games are all innovations that have survived from a time when a majority of the current crop of cricketers had not even contemplated playing the game. Why, in the past couple of years alone, we have seen the introduction of Power Play and Super Sub – the latter has been mercifully been done away with now – in a bid to infuse more excitement into an already exciting format.

There's really no harm in trying to make the game more exciting for the public, in order to attract a wider audience. But you want to be careful not to eliminate certain skills from the game. A lot of the time, innovations tend to be lopsided and take out certain skills from the game. You want to add to the excitement, but you don't want the game to become one-sided; you don't want batting sides to score 375–400 runs regularly, taking the bowlers completely out of the picture. Nowadays, one-day cricket is anyway batsman-dominated and you want to be careful not to make it even more weighted in their favour.

Even then, teams have had to evolve constantly, seeking new strategies and challenging their own players by giving them the opportunities to excel in different roles. We have seen some astonishing displays of batsmanship, what with teams chasing large scores with some success. We have also seen bowlers hold their own despite the mayhem unleashed by strokeplayers and we have quietly marvelled at the vast improvement in fielding standards the world over. What's more, the rub-off of limited-overs cricket on Tests is there for all to see.

The World Cup has been an elusive dream for us since India won the prize in 1983. I remember watching that final against the West Indies at home on TV in Bangalore as a 10-year-old. After 1983, people really believed we could be good at cricket, especially the one-day game. This victory did a lot to inspire young kids in India to take to the game. I have pleasant memories of the 1999 World Cup in England despite our failure to make it to the semi-finals. The 2003 campaign was even better, with us going through to the final against Australia after a none-too-happy start. We have worked towards being a competitive side in the 2007 edition in the West Indies.

Mention of the West Indies brings me to what many, including Ashis Ray in this book, reckon to be the turning point in the history of India's limited-overs cricket. For years, we have heard of how the seeds of India's World Cup conquest were laid in Berbice in March 1983 when the team beat the West Indies in a one-day international. For many, this will be a comprehensive account of a landmark game that inspired a dream and a revolution in a nation that has always been extremely passionate about its cricket.

Come to think of it, India may have been somewhat slow to embrace the one-day format, let alone come to terms with it. But there is no doubt that over the past 25 years or so, successive teams have coped quite well. We have had some memorable conquests that have made India's collective adrenaline race quicker. I remember the World Championship of Cricket in 1985 when India was on a roll, some fantastic games in Sharjah, the NatWest Trophy win in England in 2002, our victories in Pakistan in 2004 and 2006, not to speak of the Champions Trophy success in 2002. There have been many books on test cricket; and this one on one-dayers will be a nice companion.

I have known Ashis for some years now and am aware that he can be a wonderful raconteur. This book features the anecdotal style that I like so much. It lends a personal touch that can make a huge difference to the quality of reading. From what I have read of the book, I have liked the manner in which Ashis has articulated his thoughts. It makes for very comfortable reading. I believe you can pick the book up at any time and start reading any chapter. Of course, you could also read it from the start to the finish and enjoy it as much. I am sure readers will find a new perspective to events that unfolded in the past and will welcome this fine addition to their collection of cricket literature.

Besides becoming aware of the rich tapestry of sporting history, I have been able to draw inspiration from some autobiographies. I believe that it gives you a chance to get outside your own head and into someone else's, to see things in a different manner, from a different perspective. It's important for me to be part of a successful team. I am fascinated when I read about great teams, like the Chicago Bulls or Manchester United, to understand what they have, this coming together to do great things. Yes, I have found it very rewarding to spend time with books. And I know when I get down to wholly reading this one, I will enjoy it a great deal.

Rahul Dravid

Preface

One-day cricket is a phenomenon within the compass of my existence. It hit the scene in 1963, when I was 12 and, therefore, old enough to appreciate such a development. It has since, needless to mention, expanded exponentially.

This book is, therefore, largely written from first-hand experience or remembrance; from meticulously following the sport over the 44 years that limited-overs cricket has endured and flourished. Fortunately, I have either been personally present at most events covered in this effort or watched these live on television. This is true of all the World Cups, bar the first – of which I have only seen highlights – as well as every Champions Trophy tournament.

Of course, I had to embark on fairly extensive reference work to either crosscheck facts or refresh my memory. For this I owe a particular debt to several volumes of the *Wisden Cricketers' Almanack* and to a certain extent to Gordon Ross's book *The Gillette Cup*, Ramachandra Guha's *The States of Indian Cricket* and the Association of Cricket Statisticians and Historians, especially Andrew Hignell; otherwise to websites like *www.icc-cricket.com* and *www.cricinfo.com*.

I must also thank my friend from school days and former India left-arm spinner, Dilip Doshi, distinguished cricket writer, Dicky Rutnagur and former Indian captains, Mansur Ali Khan of Pataudi and Srinivasaraghavan Venkataraghavan for clarifying matters. I should mention Chris Dehring of the ICC Cricket World Cup West Indies 2007 Inc., as well, for his useful briefing regarding the next World Cup.

The first chapter traces the roots of one-day cricket, before tackling the first two World Cups in the next. The third chapter is a dissertation on the defining moment for India in their acquisition of self-belief in over-limit cricket, which was a forerunner to their most glorious hour in one-day cricket – the winning of the 1983 World Cup. The 1987, 1992, 1996 and 1999 World Cups are dealt with in a composite chapter: an indifferent phase for India, though successful for two other subcontinental sides (Pakistan and Sri Lanka) and even more so for Australia. The 2003 World Cup, in which India entered the final, is embodied in an independent chapter. Finally, the book examines the preparations and prospects of the 2007 World Cup.

In between, the Champions Trophy and other noteworthy championships are evaluated separately over three chapters. Indeed, one of these touches on the aspect of tobacco companies, once prominent sponsors of one-day cricket, now extinct as backers. In so doing, this focuses on, among other events, the Benson & Hedges 'World Championship of Cricket' held in 1985.

The pattern of presentation has been to narrate every Indian engagement and the semi-finals and final in each competition. This is undertaken in varying detail, with the matches in 1983 recounted more graphically. Scorecards (with the number of balls played by each batsmen – to give a correct reflection of the effectiveness of innings) are also provided for such fixtures, so as to complete the picture. The Rothmans Four-Nation Cup, the AustralAsia Cup and the 2002 NatWest Series final as well as some outstanding one-day internationals (ODIs), irrespective of whether or not India were involved in these, are likewise treated.

I have been attached to cricket since my childhood. But my professional experience and training have increasingly transformed me into a hard-nosed observer, who has encountered the most delicate and sensitive of situations – political, economic, diplomatic, humanitarian – where it has been essential to dispense with emotion and be nothing other than accurate, fair and responsible. Therefore, in celebrating one-day cricket, I have perforce not avoided a critical analysis.

Any criticism, though, is without malice; indeed, sometimes in the framework of respect for an individual or an institution. My disappointment with Sunil Gavaskar's batting in the match against England in the 1975 World Cup is, for example, against the background of my conviction that he is the greatest Indian batsman I have seen. In the last three or four years of his international career, when he applied himself to limited-overs cricket, he was as brilliant and consistent as any – his several Man of the Match awards merely confirming this view. However, his dominance of Indian cricket notwithstanding, he never got an opportunity to captain India in the World Cup.

Similarly, my anguish over the Board of Control for Cricket in India (BCCI) is not aimed at any particular official, but against its structure, which is wholly outdated and lacks professional systems. The world's wealthiest cricketing body – with an annual revenue now running in excess of a quarter of a billion US dollars – needs to be more accountable and efficient, so as to facilitate greater success for Indian cricket.

I was at an Anglican public school – St Paul's, Darjeeling, founded in 1823 – when the Gillette Cup, the first one-day competition, was launched in England. This was also the year – 1963 – that cricket probably made a major impact on me, with the West Indies, led by the inimitable Sir Frank Worrell steam-rolling Ted Dexter's Englishmen 3–1 in a test series.

The international information order still being under the control of British-owned media, West Indians like Garry Sobers, Rohan Kanhai, Conrad Hunte, Basil Butcher, Wesley Hall, Charlie Griffith and Lance Gibbs, not to mention Worrell himself, became household names among close followers of the game anywhere in the world. I was one such, as I assembled with friends in one of the masters', O. A. Gregory's, flat near our dormitory to listen to live running commentary on the England–West Indies tests on the short-wave transmission of BBC's World Service, and then devour reports on each day's play in *The Statesman* of Calcutta (now Kolkata), flown up every day to our Himalayan abode, 7500 feet above sea level.

Thereafter, two of my uncles, Subimal Ghosh and Subroto Ghose, played a part in fostering my interest in cricket in my formative years. My friendship with Raju Mukherji, a classmate at St Xavier's school, Kolkata, who later captained Bengal and East Zone, also helped to formulate my understanding of the game.

Admittedly, the Gillette Cup did not attract my attention as much as Indian cricket or test cricket elsewhere, but it didn't go unnoticed either, as the sports pages of *The Statesman*, once wholly owned by a Kolkata-headquartered British agency house, Andrew Yule and Company, faithfully carried scores and summaries of English county cricket (generally disseminated by the British wire service, Reuters), including, from 1963, round-ups of the Gillette Cup. Also, BBC World Service Sport frequently touched on this tournament in the second half of the summer, when it was generally held.

Another reason for the Gillette Cup entering my consciousness was, perhaps, the fact that Sussex, captained by Dexter won the inaugural tourney. This aristocratic batsman had made an impression on me a year and a half earlier, when he skippered the Marylebone Cricket Club or MCC (as England touring teams were then called) to India. The tourists lost the test series that winter 2–0 – the first time the MCC had been inflicted such a defeat by India – but Dexter, with his driving off the Indian fast-medium bowlers in front of the wicket, had, in particular, aroused awe among spectators.

Besides, it came to be highlighted around the time of the visit that he had married Susan Longfield, the daughter of a former captain of Bengal, Thomas Longfield, under whom the state had the distinction of winning the Ranji Trophy. This, if anything, cemented Dexter's ties with Bengalis. My curiosity about him was also increased by the fact that the charismatic Tiger Pataudi was his teammate at Sussex. Pataudi, incidentally, made his test debut against Dexter's MCC side.

Just as much as the embrace of one-day cricket was an economic necessity, so was, to a certain extent, the unveiling of the World Cup. In both cases, triggering this need was the incompetence and inflexibility of the MCC, then, directly or indirectly, the governors of the game globally. Blind to reality, resistant to change and obstructive to expansion, this organization took the game to the brink of bankruptcy before it was rescued by the appearance of sponsorship and the common denominator of one-day cricket.

For England, switching to a fast-paced existence in the 1960s and 1970s and, consequently, time constraints, the birth of over-limit cricket was at the right place and at the right time. One-day cricket was also an ideal recipe for New Zealand, where the five-day exercise had never really energized a nation obsessed with rugby. But Australia's inseparable entanglement with the abridged format occurred only after strident promotion of it by television tycoon, Kerry Packer's World Series Cricket (WSC). The West Indians, with cavalier cricket in their blood vessels, were always natural takers of this version; while Pakistan, with a majority of their regular test players engaged in county cricket as well as WSC, were also familiar with, and enthusiastic about, the concept. Ironically, India, where the shorter discipline has today become a matter of faith, were virtually the last of the test-playing entities to endorse it. Indeed, this only happened after they, sensationally and surprisingly, won the 1983 Prudential World Cup.

As the only Indian, nay Asian, ball-by-ball commentator on host broadcaster BBC's panel for the 1983 World Cup, it was, perhaps, an enviable experience to describe India's march through the tournament, including the famous victory at Lord's. But I have had mixed feelings ever since about the fallout of this incident on Indian cricket.

In a country rarely accustomed to any significant international sporting success, other than in hockey, India's triumph in 1983 was perceived by the general public as the country becoming world champions in cricket. The BCCI, conveniently, made no effort to correct this misconception; and Indian media, by and large, made little attempt to contradict it either.

Sensing a cash cow, the BCCI, rather damagingly, distanced themselves from test cricket (the supreme level of competition) and poured their efforts into promoting and capitalizing on one-day cricket – a contest loaded in favour of batsmen and an incomplete test of their skill and, otherwise, somewhat unfair to bowlers. But it was perfect for the uninitiated as well as for those lacking the patience for, and/or understanding of, the five-day format.

Indian newspapers and magazines, driven by revenue considerations rather than answerability, joined the bandwagon. Worst of all, the public service broadcaster, Doordarshan, ignorantly and irresponsibly, began treating limited-overs cricket as a sort of listed item instead of according this honour to tests.

The net result was, one-day cricket in India expanded beyond recognition; and with Indian commercial firms, increasingly, inclined to invest colossal sums of money in it, the honey-comb of the game came to nest in India.

Limited-overs cricket, as it has evolved, is generally played on good batting wickets. It's not just partial to batsmen, but effectively an exhibition by wielders of the willow, with bowlers relegated to almost the role of slaves. This skewed scenario, while entertaining to many, vitiates the basic tenets of the game, which its founders envisioned as an even contest between bat and ball.

Mercifully, the International Cricket Council (ICC), which today controls the sport, are not oblivious of the need to review the rules so as to reduce the one-sidedness. The creation of 'power play' or an extended (from 15 to 20 overs) but more flexible existence of overs when restrictions on field placements apply has lent variety and is a move in the right direction. Even greater elasticity in the employment of such tactics can, however, be explored. Also, at least one of the bowlers can perhaps be permitted to send down more than the fixed quota of 10 overs. Such modifications would, I feel, rectify the current imbalance.

I would also love to see a debate on Law 1.2 (Nomination of Players) of the game, which states: 'Each captain shall nominate his players in writing to one of the umpires before the toss. No player may be changed after the nomination without the consent of the opposing captain.' The ICC and the MCC could consider amending this regulation so as to allow the sides losing the toss to make one switch in their eleven. They would, thus, have the option of playing an extra bowler (perhaps a seamer to exploit morning conditions) if they field first or an extra batsmen if they are sent in to bat in adverse circumstances. With so much money at stake, the spin of the coin should, ideally, not be over-influential in any match (and this includes tests). In effect, the change in the law could emerge as a refined version of the failed 'Super Sub' (a player who replaced one in the original eleven in course of a match and enjoyed a right to bat or bowl and not just field, as a 12th man does) experiment.

The situation swings from one extreme to another when bowlers collect easy wickets, especially in the slog overs. Batsmen sometimes attempt ungainly shots, which result in unplanned, unflattering dismissals. The game, thus, becomes a comedy of errors. A fast bowler's prescribed role is to get a batsman out caught close to the wicket, leg before wicket or off a mistimed hook or pull. Yet, in one-day cricket, batters often hole out at long-off or long-on to pacemen. Traditionally, it's been considered a gross insult to an express bowler to be walloped that far. Of course, the quality of modern bats plays a part in despatching the ball to distances previously unimaginable.

On 12 March 2006, Australia and South Africa played an incredible ODI at Johannesburg. But for the fact that it actually occurred, it would have been the stuff of cricketing fiction. Batting first after winning the toss, Australia scored 434 for four in their 50 overs. The match, to any knowledgeable person, was over. But to everyone's amazement, the South Africans reached their target with a ball to spare. This represented a monstrous aggregate of 872 runs in a day. Mike Lewis, one of the Australian bowlers, went for 113 in his 10 overs.

Toss: Australia
Umpires: Aleem Dar (Pak) and BG Jerling
TV Umpire: KH Hurter
Match Referee: BC Broad (Eng)
Men of the Match: HH Gibbs and RT Ponting
Player of the Series: SM Pollock (SA)

Australia innings (50 overs maximum)			R	B
+AC Gilchrist	c Hall	b Telemachus	55	44
SM Katich	c Telemachus	b Ntini	79	90
*RT Ponting	c Dippenaar	b Telemachus	164	105
MEK Hussey	c Ntini	b Hall	81	51
A Symonds	not out		27	13
B Lee	not out		9	7

Extras (lb 4, w 5, nb 10) 19
Total (4 wickets, 50 overs, 234 mins) 434

DNB: DR Martyn, MJ Clarke, NW Bracken, SR Clark, ML Lewis.

FoW: 1-97 (Gilchrist, 15.2 ov), 2-216 (Katich, 30.3 ov),
3-374 (Hussey, 46.1 ov), 4-407 (Ponting, 47.4 ov).

Bowling	O	M	R	W
Ntini	9	0	80	1 (1w)
Hall	10	0	80	1 (2nb)
van der Wath	10	0	76	0 (1nb, 1w)
Telemachus	10	1	87	2 (7nb, 3w)
Smith	4	0	29	0
Kallis	6	0	70	0
Kemp	1	0	8	0

South Africa innings (target: 435 runs from 50 overs)			R	B
*GC Smith	c Hussey	b Clarke	90	55
HH Dippenaar		b Bracken	1	7
HH Gibbs	c Lee	b Symonds	175	111
AB de Villiers	c Clarke	b Bracken	14	20
JH Kallis	c & b Symonds		20	21
+MV Boucher	not out		50	43
JM Kemp	c Martyn	b Bracken	13	17

(contd.)

JJ van der Wath	c Ponting	b Bracken	35	18
R Telemachus	c Hussey	b Bracken	12	6
AJ Hall	c Clarke	b Lee	7	4
M Ntini	not out		1	1

Extras (b 4, lb 8, w 4, nb 4) 20
Total (9 wickets, 49.5 overs, 228 mins) 438

FoW: 1-3 (Dippenaar, 1.2 ov), 2-190 (Smith, 22.1 ov),
3-284 (de Villiers, 30.5 ov), 4-299 (Gibbs, 31.5 ov),
5-327 (Kallis, 37.4 ov), 6-355 (Kemp, 42.1 ov),
7-399 (van der Wath, 46.3 ov), 8-423 (Telemachus, 48.2 ov),
9-433 (Hall, 49.3 ov).

Bowling	*O*	*M*	*R*	*W*
Lee	7.5	0	68	1 (3nb, 1w)
Bracken	10	0	67	5
Clark	6	0	54	0
Lewis	10	0	113	0 (1nb, 1w)
Symonds	9	0	75	2
Clarke	7	0	49	1

Ardent devotees of one-day cricket were bowled over by the feat. Sections of media almost everywhere went overboard in their appreciation of it. Was this the greatest game of cricket or at least the greatest ODI of all time, they asked? I, on the other hand, felt a little disturbed by the development. It was sacrilegious to even contemplate that it was the greatest game of cricket, for this could only be in the realm of test cricket, or in a fair battle between bat and ball on a sporting wicket at the highest level of the sport. As a limited-overs contest, though, it would have to rank as astonishing. In one respect it was possibly unparalleled – a dream batting pitch.

The reason for my disquiet was very simple. Why would anyone aspiring to play cricket – after watching or learning of the mayhem – want to become a bowler? As it is, there is evidence to suggest that, as a result of one-day cricket, youngsters adopt batsmen rather than bowlers as role models. After sensing such a hammering – in addition to imbibing day in and day out that bowlers are only meant to facilitate a hit for batsmen, for this is what a majority of over-limit matches transpire to be – they are likely to be even more dissuaded from rolling their arm over. The net result of such lopsidedness – already prevalent – will be less skilful bowlers as compared to batsmen. As it is, even in tests, the balance since the 1970s has gradually tilted towards batsmen, with provision of covered wickets and better pitch preparation overall.

In contrast, Bangladesh slaying Australia at Cardiff in the NatWest Series in June 2005, one of the greatest upsets in the history of ODIs, was a stimulating reminder of cricket being a game of glorious uncertainties. Mohammad Ashraful's mother is said to have been concerned about her short and slender son taking on the tall and well-built Aussies. But he set the Welsh capital alight with a deft, run-a-ball hundred.

Toss: Australia
Umpires: BF Bowden (NZ) and DR Shepherd
TV Umpire: MR Benson
Match Referee: JJ Crowe (NZ)
Man of the Match: Mohammad Ashraful

Australia innings (50 overs maximum)			R	B
+AC Gilchrist	bw	b Mashrafe Mortaza	0	2
ML Hayden		b Nazmul Hossain	37	50
*RT Ponting	lbw	b Tapash Baisya	1	16
DR Martyn	c Nafees Iqbal	b Tapash Baisya	77	112
MJ Clarke	c Mashrafe Mortaza	b Tapash Baisya	54	84
MEK Hussey	not out		31	21
SM Katich	not out		36	23

Extras (lb 3, w 2, nb 8) 13

Total (5 wickets, 50 overs, 205 mins) 249

DNB: GB Hogg, JN Gillespie, MS Kasprowicz, GD McGrath.

FoW: 1-0 (Gilchrist, 0.2 ov), 2-9 (Ponting, 5.2 ov),
3-57 (Hayden, 15.4 ov), 4-165 (Martyn, 41.4 ov),
5-183 (Clarke, 43.3 ov).

Bowling	O	M	R	W
Mashrafe Mortaza	10	2	33	1 (1w)
Tapash Baisya	10	1	69	3 (8nb)
Nazmul Hossain	10	2	65	1
Mohammad Rafique	0	0	31	0 (1w)
Aftab Ahmed	10	0	48	0

Bangladesh innings (target: 250 runs from 50 overs)			R	B
Javed Omar	c Hayden	b Kasprowicz	19	51
Nafees Iqbal	c Gilchrist	b Gillespie	8	21
Tushar Imran	c Katich	b Hogg	24	35
Mohammad Ashraful	c Hogg	b Gillespie	100	101
*Habibul Bashar	run out (Gillespie)		47	72
Aftab Ahmed	not out		1	13
Mohammad Rafique	not out		9	7

Extras (b 1, lb 11, w 6, nb 4) 22
Total (5 wickets, 49.2 overs, 199 mins) 250

DNB: +Khaled Mashud, Mashrafe Mortaza, Tapash Baisya, Nazmul
Hossain.

FoW: 1-17 (Nafees Iqbal, 7.1 ov), 2-51 (Tushar Imran, 15.4 ov),
3-72 (Javed Omar, 20.5 ov), 4-202 (Habibul Bashar, 43.5 ov),
5-227 (Mohammad Ashraful, 47.1 ov).

Bowling	O	M	R	W
McGrath	10	1	43	0 (2nb)
Gillespie	9.2	1	41	2 (2w)
Kasprowicz	10	0	40	1 (2nb)
Hogg	9	0	52	1 (1w)
Clarke	6	0	38	0 (1w)
Hussey	5	0	24	0

Any limited-overs contest decided in the last over can be deemed to have provided one's money's worth. More so, if it really goes to the wire and is determined off the last ball. A tie is, of course, an even greater thrill.

Of the 2500 odd ODIs staged till date, only a handful fall into the category of sustained suspense. The problem of one-day cricket is, it's only interesting if it's a close contest. A one-sided one-day match is horribly boring.

The Australia–South Africa match at Johannesburg and the Australia–Bangladesh meeting at Cardiff, unless eclipsed, are likely to be recognized from several aspects as the pinnacles of ODIs. Others at that lofty level could be Pakistan versus West Indies in the 1975 World Cup, Kenya versus West Indies in the 1996 World Cup, Australia versus West Indies in the semi-finals of the same World Cup, Australia versus South Africa in the 1999 World Cup and South Africa versus West Indies in the 2002 Champions Trophy; and, perhaps, India versus Pakistan in the AustralAsia Cup at Sharjah in 1985–86 and England versus India in the 2002 NatWest Series final at Lord's. These have all been woven into the canvas of this work in some form.

Such a list, given the sheer volume of ODIs, is, undoubtedly, incomplete, and is, obviously, a subjective selection rather than an objective one. I have taken the liberty of exercising a writer's licence to pick and choose. The rationale has been to extend weight to the criticality of a contest, such as a match in a World Cup or a Champions Trophy, rather than a less crucial tie.

On the credit side, one-day cricket has injected a positive outlook among batsmen and improved fielding immeasurably. Such affirmative tendencies have permeated the arena of tests and – together with the 90-overs-a-day rule – made the five-day game even more absorbing and result-oriented.

I don't pretend to be an historian; and this book does not claim to be a history of one-day cricket. It is an attempt to chronicle the one-day game from the prism of an Indian perspective; bearing in mind that Indians now constitute more avid adherents of the sport than all other cricket-loving nationalities put together.

While the Anglo–Australian tussle over the Ashes is the game's oldest rivalry, this (partly because of the inequitable nature of contests in the 17 years preceding 2006 and the Australians beginning to relish the fight with India more) has been rather overtaken by the antagonism generated by an India–Pakistan clash. An ODI between these two sides, in particular, spawns a competitiveness, which has become one of the most arresting among all sports. When the two teams locked horns in the 2003 World Cup, not just the subcontinent, but many other regions, too, came to a standstill. I have never been enthusiastic about Indo–Pak matches, because a political atmosphere overrides them. But I cannot deny that almost every time the two confront each other, a surge of electric current is transmitted across the cricketing world.

Given the pressures involved in such a stand-off, India have acquitted themselves invincibly in the World Cups. The two have cross swords in every World Cup starting with the one in 1992; yet the Indians have an unblemished record. In their only clash in the Champions Trophy, though, Pakistan beat India at Birmingham in 2004. An Indo–Pak ODI fills the coffers of the BCCI and the Pakistan Cricket Board as no other contest. But the former nearly killed the goose that lays the golden eggs with an overabundance of 17 such matches in 20 months in each other's territories since 2004.

I sympathize with cricket connoisseurs, who suffer in silence as an excess of one-day cricket is stockpiled on them. But this form of the game has not only come to stay, but also contributes huge revenues, which are essential to the survival of the game (including the sustenance of tests) and to providing the relatively handsome remuneration that players receive these days. A further dumbing down, but, perhaps, greater profitability, may be upon us, what with the espousal of a 20: 20 World Cup by the ICC.

My fascination with Richie Benaud began when he led Australia on a tour to India in 1959–60. Since making his acquaintance in the 1980s, I have admired his equanimity yet firmness and the ease with which he straddled the old and the new, conformism and reformation, custom and change, and indeed continued to broadcast for the establishment (BBC) in England, while identifying conspicuously with the Packer revolution in Australia, not to mention the fact that he is probably one of the finest cricketing brains ever. After nearly 60 years as a successful cricketer, captain and broadcaster, he is in the eyes of many 'Mr Cricket'. I am flattered by the words he has so kindly provided for this publication.

Similarly, I have come to appreciate Rahul Dravid as a pre-eminent batsman of his generation, a gentleman and as good at offering an impregnable bat to media as to the meanest bowlers. I am delighted he agreed to write the Foreword. I thank Lokesh Sharma and Jasmeet Kochar for arranging this piece.

Ashish Bagga, the CEO of the *India Today* Group, introduced me to HarperCollins India, who gave me a stiff deadline to complete the writing of this book. I managed to extract 10 weeks in three stages to do so. More time to reflect, rather than rush with the manuscript, would have been comforting. At the same time, had I not been under starter's orders from P. M. Sukumar, chief executive, and K. J. Ravinder, the non-fiction editor, at HarperCollins India, I would probably not have been galvanized to execute what I have envisioned for some time – to encapsulate my thoughts on cricket in the form of a book. Therefore, they deserve kudos for their insistence. I also appreciate Saugata Mukherjee's role in completing the production process of this book.

London, Christmas 2006   **Ashis Ray**

1

The Genesis

JAWAHARLAL NEHRU, INDIA'S ENGLAND-EDUCATED PRIME MINISTER since the country's independence in August 1947, was still in office when the world's first major limited-overs cricket competition – 65 overs a side – was launched in England in 1963. It was called 'The Knockout Cup' in the first year; thereafter the Gillette Cup, following the Gillette Safety Razor Company of the United Kingdom agreeing to underwrite the event – providing counties, in effect, with insurance against bad weather. (A major stumbling block to a one-day tournament had been costs, especially if contests were to be interrupted by the notorious English climate.) It was conceived as a tournament involving the then 17 first-class counties (now 18, with the addition of Durham). Indeed, a trial run had taken place the previous year in the Midlands (so called because it constitutes the midriff of England), in which four of the counties participated.

In the early 1960s – notwithstanding the revitalizing effect of the 1960–61 Australia–West Indies series, which, thrillingly, threw up the first-ever tie in a test match, at Brisbane – cricket in England was somewhat in decline. Attendances at county matches had slumped from nearly two million in 1950 to 700,000 in 1962.

★

A shorter version of the game had, in fact, been mooted a decade-and-a-half earlier. During World War II, the three-day county championship as well as test matches – both suspended – had given way to a flurry of one- or two-day cricket. This prompted some discussion about promoting a one-day knockout tourney between the counties. The innovation of overs being restricted, though, was not integral to such exploration.

Interestingly, the formula had, a little half-heartedly, been tried as far back as in 1873 when the Marylebone Cricket Club (MCC) had examined means of popularizing the county game in an effort to boost finances. In that milieu, the sport was still adrift and far from blossoming into the widespread 'way of life' it evolved into by the end of the nineteenth century. Indeed, the institution of the County Championship was, then, still 17 years away. Fixtures were fitful and often personality-dictated – the latter to cater to public demand. (Remember the folklore of Dr William Gilbert Grace knocking back the stumps after being clean bowled, with the famous remark to the flabbergasted bowler that the crowd had come to see him bat, not to see his opponent bowl?)

Anyhow, the MCC proposed a 'County Championship Cup', a knockout tournament for the leading counties to be played over two days; five of them readily agreed to partake. However, when wider membership of the respective counties was consulted, two of them were forced to withdraw as 'the liberal views of the committee did not meet with general support'. The others – Middlesex, Kent and Sussex – remained; but, rather piqued at the rejection, the MCC declined to redeem their offer of a silver cup for the winners. Indeed, it was only because Sussex had already committed to being in London that any matches were held at all.

To be precise, only one match took place, that between Kent and Sussex. The problem was the pitch. Lord's, home to MCC, at the time, was in the middle of being completely relaid, as the playing surface had become a virtual disgrace. In 1868, a batsman, George Summers, died at the venue after being struck on the head by a ball that had reared off a length.(This tragedy triggered an urgent makeover, which began in 1869 and was finally completed in 1875.) The track selected for the Kent–Sussex match – when this work had barely begun – sadly turned out to be one of the worst.

The state of the wicket – described by *Wisden Cricketers' Almanack* as 'dangerously bad' – soon became obvious and as *The Times* of Britain reported: 'several of the players received ugly blows' from pacemen James Lillywhite and Richard Fillery. The pair sent down 66 four-ball overs unchanged, as Kent were bowled out for a paltry 122.

But Sussex's chuckle soon became a scowl. They were brought down to earth by George Coles, a 22-year-old fast bowler from the Royal Indian Civil Engineering College (which trained engineers for the Indian Public Works Department) at Cooper's Hill in Surrey, making his debut, who repeatedly struck the batsmen, and with Edgar Willsher, who finished his spell with ten successive maidens, bundled out Sussex for an even more humbling 45.

Kent batted again and were dismissed cheaply for a second time by Lillywhite and Fillery bowling without a breather. Sussex eventually needed 153 to win. But they stood no chance as Coles battered the batsmen into submission and Kent won by 52 runs. The match was over by early afternoon of the second day.

Thus, the County Championship Cup was consigned to history before it ever really got underway. None of the counties was particularly keen to continue. MCC wilted under criticism of the playing conditions, incurred losses because of a poor public response and were miffed by the lack of interest on the part of the counties.

As for Coles, the man who had caused the most damage, he only made one more appearance for Kent later that summer, when the team returned to London to take on Surrey; but had little success. He soon left for India where he spent the rest of his life.

Another 90 years were to pass before Lord's could host a top-order knockout match again.

In 1956, the MCC constituted a committee to investigate ways of galvanizing the game. This group recommended a one-day knockout championship. Interest was at first lukewarm; but after the experiment with four counties in 1962, the seed was sown for a more inclusive re-enactment the next summer.

Sussex, under the leadership of Ted Dexter, won the inaugural tournament, beating Worcestershire in the final. It was the first title in the county's 124-year history. The match was held in front of a full house at Lord's. Thus, an event that had begun with trepidation ended as a resounding success. The total prize money awarded that year was £6500. (In 2006, this amount had been raised by the tournament's current sponsors, Cheltenham & Gloucester, to £139,400, with the winners receiving £43,000 and the runners-up £22,000 pounds.)

India's young Nawab Mansur Ali Khan of Pataudi, although a member of the Sussex staff, was not a part of this county's Gillette Cup-winning squad in 1963. Growing up in England, he had captained his Winchester School and Oxford University before joining the southern county, where the illustrious Kumar Shri Ranjitsinhji (in the late nineteenth and early twentieth centuries) and his nephew Kumar Shri Duleepsinhji (in the 1920s and 1930s) had paved the way for other Indians to follow.

In 1961, as a 20-year-old, Pataudi hit centuries in both innings for Oxford at the expense of a formidable Yorkshire attack, which contained, among others, the fiery England fast bowler, Freddie Trueman, then at his prime. But the nawab was involved in a car accident soon after, which irreparably impaired the sight in his right eye (giving him double vision). Though he returned to Oxford and Sussex in 1963 – after making his debut for India against Dexter's MCC side in 1961–62 and then touring the West Indies in 1962 – his appearances for the county were irregular. He, however, captained them in 1966 and featured in their only outing in the Gillette Cup that year against Somerset, in which he top-scored with 42 in a losing cause. 'Tiger', as he was nicknamed by his parents for his style of crawling as a child and as he is generally known to friends, caused a stir in the 1960s by turning professional. British dailies were moved to exclaim: 'A prince plays for money.'

The nawab was the hereditary ruler of the principality of Pataudi (all of 53 square miles), now a part of the state of Haryana, which adjoins the Indian capital, New Delhi. Appointed vice-captain for the 1962 tour of West Indies, he was compelled to take over the captaincy of his country within months of playing his first test when the incumbent, Nari Contractor, had to withdraw after being struck a life-threatening blow on the temple by a Charlie Griffith delivery in the Barbados match. In India, Pataudi initially turned out for Delhi in the Ranji Trophy and, consequently, the North Zone in the Duleep Trophy, but thereafter switched to Hyderabad and the South Zone. He was more at home in his new habitat. The atmosphere of Delhi cricket, one of the worst in India, had been a veritable culture shock for his genteel, Anglicized sensitivities.

Other Indian test cricketers who figured in the Gillette Cup were Farokh Engineer of Bombay (now Mumbai), who played in four finals (1970, 1971, 1972 and 1975) for Lancashire, all of which this county won to implant themselves as the most successful team in this tourney. Engineer's best batting performance was 31 not out in the 1970 final. Bishan Singh Bedi of Delhi turned out for Northamptonshire and was, in fact, conspicuous in their victory over Lancashire in the ultimate stage in 1976, returning figures of three for 52 in 11 overs. Srinivasaraghavan Venkataraghavan of Tamil Nadu rendered service to Derbyshire from 1973 to 1975. But the only Indian to win a Man of the Match award in the pioneering limited-overs competition was Dilip Doshi of Bengal, who, wearing the colours of a minor county, Hertfordshire, in 1976, took four for 23 against Essex to win the game for his side.

In 1964, the previous season's top five minor counties were added to the 17 first-class sides, and the overs were reduced to 60 a side before being decreased further in 1999 to 50, thus making them the same length as one-day internationals. Ireland joined in 1980 and Scotland in 1983, when the number of minor counties was also increased. Holland was incorporated in 1995. In 1981, the Gillette Cup became The NatWest Trophy; and since 2001, it has come to be known as the Cheltenham & Gloucester Trophy. A new company will take over the sponsorship from 2007.

In the 1990s, the tournament began to lose some of its appeal. Where sell-outs were previously taken for granted, these became harder to achieve. A glut of one-day cricket, its saturation coverage on TV and rising ticket prices caused a fall in spectator presence. In 2005, coloured clothing was introduced, and the following year, the event's authors abolished its entirely knockout format to adopt a partially league style, dividing participants into two groups, prior to reaching the decisive phase.

In the first 43 years of the Gillette Cup and its successors, Lancashire with four successes had lifted the trophy more than any other county. This was mainly because of their strength in the first half of the 1970s, when the West Indian, Clive Lloyd, was in cracking form as a batsman. He was, of course, backed by a penetrative attack comprising Peter Lever and Ken Shuttleworth, both of whom played for England.

The first one-day tournament outside England was staged in Australia during the 1969–70 season and was known as the Vehicle & General Knockout. Simultaneously, South Africa launched their version of the Gillette Cup. Then in 1971–72, New Zealand set into motion the Motor Corporation Tournament. In India, the Deodhar Trophy has been organized for the five zonal teams only (that is, not for all first-class players) since 1973–74. This trophy is named after Dinkar Balwant Deodhar, a celebrated first-class cricketer whose 146 in an unofficial test against Arthur Gilligan's MCC at Mumbai in 1926–27 was the first century by an Indian against a touring side. Deodhar, who hailed from Poona (now Pune), was also a respected coach and a college professor of Sanskrit, the ancient language from which many Indian tongues, including India's national language, Hindi, are derived.

Notably, West Indies were the last of the then six test-playing sides to embark on a domestic one-day competition; they got theirs – also known as the Gillette Cup – in 1975–76. Some might argue they didn't need one as most of their players were then contracted by English counties, which gave them enough practice in the art of limited-overs cricket.

2

Before 1983

THE 1975 WORLD CUP

IN 1964, THE IMPERIAL CRICKET CONFERENCE, THE GOVERNING body of the game, renamed themselves the International Cricket Conference (ICC). (This also signalled the opening up of the organization to non-test-playing sides as members, under an 'associate' category. Among the first such members was Ceylon, now Sri Lanka.) As the previous nomenclature suggested, it was an entity born in an age when the sun never set on the British Empire and, therefore, of an imperious mindset. Cricket was treated by the English, especially the MCC, as a private fiefdom, with the president of this club automatically the ICC's ex-officio chairman (a convention that continued until suspended in 1989). No one questioned this practice or, if anyone did, such challenges were promptly shot down. The fact that a great pastime – which the MCC, admittedly, created and must be accorded full credit for this – was stagnating commercially as well as in terms of its popularity, without any imagination on the part of its administrators to enhance its appeal and expand it beyond the shores of a handful of participants, appeared to be of no consequence to people preoccupied with clinging to the past. These Little Englanders with myopic vision had clearly outlived their utility, and were seen by progressive forces to be acting in a manner that protected Anglo–Saxon interests.

In Australia and New Zealand, England had active and dependable allies. They were, after all, nothing but an extension of the Anglo–American conglomerate, owing allegiance to the British Queen and echoing London and Washington's worldview. The façade of the Ashes rivalry between England and Australia rapidly melted in the boardrooms of Lord's, as the duo closed ranks in a spirit of mutual back scratching. In fact, until 2000, both England and Australia had to agree on an ICC decision before this could be executed, which, effectively gave them veto powers over other members. Then, there was a sure bet in the support of the West Indies, who were heavily reliant on England financially, apart from some of their constituents still being actual colonies of the United Kingdom.

In other words, the poor sods from the subcontinent, India and Pakistan, were voiceless. In any case, if one of them raised an issue, the chances were the other – because of the hostility between the two for political reasons – would automatically side with the majority foursome. This was particularly true of Pakistan's policy dictated as it was by military hawks. It was in such an environment that the concept of a World Cup played on over-limit lines was mooted in 1971 at an ICC meeting and approved in 1973. 1975 was chosen as the year of the inaugural tournament, with England as the venue. (Not that this incident had anything to do with the decision, but in December 1971, after nearly a year of high tension between them, India and Pakistan went to war, leading to the liberation of the latter's eastern half by the Indian army and the emergence of Bangladesh.)

When the first one-day summit was held, only those who were representing first-class county teams in England were really accustomed to limited-overs cricket. Was the first football World Cup hosted without any player in any team not being more or less equally familiar with the duration and rules of the contest? Was the hockey World Cup organized likewise? There was a sneaking suspicion that the intelligent English cricket administrator saw an opportunity to obtain an advantage by springing a 'World Cup' – whose branding was bound to capture the imagination of cricket lovers internationally – on sides comparatively uninitiated in the abbreviated format.

For instance, as compared to England, who had chalked up 15 one-day international (ODI) appearances (and their players, countless limited-overs outings domestically since 1963), Australia, West Indies, New Zealand, Pakistan and India had only seven, two, seven, three and two instances, respectively, of familiarity with the ODIs. West Indies and Pakistan were relatively less affected, as most of their players were engaged in English county cricket over the summer, while Australia had their own one-day domestic tournament for six years and New Zealand theirs for four years. India, therefore, were the ones who were really left high and dry, and this plight could, of course, be equally attributed to a lack of alertness and inclination on the part of the Board of Control for Cricket in India (BCCI).

However, over 30 years have elapsed; yet, the apparently carefully laid plan has not borne fruit for England. Even Sri Lanka, only an associate member of the ICC in the first two World Cups, have lifted the trophy, but not the founder-member who probably foresaw easy success!

But the event has grown in stature quadrennially as well as in terms of mass appreciation. It has also, from its humble beginnings, become comparatively, a huge financial success. This upsurge has, of course, taken place largely because of the accident of India winning the World Cup in 1983, and the BCCI riding piggyback on the frenzy for the one-day game that overtook Indians. Limited-overs cricket in general and the World Cup in particular are international monetary marvels today because of the unforeseen but fortuitous shift in the balance of power in world cricket consequent to this outcome. Right of entry into the competition would probably have remained restricted; and the derivation and distribution of greater revenues, unambitious. Before 1983, the commercial success of the Olympics, football, golf and tennis had, in fact, eluded cricket because of the stubbornness of the game's controllers.

★

In the 1975 World Cup, sponsored by Prudential Assurance, the eight invited sides were split into two equal bunches, with each team pitted against the other three on a league basis. In Group A were England, New Zealand, India and East Africa; the stronger Group B was comprised of West Indies, Australia, Pakistan and Sri Lanka. The top two on points in each cluster would qualify for the semi-finals, with the champions of one clashing with the runners-up of the other. It envisaged 15 matches with each side restricted to 60 overs.

Grey clouds had, by this stage, gathered over the Indian political scene; the country was smouldering. Jayaprakash Narayan, a contemporary of Jawaharlal Nehru, had, since 1974, spearheaded a campaign of civil disobedience against the Central Government, which now had the latter's daughter, Indira Gandhi, as prime minister. By June 1975, this movement had reached a crescendo.

Against such a backdrop, Srinivasaraghavan Venkataraghavan (almost universally abridged to 'Venkat'). The elevation of this Tamil Brahmin (or an upper caste Hindu), was prompted by a vacuum created by the premature retirement of Ajit Wadekar, and by Tiger Pataudi revealing himself to be over the hill. The former received a rather rumbustious reception in Mumbai upon India being whitewashed in a three-test series in England in 1974, which provoked his hasty departure. As for Pataudi, then 34, he had virtually ruled himself out by struggling as a batsman against the pace of Andy Roberts in the 1974–75 home season. Venkat, the off-spinner from the southern Indian state of Tamil Nadu, who made his test debut in 1965, was among the senior players still available and suitable for selection. He was credited with a fairly sharp cricketing brain – being his state's skipper – but also reputed to have an impatient streak.

Bishan Singh Bedi, a Sikh, who migrated from the northern state of Punjab to Delhi and who became captain of his country in 1976, could have been in the reckoning. Indeed, this left-arm spin bowler was a more regular member of the test eleven than Venkat. The latter, despite being a high-quality performer, was often sidelined because of his competition for a place in the side with another off-spinner, Erapalli Prasanna, from Mysore (later Karnataka) state, who fainly spun the ball like a top, with masterly control over flight and variation. But Bedi, reportedly, behaved rebelliously during the 1974 tour to England, which probably postponed his promotion. Venkat, on the other hand, was uncontroversial, a better batsman than either Bedi or Prasanna, an excellent fieldsman and had some experience of limited-overs cricket as a result of playing for Derbyshire. Besides, he had an influential southern Indian lobby, led by industrialist and BCCI heavyweight, M. A. Chidambaram, to endorse his candidature.

7 June: Lord's, London

India's unpreparedness was soon confirmed. On the opening day of the competition at the Mecca of world cricket, they collided against England, as if bumping into a brick wall in a dark corridor.

With Dennis Amiss, a technically correct opening batsman but not noted for flair in strokeplay, in exceptional form and Keith Fletcher, too, in excellent touch, England amassed a record total for a 60-over ODI. The pipe-smoking Warwickshire opener, later this county's chief executive, powered to 137, with 18 fours and put on 176 for the second wicket with the Essex man. To rub salt into the wound, Yorkshire fast bowler, Chris Old, also enjoyed a salad day, helping himself to 51 off a mere 30 balls. England's score was – for that era – a staggering 334 for four.

India – or more precisely, Sunil Gavaskar – made no effort to respond in the spirit of one-day cricket, let alone pick up the gauntlet. Indeed the Bombay batsman batted out the entire 60 overs as if entrusted to save a test match, remaining not out on 36. And India, in course of their innings, procured a pathetic 132 for three. As the *Wisden Cricketers' Almanack* succinctly put it, Gavaskar 'sat on the splice' throughout the innings.

Both the Indian manager, Gulabai Ramchand, and Venkat (the only Indian bowler, incidentally, who conceded less than 50 runs in the allotted 12 overs per bowler) criticized Gavaskar for his cynicism. But no action was ever taken by the BCCI against him. Many years later – after Gavaskar had retired – Raj Singh, a stakeholder in the Indian princely state of Dungarpur, in Rajasthan, former chairman of Indian selectors, president of the BCCI and, most honourably, a distinguished president of the Cricket Club of India (India's MCC), which he has made more magnificent under his leadership, raised this issue in the middle of a public spat with the Mumbai legend. The truth is he and his colleagues in the BCCI had remained silent when the outrageous display actually occurred.

Gavaskar, in his defence, argued, since there was no possibility of India surpassing England's compilation, he used the opportunity to obtain some batting practice! On hindsight, I am sure he regrets his attitude that day. But then, his training was to secure matches first, before trying to win them — which he did with the historical valour and heroism of the Marathas (of whom he was one)on innumerable occasions in tests. The win-or-lose circumstance of the one-day scenario was alien to his nature.

India, incidentally, excluded Bedi from their eleven. This omission raised a few eyebrows, since the spinner had indulged in a fair amount of over-limit stuff for Northamptonshire, where he was contracted for six years from 1972. Instead, the Indians plumped for five medium pacers, all of whom could bat in varying degrees — Madan Lal Sharma, Mohinder Amarnath, Syed Abid Ali, Karsen Ghavri and Eknath Solkar. Venkat, too, pushed his off-breaks through faster than usual. Tilting towards seam in the first half of an English summer was correct thinking. But none of the quicker bowlers possessed much quality and were, predictably, treated with disdain by the English batsmen.

Toss: England
Umpires: DJ Constant and JG Langridge
ODI Debuts: M Amarnath, AD Gaekwad, KD Ghavri (Ind).
Man of the Match: DL Amiss

England innings			R	B
JA Jameson	c Venkataraghavan	b Amarnath	21	42
DL Amiss		b Madan Lal	137	147
KWR Fletcher		b Abid Ali	68	107
AW Greig	lbw	b Abid Ali	4	8
*MH Denness	not out		37	31
CM.Old	not out		51	30

Extras: (lb 12, w 2, nb 2) 16
Total: (4 wickets, 60 overs) 334

DNB: B Wood, +APE Knott, JA Snow, P Lever, GG Arnold.
FoW: 1-54 (Jameson), 2-230 (Fletcher), 3-237 (Greig), 4-245 (Amiss).

Bowling	O	M	R	W
Madan Lal	12	1	64	1
Amarnath	12	2	60	1
Abid Ali	12	0	58	2
Ghavri	11	1	83	0
Venkataraghavan	12	0	41	0
Solkar	1	0	12	0

India innings (target: 335 runs from 60 overs)			R	B
SM Gavaskar	not out		36	174
ED Solkar	c Lever	b Arnold	8	34
AD Gaekwad	c Knott	b Lever	22	46
GR Viswanath	c Fletcher	b Old	37	59
BP Patel	not out		16	57

Extras: (lb 3, w 1, nb 9) 13
Total: (3 wickets, 60 overs) 132

DNB: M Amarnath, +FM Engineer, S Abid Ali, Madan Lal,
† S Venkataraghavan, KD Ghavri.
FoW: 1-21 (Solkar), 2-50 (Gaekwad), 3-108 (Viswanath).

* Captain; † wicketkeeper.

Bowling	O	M	R	W
Snow	12	2	24	0
Arnold	10	2	20	1
Old	12	4	26	1
Greig	9	1	26	0
Wood	5	2	4	0
Lever	10	0	16	1
Jameson	2	1	3	0

11 June: Headingley, Leeds

After being slaughtered by England, India breathed a sigh of relief at being squared off against part-timers from East Africa, whose players were mostly of subcontinental origin. There was, however, an Englishman in Donald Pringle, father of Derek Pringle, who played for England principally as a medium pacer but was also a decent lower order batsman and is now cricket correspondent of *The Daily Telegraph* of the UK.

Not unexpectedly, India flourished against such modest opposition. The East Africans won the toss and batted first. There was no venom in the pitch, but they lacked the wherewithal to combat good line and length. India, on their part, fielded well. East Africa scored just 36 runs in their first 22 overs and could eventually muster a total of only 120. Indeed, it was a scramble for the ball between the bowlers, as Bedi, returning to the fold with a vengeance, posted figures of 12-8-6-1. Jawahir Shah, though, stood valiantly on the burning deck with an attacking 37, resplendent with cover drives, before he was bowled by Amarnath.

Farokh Engineer, too, was back in the side after missing the first outing due to injury. A batsman-wicketkeeper for Lancashire and, therefore, vastly seasoned in the shorter version of the game, he quite naturally slipped into this role for his country. He (with seven fours) and Gavaskar (with nine) duly reached the team's target in the 30th over without any mishap. Frasat Ali, who opened the batting and bowling for East Africa, exhibited an accurate opening spell for his team, but Pringle, who shared the new ball with him, proved to be expensive and was taken off after only three overs. Tragically, he died in a car accident when only 43.

Toss: East Africa
Umpires: HD Bird and A Jepson
ODI Debuts: PS Mehta, DJ Pringle, Yunus Badat (EA).
Man of the Match: FM Engineer

East Africa innings (60 overs maximum)			*R*	*B*
Frasat Ali		b Abid Ali	12	36
S Walusimbi	lbw	b Abid Ali	16	50
+PS Mehta	run out		12	41
Yunus Badat		b Bedi	1	4
Jawahir Shah		b Amarnath	37	84
*Harilal Shah	c Engineer	b Amarnath	0	2
RK Sethi	c Gaekwad	b Madan Lal	23	80
Mehmood Quaraishy		run out	6	25
Zulfiqar Ali	not out		2	5
PG Nana	lbw	b Madan Lal	0	2
DJ Pringle		b Madan Lal	2	3

Extras: (lb 8, nb 1) 9
Total: (all out, 55.3 overs) 120

FoW: 1-26 (Frasat Ali), 2-36 (Walusimbi), 3-37 (Yunus Badat), 4-56 (Mehta), 5-56 (Harilal Shah), 6-98 (Jawahir Shah), 7-116 (Sethi), 8-116 (Mehmood Quaraishy), 9-116 (Nana), 10-120 (Pringle).

Bowling	*O*	*M*	*R*	*W*
Abid Ali	12	5	22	2
Madan Lal	9.3	2	15	3
Bedi	12	8	6	1
Venkataraghavan	12	4	29	0
Amarnath	10	0	39	2

India innings (target: 121 runs from 60 overs)		R	B
SM Gavaskar	not out	65	86
+FM Engineer	not out	54	93

Extras: (b 4) 4
Total: (0 wickets, 29.5 overs) 123

DNB: AD Gaekwad, GR Viswanath, BP Patel, ED Solkar, S Abid Ali,
S Madan Lal, M Amarnath, *S Venkataraghavan, BS Bedi.

Bowling	O	M	R	W
Frasat Ali	6	1	17	0
Pringle	3	0	14	0
Zulfiqar Ali	11	3	32	0
Nana	4.5	0	36	0
Sethi	5	0	20	0

Meanwhile...

England built on their overwhelming win over India by eclipsing East
Africa by 181 runs and then New Zealand by 80 runs. They, therefore,
comfortably occupied the foremost position in their group.

14 June: Old Trafford, Manchester

This was the make-or-break match, with the winners qualifying for
the semi-finals. India won the toss on a palatable pitch. However,
Gavaskar, who notched a notable test hundred on the same ground
a year earlier, failed to ignite, caught as he was by Richard Hadlee
off elder brother Dayle Hadlee, who proved to be the pick of the
New Zealand bowlers. Engineer set off with characteristic briskness,
but was trapped leg before wicket by Richard, later to emerge as
one of the greatest fast bowlers of all time.

Although Anshuman Gaekwad produced a useful 37, India
fragmented to 101 for six, before Abid Ali, an all-purpose man from
the southern Indian city of Hyderabad, with a doughty innings of
70 at number seven, restored respectability. This effort included a
six and five fours. Madan Lal provided some support to Abid, as did
Venkat, who remained not out on 26 as India finished with a
reasonably defendable total.

Man to man, India were not inferior to the Kiwis even on the alien stage of one-day cricket. But the person who made the difference was Glen Turner. A batsman in the Gavaskar mould, he was by no means a natural in the one-day realm. Yet, his long stint with Worcestershire had honed his skills for limited-overs requirements. His undefeated 114 off 177 balls, with 13 boundaries, essentially settled the issue for the New Zealanders.

India chipped away at the other end. Abid Ali, a Muslim educated in a Christian school, whose nephew, Mohammed Azharuddin, was to later captain India, capped his batting display with an impressive bowling stint. And Bedi was again economical. New Zealand were at one point 70 for three. But with Turner, unruffled and collecting runs crisply, they cruised home by four wickets with seven balls to spare. India, thus, made an early exit from the first World Cup.

Toss: India
Umpires: WL Budd and AE Fagg
Man of the Match: GM Turner

India innings (60 overs maximum)			R	B
SM Gavaskar	c RJ Hadlee	b DR Hadlee	12	14
+FM Engineer	lbw	b RJ Hadlee	24	36
AD Gaekwad	c Hastings	b RJ Hadlee	37	51
GR Viswanath	lbw	b McKechnie	2	9
BP Patel	c Wadsworth	b HJ Howarth	9	32
ED Solkar	c Wadsworth	b HJ Howarth	13	10
S Abid Ali	c HJ Howarth	b McKechnie	70	98
S Madan Lal	c & b McKechnie		20	44
M Amarnath	c Morrison	b DR Hadlee	1	3
*S Venkataraghavan	not out		26	58
BS Bedi	run out		6	10

Extras (b 5, w 1, nb 4) 10
Total: (all out, 60 overs) 230
FoW: 1-17 (Gavaskar), 2-48 (Engineer), 3-59 (Viswanath),
4-81 (Gaekwad), 5-94 (Solkar), 6-101 (Patel),
7-156 (Madan Lal), 8-157 (Amarnath), 9-217 (Abid Ali),
10-230 (Bedi).

Bowling	O	M	R	W
Collinge	12	2	43	0
RJ Hadlee	12	2	48	2
DR Hadlee	12	3	32	2
McKechnie	12	1	49	3
HJ Howarth	12	0	48	2

New Zealand innings (target: 231 runs from 60 overs)			R	B
*GM Turner	not out		114	177
JFM Morrison	c Engineer	b Bedi	17	34
GP Howarth	run out		9	13
JM Parker	lbw	b Abid Ali	1	6
BF Hastings	c Solkar	b Amarnath	34	49
+KJ Wadsworth	lbw	b Madan Lal	22	38
RJ Hadlee		b Abid Ali	15	30
DR Hadlee	not out		8	7

Extras: (b 8, lb 5) 13
Total: (6 wickets, 58.5 overs) 233

DNB: BJ McKechnie, HJ Howarth, RO Collinge.

FoW: 1-45 (Morrison), 2-62 (GP Howarth), 3-70 (Parker), 4-135 (Hastings), 5-185 (Wadsworth), 6-224 (RJ Hadlee).

Bowling	O	M	R	W
Madan Lal	11.5	1	62	1
Amarnath	8	1	40	1
Bedi	12	6	28	1
Abid Ali	12	2	35	2
Venkataraghavan	12	0	39	0
Solkar	3	0	16	0

Elsewhere...

It was a resurgent West Indies after their travails in the late 1960s and early 1970s. This revival was first felt in India, with the flowering of Andy Roberts, Gordon Greenidge and Vivian Richards, in addition to the endurance of Clive Lloyd and Alvin Kalicharran. Now, they stamped their authority by defeating Sri Lanka by nine wickets and Australia by seven wickets, but were lucky to get the better of Pakistan, the winning run being scored off the fourth ball of the last over – in what's looked upon as one of the great ODIs. This riveting encounter hung in the balance until the very end, and the West Indies could not have been confident when their eighth wicket fell on 166 and their ninth at 203. But amazingly, the last pair of Deryck Murray and Andy Roberts, who came together in the 46th over, scored the necessary 64 runs for victory. The Pakistani batsmen followed Majid Khan's example, punishing anything not on a length and going boldly for their strokes. But Mushtaq Mohammad and Wasim Raja, who prematurely passed away in August 2006, were unfortunate to playon when both threatened to dominate the bowling. The West Indies batsmen showed almost indecent haste and, with the exception of Lloyd and Murray, lacked the patience to build a major innings. Murray's brand of discipline and the courage of Roberts eventually carried them through.

Toss: Pakistan
Umpires: DJ Constant and JG Langridge
ODI Debuts: CG Greenidge (WI); Javed Miandad, Pervez Mir (Pak).
Man of the Match: Sarfraz Nawaz

Pakistan innings (60 overs maximum)			R	B
*Majid Khan	c Murray	b Lloyd	60	108
Sadiq Mohammad	c Kanhai	b Julien	7	23
Zaheer Abbas	lbw	b Richards	31	56
Mushtaq Mohammad		b Boyce	55	84
Wasim Raja		b Roberts	58	57
Javed Miandad	run out		24	32
Pervez Mir	run out		4	9
+Wasim Bari	not out		1	1
Sarfraz Nawaz	not out		0	0

Extras: (b 1, lb 15, w 4, nb 6) 26
Total: (7 wickets, 60 overs) 266

DNB: Asif Masood, Naseer Malik.

FoW: 1-21 (Sadiq Mohammad), 2-83 (Zaheer Abbas),
3-140 (Majid Khan), 4-202 (Mushtaq Mohammad),
5-249 (Wasim Raja), 6-263 (Pervez Mir),
7-265 (Javed Miandad).

Bowling	O	M	R	W
Roberts	12	1	47	1
Boyce	12	2	44	1
Julien	12	1	41	1
Holder	12	3	56	0
Richards	4	0	21	1
Lloyd	8	1	31	1

West Indies innings (target: 267 runs from 60 overs)			R	B
RC Fredericks	lbw	b Sarfraz Nawaz	12	11
CG Greenidge	c Wasim Bari	b Sarfraz Nawaz	4	6
AI Kallicharran	c Wasim Bari	b Sarfraz Nawaz	16	25
RB Kanhai		b Naseer Malik	24	42
*CH Lloyd	c Wasim Bari	b Javed Miandad	53	58
IVA Richards	c Zaheer Abbas	b Pervez Mir	13	23
BD Julien	c Javed Miandad	b Asif Masood	18	40
+DL Murray	not out		61	76
KD Boyce		b Naseer Malik	7	6
VA Holder	c Pervez Mir	b Sarfraz Nawaz	16	28
AME Roberts	not out		24	48

Extras: (lb 10, w 1, nb 8) 19
Total: (9 wickets, 59.4 overs) 267

FoW: 1-6 (Greenidge), 2-31 (Fredericks), 3-36 (Kallicharran),
4-84 (Kanhai), 5-99 (Richards), 6-145 (Julien),
7-151 (Lloyd), 8-166 (Boyce), 9-203 (Holder).

Bowling	O	M	R	W
Asif Masood	12	1	64	1
Sarfraz Nawaz	12	1	44	4
Naseer Malik	12	2	42	2
Pervez Mir	9	1	42	1
Javed Miandad	12	0	46	1
Mushtaq Mohammad	2	0	7	0
Wasim Raja	0.4	0	3	0

On the basis of this win, the West Indies headed their group, with the Aussies securing second place after beating Pakistan and Sri Lanka by 73 runs and 52 runs, respectively.

Semi-final, 18 June: Headingley, Leeds

If it was sunny at the headquarters of Yorkshire County Cricket Club, it was generally heavenly for batting. But once an overcast sky enveloped the industrial pollution that hung in the air, conditions became beastly for batsmen. Apart from aiding movement in the air, such an environment assisted a greening of the pitch, converting it into a quicker bowler's paradise. Sometimes an uneven bounce made life more miserable for batsmen.

The wicket was the same as the one used for the Australia–Pakistan game, in which 483 runs were scored. But 10 days later, it looked grassy and the players complained it was also damp.

Australia won the toss and unhesitatingly inserted England. Indeed, the Aussies ran rather than walked to change ends (much in the style of today's 20:20 cricket) to get through as many overs as possible before the wicket dried out. England were soon 37 for seven and then 93 all out in 36.2 overs. Gary Gilmour, left-arm fast medium, tore through the English line-up. Bowling a good length, he swung and cut the ball disconcertingly in the heavy atmosphere. Four of his victims were trapped leg before wicket to incoming deliveries, including Amiss and Fletcher, while Tony Greig was caught behind. Bowling unchanged for his 12 overs, he finished with quite sensational figures of six for 14. Captain Mike Denness and the tail staged a slight rally from 52 for eight; otherwise, it would have been worse.

But there was excitement yet in the encounter. At first, there was relative calm as the Australian openers resisted inroads by the England new ball operators for the first seven overs. But Geoff Arnold, John Snow and Chris Old – all adept at swinging and seaming the ball – performed predictably. The conditions were less challenging for batsmen than in the morning. Yet the trio had the Australians tottering on 39 for six. At this stage, though, Gilmour joined Doug Walters and this pair ensured England made no further headway. They added 55 and the Aussies won quite comfortably by four wickets, with 31 overs to spare.

Recrimination followed, as both sides castigated the strip, particularly England. Such reactions even raised questions about Headlingley's suitability as an international venue.

Toss: Australia
Umpires: WE Alley and DJ Constant
Man of the Match: GJ Gilmour

England innings (60 overs maximum)			*R*	*B*
DL Amiss	lbw	b Gilmour	2	11
B Wood		b Gilmour	6	19
KWR Fletcher	lbw	b Gilmour	8	45
AW Greig	c Marsh	b Gilmour	7	25
FC Hayes	lbw	b Gilmour	4	6
*MH Denness		b Walker	27	60
+APE Knott	lbw	b Gilmour	0	5
CM Old	c GS Chappell	b Walker	0	3
JA Snow	c Marsh	b Lillee	2	14
GG Arnold	not out		18	30
P Lever	lbw	b Walker	5	13

Extras: (lb 5, w 7, nb 2) 14
Total: (all out, 36.2 overs) 93

FoW: 1-2 (Amiss), 2-11 (Wood), 3-26 (Greig), 4-33 (Hayes),
5-35 (Fletcher), 6-36 (Knott), 7-37 (Old), 8-52 (Snow),
9-73 (Denness), 10-93 (Lever).

Bowling	O	M	R	W
Lillee	9	3	26	1
Gilmour	12	6	14	6
Walker	9.2	3	22	3
Thomson	6	0	17	0

Australia innings (target: 94 runs from 60 overs)			R	B
A Turner	lbw	b Arnold	7	20
RB McCosker		b Old	15	50
*IM Chappell	lbw	b Snow	2	19
GS Chappell	lbw	b Snow	4	9
KD Walters	not out		20	43
R Edwards		b Old	0	3
+RW Marsh		b Old	5	8
GJ Gilmour	not out		28	28

Extras: (b 1, lb 6, nb 6) 13
Total: (6 wickets, 28.4 overs) 94

DNB: MHN Walker, DK Lillee, JR Thomson.

FoW: 1-17 (Turner), 2-24 (IM Chappell), 3-32 (GS Chappell),
4-32 (McCosker), 5-32 (Edwards), 6-39 (Marsh).

Bowling	O	M	R	W
Arnold	7.4	2	15	1
Snow	12	0	30	2
Old	7	2	29	3
Lever	2	0	7	0

Semi-final, 18 June: The Oval, London

Two hundred miles south of Leeds, the West Indies took on New
Zealand in the last four. Possessing an all-pace attack, it was no
surprise the former's captain Clive Lloyd invited the opposition to

bat. Thus, New Zealand took first strike and initially fared quite well against some sustained hostility. Their run rate of around three an over was sluggish, but they, adequately advanced to 98 for one. Geoff Howarth pushed the score along as best he could, playing some delightful shots en route to a well-deserved 50. But Turner, on whom New Zealand banked heavily after his two centuries in the championship, rather essentially failed to cut loose, his technical competence notwithstanding. With his departure and then Howarth's in the following over – both dismissed by Andy Roberts – the Kiwis were disembodied like a pack of cards.

Left-arm fast-medium exponent, Bernard Julien, swung the ball both ways to return four for 27 in his 12 overs; Roberts dug it in awkwardly and Vanburn Holder and Keith Boyce provided equally disobliging support. The Kiwis folded up for 158.

When the Windies began the chase, Roy Fredricks left early to a lackadaisical stroke; but Greenidge and Kalicharran realized 125 runs for the second wicket to largely put the issue beyond doubt. Richard Collinge created a stir by capturing three quick wickets. But the evergreen Rohan Kanhai, recalled for the World Cup, was in attendance to steer the West Indians past the finishing line by five wickets.

Toss: West Indies
Umpires: WL Budd and AE Fagg
Man of the Match: AI Kallicharran

New Zealand innings (60 overs maximum)			R	B
*GM Turner	c Kanhai	b Roberts	36	74
JFM Morrison	lbw	b Julien	5	26
GP Howarth	c Murray	b Roberts	51	93
JM Parker		b Lloyd	3	12
BF Hastings	not out		24	57
+KJ Wadsworth	c Lloyd	b Julien	11	21
BJ McKechnie	lbw	b Julien	1	9
DR Hadlee	c Holder	b Julien	0	10
BL Cairns		b Holder	10	14
HJ Howarth		b Holder	0	1
RO Collinge		b Holder	2	4

Extras: (b 1, lb 5, w 2, nb 7) 15
Total: (all out, 52.2 overs) 158

FoW: 1-8 (Morrison), 2-98 (Turner), 3-105 (GP Howarth),
4-106 (Parker), 5-125 (Wadsworth), 6-133 (McKechnie),
7-139 (Hadlee), 8-155 (Cairns), 9-155 (HJ Howarth),
10-158 (Collinge).

Bowling	O	M	R	W
Julien	12	5	27	4
Roberts	11	3	18	2
Holder	8.2	0	30	3
Boyce	9	0	31	0
Lloyd	12	1	37	1

West Indies innings (target: 159 runs from 60 overs)			R	B
RC Fredericks	c Hastings	b Hadlee	6	14
CG Greenidge	lbw	b Collinge	55	95
AI Kallicharran	c & b Collinge		72	92
IVA Richards	lbw	b Collinge	5	10
RB Kanhai	not out		12	18
*CH Lloyd	c Hastings	b McKechnie	3	8
BD Julien	not out		4	5

Extras: (lb 1, nb 1) 2
Total: (5 wickets, 40.1 overs) 159
DNB: +DL Murray, KD Boyce, VA Holder, AME Roberts.

FoW: 1-8 (Fredericks), 2-133 (Kallicharran), 3-139 (Richards),
4-142 (Greenidge), 5-151 (Lloyd).

Bowling	O	M	R	W
Collinge	12	4	28	3
Hadlee	10	0	54	1
Cairns	6.1	2	23	0
McKechnie	8	0	37	1
HJ Howarth	4	0	15	0

Final, 21 June: Lord's, London

With no spinner in his ranks, Ian Chappell asked West Indies to bat and the decision seemed to be justified. The left-handed Fredricks hooked a bouncer for six only to loose his balance and swivel on to his stumps. Greenidge just could not get going and Kalicharran essayed an indiscreet cut. Both were caught behind. West Indies were, thus, 50 for three.

But Lloyd filled the breach and with Kanhai, his Guyanese compatriot, put on 149 runs for the fourth wicket to radically reverse the Australian advantage. While the tall, bespectacled left-hander bludgeoned the ball, Kanhai anchored his way to a half century. However, the day really belonged to the former as he sculpted a sizzling hundred off 85 balls, punctuated by a brace of sixes and a dozen fours. Boyce and Julien, then, took over from where the skipper left off to set their opponents a stiff target.

But the Aussies, with their never-say-die approach, were undeterred. Chappell led the way with a skilful 62, but he was one of five to be run out, which, arguably, cost Australia the match. Vivian Richards, unsuccessful with the willow, twice hit the stumps from square leg and was also involved in a third dismissal. Yet, Jeff Thomson and Dennis Lillee, generally feared for their bowling, batted like a trigger-happy twosome emerging from an under-siege saloon in a Hollywood western. Australia perished, but they went down guns blazing, as the pace partners rattled up 41 for the last wicket. The West Indies were generally dominant and edged home by 17 runs, but the Australians had made a match of it.

As finals go, this unquestionably lived up to its billing. It was the longest day of the year and possibly the most extended day in cricket history. The match started at 11 a.m. and concluded at 8.43 p.m., when the light was just about adequate on a luminous evening. The cavaliers from the Caribbean had jousted with the dashers from Down Under. It had proved to be a classic and secured the future of the World Cup!

Millions watched the tournament on television. A full house witnessed the final, which produced gate receipts of £66,950, a record for a one-day match in England at the time. The 15-day extravaganza, governed by good weather, was underwritten by Prudential to the tune of £100,000. The sale of tickets fetched over £200,000, as 158,000 spectators waded through the turnstiles. The winners received £4000 and the runners-ups £2000. England and New Zealand went home with £1000 each.

Ten per cent of the profits was retained by the UK. The other seven participating sides were each allocated 7.5 per cent of the surplus. The rest went to the ICC.

Toss: Australia
Umpires: HD Bird and TW Spencer
Man of the Match: CH Lloyd

West Indies innings (60 overs maximum)			R	B
RC Fredericks	hit wicket	b Lillee	7	13
CG Greenidge	c Marsh	b Thomson	13	61
AI Kallicharran	c Marsh	b Gilmour	12	18
RB Kanhai		b Gilmour	55	105
*CH Lloyd	c Marsh	b Gilmour	102	85
IVA Richards		b Gilmour	5	11
KD Boyce	c GS Chappell	b Thomson	34	37
BD Julien	not out		26	37
+DL Murray	c & b Gilmour		14	10
VA Holder	not out		6	2

Extras: (lb 6, nb 11) 17
Total: (8 wickets, 60 overs) 291

DNB: AME Roberts.

FoW: 1-12 (Fredericks), 2-27 (Kallicharran), 3-50 (Greenidge), 4-199 (Lloyd), 5-206 (Kanhai), 6-209 (Richards), 7-261 (Boyce), 8-285 (Murray).

Bowling	O	M	R	W
Lillee	12	1	55	1
Gilmour	12	2	48	5
Thomson	12	1	44	2
Walker	12	1	71	0
GS Chappell	7	0	33	0
Walters	5	0	23	0

Australia innings (target: 292 runs from 60 overs)		R	B
A Turner	run out (Richards)	40	54
RB McCosker	c Kallicharran b Boyce	7	24
*IM Chappell	run out (Richards/Lloyd)	62	93
GS Chappell	run out (Richards)	15	23
KD Walters	b Lloyd	35	51
+RW Marsh	b Boyce	11	24
R Edwards	c Fredericks b Boyce	28	37
GJ Gilmour	c Kanhai b Boyce	14	11
MHN Walker	run out (Kallicharran/Holder)	7	9
JR Thomson	run out (Kallicharran/Murray)	21	21
DK Lillee	not out	16	19

Extras: (b 2, lb 9, nb 7) 18
Total: (all out, 58.4 overs) 274

FoW: 1-25 (McCosker), 2-81 (Turner), 3-115 (GS Chappell),
4-162 (IM Chappell), 5-170 (Walters), 6-195 (Marsh),
7-221 (Gilmour), 8-231 (Edwards), 9-233 (Walker),
10-274 (Thomson).

Bowling	O	M	R	W
Julien	12	0	58	0
Roberts	11	1	45	0
Boyce	12	0	50	4
Holder	11.4	1	65	0
Lloyd	12	1	38	1

★

About a week after the finals, the ICC assembled for their annual meeting to discuss, among other business, proposals for the next World Cup. The BCCI submitted that they were enthusiastic about hosting the event. Not surprisingly, there were no takers for this bid, as most members concurred 'it was hard to beat England as the venue'.

It was, of course, true that India's shorter daylight hours would have made it impossible to stage 120 overs of cricket in a day.

Within days of the first World Cup coming to an end, Prime Minister Indira Gandhi imposed an 18-month state of Emergency, during which she imprisoned her political opponents and suspended civil liberties in India. This rather drastic move followed a judgment in the High Court of Allahabad, a city in India's most densely and populated province of Uttar Pradesh, which upheld an application regarding misuse of government machinery in her 1971 election campaign and unseated her from Parliament. When she finally called elections in March 1977 – postponed by a year – the Indian electorate voted her out of office. Her rival for over a decade, Morarji Desai , became prime minister.

THE 1979 WORLD CUP

The summer of 1979 was a significant one for Indian cricketers. This was the first time they were returning to play test matches in England after the dreadful tour of 1974 – when, among other indignities, the visitors were shot out for 42 in an innings at Lord's. But before the test series, there was the business of the second World Cup, again sponsored by Prudential Assurance.

Indeed, it was *déjà vu*. Venkataraghavan was again, unexpectedly, retained as captain; and India appeared to be as unripe for the task as four years ago. In the autumn of 1978, the Indians had resumed cricket relations with Pakistan after 17 years. Playing away, they lost a three-test series 2–0. Following this defeat, Bishan Bedi was forthwith relieved of the captaincy and his second in command, Sunil Gavaskar, assumed charge. By this stage, Kerry Packer, an Australian tycoon, piqued by the Australian Cricket Board's refusal to award television rights to his Channel Nine network, had retaliated by lucratively luring three dozen top players from Australia, England, West Indies, New Zealand and Pakistan to participate in his 'World Series Cricket' Down Under, in defiance of cricket approved by, and under the auspices of, the ICC or its member boards. For the first time, it was cricket in coloured clothing, under floodlights and with a white, rather than a red, ball.

In the winter of 1978–79, therefore, a second-string West Indies squad under Alvin Kalicharran – for the bulk of their leading lights had gone over to Packer – visited India. The depth of talent in the Caribbean in that period was such that even a side without stars consisted of exponents who were strongly competing for places in the first XI, among them the effervescent Barbadian fast bowler, Malcolm Marshall. But the Indians duly recorded their maiden series victory over the West Indians at home; and Gavaskar, unaffected by the burden of leadership, aggregated 732 runs in the six tests at an average of 91.50.

Yet he was relieved of the captaincy for the trip to England. None of the Indian cricketers had been tempted to join Packer. But it was widely rumoured that Gavaskar had been approached and the BCCI feared he would cross over. While this has never been officially confirmed, it was surmised that Indian officials, not wanting to be embarrassed if he announced his departure after being retained as skipper, pre-emptively stripped him of his job. As it transpired, their apprehensions were misplaced, as Gavaskar never signed up with Packer. Indeed, he was probably never seriously approached, as a criterion for consideration was ability to play limited-overs cricket; and in this respect, the Indian run-glutton had not shown himself to be particularly enthusiastic.

The 'coup d'état' by Packer, who died in December 2005, aged 68, turned the modern game upside down. At the time, cricket's authorities and conservatives (and I must admit I was one such) condemned him. I ventilated my opinion several times on BBC radio. At the time, I felt it was unacceptable that he should hold international cricket to ransom because of a domestic dispute. If action was justified, this ought to have been confined to Australia. But then, money power in a capitalist environment knows no boundaries.

Nonetheless, when Packer died, there were black armbands and a minute's silence during a test match at Melbourne and tributes flowed from the president of the ICC. His Channel Nine has now been a notably powerful force in Australian cricket for over a quarter of a century, and the bad blood generated by him has long dissolved. There is, in fact, widespread, if not universal, appreciation of what he did, with the players he helped particularly indulgent in their praise.

Packer saw Australian cricket as ready for glamorization. But the Australian Cricket Board (ACB) were content with their, if not high-income, then historical, relationship with the Australian Broadcasting Corporation (ABC). In 1976, the ACB had agreed to, but not signed, a three-year contract with this public broadcaster. Channel Nine was, on the other hand, casually promised the possibility of some kind of shared arrangement in future. Packer had offered $A500,000 (seven times the rival bid) for a three-year licence in lieu of ABC; and he wanted the deal immediately. He was spurned.

The administrators were complacent in their belief that all was well in the cricket world, with a celebratory England–Australia match to mark the centenary of tests staged at Melbourne in March 1977. They were out of touch with the reality of cricketers being a dissatisfied lot as a result of low remuneration as compared to some of the other sports, not to mention insecure careers. Packer sensed this discontent and took advantage of it. He offered them, by the standards of those days, quite a princely sum of $A25,000 for 12 weeks' performance. There were very few 'nays'. The behind-the-scenes story of the Centenary Test was, in fact, the real one. Almost the entire Australian team signed in confidence with Packer. Next, the then England captain, Tony Greig, was contacted; and the inducement spread to all test-playing countries, other than India.

News of the exodus to Packer broke in May 1977 and stunned the cricketing world. The indignation was the most pronounced in England. It was a traditionalist reaction coloured by colonial arrogance. The alleged disloyalty of the South African-born Greig was noticeably highlighted. In their anger, England's Test and County Cricket Board (TCCB) and other governing bodies underestimated the soundness of Packer and his players' legal position. They made the error of disbarring the rebels from tests and, in England, also from county cricket, although none had broken any contracts. Predictably, Packer and some players sued the TCCB in the High Court in London. The concerned judge quashed the bans on the grounds that the authorities were guilty of restraining the trade practices of the cricketers.

Packer's 'circus', as opponents branded his World Series Cricket, failed to attract much attention in its first season (1977–78). Australia's major grounds debarred entry to the enterprise and TV audiences were nothing to write home about, either. But the first match under floodlights at Melbourne's VFL (Victorian Football League) Park, better known as an Australian Rules football venue, enticed a heartening crowd of 7000. Then, political intervention symbolically facilitated the first day/night match at the Sydney Cricket Ground. The ground was full except the members' stand. This, against the backdrop of poor attendances in the concurrent 1978–79 Ashes series, in which a debilitated official Australian side were quite easily defeated by Mike Brearley's England team. Packer's jingle of 'C'mon, Aussie, c'mon' was later adopted by the ACB and was still in currency when the Indians toured Australia in 1980–81.

In May 1979, the ACB threw in the towel and extended significantly better terms to Packer than he had bargained for earlier. And floodlit cricket became his lasting legacy. Also, a quantum increase in one-day cricket, broadcast by Channel Nine with matching technical brilliance, became the order of the day. Indeed, other than between 1987 and 1990 – when he sold and bought back his TV interests – and until his death Packer held an effective veto over Australian cricket.

In 1996, Packer lay clinically dead for eight minutes after having a heart attack playing polo. One night, he reportedly, won US$24 million at a Las Vegas casino, following which, at The Ritz in London, he lost two million pounds one evening, only to recover three million pounds before the night was out.

As a result of his intercession, England players' fees rapidly quintupled because sponsorship of the official game increased, including even test match being underwritten. Although unaffected, the BCCI, too, were unwilling to take chances. They doubled test match fees for Indian players.

As in 1975, eight sides took part in the 1979 World Cup, the six test-playing ones, namely, England, Australia, West Indies, New Zealand, India and Pakistan, and two associate members of the ICC, Sri Lanka (who had also partaken four years earlier) and Canada, both of whom emerged from the ICC Trophy qualifying tournament. As per the draw, England, Australia, Pakistan and Canada featured in Group A; West Indies, New Zealand, India and Sri Lanka figured in Group B.

The English establishment's heart bled that South Africa had been spurned for a second time. It was astonishing that such elements could be so insensitive to the heinous crimes being systematically committed against human beings under institutionalized brutality – that, too, on a majority by a minority, racist government. For such behaviour, South Africa had become the pariah of the world. Yet, a majority of MCC members, the TCCB and the right wing of British media were advocating contravention of the 1977 Gleneagles Agreement, reached between Commonwealth Heads of Government (India had been represented at this meeting by Prime Minister Morarji Desai, with the then External Affairs Minister Atal Bihari Vajpayee in attendance), which imposed a ban on all sporting links with Pretoria that was binding on all Commonwealth countries. Indeed, it took the reluctant ICC 12 years to ratify the Gleaneagles resolution, when, in 1989, it finally debarred cricketers with South African ties from playing tests and ODIs.

The world of cricket was undoubtedly poorer for the likes of Graeme Pollock (who, Richie Benaud once rated as a better batsman than Garry Sobers), Barry Richards, Eddie Barlow and Peter Pollock (Graeme's elder brother and Shaun's father) being denied greater international exposure and more interaction with the best talent elsewhere. As a matter of fact, South Africa whitewashed Bill Lawry's Australians 4–0 in 1970, soon after the latter had convincingly won a series in India 3–1. But the issue of dismantling apartheid was far more important for the global community than indulging in the comparatively petty business of playing cricket. Sadly for the Springboks – as the South African cricketers were then labelled as a variation – it was a price they had to pay for the crimes of their government and the relative silence of their cricket authorities. Besides, the expulsion had the intended effect. The repugnant regime finally came to its senses; Nelson Mandela, father of the freedom struggle, was released in February 1990 after being imprisoned for 27 years, and the white-only authority transferred power to a democratically elected multiracial government, which promptly paved the way for the emancipation of South African cricketers from their isolation.

Before the curtain ascended on the 1979 World Cup, India had featured in 10 ODIs, as compared to England's 36, Australia's 22, West Indies' 14 and Pakistan and New Zealand's 16 apiece. The Pakistani and West Indian cricket boards had forgotten and forgiven their Packer rebels; so, they were at full strength. England too had recovered from the likes of Tony Greig deserting them. But Australia continued to be without, among others, Greg Chappell and Dennis Lillee. Most were, however, more attuned to the needs of one-day cricket, especially those with the additional experience of the quite competitive limited-overs matches in Packer's World Series Cricket. The Indians had neither much practice in domestic competition nor the privilege of figuring in over-limit cricket in England. Only Bedi and Venkat in the Indian squad had experience of playing for English counties.

As the event got underway, India was again facing political instability. India's prime minister, Morarji Desai, who had earlier succeeded in defeating his *bête noire*, Indira Gandhi, was now at his wit's end trying to keep his flock together. Juxtaposed with India's cricketing predicament at this juncture, one could aptly reiterate that it never rains, but pours!

9 June: Edgbaston, Birmingham

To India's misfortune, their very first outing was a stern challenge – against the defending champions, no less, now approaching the height of their powers. Clive Lloyd won a significant toss and was able to unlatch his fearsome foursome – Andy Roberts, Michael Holding, Joel Garner and Colin Croft – on a wicket with residual moisture. With an umbrella field plucking catches as India slipped to 77 for five, the action paralleled more a test match than a one-day game. Only Gundappa Viswanath tackled with any conviction such sustained hostility, which was characterized by an overdose of bouncers, ignored by umpires David Evans and John Langridge – those were the days of all-English officials supervising World Cup fixtures!.

It was, obviously, not a case of bias, but a lack of vigilance. The umpires appeared to solely interpret the situation on the basis of whether it was intimidation or not, forgetting that deliveries sailing well over a batsman's head – and 'Vishy', as the Bangalore batsman 'without an enemy in the world' was popularly addressed, was barely five foot five even with his spikes – were impossible to score of and should, therefore, have been penalized. Thus, the West Indies – not that they needed any help – not only benefited from the life in the pitch, but also from the benevolence of the umpires. As conditions eased, the Indian tail mustered a slight resistance, but overall the effort was insufficient.

At the customary cocktails after the match, Venkat expressed his displeasure with the umpiring in no uncertain terms. I immediately sensed a 'scoop'. Reporting for United News of India (UNI) – an Indian wire service – I carried his comments verbatim, which were published by newspapers in various parts of India, including his home city of Madras (now Chennai). Before the next match, though, I noticed Venkat had turned rather grumpy and sneerful. The manager of the team, Coimbatarao Gopinath, a former test player also from Chennai, explained the captain's remarks were not meant to be quoted. I remonstrated he never qualified his remarks by saying so. I also offered to despatch a denial, if this is what either he or Venkat desired. He didn't accept this offer. He elucidated it was not that Venkat did not make the remarks, but he was upset about these being sourced to him.

As a stickler for journalistic ethics and diligent about not attributing remarks which are meant to be off-the-record, I was fairly clear in my mind Venkat's observations were not provided as background information. His subsequent stance, I felt, stemmed from

his corporate and cricketing bosses in Chennai, with strong business
links with Britain, censuring him for his criticism of umpires, that,
too, English officials. I understood his circumstances and, therefore,
my attitude towards him remained unaltered. But it took him four
years – until half way through India's 1983 tour of the West Indies,
for which he had been recalled – to snap out of his sulk. As far as I
am concerned, I have never had any ill-feeling towards him before,
during or since the incident; and I watched in admiration as he became
the first Indian test player to don an umpire's coat (which many of
his predecessors and peers deemed unsuitable for them) and
established himself, for a spell, as the best in this trade. Not that it
matters, but I hope that if 'Venky' ever writes his memoirs, he will
reiterate what he told me that evening at Edgbaston – to put the
record straight.

In reply, the West Indies batted exactly the same number of lawful
deliveries as India. Despite some disciplined bowling by Kapil Dev
and Karsen Ghavri, Gordon Greenidge took charge, completing a
century, and realizing 138 runs for the opening partnership with his
fellow Barbadian Desmond Haynes, before Viv Richards helped to
finish the job. The West Indians cruised home by nine wickets.

Toss: West Indies
Umpires: DGL Evans and JG Langridge
ODI Debuts: SC Khanna (Ind).
Man of the Match: CG Greenidge

India innings (60 overs maximum)			R	B
SM Gavaskar	c Holding	b Roberts	8	7
AD Gaekwad	c King	b Holding	11	30
DB Vengsarkar	c Kallicharran	b Holding	7	7
GR Viswanath		b Holding	75	134
BP Patel	run out		15	33
M Amarnath	c Murray	b Croft	8	15
N Kapil Dev		b King	12	12
+SC Khanna	c Haynes	b Holding	0	12
KD Ghavri	c Murray	b Garner	12	26
*S Venkataraghavan	not out		13	30
BS Bedi	c Lloyd	b Roberts	13	23

Extras: (b 6, lb 3, w 3, nb 4) 16
Total: (all out, 53.1 overs) 190

FoW: 1-10 (Gavaskar), 2-24 (Vengsarkar), 3-29 (Gaekwad),
4-56 (Patel), 5-77 (Amarnath), 6-112 (Kapil Dev),
7-119 (Khanna), 8-155 (Ghavri), 9-163 (Viswanath),
10-190 (Bedi).

Bowling	O	M	R	W
Roberts	9.1	0	32	2
Holding	12	2	33	4
Garner	12	1	42	1
Croft	10	1	31	1
King	10	1	36	1

West Indies innings (target: 191 runs from 60 overs)		R	B
CG Greenidge	not out	106	173
DL Haynes	lbw b Kapil Dev	47	99
IVA Richards	not out	28	44

Extras: (lb 6, nb 7) 13
Total: (1 wicket, 51.3 overs) 194

DNB: AI Kallicharran, *CH Lloyd, CL King, +DL Murray,
AME Roberts, J Garner, MA Holding, CEH Croft.

FoW: 1-138 (Haynes).

Bowling	O	M	R	W
Kapil Dev	10	1	46	1
Ghavri	10	2	25	0
Venkataraghavan	12	3	30	0
Bedi	12	0	45	0
Amarnath	7.3	0	35	0

13 June: Headingley, Leeds

Under sullen skies and given a slightly moist pitch, it was small wonder New Zealand's captain Mark Burgess invited India to bat. Sunil Gavaskar offered a difficult return catch to Richard Hadlee, but otherwise batted meticulously. However, Anshuman Gaekwad, Dilip Vengsarkar and Viswanath failed to forge any significant partnerships with him and India were soon 53 for three. Furthermore, their run rate was an indolent 2.5 an over. At this point though, Brijesh Patel filled the breach more inventively. This also instigated Gavaskar to take the cue. Kapil Dev and Ghavri, then, delivered a few lusty blows. But the Kiwis made the best of the conditions, which were not dissimilar to what one often encountered at Wellington or in their South Island. Richard Hadlee conceded only 20 runs in 10 overs, capturing two wickets, including the prized scalp of Gavaskar.

John Wright, later India's coach, and Bruce Edgar posted three figures for the opening wicket for the New Zealanders, which laid a launch pad for victory. At one stage they fell behind in their run rate, only to be reinvigorated by Glen Turner, who, with an undefeated 43, featured in an unbroken partnership of 80 with Edgar. New Zealand won by eight wickets.

Toss: New Zealand
Umpires: WL Budd and AGT Whitehead
Man of the Match: BA Edgar

India innings (60 overs maximum)			R	B
SM Gavaskar	c Lees	b Hadlee	55	144
AD Gaekwad		b Hadlee	10	31
DB Vengsarkar	c Lees	b McKechnie	1	2
GR Viswanath	c Turner	b Cairns	9	17
BP Patel		b Troup	38	60
M Amarnath		b Troup	1	5
N Kapil Dev	c & b Cairns		25	24
KD Ghavri	c Coney	b McKechnie	20	22
+SC Khanna	c Morrison	b McKechnie	7	16
*S Venkataraghavan	c Lees	b Cairns	1	2
BS Bedi	not out		1	2

Extras: (lb 8, w 5, nb 1) 14
Total: (all out, 55.5 overs) 182

FoW: 1-27 (Gaekwad), 2-38 (Vengsarkar), 3-53 (Viswanath),
4-104 (Patel), 5-107 (Amarnath), 6-147 (Kapil Dev),
7-153 (Gavaskar), 8-180 (Khanna), 9-181 (Ghavri),
10-182 (Venkataraghavan).

Bowling	O	M	R	W
Hadlee	10	2	20	2
Troup	10	2	36	2
Cairns	11.5	0	36	3
McKechnie	12	1	24	3
Coney	7	0	33	0
Morrison	5	0	19	0

New Zealand innings (target: 183 runs from 60 overs)		R	B
JG Wright	c & b Amarnath	48	94
BA Edgar	not out	84	167
BL Cairns	run out	2	4
GM Turner	not out	43	76

Extras: (lb 3, nb 3) 6
Total: (2 wickets, 57 overs) 183

DNB: JV Coney, *MG Burgess, JFM Morrison, BJ McKechnie, +WK Lees,
RJ Hadlee, GB Troup.

FoW: 1-100 (Wright), 2-103 (Cairns).

Bowling	O	M	R	W
Amarnath	12	1	39	1
Bedi	12	1	32	0
Venkataraghavan	12	0	34	0
Ghavri	10	1	34	0
Kapil Dev	11	3	38	0

16 and 18 June: Old Trafford, Manchester

In 1979, Sri Lanka were only an associate member of the ICC or, in other words, had not yet been granted test status. Indeed, at this juncture, they still figured in an annual clash alternately at home and away across the Palk Straits – 22 miles of sea that separates the Indian Ocean island from mainland India – for what was called the Gopalan Trophy (named after M. J. Gopalan, who played his only test for India at Calcutta, now Kolkata, against England in 1933–34) with the southern Indian state of Tamil Nadu, a first-class side, that too, not among the topmost Ranji Trophy teams. And Sri Lanka did not always win, either. Moreover, on this occasion at the World Cup, they were without the services of their skipper, Anura Tenekoon, who had pulled a hamstring at practice the day before the match. To top it all, they lost the toss and were asked to bat.

It was a Saturday and overcast as only Lancashire's commercial and cultural hub – notorious for its inclement weather – can be. Indeed, commencement of play had been delayed by drizzles. But the pitch was unharmed and against a blunt Indian attack, which, additionally, underperformed, the Sri Lankans batted in a spirit of nothing-to-lose. Sidath Wettimuny and Roy Dias, both to subsequently acquit themselves with credit in official tests, erected a foundation with a 96-run second-wicket association at around four runs an over, before Duleep Mendis, another batsman to catch the eye in tests in 1980s, drove home the advantage.

Wettimuny played correctly as befits an opener, driving with precision; Dias worked the ball away wristily, while the thickset Mendis carted the Indian seamers to distant corners on the leg side. Kapil, Ghavri and Amarnath were each despatched for six. All three Sri Lankan batsmen registered half centuries. Even Sudath Pasqual, a left-handed schoolboy and the youngest participant in the 1979 World Cup, partook of the jollity, adding 52 runs in seven overs for the fifth wicket with Mendis, before the latter, not the swiftest over 22 yards, was run out.

Although secular in practice, Britain is on paper a Christian state; and, in the 1970s, Sundays were strictly a day of rest, when test and county championship matches would come to a standstill only to resume on Mondays. Whether cricketers attended church or not – some notably did – they were, by tradition, not meant to be seen frolicking in a cricket field, or anywhere else for that matter. But confronted by commercial realities, English authorities were compelled to relax such rigidity by permitting cricket on Sunday afternoons after religious services in the morning. The popularity of the Gillette Cup prompted administrators to conceive of another limited-overs tournament – a 40-overs-a-side competition between the first-class counties – christened the John Player League. Given the extended daylight in England's summer months, this was easily accommodated. Indeed, the urbane utterances of John Arlott accompanied by the pleasant cockney of Jim Laker on BBC TV would lift the boredom of a sleepy Sabbath.

But full-day cricket had not yet been introduced on a Sunday; therefore, a 60-over match, which is what a World Cup game then amounted to and which would consume both morning and afternoon, was still not admissible. Consequently, the India–Sri Lanka match, which could not be finished in a Saturday because of the late start, was held over until the following Monday.

Gavaskar and Gaekwad put on 60 for the first wicket and India needed 4.88 runs an over off the last 25 with eight wickets in hand. But no worthwhile stand bloomed to tackle this task. Somachandra de Silva, a leg spinner, enticed the Indian middle order to their doom. Tony Opatha, a medium pacer, who had made no impact with the new ball, then extinguished the tail. India crashed to an ignoble surrender by 47 runs. It was Sri Lanka's first victory in two World Cups.

It was the only upset by a non-test-playing side in the tourney. As for India, far from progressing from their display in the previous World Cup, they had actually retarded. Indeed, if 1975 had been an embarrassment, 1979 now turned out to be an unalloyed contretemps.

Toss: India
Umpires: KE Palmer and AGT Whitehead
ODI Debuts: FRMD Gunatilleke, RS Madugalle (SL)
Man of the Match: LRD Mendis
Close of Play: Day 1: Sri Lanka 238/5 (60 ov)

Sri Lanka innings (60 overs maximum)			R	B
*B Warnapura	c Gaekwad	b Amarnath	18	51
SRD Wettimuny	c Vengsarkar	b Kapil Dev	67	120
RL Dias	c & b Amarnath		50	88
LRD Mendis	run out		64	57
RS Madugalle	c Khanna	b Amarnath	4	16
SP Pasqual	not out		23	26
DS de Silva	not out		1	4

Extras: (lb 8, w 2, nb 1) 11
Total: (5 wickets, 60 overs) 238

DNB: +SA Jayasinghe, ARM Opatha, DLS de Silva, FRMD Gunatilleke.

FoW: 1-31 (Warnapura), 2-127 (Wettimuny), 3-147 (Dias),
4-175 (Madugalle), 5-227 (Mendis).

Bowling	O	M	R	W
Kapil Dev	12	2	53	1
Ghavri	12	0	53	0
Amarnath	12	3	40	3
Bedi	12	2	37	0
Venkataraghavan	12	0	44	0

India innings (target: 239 runs from 60 overs)			R	B
SM Gavaskar	c Dias	b Warnapura	26	54
AD Gaekwad	c sub (GRA de Silva)	b DLS de Silva	33	52
DB Vengsarkar	c DLS de Silva	b DS de Silva	36	57
GR Viswanath	run out		22	55
BP Patel		b DS de Silva	10	13
N Kapil Dev	c Warnapura	b DLS de Silva	16	19
M Amarnath		b DS de Silva	7	15
KD Ghavri	c Warnapura	b Opatha	3	8
+SC Khanna	c Dias	b Opatha	10	17
*S Venkataraghavan	not out		9	9
BS Bedi	c Jayasinghe	b Opatha	5	8

Extras: (lb 10, w 3, nb 1) 14

Total: (all out, 54.1 overs) 191

FoW: 1-60 (Gavaskar), 2-76 (Gaekwad), 3-119 (Viswanath),
4-132 (Patel), 5-147 (Vengsarkar), 6-160 (Kapil Dev),
7-162 (Amarnath), 8-170 (Ghavri), 9-185 (Khanna),
10-191 (Bedi).

Bowling	O	M	R	W
Opatha	10.1	0	31	3
Gunatilleke	9	1	34	0
Warnapura	12	0	47	1
DLS de Silva	12	0	36	2
DS de Silva	11	1	29	3

To add to India's discomfiture, Morarji Desai was forced to quit as prime minister in July 1979. In his place was sworn in one of his cabinet colleagues, Charan Singh, an ambitious farmer, who held the reins for a few months without ever proving his majority in Parliament, before himself becoming a victim of intrigue.

Earlier...

The points from India were not the only ones acquired by the Sri Lankans. They obtained two more from their match against the West Indies, which even after three days of efforts – 13, 14 and 15 June – was abandoned without a ball being bowled. Unrelentingly heavy downpours at The Oval left the outfield waterlogged and unsuitable for play even when there were a few dry spells.

The misfortune, though, did not prevent the West Indians from topping their group, with New Zealand finishing as runners-up. In the other cluster, England won all three of their games, while Pakistan edged out Australia. The two, thus, qualified for the semi-finals.

Semi-final, 20 June: Old Trafford, Manchester

Burgess won the toss for New Zealand and sent England into bat; and Hadlee restrained as well as threatened immediately. He had

Geoffrey Boycott caught at third slip in the fifth over. But both skipper Mike Brearley and Graham Gooch chiselled half centuries, the latter more aggressively. Indeed, stepping out, he sent Brian McKechnie sailing over the sightscreen before being bowled by the same bowler. Brearley had departed by then, snicking Jeremy Coney to the wicketkeeper. So, as most of the middle order collapsed – David Gower was run out and Ian Botham was lbw to one that kept low – Derek Randall, at number seven, conjured a neat cameo, playing sensibly rather than flamboyantly, while Bob Taylor chipped in with a six to long on off Lance Cairns. The Englishmen, thus, scrambled 25 runs in the last three overs.

The left-handers, Wright and Edgar, launched New Zealand's chase. But none, other than the former, even crossed 50 and only Turner made a meaningful contribution before he became Bob Willis' only victim. They ought to have done better, as the Warwickshire paceman had an injured leg and Botham and Mike Hendrick (the most successful of the English bowlers), too, had niggles. The attack (which included Boycott with his gentle medium pacers and he had Geoff Howarth lbw with a full toss bowled round the wicket) lacked a single spinner, as left-armer, Phil Edmonds, had been left out amidst some criticism in the English media. Wright kept the Kiwis' hopes alive until Randall brilliantly ran him out from square leg. Warren Lees and Cairns struck a six each at the expense of Hendrick and Botham, respectively, and took the New Zealanders close, but these were only the last strokes of a drowning swimmer.

As Botham began the last over, New Zealand needed 14 runs to win. They ultimately got only four of them, thereby losing by nine runs. It was a well-contested game played at an unusually sunny Old Trafford. For the near-capacity crowd, it was quite pulsating as the pendulum swung from one end to the other before coming to rest in the home side's favour.

Toss: New Zealand
Umpires: JG Langridge and KE Palmer
ODI Debuts: W Larkins (Eng).
Man of the Match: GA Gooch

England innings (60 overs maximum)			R	B
*JM Brearley	c Lees	b Coney	53	115
G Boycott	c Howarth	b Hadlee	2	14
W Larkins	c Coney	b McKechnie	7	37
GA Gooch		b McKechnie	71	84
DI Gower	run out		1	1
IT Botham	lbw	b Cairns	21	30
DW Randall	not out		42	50
CM Old	c Lees	b Troup	0	2
+RW Taylor	run out		12	25
RGD Willis	not out		1	2

Extras: (lb 8, w 3) 11
Total: (8 wickets, 60 overs) 221

DNB: M Hendrick.

FoW: 1-13 (Boycott), 2-38 (Larkins), 3-96 (Brearley),
4-98 (Gower), 5-145 (Botham), 6-177 (Gooch), 7-178 (Old),
8-219 (Taylor).

Bowling	O	M	R	W
Hadlee	12	4	32	1
Troup	12	1	38	1
Cairns	12	2	47	1
Coney	12	0	47	1
McKechnie	12	1	46	2

New Zealand innings (target: 222 runs from 60 overs)			R	B
JG Wright	run out		69	137
BA Edgar	lbw	b Old	17	38
GP Howarth	lbw	b Boycott	7	12
JV Coney	lbw	b Hendrick	11	39
GM Turner	lbw	b Willis	30	51
*MG Burgess	run out		10	13
RJ Hadlee		b Botham	15	32
+WK Lees		b Hendrick	23	20
BL Cairns	c Brearley	b Hendrick	14	6
BJ McKechnie	not out		4	9
GB Troup	not out		3	3

Extras: (b 5, w 4) 9
Total: (9 wickets, 60 overs) 212

FoW: 1-47 (Edgar), 2-58 (Howarth), 3-104 (Coney), 4-112 (Wright),
5-132 (Burgess), 6-162 (Turner), 7-180 (Hadlee),
8-195 (Cairns), 9-208 (Lees).

Bowling	O	M	R	W
Botham	12	3	42	1
Hendrick	12	0	55	3
Old	12	1	33	1
Boycott	9	1	24	1
Gooch	3	1	8	0
Willis	12	1	41	1

Semi-final, 20 June: The Oval, London

The other clash amongst the last four – staged simultaneously – also
lived up to the occasion. Pakistan, perhaps wanting as much to avoid
the opposition's quartet of serious quicks as to exploit the morning
conditions with Imran Khan, Sarfraz Nawaz and Sikander Bakht,
inserted the West Indies; but came up against the roadblock of inform Caribbeans.

Greenidge and Haynes posted an opening stand of 132, although
the latter was lucky to be dropped by Imran at long leg off the amiable
pace of Mudassar Nazar when he was 32. Eventually the slow but
slippery medium pace of Asif Iqbal, vastly seasoned in the art of
one-day cricket by virtue of his long stint at Kent, collected four of
the six wickets that fell; indeed the top four, but not before Richards
and Lloyd had sprayed the field with an array of shots. Sarfraz was a
particular spendthrift, donating 71 runs in his 12 overs before he
had Collis King caught and bowled. The West Indians set their
opponents a target of 294. Match over? Not yet.

Sadiq Mohammad, the left-handed brother of the more famous
Hanif and Mushtaq, was snuffed out peremptorily by the hostility
of Holding, as he attempted to ward off a bouncer. But his dismissal

brought together Majid Khan and Zaheer Abbas in the most exhilarating partnership of the day. As the sun bathed this lustrous ground on a glorious south London afternoon, the two Pakistani stroke players, adept at the one-day game, having spent years at Glamorgan and Gloucestershire respectively, mirrored nature's splendour. Admittedly, Majid was given a life by Greenidge off Holding when only 10, but the duo added 166 runs for the second wicket in 36 overs to give their side an even chance of victory. Trevor MacDonald, Britain's Independent Television News' newscaster of Trinidadian origin and an occasional cricket writer, was on his feet in the Long Room of the pavilion, smiling nervously, tankard in hand. But where Roberts, Holding and Garner were seen off by the skill of a talented twosome, ultimately the West Indians' bowling depth had the last say.

Colin Croft, as awkward a speedster as any, was brought back from the Vauxhall end – the side of the river Thames. He had Zaheer and Majid caught and trapped Javed Miandad, a potential match winner, leg before in 12 balls for four runs. Pakistan never recovered from this. More importantly, the West Indies reached the World Cup final for the second time running.

Toss: Pakistan
Umpires: WL Budd and DJ Constant
Man of the Match: CG Greenidge

West Indies innings (60 overs maximum)			*R*	*B*
CG Greenidge	c Wasim Bari	b Asif Iqbal	73	107
DL Haynes	c & b Asif Iqbal		65	115
IVA Richards		b Asif Iqbal	42	62
*CH Lloyd	c Mudassar Nazar	b Asif Iqbal	37	38
CL King	c sub	b Sarfraz Nawaz	34	25
AI Kallicharran		b Imran Khan	11	14
AME Roberts	not out		7	4
J Garner	not out		1	1

Extras: (b 1, lb 17, w 1, nb 4) 23
Total: (6 wickets, 60 overs) 293

DNB: +DL Murray, MA Holding, CEH Croft.

FoW: 1-132 (Greenidge), 2-165 (Haynes), 3-233 (Richards),
4-236 (Lloyd), 5-285 (Kallicharran), 6-285 (King).

Bowling	O	M	R	W
Imran Khan	9	1	43	1
Sarfraz Nawaz	12	1	71	1
Sikander Bakht	6	1	24	0
Mudassar Nazar	10	0	50	0
Majid Khan	12	2	26	0
Asif Iqbal	11	0	56	4

Pakistan innings (target: 294 runs from 60 overs)			R	B
Majid Khan	c Kallicharran	b Croft	81	124
Sadiq Mohammad	c Murray	b Holding	2	7
Zaheer Abbas	c Murray	b Croft	93	122
Haroon Rashid	run out		15	22
Javed Miandad	lbw	b Croft	0	1
*Asif Iqbal	c Holding	b Richards	17	20
Mudassar Nazar	c Kallicharran	b Richards	2	9
Imran Khan	c & b Richards		6	4
Sarfraz Nawaz	c Haynes	b Roberts	12	15
+Wasim Bari	c Murray	b Roberts	9	12
Sikander Bakht	not out		1	4

Extras: (lb 9, w 2, nb 1) 12
Total: (all out, 56.2 overs) 250

FoW: 1-10 (Sadiq Mohammad), 2-176 (Zaheer Abbas),
3-187 (Majid Khan), 4-187 (Javed Miandad),
5-208 (Haroon Rashid), 6-220 (Mudassar Nazar),
7-221 (Asif Iqbal), 8-228 (Imran Khan), 9-246 (Wasim Bari),
10-250 (Sarfraz Nawaz).

Bowling	O	M	R	W
Roberts	9.2	2	41	2
Holding	9	1	28	1
Croft	11	0	29	3
Garner	12	1	47	0
King	7	0	41	0
Richards	8	0	52	3

Finals 23 June: Lord's, London

The home of cricket was filled to the rafters as a clear blue sky provided a magnificent canopy over proceedings. Many who had come to St John's Wood, the north London quarter that houses the ground, in expectation of picking up returned tickets left disappointed.

That no side relished facing the West Indian pacemen of the late 1970s' vintage in the freshness of an English forenoon was once again testified to by Brearley, a shrewd judge of the game, who invited Lloyd to bat. England were handicapped by the absence of Willis. But Edmonds, Brearley's Middlesex teammate, replacing him, emerged as the most economical of the English bowlers. This performance was offset, though, by Boycott, Gooch and Will Larkins, combining to bowl 12 overs, haemorrhaging 86 runs without any purchase.

Earlier, England's bowlers had got off to a dream start, as Botham, Hendrick and Chris Old – and an under-arm run out from mid-wicket by Randall – reduced the favourites to 99 for four. Richards was in control, but by his sublime standards, not his contemptuous self. The man who joined him at this point, though, evidently was. In about an hour and a quarter, King smashed three sixes and 10 fours in an awesome power play. He drove, hooked and pulled en route to 86 in a fifth-wicket association of 139 with Richards, and by the time he holed out at square leg off Edmonds, he had all but taken the game away from England.

Richards thereafter completed his hundred and famously flicked Old's last ball of the innings over square leg for six to remain unconquered on 138, with three hits over the fence and 11 fours.

A dry pitch under a salubrious afternoon glow was perfect for batting. But while Boycott and Brearley, opening for England, both crossed 50 and were unseparated for 130 minutes, they never managed to stamp their authority on the West Indian bowling. Indeed, Boycott spent 17 overs just to reach double figures. After Brearley left – caught off Holding – for 64, England required 158 runs in 22 overs, too tall an order by any definition. Gooch made a valiant attempt to step up the scoring, but in vain. In hot pursuit of their target, the Englishmen crumbled. In a sensational spell, the 6-ft-8-inch Garner snapped up five wickets for four runs in 11 balls and was twice on a hat trick.

As the giant Barbadian tightened his team's grip on the match, the music and dancing among the West Indian supporters in the stands grew in magnitude. And when the West Indies completed their 97-run win to retain the Prudential World Cup, their compatriots fittingly converted the hallowed abode of cricket into an arena for a Caribbean carnival.

Toss: England
Umpires: HD Bird and BJ Meyer
Man of the Match: IVA Richards

West Indies innings (60 overs maximum)			*R*	*B*
CG Greenidge	run out (Randall)		9	31
DL Haynes	c Hendrick	b Old	20	27
IVA Richards	not out		138	157
AI Kallicharran	b Hendrick		4	17
*CH Lloyd	c & b Old		13	33
CL King	c Randall	b Edmonds	86	66
+DL Murray	c Gower	b Edmonds	5	9
AME Roberts	c Brearley	b Hendrick	0	7
J Garner	c Taylor	b Botham	0	5
MA Holding		b Botham	0	6
CEH Croft	not out		0	2

Extras: (b 1, lb 10) 11
Total: (9 wickets, 60 overs) 286

FoW: 1-22 (Greenidge), 2-36 (Haynes), 3-55 (Kallicharran), 4-99 (Lloyd), 5-238 (King), 6-252 (Murray), 7-258 (Roberts), 8-260 (Garner), 9-272 (Holding).

Bowling	O	M	R	W
Botham	12	2	44	2
Hendrick	12	2	50	2
Old	12	0	55	2
Boycott	6	0	38	0
Edmonds	12	2	40	2
Gooch	4	0	27	0
Larkins	2	0	21	0

England innings (target: 287 runs from 60 overs)			R	B
*JM Brearley	c King	b Holding	64	130
G Boycott	c Kallicharran	b Holding	57	105
DW Randall		b Croft	15	22
GA Gooch		b Garner	32	28
DI Gower		b Garner	0	4
IT Botham	c Richards	b Croft	4	3
W Larkins		b Garner	0	1
PH Edmonds	not out		5	8
CM Old		b Garner	0	2
+RW Taylor	c Murray	b Garner	0	1
M Hendrick	b Croft		0	5

Extras: (lb 12, w 2, nb 3) 17
Total: (all out, 51 overs) 194

FoW: 1-129 (Brearley), 2-135 (Boycott), 3-183 (Gooch),
4-183 (Gower), 5-186 (Randall), 6-186 (Larkins),
7-192 (Botham), 8-192 (Old), 9-194 (Taylor),
10-194 (Hendrick).

Bowling	O	M	R	W
Roberts	9	2	33	0
Holding	8	1	16	2
Croft	10	1	42	3
Garner	11	0	38	5
Richards	10	0	35	0
King	3	0	13	0

Although the second World Cup did not enjoy the fairly uninterrupted sunshine of four year earlier, it was still an unqualified success. Prudential contributed £250,000 and revenues from ticket sales fetched £359,700 – almost double the takings in the first competition. But because of the sketchy weather, spectator presence dropped from 160,000 in 1975 to 132,000 in 1979. Eventually, the profit of £350,000 was shared between the full and associate members of the ICC.

Out of the £25,900 reserved for prize money, the West Indies received £10,000 and England £4000. New Zealand and Pakistan, the losing semi-finalists, went home with £2000 each, while winners of group matches got £500. Richards won £300 for his Man of the Match award in the finals; £200 were paid out in each of the semi-finals and £100 in the league matches to such nominated players.

With this championship, the ICC formally resolved to make the World Cup a four-yearly event, with the 1983 tournament once again allocated to England.

3

The Turning Point

GUYANA, SITUATED IN THE NORTHEAST OF SOUTH AMERICA, WITH
Venezuela to its west, Suriname to its east and Brazil to the south, is
a country of around one million people. The Dutch, who founded
colonies in the region in the seventeenth and eighteenth centuries,
imported African slaves for plantations producing sugar, coffee and
cotton. The territories were, then, ceded to Britain in 1814.

With the abolition of slavery in 1834, labourers were imported
from India, mainly from the northern provinces of Bihar and Uttar
Pradesh, many of whom settled in the country after their indentures.
As a result, people of Indian decent are in a slight majority in the
country, with Afro-Caribbeans largely constituting the rest of the
population.

Racial distinction has increasingly divided the country since the
1950s and more so after its independence in 1966. Dr Cheddi Jagan,
India's preferred choice as Guyanese head of government and an
approachable man, whom I encountered as a grey-haired person in
his mid-sixties at a reception at the Indian high commissioner's
residence in 1983, was the most widely accepted political leader in
Guyana. His Indo-Caribbean support base – he being of Indian origin
– was the backbone of his strength. He led his People's Progressive
Party (PPP) to victory in Guyana's first three elections under
universal suffrage – in 1953, 1957 and 1961 – but, because of his

radically left-wing views – which were shared by his American wife, Janet – was rather undemocratically relieved of office.

Many Afro-Caribbeans, who voted for the PPP in the first poll, shifted allegiance to Forbes Burnham, a black colleague of Jagan, who quit this party to form the People's National Congress. Following this, Britain and the United States pushed through proportional representation and, coupled with a plot to oust Jagan, manoeuvred Burnham into government. Indeed, when the Indian team toured the Caribbean in 1983, it was the latter who occupied the President's House, but, by this stage, even more controversially.

International observers had declared the 1980 election as fraudulent. After Burnham's death in 1985, though, Jagan was again duly elected. In March 1997, he died in harness at Washington D.C., where he had been taken for medical treatment after suffering a severe heart attack. Around 100,000 people, or practically 10 per cent of Guyana's population, attended his cremation.

The ethnic tension enveloped Guyanese cricket as well. Yet, this only non-island state in the cricketing consortium that comprises the West Indies has sprouted exceptional talent. Among the Afro-Caribbeans, there have been Basil Butcher, Lance Gibbs, Roy Fredericks, Clive Lloyd, Colin Croft and Carl Hooper, while the Indo-Caribbeans have included Rohan Babulal Kanhai, Alvin Kallicharran, Shivnarine Chanderpaul and Ramnaresh Sarwan. Typically, the blacks came from the country's coastal areas, including the capital Georgetown, which are generally inhabited by people of their background, whereas the Indians hailed from the 'interior', a term commonly used for inland areas.

The third leg of the visit by Kapil Dev's team in 1983 – the first two having been Jamaica and Trinidad in that order – was Guyana, which was, then, in a rather impoverished and lawless condition. The Dutch colonial architecture of the country was in a state of disrepair. Food was in short supply, of dodgy quality and quite unvaried even in the towering Pegasus Hotel at Georgetown overlooking the Atlantic Ocean where the two sides stayed – the best in the country. A phenomenon known as 'choke and rob' made it hazardous to venture onto the streets. But the hospitality of the local Indians, notably that of Dr B. P. Bhattacharyya, Guyana's most eminent gynaecologist, and his half-English daughter, enlivened the evenings.

On the morning of 29 March, the Indian and West Indians players as well as mediapersons were transported on military aircraft from Georgetown, which was also on the mouth of the Demerara (of sugar fame) river to Albion town in the rice-bowl region of Berbice (otherwise a five-hour drive), for – in those days – the less important business of playing a one-day international. The West Indians were, at the time, not only by far the most dominant force in tests, but also the best at limited-overs cricket, for which they had a natural propensity. They had, in fact, won both the Prudential World Cups held up to this juncture – in 1975 and 1979 – and were odds-on favourites to complete a hat trick in the one scheduled for June of that year.

In contrast, the Indians, who had performed abysmally in the two events and also been soundly beaten in the first one-dayer of this tour at Port of Spain, Trinidad, gave the impression of being unenthusiastic about the shorter format. They were, thus, only expected to serve as cannon fodder in the Guyanese countryside.

India's reticence in respect of one-day cricket stemmed from the fact that Sunil Gavaskar had either been their pre-eminent batsman or captain during the evolution of the limited-overs game onto the international stage. At a time when test cricket held centre-stage, his percentage batting was crafted to India's needs. It was not because he lacked flair, but because he hated to lose. And India were devoid of depth in both batting and bowling to be aggressive, as is necessary in one-day cricket.

For the greater part of the 1970s, compilation of runs by India depended heavily on him and his brother-in-law, Gundappa Viswanath. There was little luxury or leeway to play shots. Gavaskar's mentality, therefore, was to save a match first and to go on the offensive only if a genuine opportunity arose. He could apply this philosophy in tests with a degree of success, but not in one-dayers, where India were ill-equipped for the compulsions of an attacking game. They were accoutred with neither the batting talent nor the bowling prowess to flourish in a one-day situation. The Mumbai maestro tried to invigorate himself in the Benson & Hedges Series with Australia and New Zealand Down Under in 1980–81, where there was an incentive of prize money. But his predetermined mindset prevailed over him.

However, in the Caribbean, in 1983, Gavaskar had been replaced as skipper by Kapil, an athletic, sports-loving member of a Chandigarh-based business family.. This all-rounder from the northern agricultural state of Haryana, bordering the capital, New Delhi, was of a different mould. He was a belligerent swing bowler and naturally strokeful in his batting. He played the game with a carefree candour, instinctively and without worrying too much about the consequences. Safety first or unentertaining cricket was alien to his thinking. He once innocently asked me after one of his pleasing performances whether I had enjoyed it. The uncomplicated character that he was, it probably never occurred to him that I hadn't been at the ground as a paying spectator, but as an unsentimental journalist. Quite simply, his doctrine was to dish out delight to anyone caring to watch.

India had just been thrashed 3–0 in a test series in Pakistan, yet the composition of the squad despatched to the West Indies under Kapil was suddenly more promising. The resurfacing of Mohinder Amarnath in a brilliant, new incarnation, the advance of Dilip Vengsarkar (later to become the world's highest ranked batsman) and the performance of the stoic utilitarian, Ravi Shastri, had lessened the burden on Gavaskar, while Balwinder Singh Sandhu, a Sikh swing bowler from the cosmopolitan metropolis of Mumbai, provided a decent foil to Kapil. (Of course, India were beaten 2–0 in the five-test series on the 1983 tour by the irrepressible West Indian bulldozer navigated by Lloyd; but went down without discredit!)

The batting of Mohinder Amarnath, the second son of Lala Amarnath, who scored India's first test century against England in Mumbai in 1933, was particularly riveting. Continuing from where he left off in Pakistan, he met fire with fire, driving and hooking the West Indian fast bowlers in a manner they had rarely been treated before. With centuries at Port of Spain and St John's,

Antigua, and four other half-centuries, including two rip-roaring innings of 91 and 80 on a characteristically bouncy track at Bridgetown, Barbados – batting with stitches after being struck on his lips – he was at that stage incomparable against pace. Vivian Richards, a premier batsman in that era, but who never had the unenviable task of facing the fearsome foursomes of West Indian cricket, had graciously conceded as much at Kapil's birthday bash at Port of Spain. He, then, mischievously added: 'I take my hats off to you maan for the runs you got in Pakistan!' Inherent in the remark was Richards' belief – which he went on to elaborate – that the Pakistanis tampered with the ball, thus obtaining movement by unfair means. Amarnath, nicknamed 'Jimmy', smiled appreciatively. He had registered three hundreds on India's neighbouring soil a few months earlier to the Antiguan's solitary three-figure knock in Pakistan in his entire career. Indeed, while batting in a test and after being beaten several times by bending deliveries, Richards demanded to see the ball to check if it had been scuffed up.

As a growing number of Indian broadcasters and writers began accompanying Indian touring teams in the second half of the 1970s, a fun event of a match between the visiting and host media became an occasional feature of the calendar. One such meeting was held at Harrogate, in England, in 1979, which ended in a draw, after the Indians managed to hold out against an English attack spearheaded by a Nottinghamshire bowler still playing first-class cricket.

This was a bit like the joke about the match between the Church of England and the Catholic Order. The former decided to be flexible with the rules by requisitioning the services of a certain Ken Barrington (a top-notch Surrey and England batsman). Quite pleased about this coup d'état, the Archbishop cheerfully rang the venue of the match mid-way through the morning to ascertain the score. He was shocked to learn, though, that his side were plunged in a serious crisis. 'Who's doing the damage?' he fumed. 'A Father Fred Trueman (the premier Yorkshire and England pace bowler),' came the reply!

Anyhow, thanks to an unflappable rearguard effort by Qamar Ahmed, a Pakistani journalist whom we co-opted on the basis of birth – he having been born in Patna, before his family migrated to Hyderabad, in Sindh – and a supporting role by yours truly, we barely managed to save blushes.

The one-day international at Albion was preceded by a limited-overs sideshow at Georgetown. This match was between the Guyanese army and cricket scribes – Indians and West Indians, for there was an insufficient number from India to make up a eleven. Whose bright idea it was to agree to this face-off, I still haven't fathomed. But reports trickling through suggested the proposal from the men in uniform – made at cocktails hosted by President Burnham on the sprawling lawns of at his palatial residence – was more in the nature of an order than an invitation. It was as if the authorities wanted to soften up a breed they disliked, for media were, then, a detested tribe in Guyana; indeed, quite nonexistent, other than state-controlled monopolies.

We lost the toss and were hoping to field. The military would have none of this. They sent us in to bat. Big, burly fast bowlers, either whistling the ball past your ears or delivering toe-crushing yorkers, took charge of proceedings. Not surprisingly, we were soon in dire straits. I had neither carried any cricket clothes nor a pair of sports shoes (let alone cricket boots) on the trip. A white shirt was permissible; wearing this, along with light grey trousers and borrowed sneakers, I turned up at the designated ground. Then, with ill-fitting pads, an unfamiliar bat and not even a cap, forget any other protective gear, I made my way to the wicket to join my West Indian colleague, Tony Cozier, who was more accustomed to the circumstances, he being a regular club cricketer in Barbados, the nursery of Caribbean express bowlers. With one eye on my young wife, Pritha (whom I had married only two months earlier and who was sitting in the stands, smiling and oblivious of the physical danger confronting her husband), and the other on a large, looming figure racing towards me with a ball in his hand, which could crack my skull (or perhaps, with both my eyes shut at the sight of the latter), I kept going half forward so as to at least to avoid the embarrassment of the timber behind me going cartwheeling. My rudimentary method amused the legendary Kanhai, whose friendly banter from the stands, in the situation, wasn't exactly confidence boosting. The Cozier–Ray partnership, however, restored some respectability. But this notwithstanding, we were bowled out for less than 150.

The soldiers bristled with brashness. But with a blend of steady bowling and miraculous out-cricket, I, too, was fortunate enough to pull off a decent catch – we, somehow, bowled out the armed forces' unit for less than our score. The commanding officer was furious and immediately challenged us to a return match. Thankfully, the Indian team's packed schedule did not permit this!

The first ODI at Queen's Park Oval, Port of Spain, had been clipped to 39 overs a side owing to wet weather. Kapil, calling correctly, put the West Indies in, but only he prospered, that too, belatedly, in the favourable conditions, returning an analysis of two for 21 in 6.5 overs. The other Indian bowlers were nowhere near as accurate. As a result, the Windies compiled 215 for four, with Desmond Haynes, the Man of the Match, top-scoring with 97 off 104 balls. Indeed, Haynes and Gordon Greenidge, one of the most successful opening pairs in cricket history, notched up 125 for the first wicket, which all but put the nail in the Indian coffin. In reply, India only mustered 163 for seven. Not a single Indian batsman reached 30 against the frightening quartet of quick bowlers – Andy Roberts, Michael Holding, Joel Garner and Malcolm Marshall – of whom the first mentioned, with two for 27 in seven overs, was in his element. But it was the innocuous off-spin of Larry Gomes that swallowed three wickets, as the risk taking against him backfired for the Indians.

Albion, located in the alluvial, foliaged plains of the Berbice region, sometimes depicted as the 'ancient county', through which the Berbice river meandered, had once been a major sugar plantation hub. Masses of East Indian faces – not the ruddy skins of indigenous Indians of the American continent – glistened in the hazy, humid sunshine. They had mushroomed as if to greet and inspect messengers from the mother country. Among others, Kanhai, who originated from here, was concurrently visiting his mother, who still lived nearby. Not surprisingly, some darker complexions bestrewed the welcome party. Basil Butcher, after all, came from the same area. What caught the eye were banana groves and coconut trees half-concealing Biswasian cottages of Naipaulian description (though this was Guyana, not Trinidad). Small, red, triangular flags – with a clearly Hindu connotation – fluttered in the breeze. A boisterous crowd of 15,000, with distinctly divided loyalties, were assembled at the town's Sports Complex.

Lloyd, the West Indian skipper, had settled in England, where he had long worn Lancashire's colours in the county scene. Now back on native soil, he won the toss. With the battery of fast bowlers at his disposal, he generally fancied unleashing them while the pitch was still fresh in the morning, regardless of the opposition. This time, too, he made no exception. He inserted India; and let loose his speed merchants, who indicated a change, with an injured Garner being rested for Winston Davis, who was making his ODI debut. But contrary to all expectations, India did not surrender a wicket until Shastri, opening the innings with Gavaskar, was caught behind off Marshall with the total on 93.

Gavaskar, a middle-class Maharashtrian groomed in the batting mill of Mumbai's Dadar Union club, had been the bane of West Indian bowlers with record-breaking aggregates in test series in 1971 and 1976. But he had, thus far on this visit, not been his normal, prolific self. Not only had he disappointed in the previous one-dayer, but also had a top score of just 32 in four test innings, which included a first ball duck at Sabina Park, Kingston, where his stumps were spectacularly sent cantering by the local limousine, Michael Holding. (Incidentally, this match was graced by the fabled, Panamanian-born Jamaican, George Headley, widely acknowledged as the 'black Bradman', though his die-hard fans preferred to refer to the Australian, Sir Donald Bradman, arguably the greatest batsman of all time, as the 'white Headley'. Headley died later that year.)

Gavaskar, nephew of a former test wicketkeeper, Madhav Mantri, was, of course, the primary target of the West Indian quicks, with Lloyd not averse to employing them around the wicket to pretty much aim every ball at his head or ribs. With no fixed ceiling on bouncers in those days, nothing, I daresay, in cricket history could have been as threatening as this four-pronged offensive against Gavaskar, not even the Douglas Jardine-inspired bodyline bowling of Harold Larwood in Australia in 1932–33 in Australia to contain Bradman. Gavaskar's absence of form, though, might also have been caused by the fact that he was yet to come to terms with being deposed as captain. To return to the ranks from a lofty pedestal is never easy. In his case, to play under someone considerably his junior could also have been a factor. Besides, relations between him and his successor, Kapil had become a little tense. This, because of an ego clash, a West Zone–North Zone rivalry that still existed in Indian cricket at the time and also because of the misleading influence of their cronies.

At Albion, though, he carved one of the most significant limited-overs knocks of his career. Indeed, by the time he was run out for 90 – and India had progressed to 152 for two – he had the Windies really worried. (A good-humoured prankster, Sunil and his wife Pammie occupied the room next to us at the hotel in Georgetown. Among his antics was to switch the notice hanging at our door from 'Please do not disturb' to 'Please clean the room'. The trick failed as the housekeeping staff either did not have a master key or ignored the sign! But it's still a mystery as to who in 1981 ordered an expensive, unsolicited full English breakfast for an All India Radio commentator in his hotel room at Adelaide or a lady escort to his room at Wellington, where his wife was present! The finger of suspicion pointed at Gavaskar, Pataudi and journalist, Dicky Rutnagur!! The case was, however, never proved!!!) More pertinently, Gavaskar was delighted with his Albion essay. It was as if he had crossed the Rubicon and proved to himself and the world that he was now ready for the one-day requirements.

Kapil replaced Gavaskar. He connected with the ball like a Muhammad Ali punch. Aware that his opponents had been softened up, he was determined not to allow them to return to their feet. With languid ease, he floated down the wicket like a butterfly but stung the bowlers, especially Gomes and Holding, like a bee! With seven fours and three sixes, he raced to a stunning 72 in 38 balls. Like the Hindu God, Hanuman torching pre-historic Lanka in the mythological epic, Ramayana, he set Albion ablaze. The match had been reduced to 47 overs for each side the West Indies, faced an uncommonly stiff target of 283.

Yet Greenidge and Haynes strode out, but were soon separated as Sandhu trapped the latter leg before wicket. The other followed not long afterwards – caught and bowled by Kapil – and Lloyd, too, perished cheaply, falling victim to Madan Lal. His exit reduced the home side to 62 for three, to which the imperious Vivian Richards had contributed the most. As far as the Indians were concerned, his was the key wicket. He majestically moved to 64, but at this point, Madan Lal shattered his stumps.

Eight years previously, I had seen the same, underrated bowler send back this burgeoning batsman with a ball that swung away to start with and then moved back at the Eden Gardens in Kolkata. It was in the final session of play – when a breeze used to emanate from the nearby Hooghly river and assist deviation in the air at this ground – on the fourth day of the third test in a best-of-five series. Tiger Pataudi, leading India, reintroduced the medium-pacer against the wind. Madan Lal disfigured Richards' sticks after the batsman had ominously progressed to 47. It was the only wicket he took in that innings – as the spinners, Bishan Bedi and Bhagwat Chandrasekhar wrapped up the match to fetch India victory after being beaten in the first two tests at Bangalore and Delhi. But the menacing Richards' was, arguably, the most valuable scalp.

At Albion, a more mature and determined West Indies did not cave in that easily. Faoud Bacchus and Jeff Dujon, with half centuries, resisted spiritedly. But Shastri, with his left-arm orthodox stuff, chipped in with three wickets. And so, the undisputed champions of both forms of cricket crashed to unprecedented defeat by 27 runs. It was the first time that a full-strength West Indian side had lost a one-day international at home. The only other instance was in

1978, when they went down to Australia by two wickets – in a match restricted to 36 overs by rain – when both teams were weakened by the exodus of a majority of their leading cricketers to Kerry Packer's rebel 'World Series'.

For India, this was their first-ever win over the West Indies in an ODI anywhere.

Tension had increased at the ground as the possibility of an Indian win intensified. Having applauded Gavaskar and Kapil in the morning, the Indo-Caribbeans in attendance could not help appreciate the combined effort of the visiting bowlers. This annoyed the Afro-Caribbeans. At one stage, scuffles spilling over from the temporary stands, not to mention the worsening light, raised fears of an abandonment, which the West Indians wouldn't have minded.

Bacchus' presence in the side notwithstanding, Guyanese Indians were generally dissatisfied with the West Indian team selection. They felt Kalicharran, among others, had received a raw deal under the Lloyd regime – a point rubbed in to me in no uncertain manner by the former, a follower of the Indian spiritual leader, Sai Baba, one evening at Birmingham (where he was stationed, playing, as he was, for Warwickshire) in 1980. Gavaskar who had turned out that season for Somerset and Dilip Doshi who was also on Warwicks' staff, were present. Whether on merit or by design, it is factually correct that very few Indo-Caribbeans wore West Indian colours under Lloyd and Richards.

The West Indies, predictably, proceeded to win the third and final ODI at Queen's Park, St George's, in Grenada. In 1979, this island state had witnessed the overthrow of a crooked and erratic government in a bloodless coup by a left-wing group, who set up a People's Revolutionary Government, with a youthful Maurice Bishop as its head. In April 1983, the bearded Bishop mixed freely at a party for the cricketers. He even expressed to me his admiration for Indira Gandhi, then back as India's prime minister. (But the United States suspected an increase in Cuban influence in Grenada and perceived the construction of an airport in the island with Havana's assistance to be a threat. In October 1983 – six months after my accidental chat with Bishop – one of his deputies and the army chief seized power. The prime minister was murdered. Without the courtesy of consulting Britain's Queen Elizabeth, who was still Grenada's head of state, the US, supposedly the UK's closest ally, invaded and overran the tiny territory.)

As for the cricket, the West Indian ploy of putting the other side in did pay off on this occasion. India were dismissed for 166 in 44.4 overs. Only Vengsarkar, with 54, staged a fight. Holding, the Jamaican Rolls Royce, was superb with a return of two for 15 in 8.4 overs. But once again, Gomes profited the most with figures of four for 38. The West Indies, then, romped home victorious by seven wickets, with Greenidge being declared the Man of the Match. It was reminiscent of the mismatch between the two sides at Edgbaston, Birmingham, in the 1979 Prudential World Cup.

The significance of the Indian triumph at Albion, though, is immeasurable. It helped the Indians to realize they were not so useless in one-day cricket; that what was hitherto deemed to be unimaginable – beating the West Indies in the abbreviated form – had, actually, been achieved, that, too, in the West Indians' backyard. The victory converted an erstwhile apathy towards the shorter version of the game into a calculated keenness for it.

While the attainment could well have been labelled a flash in the pan, it soon became obvious that the psychological gain from it was enormous. It signified that India entered the Prudential World Cup less than three months later in a completely different frame of mind as compared to the two previous such competitions. They were more self-assured against all teams, including the formidable West Indies. This aspect was, in fact, to manifest itself in their very first outing against the defending champions at Old Trafford, Manchester.

In more ways than one, therefore, the ascent at Albion was the turning point in India's odyssey in limited-overs cricket, which was soon to lead to a lustrous display in the 1983 Prudential World Cup.

Toss: West Indies
Umpires: DM Archer and MN Baksh
ODI Debuts: WW Davis (WI).
Man of the Match: N Kapil Dev

India innings (47 overs maximum)			R	B
SM Gavaskar	run out		90	117
RJ Shastri	c Dujon	b Marshall	30	56
M Amarnath		b Richards	30	34
*N Kapil Dev		b Roberts	72	38
Yashpal Sharma	c Greenidge	b Davis	23	26
DB Vengsarkar	not out		18	19
AO Malhotra	not out		1	3

Extras: (b 1, lb 9, w 4, nb 4) 18
Total: (5 wickets, 47 overs) 282

DNB: S Madan Lal, +SMH Kirmani, BS Sandhu, S Venkataraghavan.
FoW: 1-93 (Shastri), 2-152 (Gavaskar), 3-224 (Amarnath),
4-246 (Kapil Dev), 5-277 (Yashpal Sharma).

Bowling	O	M	R	W
Holding	7	0	49	0
Roberts	9	0	44	1
Davis	8	0	40	1
Marshall	7	0	23	1
Gomes	10	0	64	0
Richards	6	0	44	1

West Indies innings (target: 283 runs from 47 overs)			R	B
CG Greenidge	c & b Kapil Dev		16	28
DL Haynes	lbw	b Sandhu	2	7
IVA Richards		b Madan Lal	64	51
*CH Lloyd	c Amarnath	b Madan Lal	8	4
SFAF Bacchus	c Yashpal Sharma	b Shastri	52	65
HA Gomes	c Kapil Dev	b Shastri	26	28
+PJL Dujon	not out		53	64
1MD Marshall	c Sandhu	b Shastri	5	6
AME Roberts		b Kapil Dev	12	10
MA Holding	c Malhotra	b Sandhu	2	8
WW Davis	not out		7	12

Extras: (lb 6, w 1, nb 1) 8
Total: (9 wickets, 47 overs) 255

FoW: 1-6 (Haynes), 2-22 (Greenidge), 3-62 (Lloyd),
4-98 (Richards), 5-154 (Gomes), 6-181 (Bacchus),
7-192 (Marshall), 8-228 (Roberts), 9-232 (Holding).

Bowling	O	M	R	W
Kapil Dev	10	0	33	2
Sandhu	10	0	38	2
Madan Lal	9	0	65	2
Venkataraghavan	10	0	63	0
Shastri	8	0	48	3

4

The Summer of 1983

'THE SUN NEVER SHINES AT OLD TRAFFORD,' HAS BEEN AN ENDLESS refrain about the opprobrious weather at this Manchester ground. This is where the Lancashire and England fast bowler, Brian Statham, flourished in the 1950s and early 1960s as the pitch acquired a greenish hue under cloud cover exacerbated by industrial pollution, but where batsmen would make hay when the sky cleared.

I have always felt attracted to Old Trafford, with its pavilion, unlike most other international cricket grounds, square to the wicket, a chaplet of red brick, Victorian masonry. This affection was triggered in my teens, when reading the *doyen* of English cricket writers, Sir Neville Cardus, himself a Mancunian. Among many gems, I came across his description of Kumar Sri Ranjitsinhji's batting, especially his leg glance – a shot he invented and even executed from off-stump – as 'esoteric *legerdemain*'. 'Ranji', the first Indian to play test cricket and later the Jam Saheb or ruler (of the princely state) of Nawanagar, in the western Indian state of Gujarat, made his debut at Old Trafford in 1896.

Not only that; he became the second batsman after W. G. Grace, the Gloucestershire doctor recognized as the father of batsmanship, to score a hundred on his maiden appearance for England – from all accounts a magical effort. In so doing, he also became the first player to complete a hundred runs before lunch in a test match. On the third morning, he took his overnight contribution of 41 to 154, thus adding 113 runs in a session and setting a record that remains unsurpassed in Ashes series.

The fact that Farokh Engineer, the Indian wicketkeeper-batsman of the 1960s and 1970s from Mumbai, joined Lancashire County Cricket Club – whose home is Old Trafford – in 1968, further enhanced my interest. 'Rooky', as he came to be called in England, was a swashbuckling cricketer who caught the imagination of many in my generation, especially after he almost reached three figures before the luncheon interval at Chennai in 1967 against the West Indies led by Garry (later Sir Garfield) Sobers. His 94 not out at the interval on the first day was no mean effort, for it was at the expense of Wesley Hall, Charlie Griffith, Sobers himself and Lance Gibbs. He went on to record 109.

Last but not the least, on a grey afternoon, within weeks of my arrival in England for the first time as an adult, I saw Greg Chappell, then Australia's captain and some three decades later India's coach, etch an innings of 112 out of a total of 218. Remembering Cardus, I was inspired to characterize his footwork against England's left-arm spinner Derek Underwood on a dodgy pitch (Australia lost the test by nine wickets) to the felicity of the Russian ballet dancer Rudolf Nureyev, whom I had just seen on the London stage.

Cardus was also the music critic of *The Manchester Guardian*, later *The Guardian*, the distinguished British daily, in addition to being its cricket correspondent. John Arlott, who succeeded Cardus as cricket correspondent, fulfilled a dual responsibility, as well. He was the wine appraiser of the paper. In the summer of 1979, he was seated immediately behind me at the old press box at Lord's, when he narrated a friendly banter between him and Cardus about who had enjoyed the better job overall. They agreed, in terms of cricket, they were at par. But what about the additional role? Arlott insisted his was the cushier circumstance since he got to savour the finest wines in the market. Cardus thought about this for a while, then retorted: 'But who would you rather spend an evening with? A drunk or a soprano?' Arlott of the gravelly Hampshire voice was stumped!

★

India had mixed memories of Manchester. Here, in 1936, Vijay Merchant, a textile tycoon and a prolific run-getter from Mumbai, and Mushtaq Ali, the light-footed Virender Sehwag of his era, put on 203 for the first wicket, but in 1952, India were bowled out for 58 and 82 to lose by an innings. India also went down in 1959, despite the elegant Hyderabadi Abbas Ali Baig posting a hundred on debut, and succumbed once more in 1974, in spite of a Sunil Gavaskar century. The Indians drew in 1982, though, when Sandip Patil, a Bombay belter, pummelled Bob Willis for six fours – a world test record – in a seven-ball over (one of which was a no-ball). His 24 runs also equalled the test record for the highest number of runs in an over held by Andy Roberts. Indeed, he fairly motored from 73 to 104 off a mere nine balls. (I was also an eyewitness to this feat being ingeminated by Ramnaresh Sarwan of the West Indies at St Kitts in June 2006 at the expense of paceman Munaf Patel.)

Patil was a natural and powerful stroke player. But practice and fitness were not his forte. Gavaskar, his captain both at state and national levels, used to virtually beseech his parents to ensure that he attended nets and training regimens. In fact, Patil had looked rather out of sorts in county games on the 1982 tour and, consequently, couldn't be accommodated in the team for the first test at Lord's. But after India lost this match, the tour selectors decided to gamble with him. That they were not exactly confident about him was reflected by him being held back to number seven in the batting order. Indeed, he walked in at 136 for five, with his side still requiring 90 runs to save the follow-on. But what an exhibition he, then, proffered! Willis, a redoubtable fast bowler, probably still wakes up with a sweat from the mauling meted out to him.

This was the second of two heroic performances from Patil I had had the pleasure of observing. The previous one was at the Adelaide Oval, a year and a half earlier.

In the first test of that series, he had been fearfully hit on the head by a Lenny Pascoe bouncer on a lively first-day wicket at the

Sydney Cricket Ground. Tiger Pataudi, sitting next to me in the press box, unconsciously grabbed my arm in a grip that left me a bit bruised. As Patil – batting on 65 (which transpired to be the top score in an innings of 201) – crumpled, Pataudi had visions of Nari Contractor being near-fatally struck on the head by a short-pitched delivery from Charlie Griffith that failed to rise in the Barbados game in 1962. Contractor, leading the side on that ill-fated trip (India lost all five tests), gave way to Pataudi, then only 21, for the rest of the tour.

As Bapu Nadkarni, the slender erstwhile test player, who was India's assistant manager on that tour, struggled to lift – let alone carry – a concussed Patil back to the pavilion, an otherwise phlegmatic Pataudi, couldn't help exclaiming loudly: 'Get help, Bapu!' When Patil came out to bat with a helmet (not yet a universal feature) in the second innings, he shakily spooned a catch close to the wicket off Dennis Lillee to be dismissed for four.

The consensus based on such evidence was: he would be hard put to make a comeback to international cricket; the question of his participation in the rest of this series was completely ruled out. Experts averred: the psychological trauma of the injury was difficult to overcome. India were defeated in the match by an innings.

Less than three weeks later was the second test at Adelaide. (Among the spectators was none other than Sir Donald Bradman, who, despite being distrustful of journalists at that stage, kindly agreed to meet me for a private chat at the local Oberoi Hotel, owned by the India-headquartered chain.) To most people's surprise, Patil was included in the eleven.

Australia piled up 528 and India were starkly looking down a barrel at 130 for four, when he entered the fray. Not unexpectedly, he was greeted by a barrage of bumpers. At first, he ducked and let them sail over his shoulders. Then, once he got set, he embarked on hooking Lillee, Pascoe and Rodney Hogg through midwicket in a fierce riposte. Indeed, he stormed to 174 off 240 balls, with 22 fours and a six. It was a remarkable rejuvenation after such a frightful jolt. India drew the match and proceeded to win the next one at the Melbourne Cricket Ground to avoid defeat in a test series in Australia for the first time.

In 1983, the third and final World Cup to be sponsored by the Prudential Assurance Company was still a 60-overs-a-side competition. A bowler was allowed a maximum of 12 overs per innings, and the umpires became perceptibly stricter in applying the rules in respect of wides and bouncers.

There were once more eight participants, who were divided into two groups. But the build-up was different from that of the preceding World Cups in that, in the preliminary phase, the sides played each other not once but twice. This was partly to enhance revenue but also to reduce the chances of a team being eliminated because of worse luck with the weather than their rivals. In actual fact, after one of the wettest Mays on record, the clouds all but disappeared in June; and of the 27 matches played, only three were not concluded in a day. The first two from each group in the league stage qualified for the semi-finals and the knockout portion, with the winners of a cluster taking on the runners-up of the other. India's section had West Indies, Australia and Zimbabwe, while the other assembly was made up of England, Pakistan, New Zealand and Sri Lanka. India, 66: 1 outsiders before the tournament began, commenced their campaign in Old Trafford's fluctuating conditions. It could not have been a more foreboding challenge, for the opposition were again the Windies!

The contrast between 1979 and 1983 was that the Indians had in the interim undergone a grinding in Australia in 1980–81 when they took part in the triangular Benson & Hedges World Series Cup, which exposed them to 10 ODIs on the trot. Ultimately they prevailed in only three of these outings, but perforce gained useful experience in the ways and means of dealing with the shorter version of the game. Indeed, they made a surprisingly good start, winning three of their first four matches, but subsequently fell away sharply to seldom look like winning another game. The batsmen seemed untuned to the urgency demanded by instant cricket. Much of the bowling was uncontrolled and the overall fielding was not up to the mark.

The evening before the opener at Old Trafford, I had driven up with Ambassador Pushkar Johari, then India's deputy high commissioner in the UK and a cricket enthusiast (who had once commentated on a match in Guyana, when he was the Indian high commissioner there), to check into a hotel in Manchester's city centre, where the Indian team had also registered. For me, it was a bit of a reunion with the boys, for we had parted company only a month earlier. Following the tour of the West Indies, I had been conscripted by the Indians (deserted by some of their team-mates) to participate in two unofficial one-day matches against the United States of America at Washington D. C. (which, needless to mention, we won quite easily). There were few barriers between the Indian players and the press in those days. While in a way it was interaction between the scanned and the scanner, the two functioned quite integrally when overseas. The meeting point was often the watering hole of the team hotel. This time, too, the old rule was in force. But the rebonding effected, next morning, it was back to the respective roles of cricketer and commentator or chronicler.

9–10 June: Old Trafford, Manchester

It was a tricolour attendance – whites, Afro-Caribbeans and Asians. The indigenous folks had come to catch a glimpse of the then most respected cricketing outfit in the planet, and the West Indians and Indians had turned up to support their respective sides – the former more unabashedly, as they were sanguine about the outcome. The latter were more subdued, indeed nervous, that their compatriots might end up as lambs for slaughter.

Greater Manchester and cities and town around it, from Liverpool in the west, Birmingham to the south and West Yorkshire to the east across the Pennine mountain range, have absorbed multitudes of immigrants from both the Caribbean and the Indian subcontinent. From upwardly mobile Afro-Caribbeans in felt hats to men in boiler suits, from Indian medical practitioners to factory workers, the stands reflected a variety of pastels and people. The West Indians were soon into their rum and music. The Indians watched in admiration and amusement, tucking into benign sandwiches.

The West Indies won the toss and – as you would expect – put India in after a delayed start owing to inclement weather. Indeed, India struggled on a damp pitch and indifferent light to lose three wickets for 79. But a splendid innings of 89 by Yashpal Sharma, Kapil Dev's Haryana team-mate, in 120 balls, before he was bowled by Michael Holding, boosted them to their highest total in three World Cups. Sharma's was, up to that point, also the best-ever contribution by an Indian batsman in the World Cup. His 73-run partnership for the sixth wicket with Roger Binny, who got 27, principally contributed to this score. Patil chipped in with a sprightly 36. As the sun filtered through the clouds, the Indian innings brightened with it. Of the first eight batsmen, only Kapil Dev did not record double figures.

In reply, Gordon Greenidge and Desmond Haynes began confidently, scoring 49 before the latter was run out. From that moment, India began to tighten their grip on the match. With play spilling over to the reserve day, the West Indies recommenced on 67 for two in the 23rd over. To India's relief, Richards departed early – caught behind off Binny – and skipper Clive Lloyd, was bowled by the same bowler. The champions rapidly collapsed to 157 for nine. Andy Roberts and Joel Garner, though, demonstrated remarkable fortitude by realizing 71 runs before wicketkeeper Syed Kirmani smartly stumped the latter off Ravi Shastri to seal the West Indies' fate.

This was their first-ever loss in the World Cup. The West Indies caved in by 34 runs; their venture lasting only 54.1 overs. It was only India's second win in the World Cup – the previous one being against an unpretentious East African side in 1975. Shastri and Binny, an Anglo-Indian all-rounder from Bangalore, were slightly expensive, but both captured three wickets apiece, while medium pacers Madan Lal and Balwinder Singh Sandhu were the most economical. Where Yashpal Sharma had found the fence nine times, the West Indians, albeit on a slow outfield, failed to hit a single four. Garner, though, struck a six.

The cricketing world, especially English media, centred around England's affairs and inattentive about developments elsewhere, was stunned. But to some of us who had witnessed the Indian win at Albion, the result, while, admittedly, unexpected, was not an absolute surprise. It suggested that Albion was probably not a fluke, and that 'Kapil's devils' could now be treated as dark horses for the tournament. The advantage India possessed, as compared to the other sides, was that they were fresh from encountering the West Indian quicks — their most potent weapon — less than a couple of months earlier and had almost come to terms with them by compiling 457 runs in an innings in the final test at Antigua. It had also dawned on the Indians that, after Albion, the West Indians were no longer impregnable.

Toss: West Indies
Umpires: B Leadbeater and AGT Whitehead
Man of the Match: Yashpal Sharma
Close of Play: **Day 1:** India 262/8,
West Indies 67/2 (Richards 12*, Bacchus 3*, 22 ov)

India innings (60 overs maximum)			*R*	*B*
SM Gavaskar	c Dujon	b Marshall	19	44
K Srikkanth	c Dujon	b Holding	14	17
M Amarnath	c Dujon	b Garner	21	60
SM Patil		b Gomes	36	52
Yashpal Sharma		b Holding	89	120
*N Kapil Dev	c Richards	b Gomes	6	13
RMH Binny	lbw	b Marshall	27	38
S Madan Lal	not out		21	22
+SMH Kirmani	run out		1	2
RJ Shastri	not out		5	3

Extras: (b 4, lb 10, w 1, nb 8) 23
Total: (8 wickets, 60 overs) 262

DNB: BS Sandhu.

FoW: 1-21 (Srikkanth), 2-46 (Gavaskar), 3-76 (Amarnath),
4-125 (Patil), 5-141 (Kapil Dev), 6-214 (Binny),
7-243 (Yashpal Sharma), 8-246 (Kirmani).

Bowling	O	M	R	W
Holding	12	3	32	2
Roberts	12	1	51	0
Marshall	12	1	48	2
Garner	12	1	49	1
Richards	2	0	13	0
Gomes	10	0	46	2

West Indies innings (target: 263 runs from 60 overs)			R	B
CG Greenidge		b Sandhu	24	55
DL Haynes	run out		24	29
IVA Richards	c Kirmani	b Binny	17	36
SFAF Bacchus		b Madan Lal	14	24
*CH Lloyd		b Binny	25	38
+PJL Dujon	c Sandhu	b Binny	7	12
HA Gomes	run out		8	16
MD Marshall	st Kirmani	b Shastri	2	5
AME Roberts	not out		37	58
MA Holding	b Shastri		8	11
J Garner	st Kirmani	b Shastri	37	29

Extras: (b 4, lb 17, w 4) 25
Total: (all out, 54.1 overs) 228

FoW: 1-49 (Haynes), 2-56 (Greenidge), 3-76 (Richards),
4-96 (Bacchus), 5-107 (Dujon), 6-124 (Gomes),
7-126 (Marshall), 8-130 (Lloyd), 9-157 (Holding),
10-228 (Garner).

Bowling	O	M	R	W
Kapil Dev	10	0	34	0
Sandhu	12	1	36	1
Madan Lal	12	1	34	1
Binny	12	1	48	3
Shastri	5.1	0	26	3
Patil	3	0	25	0

The result at Old Trafford was not the only upset in the opening round of matches. More sensationally, Australia lost to Zimbabwe by 13 runs (starring in this win was skipper Duncan Fletcher, later England's coach, who with an unbeaten 69 and four wickets for 42, almost single-handedly overcame the Aussies and was, duly, made Man of the Match).

11 June: Leicester

India's next engagement was at Leicester, a central England town, which is home to Leicestershire County Cricket Club, whose colours the languorously graceful left-handed batsman, David Gower, once wore. It had also become a sanctuary for people of Indian origin fleeing persecution in East Africa, notably at the hands of the Ugandan dictator, Idi Amin. India, thus, expected exuberant support from the crowd; and this was commensurately extended.

The opposition were Zimbabwe, who were taking part in a World Cup for the first time, having qualified by virtue of winning the ICC Trophy in 1982. Though still not a test-playing nation, they were fresh from toppling Australia. Their side included several players with first-class experience, acquired from representing Rhodesia (as Zimbabwe was previously known) – in the quite competitive Currie Cup of South Africa. As a matter of fact, in the 1960s, Colin Bland, a Rhodesian, was a conspicuous member of the South African test team, he being the Jonty Rhodes of his generation or a fielder *par excellence*.

Indeed, in 1965, before the start of South Africa's match with Sussex, a contest had been arranged between him and Pataudi, then on this county's staff, to determine the world's best fieldsman. Reportedly, a delayed arrival on the part of the nawab, forced a cancellation. The moral of the story: Zimbabwe could not to be taken lightly.

A drizzle postponed start of play until after lunch. Then, having to bat first, the Zimbabweans were shaken by the extent of swing and bounce extracted by the Indian medium pacers, notably Madan Lal. This Delhi all-rounder boasted an analysis of three for 27, as Zimbabwe were bundled out cheaply. The Indian fielding was frail, but Kirmani, a Bangalorean Muslim with a Telly Savalas-style shaven head – 'Kiri' to his mates and the best Indian wicketkeeper I have ever seen – took five catches to establish a new World Cup record, improving on the West Indian Deryck Murray's four victims against Sri Lanka in the inaugural event.

In persistently murky conditions, India slumped to 32 for two, as the fast-medium, Peter Rawson, too, exploited the heaviness in the air; and the 36-year-old off-spinner John Traicos, who played for South Africa in tests in 1970 – more than 22 years before he did so for Zimbabwe – bowled a tight spell. At this point in the Indian innings, one of my colleagues, the Zimbabwean commentator in the host broadcaster, BBC's panel, jumped the gun a bit, thinking a second upset was in the offing. But a 69-run association between Mohinder Amarnath and Patil, who was dropped at 12, cleared the mist. India ultimately cruised home by five wickets with 22.3 overs to spare.

Toss: India
Umpires: J Birkenshaw and R Palmer
ODI Debuts: RD Brown (Zim).
Man of the Match: S Madan Lal

Zimbabwe innings (60 overs maximum)			R	B
AH Omarshah	c Kirmani	b Sandhu	8	32
GA Paterson	lbw	b Madan Lal	22	51
JG Heron	c Kirmani	b Madan Lal	18	30
AJ Pycroft	c Shastri	b Binny	14	21
+DL Houghton	c Kirmani	b Madan Lal	21	47
*DAG Fletcher	b Kapil Dev		13	32
KM Curran	run out		8	16
IP Butchart	not out		22	35
RD Brown	c Kirmani	b Shastri	6	27
PWE Rawson	c Kirmani	b Binny	3	6
AJ Traicos	run out		2	13

Extras: (lb 9, w 9) 18
Total: (all out, 51.4 overs) 155

FoW: 1-13 (Omarshah), 2-55 (Heron), 3-56 (Paterson),
4-71 (Pycroft), 5-106 (Fletcher), 6-114 (Houghton),
7-115 (Curran), 8-139 (Brown), 9-148 (Rawson),
10-155 (Traicos).

Bowling	O	M	R	W
Kapil Dev	9	3	18	1
Sandhu	9	1	29	1
Madan Lal	10.4	0	27	3
Binny	11	2	25	2
Shastri	12	1	38	1

India innings (target: 156 runs from 60 overs)			R	B
K Srikkanth	c Butchart	b Rawson	20	27
SM Gavaskar	c Heron	b Rawson	4	11
M Amarnath	c sub	b Traicos	44	79
SM Patil		b Fletcher	50	54
RJ Shastri	c Brown	b Omarshah	17	27
Yashpal Sharma	not out		18	19
*N Kapil Dev	not out		2	8

Extras: (w 2) 2
Total: (5 wickets, 37.3 overs) 157

DNB: RMH Binny, S Madan Lal, +SMH Kirmani, BS Sandhu.

FoW: 1-13 (Gavaskar), 2-32 (Srikkanth), 3-101 (Amarnath),4-128 (Patil),
5-148 (Shastri).

Bowling	O	M	R	W
Rawson	5.1	1	11	2
Curran	6.5	1	33	0
Butchart	5	1	21	0
Traicos	11	1	41	1
Fletcher	6	1	32	1
Omarshah	3.3	0	17	1

June 13: Trent Bridge, Nottingham

I have fond memories of Trent Bridge, Nottinghamshire County Cricket Club's seat of power and where Harold Larwood – a collier from the county's mineral belt – first caught the attention of England's selectors to go on to shatter the serenity of cricket with superfast deliveries at batsmen's bodies at the behest of his captain, Douglas Jardine, in the 1932–33 tests Down Under.

It was here that I was for the first time invited to join BBC's Test Match Special (TMS) broadcast at lunch in the 1977 Ashes test to answer questions from listeners. The other two on the panel were the well-known English commentators, John Arlott and Christopher Martin-Jenkins. I cite this episode only because it was, then, uncommon, possibly unheard-of, for a broadcaster from a third country to figure on TMS during an Anglo–Australian contest. The English, in particular, were rather protective of what they perceived as a kind of private battle.

Indeed, when I entered the Lord's press box (which used to be beside the pavilion at the time, before the spaceship facility shot up at the nursery end) for the first test of that series, I was met with quizzical stares from the middle rows, generally occupied by tabloid scribes. One of them, in fact, throwing politeness to the wind, asked: 'What's this got to do with you?'

Six year later at Trent Bridge, I was lined up against the wall before start of play in the same commentary box I had shared with John and Chris six years earlier by the wife of another English cricket commentator, Brian Johnston, to be photographed for a book BBC was rushing to print. The commentary team for the match included a representative of the Australian Broadcasting Commission, as the broadcast was being relayed live in Australia.

But India's remembrance of Trent Bridge wasn't exactly inspiring. In 1959, they had been thrashed by an innings and 59 runs. Now, though, they took the field, still maintaining a clean slate in the tourney. Australia, however, won the toss and capitalized on a gloriously sunny East Midland morning and a beautiful batting wicket. Trevor Chappell was dropped by Binny off his own bowling when

27 and this youngest of three brothers – the others being the more eminent Ian and Greg – to wear the baggy green cap made the Indians pay with a stroke-filled 110. With his captain, Kim Hughes, he put on 144 runs for the second wicket in 29 overs, which laid the foundation of a demanding total. Graham Yallop, then, proceeded to post an unbeaten 66. Only Kapil made any impression on the Aussies, finishing with five for 45, which included four in his last three.

A sidelight remains engraved in memory. When towards the closing stages of the Aussie innings, a batsman holed out to Kapil near the boundary, far from celebrating – as quick bowlers do in such circumstances these days – he hardly smiled. It wasn't the grimness of India's situation that precluded happiness. It was considered to be an insult for a fast bowler to be lofted that far afield. Kapil, with an instinctive grasp of the finer points of the game, was conscious of this aspect and he conveyed it in unmistakable terms.

India were without Gavaskar – officially injured, although some suspected he had been dropped – and when they batted, the sky turned surly, and stoppages caused by indifferent light, intermittent drizzle or both, made their monumental task even more difficult. With the wicket freshening, the young fast-medium bowler, Ken MacLeay, reaped a harvest of six for 39. Kapil, rounding off a singular resistance, reached a quickfire 40 until he was bowled by the left-arm slow bowler, Tom Hogan, who had replaced the out-of-form Dennis Lillee in the Australian eleven. India were cut to size by 162 runs.

Toss: Australia
Umpires: DO Oslear and R Palmer
Man of the Match: TM Chappell

Australia innings (60 overs maximum)			R	B
KC Wessels		b Kapil Dev	5	11
TM Chappell	c Srikkanth	b Amarnath	110	131
*KJ Hughes	b Madan Lal		52	86
DW Hookes	c Kapil Dev	b Madan Lal	1	4
GN Yallop	not out		66	73
AR Border	c Yashpal Sharma	b Binny	26	23
+RW Marsh	c Sandhu	b Kapil Dev	12	15
KH MacLeay	c & b Kapil Dev		4	5
TG Hogan		b Kapil Dev	11	9
GF Lawson	c Srikkanth	b Kapil Dev	6	3
RM Hogg	not out		2	2

Extras: (b 1, lb 14, w 8, nb 2) 25
Total: (9 wickets, 60 overs) 320

FoW: 1-11 (Wessels), 2-155 (Hughes), 3-159 (Hookes),
4-206 (Chappell), 5-254 (Border), 6-277 (Marsh),
7-289 (MacLeay), 8-301 (Hogan), 9-307 (Lawson).

Bowling	O	M	R	W
Kapil Dev	12	2	43	5
Sandhu	12	1	52	0
Binny	12	0	52	1
Shastri	2	0	16	0
Madan Lal	12	0	69	2
Patil	6	0	36	0
Amarnath	4	0	27	1

India innings (target: 321 runs from 60 overs)			R	B
RJ Shastri	lbw	b Lawson	11	18
K Srikkanth	c Border	b Hogan	39	63
M Amarnath	run out		2	17
DB Vengsarkar	lbw	b MacLeay	5	14
SM Patil		b MacLeay	0	7
Yashpal Sharma	c & b MacLeay		3	11
*N Kapil Dev		b Hogan	40	27
S Madan Lal	c Hogan	b MacLeay	27	39
RMH Binny	lbw	b MacLeay	0	6
+SMH Kirmani		b MacLeay	12	23
BS Sandhu	not out		9	12

Extras: (b 1, lb 4, w 3, nb 2) 10
Total: (all out, 37.5 overs) 158

FoW: 1-38 (Shastri), 2-43 (Amarnath), 3-57 (Vengsarkar),
4-57 (Patil), 5-64 (Yashpal Sharma), 6-66 (Srikkanth),
7-124 (Madan Lal), 8-126 (Binny), 9-136 (Kapil Dev),
10-158 (Kirmani).

Bowling	O	M	R	W
Lawson	5	1	25	1
Hogg	7	2	23	0
Hogan	12	1	48	2
MacLeay	11.5	3	39	6
Border	2	0	13	0

Elsewhere...

In Group A, England won all their three matches in the opening
round in convincing fashion and New Zealand beat Pakistan; the
latter's only victory being against Sri Lanka. While in India's group,
West Indies, after the embarrassment of the first outing, brushed
aside Australia and Zimbabwe.

15 June: The Oval, London

The world's first two cricket tests were played in March and April of
1877 and the third in January 1879 – all at the Melbourne Cricket
Ground. The maiden test in England was held at The Oval, south of
London's River Thames, in September 1880.

India's saga at this venerable venue had been one of agony and
ecstasy. In 1936, India lost a test to England by nine wickets, were
thumped by an innings and 27 runs in 1959, won by four wickets in
1971 and almost pulled off an amazing run chase in 1979. Set 438 to
win in 498 minutes, India failed to reach their target by nine runs
with two wickets to spare. The man instrumental in making the
impossible nearly possible was Gavaskar, whose 221 was hailed by
Sir Leonard Hutton, the former England captain and superlative
opening batsman, in Britain's *Observer* newspaper, as the greatest
innings he had ever seen.

I had commentated ball-by-ball on this match and to me it was certainly something special. Later, I asked Hutton if he was really sure of what he had expressed. He put his hand on my shoulder and said he had fielded in the covers for most of Stan McCabe's 232 in 235 minutes at Trent Bridge in 1938 — considered by many cricket historians to be the greatest test innings ever played — and was, therefore, in an enviable position to judge which was the better effort. Bradman, captaining Australia, reportedly, ordered his players on to the dressing room to see McCabe in action, telling them: 'You'll never see the like of it again!' Hutton himself responded with 364 in the final test of that series at The Oval to establish a new record for the highest individual score in tests before this was surpassed by Garry Sobers' 365 not out against Pakistan in 1958.

The ground is in the vicinity of the Afro-Caribbean district of Brixton. Buoyed by calypsos, improvised steel bands, salutations and taunts, Richards uncoiled an uncharacteristic sheet-anchor innings of 119. He had contributed a mere 40 runs in three visits to the crease in the competition and was determined not to miss out again. The Indian bowlers, Binny and Amarnath, cooperated fully by bowling an untidy line and length. With Haynes keeping the Antiguan company to stitch a 101-run second-wicket partnership and Lloyd — injecting a sledge-hammer 41— adding 80 with him for the third wicket in 14 overs, the West Indians were virtually supreme.

However, it was interesting that Lloyd, contrary to his practice, had refrained from giving use of the morning wicket to his fast bowlers. Twice bitten — at Albion and Old Trafford — he was third time shy. India had, thus, already made inroads into the psychological ascendancy of the West Indies.

In reply, India lost openers Srikkanth and Shastri for 21, but Amarnath and Vengsarkar were showing symptoms of a recovery — which raised excitement among the relatively smaller contingent of Indian supporters — when the latter was struck on the mouth by a viciously lifting delivery from Malcolm Marshall. He retired hurt with the score on 89 for two.

A degree of animosity had existed between the Mumbai batsman, also from the Dadar Union club, and the West Indians for some time. They reckoned Vengsarkar had once or twice not respected the spirit of the game, and it was rumoured, they were out to teach him a lesson. The Barbadian, then the speediest of his team's bowlers, possibly sent down his fastest and nastiest spell of the tournament. Indeed, when he persisted with his short-pitched stuff to Patil, who replaced Vengsarkar, umpire David Shepherd had no alternative to cautioning him. Though he was not given the Man of the Match award, Amarnath's knock of 80 was really the pick of the day. Once he and a vigorous Kapil departed – both to Holding – wickets fell in a heap, with India folding up after being 193 for four. West Indies, thereby, reasserted their authority by a margin of 66 runs.

Toss: West Indies
Umpires: BJ Meyer and DR Shepherd
Man of the Match: IVA Richards

West Indies innings (60 overs maximum)			R	B
CG Greenidge	c Vengsarkar	b Kapil Dev	9	13
DL Haynes	c Kapil Dev	b Amarnath	38	93
IVA Richards	c Kirmani	b Sandhu	119	146
*CH Lloyd	run out		41	42
SFAF Bacchus		b Binny	8	8
+PJL Dujon	c Shastri	b Binny	9	13
HA Gomes	not out		27	22
AME Roberts	c Patil	b Binny	7	9
MD Marshall	run out		4	7
MA Holding	c sub	b Madan Lal	2	5
WW Davis	not out		0	2

Extras: (lb 13, w 5) 18
Total: (9 wickets, 60 overs) 282

FoW: 1-17 (Greenidge), 2-118 (Haynes), 3-198 (Lloyd),
4-213 (Bacchus), 5-239 (Dujon), 6-240 (Richards),
7-257 (Roberts), 8-270 (Marshall), 9-280 (Holding).

Bowling	O	M	R	W
Kapil Dev	12	0	46	1
Sandhu	12	2	42	1
Binny	12	0	71	3
Amarnath	12	0	58	1
Madan Lal	12	0	47	1

India innings (target: 283 runs from 60 overs)			R	B
K Srikkanth	c Dujon	b Roberts	2	9
RJ Shastri	c Dujon	b Roberts	6	15
M Amarnath	c Lloyd	b Holding	80	139
DB Vengsarkar	retired hurt		32	59
SM Patil	c & b Gomes		21	31
Yashpal Sharma	run out		9	10
*N Kapil Dev	c Haynes	b Holding	36	46
RMH Binny	lbw	b Holding	1	4
S Madan Lal	not out		8	15
+SMH Kirmani		b Marshall	0	2
BS Sandhu	run out		0	2

Extras: (b 3, lb 13, nb 5) 21
Total: (all out, 53.1 overs) 216

FoW: 1-2 (Srikkanth), 2-21 (Shastri), 3-130 (Patil),
4-143 (Yashpal Sharma), 5-193 (Amarnath), 6-195 (Binny),
7-212 (Kapil Dev), 8-214 (Kirmani), 9-216 (Sandhu).

Bowling	O	M	R	W
Roberts	9	1	29	2
Holding	9.1	0	40	3
Marshall	11	3	20	1
Davis	12	2	51	0
Gomes	12	1	55	1

18 June: Tunbridge Wells

The Nevill county ground at Tunbridge Wells is a magical cricketing *mise en scène*. Surrounded by blooming rhododendron bushes, colourful marquees and neatly erected wooden stands, this became the setting of a great escape by India, prompted by a landmark personal performance.

The train from London's Charring Cross station to Tunbridge was late; and by the time I surfaced at the park, India were six for two, with openers Gavaskar and Srikkanth already back in the pavilion without bothering the scorers. Fortunately, mine was not the first stint on the commentary rota. By the time my turn came, India had crumbled to 17 for five, with Rawson and Kevin Curran ruling the roost.

India had misread the pitch, for the ball moved both in the air and off the wicket, but, as Binny now joined Kapil, it was the captain who stood Horatio-like as the last brown hope in the Kent countryside. Zimbabwe, though, were devoid of that extra bit of experience as well as bowling depth to deliver a *coup de grâce;* and the wicket was also drying rapidly under a hot sun. Besides, Binny, who had opened for both his state, Karnataka, and country, was not incapable of negotiating the lateral movement.

So, with his partner an ideal foil, not failing to get behind the line of the ball, Kapil unfurled one of the most astonishing innings in limited-overs history. It was a scientific assault, not a slog. He pierced the off-side field with perfect technique. With Binny and then Madan Lal, he boosted the score to 140. Thereafter, with Kirmani proving to be a sensible prop for an unbroken ninth wicket stand of 126 in 16 overs, he hoisted the total to 266 for eight. Once in full flow and using his feet, he unleashed a barrage of sixes, hitting half a dozen altogether, in addition to 16 fours. His unconquered 175 extinguished the previous highest for the World Cup – New Zealander, Glenn Turner's 170 against East Africa at Edgbaston in 1975.

But the match was far from decided. The undaunted Zimbabweans continued to defy the odds. Six of their batsmen perished for a paltry 116, but for Curran it wasn't over yet. He kept India at bay with an adventurous innings of 73 before paying the penalty of skiing the ball once too often. Zimbabwe were eventually bowled out for 235 in 56.5 overs, leaving their opponents victors by 31 runs. The fact is, notwithstanding the rope trick the Indians pulled off in the first half of the day, they remained on tenterhooks until the ninth Zimbabwean wicket – that of Curran – fell.

Toss: India
Umpires: MJ Kitchen and BJ Meyer
Man of the Match: N Kapil Dev

India innings (60 overs maximum)			R	B
SM Gavaskar	lbw	b Rawson	0	2
K Srikkanth	c Butchart	b Curran	0	13
M Amarnath	c Houghton	b Rawson	5	20
SM Patil	c Houghton	b Curran	1	10
Yashpal Sharma	c Houghton	b Rawson	9	28
*N Kapil Dev	not out		175	138
RMH Binny	lbw	b Traicos	22	48
RJ Shastri	c Pycroft	b Fletcher	1	6
S Madan Lal	c Houghton	b Curran	17	39
+SMH Kirmani	not out		24	56

Extras: (lb 9, w 3) 12
Total: (8 wickets, 60 overs) 266

DNB: BS Sandhu.

FoW: 1-0 (Gavaskar), 2-6 (Srikkanth), 3-6 (Amarnath),
4-9 (Patil), 5-17 (Yashpal Sharma), 6-77 (Binny),
7-78 (Shastri), 8-140 (Madan Lal).

Bowling	O	M	R	W
Rawson	12	4	47	3
Curran	12	1	65	3
Butchart	12	2	38	0
Fletcher	12	2	59	1
Traicos	12	0	45	1

Zimbabwe innings (target: 267 runs from 60 overs)			R	B
RD Brown	run out		35	66
GA Paterson	lbw	b Binny	23	35
JG Heron	run out		3	8
AJ Pycroft	c Kirmani	b Sandhu	6	15
+DL Houghton	lbw	b Madan Lal	17	35
*DAG Fletcher	c Kapil Dev	b Amarnath	13	23
KM Curran	c Shastri	b Madan Lal	73	93
IP Butchart	b Binny		18	43
GE Peckover	c Yashpal Sharma	b Madan Lal	14	18
PWE Rawson	not out		2	6
AJ Traicos	c & b Kapil Dev		3	7

Extras: (lb 17, w 7, nb 4) 28
Total: (all out, 57 overs) 235

FoW: 1-44 (Paterson), 2-48 (Heron), 3-61 (Pycroft), 4-86 (Brown),
5-103 (Houghton), 6-113 (Fletcher), 7-168 (Butchart),
8-189 (Peckover), 9-230 (Curran), 10-235 (Traicos).

Bowling	O	M	R	W
Kapil Dev	11	1	32	1
Sandhu	11	2	44	1
Binny	11	2	45	2
Madan Lal	11	2	42	3
Amarnath	12	1	37	1
Shastri	1	0	7	0

20 June: Chelmsford

Chelmsford, less than an hour to the east of London, is Essex county's
cricketing headquarters. From here have sprung the likes of Trevor
Bailey, Graham Gooch and Nasser Hussain. The first mentioned,
though, whose company as an expert commentator on BBC I
cherished, for he was not only an accurate judge of ability, but lucid
in elaborating on it, actually came from Southend-on-Sea on the
English coast.

The clash between India and Australia here would decide the
qualifier with the West Indies from Group B in the semi-finals. The
former had three wins from the five outings. Their opponents had
two, but a faster overall run rate, which meant a win would clinch
them a place in the last four.

It was another day of bright sunshine; and the temperature, too,
had begun to soar by this stage of the competition. India had no
hesitation in batting, but after losing three wickets for 65, they were
rather forced into reconstruction mode. Indeed, it was a collaborative
effort – for the highest individual score was Yashpal's 40 – that saw
them attain a respectable total. The Australian bowlers helped

undistinguishedly with 15 no-balls and nine wides in an extras tally of 37 – the second highest score of the innings.

The wicket was a featherbed, but Australia were missing captain and leading batsman Hughes, absent because of a thigh strain. In his place, they selected an extra bowler. Binny, introduced in the 16th over, swung the ball just enough to consistently find the edge, and with Madan Lal an able ally, the Aussies nose-dived from 46 for one to 78 for seven, never to recover. It was nothing short of a crushing victory for India. Those in Anglo–Australian media who complained that the men from the Antipodes gave a 'poor performance' were pandering to a preconceived notion that Australia were a superior side vis-à-vis India. Admittedly, form on the day counts in over-limit cricket. But at the juncture of the 1983 World Cup, India's hardening experience in the West Indies just a few months earlier, enriched them with the capability of beating the Australians of that generation. Certainly, batting-wise, on that decisive day at Chelmsford, Australia were as good as they were allowed to be.

Toss: India
Umpires: J Birkenshaw and DR Shepherd
Man of the Match: RMH Binny

India innings (60 overs maximum)			R	B
SM Gavaskar	c Chappell	b Hogg	9	10
K Srikkanth	c Border	b Thomson	24	22
M Amarnath	c Marsh	b Thomson	13	20
Yashpal Sharma	c Hogg	b Hogan	40	40
SM Patil	c Hogan	b MacLeay	30	25
*N Kapil Dev	c Hookes	b Hogg	28	32
KBJ Azad	c Border	b Lawson	15	18
RMH Binny	run out		21	32
S Madan Lal	not out		12	15
+SMH Kirmani	lbw	b Hogg	10	20
BS Sandhu		b Thomson	8	18

Extras: (lb 13, w 9, nb 15) 37
Total: (all out, 55.5 overs) 247

FoW: 1-27 (Gavaskar), 2-54 (Srikkanth), 3-65 (Amarnath),
4-118 (Patil), 5-157 (Yashpal Sharma), 6-174 (Kapil Dev), 7-207 (Azad),
8-215 (Binny), 9-232 (Kirmani), 10-247 (Sandhu).

Bowling	O	M	R	W
Lawson	10	1	40	1
Hogg	12	2	40	3
Hogan	11	1	31	1
Thomson	10.5	0	51	3
MacLeay	12	2	48	1

Australia innings (target: 248 runs from 60 overs)			R	B
TM Chappell	c Madan Lal	b Sandhu	2	5
GM Wood	c Kirmani	b Binny	21	32
GN Yallop	c & b Binny		18	30
*DW Hookes		b Binny	1	2
AR Border		b Madan Lal	36	49
+RW Marsh	lbw	b Madan Lal	0	2
KH MacLeay	c Gavaskar	b Madan Lal	5	6
TG Hogan	c Srikkanth	b Binny	8	10
GF Lawson		b Sandhu	16	20
RM Hogg	not out		8	12
JR Thomson		b Madan Lal	0	5

Extras: (lb 5, w 5, nb 4) 14
Total: (all out, 38.2 overs) 129

FoW: 1-3 (Chappell), 2-46 (Wood), 3-48 (Hookes), 4-52 (Yallop),
5-52 (Marsh), 6-69 (MacLeay), 7-78 (Hogan), 8-115 (Lawson),
9-129 (Border), 10-129 (Thomson).

Bowling	O	M	R	W
Kapil Dev	8	2	16	0
Sandhu	10	1	26	2
Madan Lal	8.2	3	20	4
Binny	8	2	29	4
Amarnath	2	0	17	0
Azad	2	0	7	0

Meanwhile...

In the other group, England slipped against New Zealand, but repeated their first round successes over Pakistan and Sri Lanka. But the Kiwis lost to Pakistan and astoundingly also to the Lankans – then the minnows of test cricket – to facilitate the Pakistanis' entry into the semi-finals behind the Englishmen.

The West Indians, on the other hand, rampaged through the second round to race past India in the final group standings. Australia finished third after staving off another energetic challenge from Zimbabwe.

Semi-final, 22 June: Old Trafford, Manchester

So, from the south-east of England the Indians drove back in their assigned coach to the north-west and to Old Trafford. It was virgin terrain for India in that they had never progressed beyond the preliminary, league stage of a World Cup, yet a beaten track, as they were back in the familiar surroundings of Old Trafford, where they had eclipsed West Indies at the start of the tournament. Many estimated, this is where the dream sequence would end. After all, England were vastly seasoned in the art and craft of one-day cricket. They had been semi-finalists in 1975 and finalists in 1979; and, not to be forgotten, enjoyed home advantage.

Unlike a fortnight earlier, the weather was luminous, even humid; and the wicket, while seaming a bit, was slow and low and not dissimilar to those in the subcontinent – as indeed were most tracks in the tournament, in general, especially after the mercury levels reflected more an Indian summer.

It was a foregone conclusion that any side winning the toss would bat first; so it was no surprise England did just that. But after openers Graeme Fowler and Chris Tavare put on 69 at four runs an over – before both became victims of Binny – England struggled against the slower part-timers, Amarnath and Kirti Azad, whose 24 overs cost a mere 55 runs and captured the wickets of Gower, Mike Gatting and the dangerous Ian Botham, while Allan Lamb was run out. With the ball not quite coming on to the bat, boundaries were difficult to come by, while lofting the ball on the sluggish pitch was also hazardous. As wickets fell at regular intervals, the Englishmen fragmented in the face of a disciplined but by no means unplayable attack. Their total was, in fact, an injustice to the conditions.

For once in the tournament, Gavaskar showed glimpses of his pedigree before he was caught at the wicket. Then, a 92-run partnership for the third wicket between Amarnath and Yashpal Sharma laid the foundation for the latter and Patil to finish the job with 5.2 overs to spare. As the Indians raised the tempo, Amarnath stepped out to clobber Vic Marks for a straight six and Sharma flicked Willis off his toes for another over boundary. Thereafter, Patil yet again feasted on Willis by despatching him thrice to the fence in an over. So, India sailed into the final with a six-wicket win.

Toss: England
Umpires: DGL Evans and DO Oslear
Man of the Match: M Amarnath

England innings (60 overs maximum)			R	B
G Fowler		b Binny	33	59
CJ Tavare	c Kirmani	b Binny	32	51
DI Gower	c Kirmani	b Amarnath	17	30
AJ Lamb	run out		29	58
MW Gatting		b Amarnath	18	46
IT Botham		b Azad	6	26
+IJ Gould	run out		13	36
VJ Marks		b Kapil Dev	8	18
GR Dilley	not out		20	26
PJW Allott	c Patil	b Kapil Dev	8	14
*RGD Willis		b Kapil Dev	0	2

Extras: (b 1, lb 17, w 7, nb 4) 29
Total: (all out, 60 overs) 213

FoW: 1-69 (Tavare), 2-84 (Fowler), 3-107 (Gower), 4-141 (Lamb), 5-150 (Gatting), 6-160 (Botham), 7-175 (Gould), 8-177 (Marks), 9-202 (Allott), 10-213 (Willis).

Bowling	O	M	R	W
Kapil Dev	11	1	35	3
Sandhu	8	1	36	0
Binny	12	1	43	2
Madan Lal	5	0	15	0
Azad	12	1	28	1
Amarnath	12	1	27	2

India innings (target: 214 runs from 60 overs)			R	B
SM Gavaskar	c Gould	b Allott	25	41
K Srikkanth	c Willis	b Botham	19	44
M Amarnath	run out		46	92
Yashpal Sharma	c Allott	b Willis	61	115
SM Patil	not out		51	32
*N Kapil Dev	not out		1	6

Extras: (b 5, lb 6, w 1, nb 2) 14
Total: (4 wickets, 54.4 overs) 217

DNB: KBJ Azad, RMH Binny, S Madan Lal, +SMH Kirmani, BS Sandhu.

FoW: 1-46 (Srikkanth), 2-50 (Gavaskar), 3-142 (Amarnath), 4-205 (Yashpal Sharma).

Bowling	O	M	R	W
Willis	10.4	2	42	1
Dilley	11	0	43	0
Allott	10	3	40	1
Botham	11	4	40	1
Marks	12	1	38	0

Simultaneously...

Semi-final: The Oval, London

Two hundred miles down south, the West Indies tackled Pakistan in the other semi-final. This match, too, turned out to be a one-sided affair. The venom of the Caribbean pacemen was too much for the

Pakistani batsmen to digest. Marshall once again bowled with utmost hostility and Holding, Roberts and Garner were almost as disconcerting. Pakistan only managed a modest score, with Mohsin Khan painstakingly collecting 70 with 43 singles and off 176 balls. The only other batsman to make an impression was Zaheer Abbas before the underrated off-spin of Gomes cut short his ambitions. Only three boundaries were logged in the innings, one of them a bye. With Imran Khan unfit to bowl, Richards swiftly took control, cutting, driving and hooking imperiously to peg an unbeaten 80. The West Indies galloped past the post by eight wickets, with 12 overs to spare.

Toss: West Indies
Umpires: DJ Constant and AGT Whitehead
Man of the Match: IVA Richards

Pakistan innings (60 overs maximum)			*R*	*B*
Mohsin Khan		b Roberts	70	176
Mudassar Nazar	c & b Garner		11	39
Ijaz Faqih	c Dujon	b Holding	5	19
Zaheer Abbas		b Gomes	30	38
*Imran Khan	c Dujon	b Marshall	17	41
Wasim Raja	lbw	b Marshall	0	3
Shahid Mahboob	c Richards	b Marshall	6	10
Sarfraz Nawaz	c Holding	b Roberts	3	12
Abdul Qadir	not out		10	21
+Wasim Bari	not out		4	7

Extras: (b 6, lb 13, w 4, nb 5) 28
Total: (8 wickets, 60 overs)184

DNB: Rashid Khan.

FoW: 1-23 (Mudassar Nazar), 2-34 (Ijaz Faqih),
3-88 (Zaheer Abbas), 4-139 (Imran Khan), 5-139 (Wasim Raja),
6-159 (Shahid Mahboob), 7-164 (Sarfraz Nawaz),
8-171 (Mohsin Khan).

Bowling	O	M	R	W
Roberts	12	3	25	2
Garner	12	1	31	1
Marshall	12	2	28	3
Holding	12	1	25	1
Gomes	7	0	29	1
Richards	5	0	18	0

West Indies innings (target: 185 runs from 60 overs)			R	B
CG Greenidge	lbw	b Rashid Khan	17	38
DL Haynes		b Abdul Qadir	29	58
IVA Richards	not out		80	96
HA Gomes	not out		50	100

Extras: (b 2, lb 6, w 4) 12
Total: (2 wickets, 48.4 overs) 188

DNB: *CH Lloyd, SFAF Bacchus, +PJL Dujon, MD Marshall,
AME Roberts, J Garner, MA Holding.

FoW: 1-34 (Greenidge), 2-56 (Haynes).

Bowling	O	M	R	W
Rashid Khan	12	2	32	1
Sarfraz Nawaz	8	0	23	0
Abdul Qadir	11	1	42	1
Shahid Mahboob	11	1	43	0
Wasim Raja	1	0	9	0
Zaheer Abbas	4.4	1	24	0
Mohsin Khan	1	0	3	0

Final, 25 June: Lord's, London

Lord's, adjoining Regent's Park and nestling in north-west London's leafy St John's Wood area, home of the Marylebone Cricket Club, founders and guardians of the game, is widely recognized as the Mecca of cricket.

It was here, in 1932, that India made their advent in the international arena and had played a test on all visits to England since, losing every time barring 1971 and 1979. A total of eight defeats rendered the venue a veritable crematorium of Indian cricket. Such a register incorporated the ignominy of being bowled out for their lowest test score ever of 42 in an incredible 77 minutes in 1974, which provoked a sneering cartoon in a British paper of a man scolding his friend: 'I told you not to go to the toilet!' Even in the 1975 World Cup, England pulverized the Indians to post a record score of 334 for four as India lost by a shameful margin of 202 runs.

Only Dilip Vengsarkar's centuries in consecutive appearances in 1979 and 1982 – which was inflated to a hat trick in 1986 – had slightly lightened the catalogue of infamy. In essence, there was cause for trepidation in the Indian camp on the eve of the 1983 World Cup final.

But Lord's, hosting its third consecutive World Cup final, was dressed to kill. To complement this, it transpired to be a radiantly sunny midsummer day.

Tickets for this finale had been sold out months in advance – bought mostly by the English. They expected England to qualify for this culmination, like they had done four years earlier. So, their hopes were rather dashed by England's capitulation to India. As a result, a flood of 'returns', officially and unofficially, became available after the semi-finals with Indians of all descriptions and from a variety of destinations – including India itself – the enthusiastic takers.

Ticket touts outside the ground – who in India are branded black marketeers – have been commonplace at English grounds, including Lord's. It was not, until recently, looked upon as an illegal activity. On this occasion, as one approached the Grace Gates (named after the illustrious W. G.), one was accosted every few yards by such peddlers, and only the flashing of a medallion – proof of media accreditation in that age, as opposed to laminated cards with photo identities of this security-conscious era – deterred their doggedness. It was, obviously, good business, for tickets – genuine or counterfeit – were exchanging hands thick and fast and at a considerable premium.

Inside was a festive atmosphere. West Indian supporters, with their improvised musical instruments, had arrived in strength, many, perhaps, from their south London base. Correspondingly, hirsute Sikhs, generally unfailing cheer leaders for India outside the country (noticeably at Olympic and World Cup hockey championships, where India used to dominate for decades until overshadowed by the Europeans and Australia), armed with bugles, stood out in the Indian section, many, presumably, descending from west London suburbs like Southall and Hounslow. Conch shells were in evidence in both segments.

While the galleries surrounding the immaculate turf were a kaleidoscope of sight and sound, a more subdued pavilion – a majestic, light brick mansion house, with three-tier seating and a spacious hall within known as the Long Room, where a tie and jacket are necessary to gain entry – presided over proceedings.

(Senior citizens, who used to serve as stewards at Lord's, were notorious for their failure to recognize non-white cricketers, including prominent figures like Gavaskar, who was once stopped at the main gate, following which he initially refused an honorary membership of the MCC. As for Tiger Pataudi, when he characteristically turned up at the pavilion entrance without a tie, it was pointed out to him that he was inadequately dressed. Tiger jestfully retorted: 'You can't stop royalty, can you?' and strode past a stupefied old age pensioner before he could recover from the remark.)

Those who had left home early were tucking into their egg and toast, washed down with coffee. Others wasted no time in bracing themselves with beer or, as both Afro- and Indo-Caribbeans often prefer, a dash of rum.

There was not much doubt about the outcome of the match among an overwhelming majority. India, they surmised, had had their moment in the sun, and even upset the titleholders at Old Trafford. Now it was time for the West Indians to monopolize the stage. Indeed, their form since the initial reverse suggested it was crunch time for the Indians. 'Thanks for coming,' a West Indian friend joked as I made my way through the aforementioned pavilion door. Only the blind, irrational India backer believed otherwise.

Ominously for India, Lloyd won the toss and, unsurprisingly, decided to give his commandos a crack at the Indians in lively morning conditions. Indeed, the ball seamed; and Joel Garner, with his extra height, consistently made the ball rise chest-high from three-quarter length. But it was the faster and flatter Andy Roberts who had Gavaskar caught behind in the third over, thus imprinting in this tournament the most barren phase of this gluttonous Indian batsman's career.

At the other end, though, Srikkanth, the buccaneer from Chennai, went about his task with a gay abandon. He hooked Roberts for four, pulled him for a six and then crashed him through the covers for another boundary. He was in full flow when he played across the line to Marshall to be trapped lbw for 38. I was on the air then. Little did I realize that I had just described the termination of most substantive innings of the match.

Amarnath, as usual, steadied a capsizing ship before he was cleaned up by Holding; Patil portrayed a flurry of shots prior to becoming a victim of greed against the innocuous Gomes. India's total appeared woefully inadequate. Yet, they didn't lose heart. Having traversed a distance they had not dreamed of travelling before the tournament, they had nothing to lose. The ball was still seaming, and while it required another minor miracle to defend the modest score, nothing was impossible. In between my commentary spells from atop the pavilion, I would scurry to the Indian dressing room one floor down to check the atmosphere therein. As the Indians took the field, Syed Abid Ali, a hero of India's maiden test series win in England in 1971 as well as a participant in the 1975 World Cup, was down on his knees in prayer.

The West Indians started inauspiciously. Greenidge shouldered arms to a ball from Sandhu he expected to leave him but which instead came back to disfigure his stumps. But this setback hardly unsettled Richards, who dismissively moved to 33 with seven fours to threaten to win the match by himself. India, though, persevered with a regimented line and length. Soon, Madan Lal impelled the Antiguan to hook; he mistimed the shot and the superb fielder that was Kapil ran back towards the midwicket boundary to take a marvellous catch over his shoulder. Haynes and Gomes, too, departed, victims of Madan, as three wickets fell in 19 balls. With Lloyd handicapped by a torn hamstring, and Bacchus not lasting long either, the West Indies plummeted to 76 for six.

But it wasn't curtains yet. Wicketkeeper Dujon was joined by Marshall, who was no novice with the willow. Uncomfortably for India, they showed no signs of relenting as the score mounted to 119. Enter Amarnath with his deceptively slow seamers. The tinge of green made the ball hurry after it pitched. Marshall was caught, Dujon played on and Holding was plumb in front to reward Amarnath with three wickets for 12 runs in seven overs. India had worthily defeated the insurmountable West Indies by 43 runs.

Akin to the history of one-day cricket, the team that had acquitted themselves more capably on the day had triumphed. Yet, this was no accident, for it was the third time India had got the better of the Windies in their last five meetings over a period spanning three months.

In the BBC commentary box, some, evidently, expected me to start jumping with joy. I disappointed them. A list of 'dos' and 'don'ts' – a creation of the BBC – thrust before me the first time I commentated on a cricket match on All India Radio in 1972 had stressed the need for detachment. I have never consciously deviated from this. My job was to describe lucidly for listeners the drama unfolding before me, not to get drawn into it.

Aaj Kaal, a Bengali daily in my home city of Kolkata and a competitor of *Ananda Bazar Patrika*, which I then represented as its London correspondent, was generous enough to carry an editorial headlined 'ABINANDAN ASHIS RAY' or 'Congratulations Ashis Ray'. It went on to say that while there were no Bengal players (Kolkata being the capital of the eastern Indian state of West Bengal) in the World Cup winning Indian squad, I had done Bengal proud with my radio commentaries on the event.

It had, obviously, been a rather low-scoring match, but this phenomenon reflected a seamer-friendly wicket. Indeed, the outcome was on knife edge until Richards left the scene. Subsequently, the match tilted inexorably towards India. Thousands among the capacity crowd of over 24,000 – mostly Indians – invaded the field to obtain a close-up of the presentation ceremony, which took place on the middle-level balcony of the three-tier pavilion. A thunderous roar rent the air as Kapil lifted the coveted trophy. It was India's day; their greatest moment till date in one-day cricket! The limited-overs game as far as India and Indians were concerned was never to be the same again!!

India's breakthrough owed much to their captain's positive frame of mind and the presence in their side of all-rounders like Kapil himself, Amarnath and Binny (the highest wicket-taker in the competition) and to the bowling of Madan Lal and Sandhu. None was express fast but of the right velocity to revel in the seaming conditions. The ball gripped even for the left-arm spin of Shastri, while, with the bat, Srikkanth, Patil and Sharma were there to be counted when the chips were down. It was an admirably collective feat.

It was a dizzy moment for the Indian players and the countless aficionados, and the intoxication had only begun. As the magnitude of the attainment sunk in, hundreds of Indian fans waited outside the pavilion to not just catch a glimpse of their heroes, but also to usher them back to their hotel across the road, then known as the Westmoreland, to continue the celebrations. The bar and lobby of this establishment have probably never seen such crowds before or since. The inebriation and impromptu *bhangra* dancing lingered late into the night. The place was awash with champagne and the cricketers, having restrained themselves for weeks, finally let their hair down. A visibly tired Kapil, but still smiling, stayed up till the end, not disappointing the innumerable well-wishers. The camaraderie between the actors and their adherents mirrored an age of accessibility. It was a delight to witness the scene, indeed cherish it.

Thus concluded the 1983 Prudential World Cup. It opened with two major shocks: when India beat West Indies and Zimbabwe defeated Australia in the opening round. And climaxed with the greatest surprise of all: when India once more trounced the West Indies. None of the eight sides that took part departed without a win.

Prudential underwrote the event to the tune of half a million UK pounds and the gate receipts were UK £1.2 million. The aggregate attendance was 232,000.

In addition to the cup and silver medals for each player, India received £20,000, West Indies got £8000 and the losing semi-finalists, England and Pakistan, took home £4000 each.

Toss: West Indies
Umpires: HD Bird and BJ Meyer
Man of the Match: M Amarnath

India innings (60 overs maximum)			R	B
SM Gavaskar	c Dujon	b Roberts	2	12
K Srikkanth	lbw	b Marshall	38	57
M Amarnath		b Holding	26	80
Yashpal Sharma	c sub (AL Logie)	b Gomes	11	32
SM Patil	c Gomes	b Garner	27	29
*N Kapil Dev	c Holding	b Gomes	15	8
KBJ Azad	c Garner	b Roberts	0	3
RMH Binny	c Garner	b Roberts	2	8
S Madan Lal		b Marshall	17	27
+SMH Kirmani		b Holding	14	43
BS Sandhu	not out		11	30

Extras: (b 5, lb 5, w 9, nb 1) 20
Total: (all out, 54.4 overs) 183

FoW: 1-2 (Gavaskar), 2-59 (Srikkanth), 3-90 (Amarnath),
4-92 (Yashpal Sharma), 5-110 (Kapil Dev), 6-111 (Azad),
7-130 (Binny), 8-153 (Patil), 9-161 (Madan Lal),
10-183 (Kirmani).

Bowling	O	M	R	W
Roberts	10	3	32	3
Garner	12	4	24	1
Marshall	11	1	24	2
Holding	9.4	2	26	2
Gomes	11	1	49	2
Richards	1	0	8	0

West Indies innings (target: 184 runs from 60 overs)			R	B
CG Greenidge		b Sandhu	1	12
DL Haynes	c Binny	b Madan Lal	13	33
IVA Richards	c Kapil Dev	b Madan Lal	33	28
*CH Lloyd	c Kapil Dev	b Binny	8	17
HA Gomes	c Gavaskar	b Madan Lal	5	16
SFAF Bacchus	c Kirmani	b Sandhu	8	25
+PJL Dujon		b Amarnath	25	73
MD Marshall	c Gavaskar	b Amarnath	18	51
AME Roberts	lbw	b Kapil Dev	4	14
J Garner	not out		5	19
MA Holding	lbw	b Amarnath	6	24

Extras: (lb 4, w 10) 14
Total: (all out, 52 overs) 140

FoW: 1-5 (Greenidge), 2-50 (Haynes), 3-57 (Richards),
4-66 (Gomes), 5-66 (Lloyd), 6-76 (Bacchus), 7-119 (Dujon),
8-124 (Marshall), 9-126 (Roberts), 10-140 (Holding).

Bowling	O	M	R	W
Kapil Dev	11	4	21	1
Sandhu	9	1	32	2
Madan Lal	12	2	31	3
Binny	10	1	23	1
Amarnath	7	0	12	3
Azad	3	0	7	0

Responsible for the coverage of the 1983 World Cup for *Ananda Bazar Patrika*, a Bengali daily with one of the largest circulations in India, I contracted Sobers to provide his comments for this paper. After each match, I would phone him wherever he was in England to secure his views. Embarrassingly, it took some time for the payment promised to him to materialize from the head office in Kolkata. When the money arrived, the all-rounder extraordinaire was, coincidentally, in London promoting tourist attractions in his beautiful island of Barbados. I seized this opportunity and handed him his dues at his government's Tourist Office in central London. He gave me a bear-like hug. 'You're a good man,' he said, thanking me for not forgetting the settlement. This was significant, for Dilip Doshi, who knew him well, told me he had often been taken for a ride by people he trusted.

As for trust, the Indian electorate had put theirs back in Indira Gandhi in early 1980. Within months of coming back to office, though, she tragically lost her younger son, Sanjay, in a plane crash. Sanjay had been demonized for his role during the Emergency, but had plotted her return to power and was her chosen heir. Now the victorious Indian cricketers put a smile back on her face, as she received them at her official residence in New Delhi and posed for photographs with the players and the Prudential World Cup trophy.

5

The Tobacco Tourneys

WHERE HAVE ALL THE TOBACCO CONGLOMERATES GONE? GONE to pasture, every one! They faded from the scene after successive government, under pressure from health lobbies, banned sponsorship of sporting events by cigarette companies.

There was a time when Benson & Hedges (B & H) in Australia and England, Rothmans in New Zealand and Sharjah, Wills in India and Pakistan and John Player in England were at the forefront of facilitating cricketing championships. Indeed, B & H went on to sponsor the 1992 World Cup, while Wills did the same in respect of this event in 1996.

As a smoker with a partiality for B & H – not since 1986, though, one should hasten to add – it was rather useful to be supplied ample cartons of the gold pack at press boxes in Australian cricket grounds in the 1980s. And if you crossed the Tasman Sea, Rothmans would be equally generous. No reflection on the latter; but switching brands was inadvisable, especially since broadcasting was a part of my assignment.

In an ideal world, promotion of smoking in the sporting arena is best avoided. At the same time, cricket is obliged to the tobacco firms that came to its rescue in difficult times and helped it straddle a hump. Indeed, it would be deficient not to acknowledge this debt, especially in the context of one-day cricket.

Anyhow, in 1985, to commemorate 150 years of the establishment of the Australian state of Victoria, the Victorian Cricket Association organized what they dubbed a 'World Championship of Cricket', sponsored by Benson & Hedges. Floodlights were installed at the Melbourne Cricket Ground at a cost of over £3 million. They were switched on for the first time for the opening match between England and Australia, which attracted a crowd of 82,000. Of the 13 matches in the tournament, four were held at Sydney, which, of course, is in the state of New South Wales, and the rest in Melbourne. Only test-playing teams were invited; and they were divided into two groups. India, Pakistan, England and Australia featured in one; West Indies, New Zealand and Sri Lanka in the other.

Sunil Gavaskar was back as captain. But this was a minor metamorphosis compared to the cataclysmic changes that had overtaken India politically. Indira Gandhi had been assassinated in October 1984 and her elder son, Rajiv, previously persuaded to resign as an Indian Airlines pilot to enter public life, was ensconced as prime minister after a landslide win in a general election.

20 February: Melbourne Cricket Ground (MCG) (Day/Night)

Pakistan won the toss and chose to bat, but struggled with their run rate, as the Indian medium pacers moved the ball around capably. Then, when Sunil Gavaskar introduced spin, Ravi Shastri was highly economical and Laxman Sivaramakrishnan (Siva for brevity among those acquainted with him) picked up two useful wickets. India also fielded assiduously. In contrast, Pakistan had a disappointing match. Briefly, though, playing his first match for Pakistan for over a year, Imran Khan threatened to turn the tables on India. In a fiery spell, he took three wickets in six overs for 13 runs as India slumped to 27 for three. But Mohammed Azharuddin and Gavaskar, coming together now, added 132 in 31 overs to pave the way for an easy Indian win. Fresh from his remarkable test debut—in course of which he posted hundreds in his first three tests against England in

India – Azharuddin created a brilliant impression on his first appearance in Australia. He survived one chance – to the wicketkeeper off Tahir Naqqash when he was on 37 – but his 93 not out came off 135 balls. India won by six wickets.

Toss: Pakistan
Umpires: RA French and PJ McConnell
ODI Debuts: L Sivaramakrishnan (Ind).
Man of the Match: M Azharuddin

Pakistan innings (50 overs maximum)			R	B
Mohsin Khan	c Viswanath	b Binny	3	13
Qasim Umar	c & b Sivaramakrishnan		57	102
Zaheer Abbas	c & b Sivaramakrishnan		25	56
*Javed Miandad	c Sivaramakrishnan	b Binny	17	35
Rameez Raja	c Shastri	b Kapil Dev	29	37
Imran Khan	c Madan Lal	b Kapil Dev	14	23
Mudassar Nazar	run out		6	8
Tahir Naqqash	c Amarnath	b Madan Lal	0	3
Rashid Khan	c Shastri	b Binny	17	16
+Anil Dalpat	c Kapil Dev	b Binny	9	8
Wasim Akram	not out		0	0

Extras: (lb 3, w 2, nb 1) 6
Total: (all out, 49.2 overs) 183

FoW: 1-8 (Mohsin Khan), 2-73 (Zaheer Abbas),
3-98 (Qasim Umar), 4-119 (Javed Miandad),
5-144 (Imran Khan), 6-151 (Mudassar Nazar),
7-155 (Tahir Naqqash), 8-156 (Rameez Raja),
9-183 (Anil Dalpat), 10-183 (Rashid Khan).

Bowling	O	M	R	W
Kapil Dev	9	1	31	2
Binny	8.2	3	35	4
Madan Lal	9	2	27	1
Amarnath	3	0	11	0
Sivaramakrishnan	10	0	49	2
Shastri	10	1	27	0

India innings (target: 184 runs from 50 overs)			R	B
RJ Shastri	c Javed Miandad	b Imran Khan	2	5
K Srikkanth	c Mohsin Khan	b Imran Khan	12	26
M Azharuddin	not out		93	135
DB Vengsarkar	c Mudassar Nazar	b Imran Khan	0	1
*SM Gavaskar	lbw	b Mudassar Nazar	54	92
M Amarnath	not out		11	16

Extras: (lb 9, w 3) 12
Total: (4 wickets, 45.5 overs) 184

DNB: N Kapil Dev, RMH Binny, S Madan Lal, +S Viswanath,
L Sivaramakrishnan.

FoW: 1-2 (Shastri), 2-27 (Srikkanth), 3-27 (Vengsarkar),
4-159 (Gavaskar).

Bowling	O	M	R	W
Imran Khan	10	1	27	3
Wasim Akram	8.5	0	38	0
Rashid Khan	7	0	38	0
Tahir Naqqash	10	0	34	0
Mudassar Nazar	10	0	38	1

26 February: Sydney Cricket Ground (SCG) (Day/Night)

Put in by David Gower, India were given a rousing start by
Krishnamachari Srikkanth, who made 42 of the first 52 runs in ten
overs. Out of the 16 boundaries hit in the match, this Tamil Nadu
opener struck 10. Indeed, England only found their feet after he was
brilliantly run out from long leg by Ashley Cowans; they bowled
and fielded much better thereafter. Then, needing 236 to win, they
seemed to be cruising until Gower hit a full toss down deep mid-
wicket's throat. After that, their last eight wickets realized just 55
runs, as Siva and Shastri exploited a much-used pitch. India won by
86 runs.

Toss: England
Umpires: RA French and BE Martin
Man of the Match: K Srikkanth

India innings (50 overs maximum)			R	B
RJ Shastri	c Fowler	b Ellison	13	38
K Srikkanth	run out		57	53
M Azharuddin	c & b Cowans		45	67
DB Vengsarkar	run out		43	62
N Kapil Dev	c Downton	b Cowans	29	23
*SM Gavaskar	not out		30	31
M Amarnath	c Lamb	b Cowans	6	11
RMH Binny	c Marks	b Foster	2	3
S Madan Lal	c Downton	b Foster	0	1
+S Viswanath	run out		8	11

Extras: (lb 2) 2
Total: (9 wickets, 50 overs) 235

DNB: L Sivaramakrishnan.

FoW: 1-67 (Shastri), 2-74 (Srikkanth), 3-147 (Azharuddin),
4-183 (Vengsarkar), 5-197 (Kapil Dev), 6-216 (Amarnath),
7-220 (Binny), 8-220 (Madan Lal), 9-235 (Viswanath).

Bowling	O	M	R	W
Cowans	10	0	59	3
Ellison	10	1	46	1
Foster	10	0	33	2
Edmonds	10	1	38	0
Marks	10	0	57	0

England innings (target: 236 runs from 50 overs)			R	B
G Fowler	c Viswanath	b Binny	26	40
MD Moxon	c & b Sivaramakrishnan		48	86
*DI Gower	c Vengsarkar	b Sivaramakrishnan	25	34
AJ Lamb		b Sivaramakrishnan	13	20
MW Gatting	c Viswanath	b Shastri	7	15
+PR Downton	c Shastri	b Kapil Dev	9	17
VJ Marks	st Viswanath	b Shastri	2	7
PH Edmonds	st Viswanath	b Shastri	5	10
RM Ellison	c Viswanath	b Madan Lal	1	5
NA Foster	c Srikkanth	b Madan Lal	1	13
NG Cowans	not out		3	5

Extras: (b 3, lb 4, w 1, nb 1) 9
Total: (all out, 41.4 overs) 149

FoW: 1-41 (Fowler), 2-94 (Gower), 3-113 (Moxon), 4-126 (Lamb),
5-126 (Gatting), 6-130 (Marks), 7-142 (Downton),
8-144 (Ellison), 9-146 (Edmonds), 10-149 (Foster).

Bowling	O	M	R	W
Kapil Dev	7	0	21	1
Binny	8	0	33	1
Madan Lal	6.4	0	19	2
Sivaramakrishnan	10	0	39	3
Shastri	10	2	30	3

3 March: MCG

The calculations were such that Australia had a dual opportunity of reaching the semi-final of the competition, both of which required them to win this match by either scoring at least 223 in 50 overs or, upon failing to do so, bowling India out for 160 or less. They came nowhere near achieving either objective. Inserted by Gavaskar (Rodney Hogg tossed the coin for Australia as Allan Border was temporarily indisposed), the Aussies were soon 37 for five – in a virtual rerun of Chelmsford 1983 – owing to a succession of loose strokes. Wayne Phillips attempted something of a recovery, but when India batted Srikkanth and Shastri made light work of maintaining their side's 100 per cent record in the group matches. India won by eight wickets and, by virtue of this victory, avoided meeting the West Indies in the last four.

Toss: India
Umpires: AR Crafter and PJ McConnell
Man of the Match: RJ Shastri

Australia innings (50 overs maximum)			R	B
GM Wood		b Binny	1	12
RB Kerr		b Kapil Dev	4	8
KC Wessels	c Madan Lal	b Kapil Dev	6	15
*AR Border		b Binny	4	16
DM Jones	c Viswanath	b Amarnath	12	21
+WB Phillips	c Amarnath	b Sivaramakrishnan	60	92
SP O'Donnell	c Amarnath	b Shastri	17	51
GF Lawson	c & b Sivaramakrishnan		0	2
RM Hogg	run out		22	39
RJ McCurdy	not out		13	25
TM Alderman		b Binny	6	19

Extras: (b 2, lb 9, w 5, nb 2) 18
Total: (all out, 49.3 overs) 163

FoW: 1-5 (Kerr), 2-5 (Wood), 3-17 (Wessels), 4-17 (Border),
5-37 (Jones), 6-85 (O'Donnell), 7-85 (Lawson), 8-134 (Hogg),
9-147 (Phillips), 10-163 (Alderman).

Bowling	O	M	R	W
Kapil Dev	10	2	25	2
Binny	7.3	0	27	3
Madan Lal	5	0	18	0
Amarnath	7	1	16	1
Sivaramakrishnan	10	0	32	2
Shastri	10	1	34	1

India innings (target: 164 runs from 50 overs)			*R*	*B*
RJ Shastri	c Phillips	b O'Donnell	51	94
K Srikkanth	not out		93	115
M Azharuddin	lbw	b Alderman	0	2
DB Vengsarkar	not out		11	16

Extras: (lb 1, w 3, nb 6) 10
Total: (2 wickets, 36.1 overs) 165

DNB: *SM Gavaskar, M Amarnath, N Kapil Dev, S Madan Lal,
RMH Binny, +S Viswanath, L Sivaramakrishnan.

FoW: 1-124 (Shastri), 2-125 (Azharuddin).

Bowling	*O*	*M*	*R*	*W*
Lawson	8	1	35	0
Hogg	6	2	16	0
McCurdy	7.1	0	30	0
Alderman	8	0	38	1
O'Donnell	7	0	45	1

Semi-final: 5 March, SCG

Gavaskar again fancied chasing rather than setting a target. On a
pensive pitch, New Zealand lost John Wright in the first over and
never really ameliorated their circumstances. There was a flicker of
defiance when Lance Cairns and Ian Smith came together at 151 for
seven in the 43rd over. But this was too little too late as the Kiwis
became the fourth successive side to be bowled out by India in the
competition. But needing 207 to win, India, initially, made rather
heavy weather of their mission. After 20 overs they managed to reach
only 46 for one. Mark Snedden was particularly impressive in giving
away only seven runs in his first five overs. But when Geoff Howarth
rested him, India slowly but surely asserted themselves, with Kapil
Dev sharing a rip-roaring stand with Dilip Vengsarkar. The turning
point was the 34th over, wherein the Haryana all-rounder cut loose
against Richard Hadlee, hitting him for four streaking 4s, besides
surviving a difficult chance to mid-off. India won by seven wickets
with 6.3 overs to spare.

Toss: India
Umpires: RA French and PJ McConnell
Man of the Match: RJ Shastri

New Zealand innings (50 overs maximum)			R	B
JG Wright	c Viswanath	b Kapil Dev	0	3
PE McEwan	c Viswanath	b Binny	9	15
JF Reid	c Kapil Dev	b Shastri	55	101
MD Crowe	c Azharuddin	b Madan Lal	9	25
*GP Howarth	run out		7	15
JV Coney	b Shastri		33	67
+IDS Smith	c Amarnath	b Madan Lal	19	35
RJ Hadlee	c Madan Lal	b Shastri	3	8
BL Cairns	c Srikkanth	b Madan Lal	39	29
MC Snedden	c Azharuddin	b Madan Lal	7	5
EJ Chatfield	not out		0	0

Extras: (lb 21, w 1, nb 3) 25
Total: (all out, 50 overs) 206

FoW: 1-0 (Wright), 2-14 (McEwan), 3-52 (Crowe), 4-69 (Howarth),
5-119 (Reid), 6-145 (Coney), 7-151 (Hadlee), 8-188 (Smith),
9-206 (Cairns), 10-206 (Snedden).

Bowling	O	M	R	W
Kapil Dev	10	1	34	1
Binny	6	0	28	1
Madan Lal	8	1	37	4
Amarnath	7	0	24	0
Sivaramakrishnan	9	1	31	0
Shastri	10	1	31	3

India innings (target: 207 runs from 50 overs)			R	B
RJ Shastri	c McEwan	b Hadlee	53	84
K Srikkanth	c Reid	b Chatfield	9	28
M Azharuddin	c Coney	b Cairns	24	54
DB Vengsarkar	not out		63	59
N Kapil Dev	not out		54	37

Extras: (b 1, lb 2, nb 1) 4
Total: (3 wickets, 43.3 overs) 207

DNB: *SM Gavaskar, M Amarnath, RMH Binny, S Madan Lal, +S Viswanath, L Sivaramakrishnan.

FoW: 1-28 (Srikkanth), 2-73 (Azharuddin), 3-102 (Shastri).

Bowling	O	M	R	W
Cairns	9	0	35	1
Hadlee	8.3	3	50	1
Chatfield	10	0	38	1
Snedden	8	1	37	0
Coney	8	0	44	0

Semi-final, 6 March: MCG (Day/Night)

Clive Lloyd, making what turned out to be his final appearance for the West Indies, won the toss against Pakistan and decided to take first strike. The West Indians had endured a rain-affected match against New Zealand and easily romped home against Sri Lanka. Consequently, they were a little short of match practice in the championship, though they were quite battle hardened and accustomed to Australian conditions at the end of a long tour of Down Under. They were, however, without Larry Gomes, who was injured and whose off-spin may have proved useful. But the truth is, they batted poorly and paid the penalty. Wasim Raja, with his leg-breaks, and Mudassar Nazar and Tahir Naqqash, with tidy medium pace, restricted the Windies. Then Wasim's brother, Rameez, with an authoritative innings, Qasim Omar, with a sprightly, unbeaten effort and Mohsin Khan with an obdurate one pole-vaulted the Pakistanis over the winning fence. For the West Indies, Malcolm Marshall and Michael Holding frequently beat the bat, but to no avail. Pakistan, thus, unexpectedly swept to victory against the favourites by seven wickets.

Toss: West Indies
Umpires: RC Isherwood and SG Randell
Man of the Match: Rameez Raja

West Indies innings (50 overs maximum)			R	B
DL Haynes	c Mudassar Nazar	b Tahir Naqqash	18	55
RB Richardson		b Tahir Naqqash	13	29
+PJL Dujon	c Anil Dalpat	b Wasim Raja	22	31
IVA Richards	c Anil Dalpat	b Tahir Naqqash	1	7
*CH Lloyd	c Javed Miandad	b Mudassar Nazar	25	41
AL Logie	c Qasim Umar	b Mudassar Nazar	8	17
MD Marshall	c Javed Miandad	b Mudassar Nazar	10	15
RA Harper	not out		25	33
MA Holding		b Wasim Akram	5	12
J Garner	c Wasim Raja	b Mudassar Nazar	13	26
WW Davis	c Javed Miandad	b Mudassar Nazar	3	8

Extras: (b 4, lb 7, w 4, nb 1) 16
Total: (all out, 44.3 overs) 159

FoW: 1-29 (Richardson), 2-44 (Haynes), 3-45 (Richards),
4-61 (Dujon), 5-75 (Logie), 6-96 (Marshall), 7-103 (Lloyd),
8-122 (Holding), 9-152 (Garner), 10-159 (Davis).

Bowling	O	M	R	W
Imran Khan	9	1	39	0
Wasim Akram	10	2	26	1
Tahir Naqqash	8	3	23	3
Wasim Raja	10	0	32	1
Mudassar Nazar	7.3	0	28	5

Pakistan innings (target: 160 runs from 50 overs)			R	B
Mudassar Nazar	c Logie	b Marshall	6	21
Mohsin Khan	c Dujon	b Garner	23	93
Rameez Raja	c & b Harper		60	88
Qasim Umar	not out		42	57
*Javed Miandad	not out		10	26

Extras: (b 3, lb 7, w 6, nb 3) 19
Total: (3 wickets, 46 overs) 160

DNB: Saleem Malik, Imran Khan, Wasim Raja, Tahir Naqqash, +Anil Dalpat, Wasim Akram.

FoW: 1-8 (Mudassar Nazar), 2-97 (Rameez Raja), 3-116 (Mohsin Khan).

Bowling	O	M	R	W
Marshall	9	2	25	1
Garner	8	3	19	1
Holding	8	3	19	0
Davis	7	0	35	0
Harper	10	1	38	1
Richards	4	0	14	0

Final, 10 March: MCG (Day/Night)

In a matter of 12 overs, Kapil Dev and Chetan Sharma had Pakistan tottering at 33 for four. Only Javed Miandad and Imran's contribution for the 5th wicket and a last wicket stand of 31 averted an annihilation. But 177 was rather a small score to defend. To illustrate this, Srikkanth and Shastri, who constituted an outstanding opening combination in the competition, made 103, the former, as usual, providing the fireworks, while his partner chugged along usefully yet unnoticeably. Following this partnership, Azharuddin contributed a-run-a-ball quarter century as India clinically finished the job. Pakistan were never really in the running. India won by eight wickets.

Indeed, India sustained the infallibility they had indicated in previous matches. Mature batting coupled with penetrative bowling, smart out-cricket and brilliant captaincy characterized their performance throughout. A 35,000 crowd provided them a lusty reception, as the Indians circled the ground in a lap of honour aboard an Audi car won by Shastri for being chosen 'champion of champions'. India's 'take-home pay' for lifting the trophy was £22,500; Pakistan raked in £11,500 for finishing as runners-up.

India had played faultless cricket, winning all their five matches comfortably. This display was in sharp contrast to their poor showing against England in the one-day series at home, which had preceded the visit to Australia. Gavaskar was a revelation. Seemingly eager to match Kapil's accomplishment of winning the World Cup, he redressed his previous allergy for one-day cricket to, first, lead India to victory in the inaugural Asia Cup tournament at Sharjah in the United Arab Emirates (UAE) in 1984 and followed this with an inspiring demonstration as captain in the 'World Championship of Cricket'.

At the age of 35, there was a new spring in his heels; he fielded superbly. Indeed he performed as if he wanted to prove a point — that he could be as good in limited-overs cricket as in test cricket, if he wanted to. That he had sufficient talent to adjust to the demands of the one-day game. As announced by him previously, he relinquished the captaincy at the end of the tournament.

For India, it was a notable double after triumphing in the World Cup. The slow turners suited them. Azhar and Siva were impressive on their overseas debuts. To Australian spectators, the latter's leg-spin provided a refreshing change from the invariableness of incessant fast bowling from the West Indians earlier in the season.

Toss: Pakistan
Umpires: AR Crafter and RC Isherwood
Man of the Match: K Srikkanth
Man of the Series: RJ Shastri

Pakistan innings (50 overs maximum)			R	B
Mudassar Nazar	c Viswanath	b Kapil Dev	14	39
Mohsin Khan	c Azharuddin	b Kapil Dev	5	17
Rameez Raja	c Srikkanth	b Sharma	4	12
Qasim Umar		b Kapil Dev	0	1
*Javed Miandad	st Viswanath	b Sivaramakrishnan	48	92
Imran Khan	run out		35	67
Saleem Malik	c Sharma	b Sivaramakrishnan	14	14
Wasim Raja	not out		21	26
Tahir Naqqash	c Viswanath	b Shastri	10	8
+Anil Dalpat	c Shastri	b Sivaramakrishnan	0	2
Azeem Hafeez	not out		7	28

Extras: (b 7, lb 8, w 1, nb 2) 18
Total: (9 wickets, 50 overs) 176

FoW: 1-17 (Mohsin Khan), 2-29 (Mudassar Nazar),
3-29 (Qasim Umar), 4-33 (Rameez Raja), 5-101 (Imran Khan),
6-131 (Saleem Malik), 7-131 (Javed Miandad),
8-142 (Tahir Naqqash), 9-145 (Anil Dalpat).

Bowling	O	M	R	W
Kapil Dev	9	1	23	3
Sharma	7	1	17	1
Madan Lal	6	1	15	0
Amarnath	9	0	27	0
Shastri	10	0	44	1
Sivaramakrishnan	9	0	35	3

India innings (target: 177 runs from 50 overs)			R	B
RJ Shastri	not out		63	148
K Srikkanth	c Wasim Raja	b Imran Khan	67	77
M Azharuddin		b Tahir Naqqash	25	26
DB Vengsarkar	not out		18	32

Extras: (lb 2, w 2) 4
Total: (2 wickets, 47.1 overs) 177

DNB: *SM Gavaskar, M Amarnath, N Kapil Dev, S Madan Lal,
C Sharma, +S Viswanath, L Sivaramakrishnan.

FoW: 1-103 (Srikkanth), 2-142 (Azharuddin).

Bowling	O	M	R	W
Imran Khan	10	3	28	1
Azeem Hafeez	10	1	29	0
Tahir Naqqash	10	2	35	1
Wasim Raja	7.1	0	42	0
Mudassar Nazar	8	0	26	0
Saleem Malik	2	0	15	0

With Gavaskar abdicating as skipper, Kapil returned to the helm. Within weeks of the 'World Championship of Cricket', Sharjah hosted a four-nation one-day knockout tournament, supported by Rothman's. Cricket in this desert state began in 1981 and was immediately supported with enthusiasm by many of the South Asians living in the UAE. A patch of green in otherwise arid surroundings boasted a stadium for 12,000 spectators. Real soil had been hauled hundreds of miles before being heaped into a gaping hole in the sand. The square was not ideal, but the pitches generally did not change character in course of a day.

The hosting of international cricket in this unlikely part of the world was the handiwork of an Arab businessman, Abdul Rahman Bukhatir. He grew to love cricket as a student in Pakistan and raised £2 million to build the stadium. He appointed Asif Iqbal, the former Pakistani captain, as cricket manager. They organized matches under the banner of Cricketers' Benefit Fund Series (CBFS), which presented retired Indian and Pakistani players with lump sums of benevolence.

In the first match of the Rothman's Four-Nation Cup, India faced Pakistan. It was an astonishing affair. On a damp wicket, Imran literally skidded the ball to take six wickets for 14 runs after India were put in. It was a day of boisterous partisanship, there being a capacity crowd of mainly Pakistanis and Indians. The Indian batsmen were undone by the pitch, which later turned sharply as soon as spin was experimented with. The most skilful innings was the 47 by Azharuddin, who ever since his stirring arrival on the international scene a few months earlier, could hardly put a foot wrong. Indeed, what seemed impossible in the morning was achieved in the afternoon as India pulled off a narrow win.

Toss: Pakistan
Umpires: HD Bird (Eng) and MW Johnson (Aus)
Man of the Match: Imran Khan

India innings (50 overs maximum)			R	B
RJ Shastri	lbw	b Imran Khan	0	1
K Srikkanth	c Saleem Malik	b Imran Khan	6	5
M Azharuddin		b Tauseef Ahmed	47	93
DB Vengsarkar	c Ashraf Ali	b Imran Khan	1	4
SM Gavaskar	c Ashraf Ali	b Imran Khan	2	9
M Amarnath		b Imran Khan	5	10
*N Kapil Dev		b Tauseef Ahmed	30	44
RMH Binny	c Javed Miandad	b Mudassar Nazar	8	19
S Madan Lal	c Ashraf Ali	b Imran Khan	11	39
+S Viswanath	not out		3	28
L Sivaramakrishnan	c Saleem Malik	b Wasim Akram	1	6

Extras: (b 5, lb 4, w 2) 11
Total: (all out, 42.4 overs) 125

FoW: 1-0 (Shastri), 2-12 (Srikkanth), 3-20 (Vengsarkar),
4-28 (Gavaskar), 5-34 (Amarnath), 6-80 (Kapil Dev),
7-95 (Binny), 8-113 (Madan Lal), 9-121 (Azharuddin),
10-125 (Sivaramakrishnan).

Bowling	O	M	R	W
Imran Khan	10	2	14	6
Wasim Akram	7.4	0	27	1
Tahir Naqqash	5	0	12	0
Mudassar Nazar	10	1	36	1
Tauseef Ahmed	10	0	27	2

Pakistan innings (target: 126 runs from 50 overs)			R	B
Mudassar Nazar	c Gavaskar	b Binny	18	18
Mohsin Khan	run out		10	9
Rameez Raja	c Gavaskar	b Kapil Dev	29	71
*Javed Miandad	c Gavaskar	b Shastri	0	15
+Ashraf Ali	c Vengsarkar	b Sivaramakrishnan	0	11
Imran Khan	st Viswanath	b Sivaramakrishnan	0	4
Saleem Malik	c Gavaskar	b Shastri	17	39
Manzoor Elahi	c & b Madan Lal		9	24
Tahir Naqqash	c Viswanath	b Kapil Dev	1	2
Tauseef Ahmed		b Kapil Dev	0	7
Wasim Akram	not out		0	0

Extras: (lb 1, w 1, nb 1) 3
Total: (all out, 32.5 overs) 87

FoW: 1-13 (Mohsin Khan), 2-35 (Mudassar Nazar),
3-40 (Javed Miandad), 4-41 (Ashraf Ali), 5-41 (Imran Khan),
6-74 (Saleem Malik), 7-85 (Rameez Raja),
8-87 (Tahir Naqqash), 9-87 (Manzoor Elahi),
10-87 (Tauseef Ahmed).

Bowling	O	M	R	W
Kapil Dev	6.5	1	17	3
Binny	3	0	24	1
Sivaramakrishnan	7	2	16	2
Shastri	10	5	17	2
Madan Lal	6	2	12	1

Next up, Australia beat England by two wickets off the last ball of the match. The Englishmen were the only ones not to take a fully representative squad to the competition; they were led by Norman Gifford, the Worcestershire left-arm spinner. Few batsmen played the slow bowling well, or adapted to the extremely slow surface.

By the time the final transpired, India were the punters' choice and lived up to such expectations. Gavaskar was adjudged Man of the Series, as much for his five brilliant catches at slip since his contribution with the bat was not special.

Toss: India
Umpires: HD Bird (Eng) and Khizer Hayat (Pak)
Man of the Match: M Amarnath
Man of the Series: SM Gavaskar

Australia innings (50 overs maximum)

			R	B
GM Wood	run out		27	37
KC Wessels	c Gavaskar	b Madan Lal	30	68
DM Jones	c Viswanath	b Madan Lal	8	10
*AR Border	c & b Amarnath		27	38
KJ Hughes	c & b Amarnath		11	24
GRJ Matthews	lbw	b Kapil Dev	11	31
SP O'Donnell	run out		3	25
+SJ Rixon	run out		4	14
MJ Bennett	lbw	b Shastri	0	2
RJ McCurdy	c Vengsarkar	b Shastri	0	5
CJ McDermott	not out		0	0

Extras: (lb 13, w 5) 18
Total: (all out, 42.3 overs) 139

FoW: 1-60 (Wood), 2-71 (Jones), 3-78 (Wessels), 4-114 (Hughes), 5-115 (Border), 6-131 (O'Donnell), 7-138 (Matthews), 8-139 (Rixon), 9-139 (Bennett), 10-139 (McCurdy).

Bowling

	O	M	R	W
Kapil Dev	6	3	9	1
Binny	5	0	25	0
Madan Lal	7	0	30	2
Sivaramakrishnan	8	1	29	0
Shastri	9.3	1	14	2
Amarnath	7	1	19	2

India innings (target: 140 runs from 50 overs)

			R	B
RJ Shastri	c Rixon	b O'Donnell	9	26
K Srikkanth	lbw	b McDermott	0	1
M Azharuddin	c Jones	b McDermott	22	44
DB Vengsarkar		b McDermott	35	43
SM Gavaskar	run out		20	50
M Amarnath	not out		24	44
*N Kapil Dev		b Matthews	1	14
RMH Binny		b Matthews	2	5
S Madan Lal	not out		7	14

Extras: (lb 9, w 7, nb 4) 20
Total: (7 wickets, 39.2 overs) 140

DNB: +S Viswanath, L Sivaramakrishnan.

FoW: 1-2 (Srikkanth), 2-37 (Shastri), 3-41 (Azharuddin),
4-98 (Gavaskar), 5-103 (Vengsarkar), 6-117 (Kapil Dev),
7-120 (Binny).

Bowling	O	M	R	W
McDermott	10	0	36	3
McCurdy	4	1	10	0
O'Donnell	4	1	11	1
Bennett	10	0	35	0
Matthews	10	1	33	2
Border	1.2	0	6	0

Pakistan beat England in the play-off for third place.

The four Boards of Control whose teams took part were satisfied that Sharjah was deserving of not being treated as a pirate outfit. Indeed, for a while, cricket flourished in the Arabian desert. The bedrock of the boom constituted India–Pakistan clashes. But the matches between the neighbours were played in a slightly unhealthy, unsporting atmosphere. The bad blood that existed between the two countries in the political spectrum spilled over to the cricketing theatre. Back in the subcontinent, people were glued to their TVs not to enjoy good cricket, but to witness another episode of hostilities between the two nations.

One such instalment was a match between the two sides in April 1986. The tournament was called the Austral-Asia Cup, and, as the name connotes, it featured Australia, New Zealand, Sri Lanka, India and Pakistan. The Australians departed in the first round while the Sri Lankas were beaten by India and the Kiwis defeated by Pakistan—thus setting the stage for a confrontation between the arch-rivals, which the UAE's expatriate community of Indians and Pakistanis and, of course, their compatriots back home had been eagerly, yet nervously, expecting.

India made light of being sent in, when Gavaskar and Srikkanth posted 116 for the first wicket and Vengsarkar, too, hit a half century. At 216 for one, the Indians were in quite an assertive state. But with Imran and Wasim returning to the attack, they slumped to the extent of setting Pakistan a target of just under five an over.

Miandad, with Abdul Qadir, who played a dab hand with the willow, realized 71 for the fifth wicket in quick time, which reduced the required rate from nine an over to five an over off the last 10. The Karachi batsman, then, maintained the momentum. Chetan Sharma was assigned to bowl the last over, which boiled down to four being needed off the last ball. As the field spread out to prevent a boundary, Miandad daringly struck this delivery for a six! His unbeaten 116, with two fours and three sixes (representing plenty of running between wickets), was strategically astute. It was, moreover, a great cricket match, played by both sides in the right spirit; but perhaps not watched by a majority of Indians and Pakistanis with the same attitude. Urban India was awash with thunderstruck citizens. Pakistanis celebrated as if they had gained revenge for the humiliation inflicted on them in the 1971 war between the two countries.

Toss: Pakistan
Umpires: DM Archer (WI) and AJ Gaynor (WI)
Man of the Match: Javed Miandad
Man of the Series: SM Gavaskar

India innings (50 overs maximum)			R	B
K Srikkanth	c Wasim Akram	b Abdul Qadir	75	80
SM Gavaskar		b Imran Khan	92	134
DB Vengsarkar		b Wasim Akram	50	64
KBJ Azad		b Wasim Akram	0	3
*N Kapil Dev		b Imran Khan	8	8
C Sharma	run out		10	10
RJ Shastri		b Wasim Akram	1	2
+CS Pandit	not out		0	2

Extras: (lb 6, w 2, nb 1) 9
Total: (7 wickets, 50 overs) 245

DNB: M Azharuddin, S Madan Lal, Maninder Singh.

FoW: 1-117 (Srikkanth), 2-216 (Vengsarkar), 3-216 (Azad),
4-229 (Kapil Dev), 5-242 (Sharma), 6-245 (Shastri),
7-245 (Gavaskar).

Bowling	O	M	R	W
Imran Khan	10	2	40	2
Wasim Akram	10	1	42	3
Manzoor Elahi	5	0	33	0
Mudassar Nazar	5	0	32	0
Abdul Qadir	10	2	49	1
Tauseef Ahmed	10	1	43	0

Pakistan innings (target: 246 runs from 50 overs)			R	B
Mudassar Nazar	lbw	b Sharma	5	22
Mohsin Khan		b Madan Lal	36	53
Rameez Raja		b Maninder Singh	10	15
Javed Miandad	not out		116	114
Saleem Malik	run out		21	37
Abdul Qadir	c sub	b Kapil Dev	34	39
*Imran Khan		b Madan Lal	7	10
Manzoor Elahi	c Shastri	b Sharma	4	5
Wasim Akram	run out		3	4
+Zulqarnain		b Sharma	0	1
Tauseef Ahmed	not out		1	1

Extras: (lb 11) 11
Total: (9 wickets, 50 overs) 248

FoW: 1-9 (Mudassar Nazar), 2-39 (Rameez Raja),
3-61 (Mohsin Khan), 4-110 (Saleem Malik),
5-181 (Abdul Qadir), 6-209 (Imran Khan),
7-215 (Manzoor Elahi), 8-236 (Wasim Akram),
9-241 (Zulqarnain).

Bowling	O	M	R	W
Kapil Dev	10	1	45	1
Sharma	9	0	51	3
Madan Lal	10	0	53	2
Maninder Singh	10	0	36	1
Shastri	9	0	38	0
Azharuddin	2	0	14	0

Gradually, though, anxiety grew that all may not be above board with the conduct of matches at Sharjah. This concern intensified when Dawood Ibrahim, – a well-known Mumbai Mafia don and the main accused in the bombings that killed more than 200 people in this city in March 1993, who had been absconding for years – surfaced prominently in an exclusive enclosure at Bukhatir's stadium and was even suspected of hobnobbing with the cricketers away from the cameras. Since illicit bookmaking is alleged to have been one of Ibrahim's innumerable illegal activities, it was reasonable to ask how he could flaunt himself so publicly?

Sharjah cricket, desperately dependent on carriage of its matches by Indian television and related revenues in order to survive (which could only happen if India took part), died a natural death as the Indian government forbade the BCCI to send teams to CBFS-organized tournaments after October 2000. The ICC and most of their constituents (not the Pakistan Cricket Board, though), reeling under the match-fixing crisis, also distanced themselves from Sharjah.

One wonders, of course, whether the BCCI were lured back through the back door in 2006 by holding offshore matches in Abu Dhabi, an UAE state bordering Sharjah.

6

After 1983

THE 1987 WORLD CUP

THE FOURTH WORLD CUP, HELD IN THE INDIAN SUBCONTINENT, attracted a much bigger audience and turned out to be more keenly contested and more glamorous than any of its three predecessors held in England. Indeed, it got off to an intoxicating start, with thrilling opening matches taking place between Pakistan, the favourites, and Sri Lanka; India, the holders, and Australia; England and the West Indies; and New Zealand and non-test-playing Zimbabwe. Even if the rest of the Reliance Cup, as it was officially known, did not quite live up to such a beginning, the foray of the World Cup into warmer climes was still seen to be an unstinting success.

As before, there were eight participants, who were divided into two groups. Australia, New Zealand, India and Zimbabwe were concentrated in one; England, West Indies, Pakistan and Sri Lanka in the other.

Outside the subcontinent, the geographical enormity of the two host countries and the policy of the India–Pakistan Joint Management Committee to spread the games around in as many as 21 venues were seen as shortcomings. It was the equivalent of staging a tournament across the European Union without quite the same infrastructure of transport and telecommunications. Fewer centres would have meant less travelling; and a shorter and more compact competition. In some cases, teams travelled for days between matches, with hours spent in unexciting airport terminals.

Nevertheless, in arduous circumstances, the organizers fared capably. The weather was hot, but unoppressive. Only one match was affected by rain, when Australia and New Zealand were reduced to 30 overs each in Indore, in India's Madhya Pradesh state. (Mercifully, the rule that a match could not be carried over to its second day was never tested.) Otherwise, the matches were 50 overs per side; and, on placid pitches, totals similar to those in previous 60-over World Cups were raised. Viv Richards, individually, and West Indies, collectively, established new records against Sri Lanka for World Cup innings.

A subcontinental World Cup, refreshingly, encouraged spin, relieving, to some extent, the recurrence of seam in previous competitions in England. The 1975 final had been wholly pace or medium pace. Australia, however, stuck to their strength, in that they did not usually risk more than 10 overs of spin; a majority of the others fielded two spinners. In the qualifying rounds, seven of the nine most economical bowlers were spinners. At the same time, the highest wicket-takers were Craig McDermott and Imran Khan, both fast bowlers. The Australian equalled the World Cup record of 18 wickets, while the Pakistani took 17 in one match less.

Shorter daylight compelled an early start of play. But the concern over dew being a disadvantage to batsmen was misplaced. Rather, batting in an exhausted state proved to be a strain. In fact, 19 of the 27 matches were won by sides batting first. The side taking first strike played normally; the side batting second seemed to panic.

As for the umpiring, even if this was not of the very highest standard, the redeeming factor was that its neutrality served to minimize grievances.

On the Indian political stage, a storm was building up. The alleged scam over the purchase of Bofors field guns from Sweden for the Indian army rocked the country and Prime Minister Rajiv Gandhi, hitherto painted as 'Mr Clean', faced a fierce onslaught from opposition politicians and the print media. (Television and radio were then virtually state controlled.) He also, damagingly, fell out with his popular finance minister, Vishwanath Pratap Singh, a stickler for probity in public life. As this burning issue engulfed the country, the tournament was afoot.

9 October: Chepauk, Chennai

The first-ever official test match in India – against England – was held at Mumbai in December 1933 at the Bombay Gymkhana Ground, which, however, ceased to be an international venue thereafter, as the next such fixture in this city was staged at the Brabourne Stadium. The third test in the same series (against Douglas Jardine's side in February 1934) took place at Chepauk, thus making it the country's third oldest test centre. For about a decade from the mid-1950s, though, tests in Chennai shifted to the Corporation Stadium, before returning to Chepauk.

Here, India won the toss, but chose to field. On a docile pitch Geoff Marsh and David Boon put on 100 at almost five runs an over. Dean Jones played quite beautifully, but the middle order lost the initiative. Marsh, in the 95-degree heat and high humidity, batted for more than three hours and hit a six and seven fours.

For India, Sunil Gavaskar (one six, six fours), Krishnamachari Srikkanth (seven fours) and Navjot Singh Sidhu (five sixes, four fours) sent India racing past 200 for the loss of only two wickets. The last-mentioned, known for his valour rather than flinging his bat, was in a new incarnation en route to becoming an effective batsman and the best Sikh wielder of the willow ever. He hailed from Patiala in Punjab, whose maharajas have been notable benefactors of cricket.

Craig McDermott's first four overs conceded 31 runs, but he came back strongly to whip out the middle order. Even so, India, with four wickets in hand, needed just 15 from the last four overs; when the last over began, the requirement was six, with the last man, Maninder Singh, taking strike. He managed two 2s, but along with his sang-froid went his off stump. Australia's innings, like India's, had been built around the top-order batsmen. Also, Kapil Dev's sportsmanship proved the deciding factor in a close-run match. One of Jones's two sixes, in his 39 from 35 balls, had been signalled a four; but between innings Kapil relented to the Australians' insistence that the ball cleared the boundary. India's target was, thus, increased by two. Australia ultimately won by a solitary run.

Toss: India
Umpires: DM Archer (WI) and HD Bird (Eng)
ODI Debuts: TM Moody (Aus); NS Sidhu (Ind).
Man of the Match: GR Marsh

Australia innings (50 overs maximum)			*R*	*B*
DC Boon	lbw	b Shastri	49	68
GR Marsh	c Azharuddin	b Prabhakar	110	141
DM Jones	c Sidhu	b Maninder Singh	39	35
*AR Border		b Binny	16	22
TM Moody	c Kapil Dev	b Prabhakar	8	13
SR Waugh	not out		19	17
SP O'Donnell	run out		7	10

Extras: (lb 18, w 2, nb 2) 22
Total: (6 wickets, 50 overs) 270

DNB: +GC Dyer, PL Taylor, CJ McDermott, BA Reid.

FoW: 1-110 (Boon), 2-174 (Jones), 3-228 (Border), 4-237 (Marsh), 5-251 (Moody), 6-270 (O'Donnell).

Bowling	*O*	*M*	*R*	*W*
Kapil Dev	10	0	41	0
Prabhakar	10	0	47	2
Binny	7	0	46	1
Maninder Singh	10	0	48	1
Shastri	10	0	50	1
Azharuddin	3	0	20	0

India innings *(target: 271 runs from 50 overs)*			R	B
SM Gavaskar	c Reid	b Taylor	37	32
K Srikkanth	lbw	b Waugh	70	83
NS Sidhu		b McDermott	73	79
DB Vengsarkar	c Jones	b McDermott	29	45
M Azharuddin		b McDermott	10	14
*N Kapil Dev	c Boon	b O'Donnell	6	10
RJ Shastri	c & b McDermott		12	11
+KS More	not out		12	14
RMH Binny	run out		0	3
M Prabhakar	run out		5	7
Maninder Singh		b Waugh	4	5

Extras: (b 2, lb 7, w 2) 11
Total: (all out, 49.5 overs) 269

FoW: 1-69 (Gavaskar), 2-131 (Srikkanth), 3-207 (Sidhu),
4-229 (Azharuddin), 5-232 (Vengsarkar), 6-246 (Shastri),
7-256 (Kapil Dev), 8-256 (Binny), 9-265 (Prabhakar),
10-269 (Maninder Singh).

Bowling	O	M	R	W
McDermott	10	0	56	4
Reid	10	2	35	0
O'Donnell	9	1	32	1
Taylor	5	0	46	1
Waugh	9.5	0	52	2
Border	6	0	39	0

14 October: Chinnaswamy Stadium, Bangalore

With the progress of Mysore, later Karnataka, in cricket, its capital
became a test centre (with a stadium dedicated to a former president
of the Karnataka State Cricket Association, M. Chinnaswamy) in
1974, with Clive Lloyd's West Indians as the first tourists. This venue
has been on the BCCI's 'A' list ever since.

New Zealand called correctly and asked India to bat in awkward conditions, on a pitch of mixed demeanour and a sluggish outfield. Besides, the Indians were not exactly helped by a suicidal Srikkanth, like Srinivas Venkataraghavan, a Tamil Brahmin, who contributed to the run-out of himself and Gavaskar. The quirky batsman was seemingly unconscious of the threat to himself when he was sent packing by Ken Rutherford. At 21 for three in the 10th over, it was certainly doom and gloom in the Indian dressing room. Sidhu (four sixes, four fours), then, lifted the spirits with an audacious use of his feet. But when he was fifth out, at 114, India still needed a major push to extend the Kiwis. This emerged in the form of Kapil (one six, four fours) and Kiran More (a protégé of the maharaja of the once princely state of Baroda, who had employed his father) realizing 82 runs off the last 51 balls.

New Zealand batted safely but did not score swiftly enough. The experienced John Wright, laid low by a virus, was missing from the New Zealand line-up. This absence entrusted onerous responsibility to Martin Crowe, the one man capable of stepping it up. But the left-arm spinner, Maninder (a Sikh like Bishan Bedi), one of three slow bowlers utilized by India, beat him with a beauty. India won by 16 runs.

Toss: New Zealand
Umpires: DM Archer (WI) and HD Bird (Eng)
Man of the Match: N Kapil Dev

India innings (50 overs maximum)			R	B
K Srikkanth	run out		9	19
SM Gavaskar	run out		2	14
NS Sidhu	c Jones	b Patel	75	71
DB Vengsarkar	c & b Watson		0	8
M Azharuddin	c Boock	b Patel	21	57
RJ Shastri	c & b Patel		22	44
*N Kapil Dev	not out		72	58
M Prabhakar	c & b Chatfield		3	5
+KS More	not out		42	26

Extras: (lb 4, w 2) 6
Total: (7 wickets, 50 overs) 252

DNB: L Sivaramakrishnan, Maninder Singh.

FoW: 1-11 (Gavaskar), 2-16 (Srikkanth), 3-21 (Vengsarkar),
4-86 (Azharuddin), 5-114 (Sidhu), 6-165 (Shastri),
7-170 (Prabhakar).

Bowling	*O*	*M*	*R*	*W*
Chatfield	10	1	39	1
Snedden	10	1	56	0
Watson	9	0	59	1
Boock	4	0	26	0
Bracewell	7	0	32	0
Patel	10	0	36	3

New Zealand innings (target: 253 runs from 50 overs)			*R*	*B*
MC Snedden	c Shastri	b Azharuddin	33	63
KR Rutherford	c Srikkanth	b Shastri	75	95
MD Crowe	st More	b Maninder Singh	9	12
AH Jones	run out		64	86
*JJ Crowe	c Vengsarkar	b Maninder Singh	7	11
DN Patel	run out		1	3
JG Bracewell	c Maninder Singh	b Shastri	8	14
+IDS Smith		b Prabhakar	10	5
SL Boock	not out		7	8
W Watson	not out		2	3

Extras: (b 5, lb 9, w 5, nb 1) 20
Total: (8 wickets, 50 overs) 236

DNB: EJ Chatfield.

FoW: 1-67 (Snedden), 2-86 (MD Crowe), 3-146 (Rutherford),
4-168 (JJ Crowe), 5-170 (Patel), 6-189 (Bracewell),
7-206 (Smith), 8-225 (Jones).

Bowling	O	M	R	W
Kapil Dev	10	1	54	0
Prabhakar	8	0	38	1
Azharuddin	4	0	11	1
Sivaramakrishnan	8	0	34	0
Maninder Singh	10	0	40	2
Shastri	10	0	45	2

17 October: Wankhede Stadium, Mumbai

International cricket moved to the Wankhede Stadium [named after S.K. Wankhede, a former president of the Mumbai Cricket Association (MCA)] and the BCCI and also Maharashtra state's finance minister) in 1975 (with the first test played against Clive Lloyd's West Indies) after a quarrel between the MCA and the Cricket Club of India at whose Brabourne Stadium such matches used to be organized.

Zimbabwe elected to bat after winning the toss. But this decision boomeranged, as on a pitch with residual moisture – it being a dewy morning – Manoj Prabhakar, a Delhi, all-rounder, swung the ball ebulliently, capturing four wickets off 17 balls. Andy Pycroft, with 61, at least ensured Zimbabwe got to three figures. India, having bowled out their opponents well within the allotted overs, deliberately raced to victory, aware of the fact that a good run-rate could have a bearing on standings, in the event of a tight finish at the end of the group stage. Gavaskar's first 36 runs were all off boundaries. Dilip Vengsarkar (tagged 'colonel' by his teammates), then, collected runs with contemptuous ease. India won by eight wickets.

Toss: Zimbabwe
Umpires: Mahboob Shah (Pak) and DR Shepherd (Eng)
ODI Debuts: KJ Arnott, MA Meman (Zim).
Man of the Match: M Prabhakar

Zimbabwe innings (50 overs maximum)

			R	B
GA Paterson		b Prabhakar	6	21
KJ Arnott	lbw	b Prabhakar	1	6
+DL Houghton		b Prabhakar	0	12
AJ Pycroft	st More	b Shastri	61	102
KM Curran	c More	b Prabhakar	0	1
AC Waller	st More	b Maninder Singh	16	42
IP Butchart	c Sivaramakrishnan	b Maninder Singh	10	23
AH Omarshah	c More	b Maninder Singh	0	1
MA Meman	run out		19	22
*AJ Traicos	c Gavaskar	b Sivaramakrishnan	0	1
MP Jarvis	not out		8	35

Extras: (b 2, lb 6, w 6) 14
Total: (all out, 44.2 overs) 135

FoW: 1-3 (Arnott), 2-12 (Houghton), 3-13 (Paterson),
4-13 (Curran), 5-47 (Waller), 6-67 (Butchart),
7-67 (Omarshah), 8-98 (Meman), 9-99 (Traicos),
10-135 (Pycroft).

Bowling

	O	M	R	W
Kapil Dev	8	1	17	0
Prabhakar	8	1	19	4
Maninder Singh	10	0	21	3
Azharuddin	1	0	6	0
Sivaramakrishnan	9	0	36	1
Shastri	8.2	0	28	1

India innings (target: 136 runs from 50 overs)

			R	B
K Srikkanth	c Paterson	b Traicos	31	38
SM Gavaskar	st Houghton	b Traicos	43	52
M Prabhakar	not out		11	41
DB Vengsarkar	not out		46	37

Extras: (lb 1, w 4) 5
Total: (2 wickets, 27.5 overs) 136

DNB: NS Sidhu, M Azharuddin, *N Kapil Dev, RJ Shastri, +KS More, L Sivaramakrishnan, Maninder Singh.

FoW: 1-76 (Srikkanth), 2-80 (Gavaskar).

Bowling	O	M	R	W
Curran	6	0	32	0
Jarvis	4	0	22	0
Butchart	3	0	20	0
Traicos	8	0	27	2
Meman	6.5	0	34	0

22 October: Feroz Shah Kotla, New Delhi

Since international cricket could not bypass the capital of India after the country became independent, the Feroz Shah Kotla has enjoyed this honour since 1948, with John Goddard's West Indians being the first visitors.

Australia asked India to take first strike here, but it was an easy batting wicket, with relatively short boundaries. Restricting the scoring was, therefore, a challenge. Indeed, with the ball coming on to the bat nicely from the Australian seamers, it was cannon fodder for the Indian batsmen. Gavaskar and Srikkanth thus helped themselves to 50 off the first 10 overs, Sidhu recorded his third successive half century and Vengsarkar and Azharuddin (who like his uncle, Abid Ali, went to a Christian school, but was groomed in cricket in the Hyderabadi tradition of wristy, short-arm flicks) batted with assurance and class, rapidly knitting 65 in 10 overs.

Marsh and Boon (seven fours) replied with 88 in 18 overs, but the advent of the left-arm trundlers, Maninder and Ravi Shastri (whose family originated from the southern state of Karnataka, but had settled in Mumbai) after 17 overs altered the tempo and the course of the match. Their accuracy, aerial control and spin were too much for the Australians to cope with. Steve Waugh was technically up to the task and also kept his head, but couldn't shake off the stranglehold as his side increasingly receded out of contention.

India prevailed by a convincing 56 runs and, with this win, the prospect of them finishing second in their group and, thus, having to play Pakistan in the semi-final faded considerably.

Toss: Australia
Umpires: Khalid Aziz (Pak) and DR Shepherd (Eng)
ODI Debuts: AK Zesers (Aus).
Man of the Match: M Azharuddin

India innings (50 overs maximum)			R	B
K Srikkanth	c Dyer	b McDermott	26	37
SM Gavaskar		b O'Donnell	61	72
NS Sidhu	c Moody	b McDermott	51	70
DB Vengsarkar	c O'Donnell	b Reid	63	60
*N Kapil Dev	c Dyer	b McDermott	3	5
M Azharuddin	not out		54	45
RJ Shastri	c & b Waugh		8	7
+KS More	not out		5	4

Extras: (b 1, lb 6, w 11) 18
Total: (6 wickets, 50 overs) 289

DNB: M Prabhakar, C Sharma, Maninder Singh.

FoW: 1-50 (Srikkanth), 2-125 (Gavaskar), 3-167 (Sidhu), 4-178 (Kapil Dev), 5-243 (Vengsarkar), 6-274 (Shastri).

Bowling	O	M	R	W
O'Donnell	9	1	45	1
Reid	10	0	65	1
Waugh	10	0	59	1
McDermott	10	0	61	3
Moody	2	0	15	0
Zesers	9	1	37	0

Australia innings (target: 290 runs from 50 overs)			R	B
GR Marsh	st More	b Maninder Singh	33	56
DC Boon	c More	b Shastri	62	59
DM Jones	c Kapil Dev	b Maninder Singh	36	55
*AR Border	c Prabhakar	b Maninder Singh	12	24
SR Waugh	c Sidhu	b Kapil Dev	42	52
TM Moody	run out		2	6
SP O'Donnell		b Azharuddin	5	10
+GC Dyer	c Kapil Dev	b Prabhakar	15	12
CJ McDermott	c & b Azharuddin		4	5
AK Zesers	not out		2	11
BA Reid	c Sidhu	b Azharuddin	1	6

Extras: (lb 11, w 8) 19
Total: (all out, 49 overs) 233

FoW: 1-88 (Marsh), 2-104 (Boon), 3-135 (Border), 4-164 (Jones), 5-167 (Moody), 6-182 (O'Donnell), 7-214 (Dyer), 8-227 (McDermott), 9-231 (Waugh), 10-233 (Reid).

Bowling	O	M	R	W
Kapil Dev	8	1	41	1
Prabhakar	10	0	56	1
Maninder Singh	10	0	34	3
Shastri	10	0	35	1
Sharma	7.1	0	37	0
Azharuddin	3.5	0	19	3

26 October: Ahmedabad

The western Indian city of Ahmedabad is a textile centre, where prohibition existed on paper, but not entirely in practice; and where there was, unfortunately, a history of Hindu–Muslim tension.

Here, Kevin Arnott, coming in at number three, patiently batted 43 overs for his 60 after Zimbabwe were put in by India. With the Indians keen to avoid a semi-final in Pakistan, the scoring rate had become a pressing issue in this group. But the Indian top-order batsmen were strokeless on a slow pitch, notwithstanding the unruly, stone-throwing crowd disturbing their concentration. Gavaskar, in fact, utilized as many as 114 balls to get 50. But Kapil, promoting himself to number five, stole the thunder with a precipitate 41, which included three towering sixes. India won by seven wickets in the 42nd over. But they were still left at a run rate of 5.18 as compared to Australia's 5.20.

Toss: India

Umpires: DM Archer (WI) and HD Bird (Eng)

Man of the Match: N Kapil Dev

Zimbabwe innings (50 overs maximum)			R	B
RD Brown	c More	b Sharma	13	52
AH Omarshah	run out		0	3
KJ Arnott		b Kapil Dev	60	126
AJ Pycroft	c More	b Sharma	2	9
+DL Houghton	c Kapil Dev	b Shastri	22	35
AC Waller	c Shastri	b Maninder Singh	39	44
IP Butchart		b Kapil Dev	13	14
PWE Rawson	not out		16	17
EA Brandes	not out		3	4

Extras: (b 1, lb 12, w 9, nb 1) 23

Total: (7 wickets, 50 overs) 191

DNB: MP Jarvis, *AJ Traicos.

FoW: 1-4 (Omarshah), 2-36 (Brown), 3-40 (Pycroft), 4-83 (Houghton), 5-150 (Arnott), 6-155 (Waller), 7-184 (Butchart).

Bowling	O	M	R	W
Kapil Dev	10	2	44	2
Prabhakar	7	2	12	0
Sharma	10	0	41	2
Maninder Singh	10	1	32	1
Shastri	10	0	35	1
Azharuddin	3	0	14	0

India innings (target: 192 runs from 50 overs)			R	B
K Srikkanth	lbw	b Jarvis	6	9
SM Gavaskar	c Butchart	b Rawson	50	114
NS Sidhu	c Brandes	b Rawson	55	61
DB Vengsarkar	not out		33	43
*N Kapil Dev	not out		41	25

Extras: (lb 6, w 3) 9
Total: (3 wickets, 42 overs) 194

DNB: M Azharuddin, RJ Shastri, +KS More, M Prabhakar, C Sharma, Maninder Singh.

FoW: 1-11 (Srikkanth), 2-105 (Sidhu), 3-132 (Gavaskar).

Bowling	O	M	R	W
Brandes	6	0	28	0
Jarvis	8	1	21	1
Omarshah	8	0	40	0
Traicos	10	0	39	0
Rawson	8	0	46	2
Butchart	2	0	14	0

31 October: Nagpur

At this commodities hub, virtually at the geographical centre of India, New Zealand chose to bat first, but did so unconvincingly. Chetan

Sharma, a state mate of Kapil, hit the timber in the last three balls of the 42nd over to record the first hat trick in the World Cup. Rutherford, Ian Smith and Ewen Chatfield comprised the dubious trio. Only a partnership of 39 between Martin Snedden and William Watson in the latter stages of the innings retrieved the situation.

The Kiwis' total of 221 meant India had to reach their destination in 42.2 overs, not impossible, but not easy either. In other words, to eclipse Australia on run-rate, India had to score at 5.25 runs an over. In Srikkanth, they had the perfect pilot. But amazingly, it was Gavaskar, reportedly, unwell on the eve of the match, who was in the most dashing form. After the pair helped themselves to 18 off the first two overs, the accumulator transformed into a Bombay bomber took 21 off Chatfield's third over as he struck the first two balls for sixes and the next two for fours. The 50 of the venture came up in the 8th over, the next 50 in another six overs. Srikkanth, not unknown to cause mayhem, lofted three sixes and clobbered nine fours in his 58-ball 75. Gavaskar, earning his 106th one-day cap for India and for whom the 1987 World Cup was his last appearance in limited-overs cricket, completed a timely maiden century in ODIs in 85 balls, adorned with three sixes and 10 fours. India, thereby, overhauled the New Zealand score with 10 overs to spare, and, as a result, qualified to meet England in the semi-finals. It was a dazzling display. India won by nine wickets, with Gavaskar and Chetan Sharma sharing the Man of the Match award.

Toss: New Zealand
Umpires: HD Bird (Eng) and DR Shepherd (Eng)
ODI Debuts: DK Morrison (NZ).
Men of the Match: SM Gavaskar and C Sharma

New Zealand innings (50 overs maximum)			R	B
JG Wright	run out		35	59
PA Horne		b Prabhakar	18	35
MD Crowe	c Pandit	b Azharuddin	21	24
KR Rutherford		b Sharma	26	54
*JJ Crowe		b Maninder Singh	24	24
DN Patel	c Kapil Dev	b Shastri	40	51
MC Snedden	run out		23	28
+IDS Smith		b Sharma	0	1
EJ Chatfield		b Sharma	0	1
W Watson	not out		12	25

Extras: (lb 14, w 7, nb 1) 22
Total: (9 wickets, 50 overs) 221

DNB: DK Morrison.

FoW: 1-46 (Horne), 2-84 (MD Crowe), 3-90 (Wright),
4-122 (JJ Crowe), 5-181 (Patel), 6-182 (Rutherford),
7-182 (Smith), 8-182 (Chatfield), 9-221 (Snedden).

Bowling	O	M	R	W
Kapil Dev	6	0	24	0
Prabhakar	7	0	23	1
Sharma	10	2	51	3
Azharuddin	7	0	26	1
Maninder Singh	10	0	51	1
Shastri	10	1	32	1

India innings (target: 222 runs from 50 overs)			R	B
K Srikkanth	c Rutherford	b Watson	75	58
SM Gavaskar	not out		103	88
M Azharuddin	not out		41	51

Extras: (lb 1, w 2, nb 2) 5
Total: (1 wicket, 32.1 overs) 224

DNB: NS Sidhu, DB Vengsarkar, *N Kapil Dev, RJ Shastri,
+CS Pandit, M Prabhakar, C Sharma, Maninder Singh.

FoW: 1-136 (Srikkanth).

Bowling	O	M	R	W
Morrison	10	0	69	0
Chatfield	4.1	1	39	0
Snedden	4	0	29	0
Watson	10	0	50	1
Patel	4	0	36	0

Semi-final, 4 November: Gaddafi Stadium, Lahore

Opting for first use of the wicket, Australia were again rendered a
good start by their openers. With Saleem Jaffer conceding 39 from
his first five overs, Marsh and Boon put on 73 in 18 overs before
Saleem Malik ran out the former with a direct hit from square leg.
However, the stocky Tasmanian continued the good work with Jones
(45 balls). They added another 82 until Pakistan removed them in
consecutive overs – the 31st and the 32nd. Boon (four fours) was
stumped by Javed Miandad, deputizing for Saleem Yousuf, who was
struck on the face by a deflection from Jones' pad. Captain Allan
Border and Michael Veletta, though, maintained the momentum with
a partnership of 60. Imran returned to snap up three for 17 in five
overs; but at the 'death', Waugh boosted the total by a valuable 18
runs as he sent the hapless Jaffer soaring over long-on.

In contrast, Pakistan started catastrophically, losing three wickets
by the 11th over. Rameez Raja could not recover his ground in the
very first over, Mansoor Akhtar failed to impress and Saleem Malik
front-edged the first ball of Waugh's spell to extra-cover. But Miandad
and Imran, four fours apiece, maturely undid the damage with 112
off 26 overs. As a result, the target whittled down to 118 from 15
overs. Much rested on the mercurial Miandad. As long as he was in,
his side had a chance. But after he left, playing across to the tall left-
arm quick, Bruce Reid, in the 44th over, 56 runs were still needed,
with only three wickets in hand. It was too much to ask for.
McDermott polished off the tail with a fast and accurate spell and,
in so doing, bagged the first five-wicket haul of the tournament.
The defeat ruined the dreams of a nation that had expected to match
India's success of four years earlier.

For the third time, a World Cup final had eluded Pakistan's grasp at the semi-final stage. Australia, unfancied at the start of the competition, handled the pressure better to rightfully enter the final round. They won by 18 runs.

Toss: Australia
Umpires: HD Bird (Eng) and DR Shepherd (Eng)
Man of the Match: CJ McDermott

Australia innings (50 overs maximum)			R	B
GR Marsh	run out		31	57
DC Boon	st +Javed Miandad	b Saleem Malik	65	91
DM Jones		b Tauseef Ahmed	38	45
*AR Border	run out		18	22
MRJ Veletta		b Imran Khan	48	50
SR Waugh	not out		32	28
SP O'Donnell	run out		0	2
+GC Dyer		b Imran Khan	0	1
CJ McDermott		b Imran Khan	1	3
TBA May	not out		0	2

Extras: (b 1, lb 19, w 13, nb 1) 34
Total: (8 wickets, 50 overs) 267

DNB: BA Reid.

FoW: 1-73 (Marsh), 2-155 (Boon), 3-155 (Jones), 4-215 (Border), 5-236 (Veletta), 6-236 (O'Donnell), 7-241 (Dyer), 8-249 (McDermott).

Bowling	O	M	R	W
Imran Khan	10	1	36	3
Saleem Jaffar	6	0	57	0
Wasim Akram	10	0	54	0
Abdul Qadir	10	0	39	0
Tauseef Ahmed	10	1	39	1
Saleem Malik	4	0	22	1

Pakistan innings *(target: 268 runs from 50 overs)*			R	B
Rameez Raja	run out		1	1
Mansoor Akhtar		b McDermott	9	19
Saleem Malik	c McDermott	b Waugh	25	31
Javed Miandad		b Reid	70	103
*Imran Khan	c Dyer	b Border	58	84
Wasim Akram		b McDermott	20	13
Ijaz Ahmed	c Jones	b Reid	8	7
+Saleem Yousuf	c Dyer	b McDermott	21	15
Abdul Qadir	not out		20	16
Saleem Jaffar	c Dyer	b McDermott	0	2
Tauseef Ahmed	c Dyer	b McDermott	1	3

Extras: (lb 6, w 10) 16
Total: (all out, 49 overs) 249

FoW: 1-2 (Rameez Raja), 2-37 (Mansoor Akhtar),
3-38 (Saleem Malik), 4-150 (Imran Khan),
5-177 (Wasim Akram), 6-192 (Ijaz Ahmed),
7-212 (Javed Miandad), 8-236 (Saleem Yousuf),
9-247 (Saleem Jaffar), 10-249 (Tauseef Ahmed).

Bowling	O	M	R	W
McDermott	10	0	44	5
Reid	10	2	41	2
Waugh	9	1	51	1
O'Donnell	10	1	45	0
May	6	0	36	0
Border	4	0	26	1

Semi-final, 5 November: Wankhede Stadium, Mumbai

Kapil inserted England, expecting the ball to swing in the sweaty conditions and the swirl of the Arabian Sea breeze. His expectations were belied, though. Instead, the slow surface responded to turn. This suited India's strength, but Graham Gooch (11 fours) and Mike Gatting (five fours) skilfully blunted the spinners. Pulling and sweeping the two left-armers, Maninder and Shastri, against the tide, they stitched together 117 off 19 overs. Srikkanth dropped a difficult chance from the Essex opener when the batsman was 82, before he finally departed caught at midwicket in the 43rd over. Gatting had exited two overs earlier. Allan Lamb, then, shepherded the lower half of the batting to add another 32.

India missed Vengsarkar, down with a tummy bug at his home ground; they received a further jolt when Philip DeFreitas uprooted Gavaskar's off stump early. Srikkanth and Sidhu, both heavy hitters, failed to produce a single boundary. Azharuddin and Chandrakant Pandit plundered 27 of Eddie Hemmings' first three overs. But Gooch was economical while his county teammate, Neil Foster, chipped in with another scalp – that of Pandit. Kapil launched a premature assault and paid the price, as Gatting, who had placed himself on the midwicket boundary, accepted the catch with a smug look on his face. In a 34-ball stint from here onwards, Hemmings captured four for 21, which included the crucial wicket of Azhar (seven fours). With five wickets in hand and a required run rate of five an over, India were still in the hunt. But with the Hyderabad artiste back in the hut, the calmness disappeared. It was largely left to Shastri to steer the steamer, but England's excellent catching, including a splendid running effort by Lamb to nip Chetan Sharma in the bud, ensured they did not relinquish the upper hand. England won by 35 runs.

Toss: India
Umpires: AR Crafter (Aus) and SJ Woodward (NZ)
Man of the Match: GA Gooch

England innings (50 overs maximum)			*R*	*B*
GA Gooch	c Srikkanth	b Maninder Singh	115	136
RT Robinson	st More	b Maninder Singh	13	36
CWJ Athey	c More	b Sharma	4	17
*MW Gatting		b Maninder Singh	56	62
AJ Lamb	not out		32	29
JE Emburey	lbw	b Kapil Dev	6	10
PAJ DeFreitas		b Kapil Dev	7	8
+PR Downton	not out		1	5

Extras: (b 1, lb 18, w 1) 20
Total: (6 wickets, 50 overs) 254

DNB: NA Foster, GC Small, EE Hemmings.

FoW: 1-40 (Robinson), 2-79 (Athey), 3-196 (Gatting),
4-203 (Gooch), 5-219 (Emburey), 6-231 (DeFreitas).

Bowling	O	M	R	W
Kapil Dev	10	1	38	2
Prabhakar	9	1	40	0
Maninder Singh	10	0	54	3
Sharma	9	0	41	1
Shastri	10	0	49	0
Azharuddin	2	0	13	0

India innings (target: 255 runs from 50 overs)			R	B
K Srikkanth		b Foster	31	55
SM Gavaskar		b DeFreitas	4	7
NS Sidhu	c Athey	b Foster	22	40
M Azharuddin	lbw	b Hemmings	64	74
CS Pandit	lbw	b Foster	24	30
*N Kapil Dev	c Gatting	b Hemmings	30	22
RJ Shastri	c Downton	b Hemmings	21	32
+KS More	c & b Emburey		0	5
M Prabhakar	c Downton	b Small	4	11
C Sharma	c Lamb	b Hemmings	0	1
Maninder Singh	not out		0	0

Extras: (b 1, lb 9, w 6, nb 3) 19
Total: (all out, 45.3 overs) 219

FoW: 1-7 (Gavaskar), 2-58 (Srikkanth), 3-73 (Sidhu),
4-121 (Pandit), 5-168 (Kapil Dev), 6-204 (Azharuddin),
7-205 (More), 8-218 (Prabhakar), 9-219 (Sharma),
10-219 (Shastri).

Bowling	O	M	R	W
DeFreitas	7	0	37	1
Small	6	0	22	1
Emburey	10	1	35	1
Foster	10	0	47	3
Hemmings	9.3	1	52	4
Gooch	3	0	16	0

As India bid adieu to the tournament, Gavaskar bowed out of international cricket only to soon reinvent himself as a handsomely remunerated writer, commentator, administrator and occasional coach or consultant.

Final, 8 November: Eden Gardens, Kolkata

Once the capital of British India and labelled as the second city of the Empire, Kolkata's Eden Gardens is the country's second oldest test venue after the Bombay Gymkhana (which has been defunct in terms of this status after hosting that first test in December 1933) and the only cricketing centre in the subcontinent that has uninterruptedly been an international venue since it hosted Douglas Jardine's England team in January 1934.

Here, a full house on a smoggy morning near the River Ganges, or the Ganga as it's called in India, witnessed a wayward opening spell from DeFreitas and Gladstone Small, which inflated Australia, who had decided to bat, to 52 in 10 overs. But Neil Foster corrected the profligacy by yielding only 16 runs in his first eight overs, which included the wicket of Marsh. Gooch, too, was steady until Border and Veletta (six fours) stepped it up by adding 73 in 10 overs after the fall of Boon, who, with his 75 (seven fours), posted his fifth half century in six innings. The last six overs proved to be even more expensive for England as they resulted in another 65 runs.

So, Australia took the field to defend a total of 253 and with the comforting thought that no side had scored 254 to win a match in this World Cup. But England, 135 for two after 31 overs, were virtually on course, with the Australian wheel appearing to wobble. But in a moment of madness, Gatting attempted to greet his counterpart's first ball with a reverse sweep. The left-arm delivery pitched on his leg stump took a top edge, glanced his shoulder, before ballooning into the wicketkeeper's gloves. The scales now tilted Australia's way. Tim Robinson found McDermott's pace too much to handle. Bill Athey figured in three partnerships of 65 in 17, 69 in 13 and 35 in eight with Gooch, Gatting and Lamb, respectively, before he was run out by Waugh while going for a third run. As England fell behind in their run rate (75 from ten overs became 46 off five), Waugh cleaned up Lamb in the 47th over. DeFreitas raised excitement as he pummelled four, six and four in McDermott's second last over. But Waugh had him caught in the next over and also conceded only two runs in it. Seventeen runs were required in the final over, but McDermott kept his cool and Australia meritoriously lifted the Reliance World Cup.

Toss: Australia
Umpires: RB Gupta (Ind) and Mahboob Shah (Pak)
Man of the Match: DC Boon

Australia innings (50 overs maximum)			*R*	*B*
DC Boon	c Downton	b Hemmings	75	125
GR Marsh		b Foster	24	49
DM Jones	c Athey	b Hemmings	33	57
CJ McDermott		b Gooch	14	8
*AR Border	run out (Robinson/Downton)		31	31
MRJ Veletta	not out		45	31
SR Waugh	not out		5	4

Extras: (b 1, lb 13, w 5, nb 7) 26
Total: (5 wickets, 50 overs) 253

DNB: SP O'Donnell, +GC Dyer, TBA May, BA Reid.

FoW: 1-75 (Marsh), 2-151 (Jones), 3-166 (McDermott), 4-168 (Boon), 5-241 (Border).

Bowling	O	M	R	W
DeFreitas	6	1	34	0
Small	6	0	33	0
Foster	10	0	38	1
Hemmings	10	1	48	2
Emburey	10	0	44	0
Gooch	8	1	42	1

England innings (target: 254 runs from 50 overs)			R	B
GA Gooch	lbw	b O'Donnell	35	57
RT Robinson	lbw	b McDermott	0	1
CWJ Athey	run out (Waugh/Reid)		58	103
*MW Gatting	c Dyer	b Border	41	45
AJ Lamb		b Waugh	45	55
+PR Downton	c O'Donnell	b Border	9	8
JE Emburey	run out (Boon/McDermott)		10	16
PAJ DeFreitas	c Reid	b Waugh	17	10
NA Foster	not out		7	6
GC Small	not out		3	3

Extras: (b 1, lb 14, w 2, nb 4) 21
Total: (8 wickets, 50 overs) 246

DNB: EE Hemmings.

FoW: 1-1 (Robinson), 2-66 (Gooch), 3-135 (Gatting),
4-170 (Athey), 5-188 (Downton), 6-218 (Emburey),
7-220 (Lamb), 8-235 (DeFreitas).

Bowling	O	M	R	W
McDermott	10	1	51	1
Reid	10	0	43	0
Waugh	9	0	37	2
O'Donnell	10	1	35	1
May	4	0	27	0
Border	7	0	38	2

The semi-finals in Bombay and Lahore had held the subcontinent transfixed; though both outcomes dashed Indian and Pakistani hopes respectively. Yet, 70,000 spectators enthusiastically mushroomed at the final; and a sporting lot they were, too, as, not inappropriately, acknowledged by Border after the match.

In retrospect, Australia benefited from batting first in five of their six qualifying games, and in the semi-finals and finals as well, on pitches that became slower and lower as the day wore on. To their credit, they appreciated this phenomenon early and also adhered to their strength – fast bowling. Besides, they didn't wilt in the heat.

Pakistan peaked too soon, winning their first five qualifying games, largely on the basis of some overwhelming bowling from Imran and Abdul Qadir, only for the dice to roll the other way in the semi-final.

India qualified for the last four without their bowling being really tested. But their batting was spectacular, though not always the most substantive. Immature crowds imploring big hits, rewards from a sponsor for every four and six, were unnecessary distractions, while the dispute between some senior Indian players and the BCCI over insignia also rumbled on.

West Indies, not as high and mighty as in the past, were without Malcolm Marshall. New Zealand missed Richard Hadlee. The Sri Lankans and the Zimbabweans returned home without a win. But for sheer bravado, the innings of the World Cup was Zimbabwean David Houghton's 142 against New Zealand.

The Australians probably worked the hardest. As his teammates placed the glistening Reliance Cup in his hands and lifted him on their shoulders in their lap of honour around the Eden Gardens, it was a personal triumph for Border who had rebuilt Australia from one of their bleakest periods earlier in the decade.

THE 1992 WORLD CUP

Much had happened in India since the previous World Cup. Rajiv Gandhi had lost office after Vishwanath Pratap Singh teamed up with the former's opponents to win a general election in late 1989.

The Bofors affair proved to be Gandhi's undoing. Then, Singh, too, was unseated in November 1990, when one of his allies, the Hindu revivalist Bharatiya Janata Party withdrew parliamentary support. Finally, while in the midst of another electoral campaign in May 1991, Gandhi was assassinated by a woman suicide bomber despatched by the Liberation Tigers of Tamil Eelam (LTTE), otherwise known as the Tamil Tigers, a militant organization fighting for a separate Tamil state in Sri Lanka. Gandhi as prime minister had sent in Indian peace-keeping forces in 1987 to contain the LTTE. After his death, his Congress party returned to government, but under the leadership of a veteran politician, Pamulaparthi Venkata Narasimha Rao, who proceeded to initiate the most dynamic economic reforms in India's history.

Oddly, since it was meant to be a quadrennial event, the World Cup, sponsored by Benson & Hedges, took place a year after it ought to have. This was because Antipodean cricket authorities, particularly the Australian Cricket Board, were unwilling to sacrifice their regular calendar of test and one-day series, which generally uncoiled from November to February; autumn (spring in the southern hemisphere) was weather-wise considered to be hazardous. But when the event did unfold a few months later, it was a further amplified occasion, jointly hosted by Australia and New Zealand. With the readmission of South Africa into the international fold, all eight test-playing teams were represented, plus Zimbabwe, who were then knocking on the door to gain full membership of the ICC. Thus, there were an unprecedented nine participants, and they were not divided into any groups. While the first two World Cups had constituted only 15 matches and the two thereafter, 27 apiece, the tournament in Australasia was enlarged to 39 fixtures – 25 in Australia and the rest in New Zealand.

Besides, the fifth World Cup fell in line with the practice initiated by Kerry Packer's World Series Cricket, in that players wore coloured clothing, white balls were used and some games were day/night and, therefore, floodlit in the latter half. Such facets were seen for the first time, but have become regulation since. However, it was again 50 overs a side, and each team played the others once before the top four in the qualifying table squared off in the semi-finals. The rules governing rain-interrupted matches, though, were debatable.

The *Wisden Cricketers' Almanack* recorded:

Recognizing the imperfection of a straight run-rate calculation when a second innings has to be shortened after rain, and unable to schedule spare days within the time-frame of the tournament, the World Cup committee adopted a scheme whereby the reduction in the target would be commensurate with the lowest-scoring overs of the side which batted first.

The tournament was infused an early tonic when New Zealand tore up the form book to beat Australia, the holders and favourites, by 37 runs at Auckland. Martin Crowe's high-quality batting – he scored a hundred in the opener – aided by the power hitting of Mark Greatbatch (who got a look-in only because John Wright was injured) at the top of the order, not to speak of Dipak Patel's off-spin with the new ball, created an impressive run of victories in the Kiwis' first seven outings on their slow pitches.

Mohammed Azharuddin was now captain of India. His city of Hyderabad and its surroundings were once ruled by a Nizam, who was reputedly the world's richest person in the first quarter of the twentieth century. Azhar wasn't a prince by birth, but was quite princely in his batting and fielding. A Muslim, he also illustrated a commendable trait in Indian cricket of no discrimination against minorities when it came to national selection. Before Azharuddin's long tenure, Ghulam Ahmed, a gifted off-spinner also from Hyderabad, and Tiger Pataudi – for an extended term – had had the honour of leading India. In 1946, a year before India's freedom, the latter's father, Nawab Iftikhar Ali Khan of Pataudi, was skipper for a tour of England.

22 February: WACA, Perth

England won the toss before a 13,000 attendance, but had difficulty coping with the pace of the wicket after playing on the slow pitches of New Zealand. Robin Smith, though, struck 91, with two sixes pulled to the long-leg boundary and Graham Gooch celebrated his 100th ODI with a half century. Yet, England lost six wickets in five overs after Neil Fairbrother's departure, only to be saved by Ian Botham at his most irrepressible.

England bowled too short, which facilitated Krish Srikkanth firing on all cylinders, hitting seven fours in his 39. Contrarily, Ravi Shastri touched the fence only twice in two and a half hours. Philip DeFreitas then dropped him off his own bowling, but broke the stumps with a direct hit to run him out. This pattern became infectious as three more such dismissals followed. After Subroto Banerjee, a seamer from the eastern Indian state of Bihar, had capitalized with a six off Derek Pringle, India needed 11 to win in the last over. The prospects were 50:50. But with the effervescent Botham effecting the last of the run outs two balls later, the issue was settled in England's favour by nine runs.

Toss: England
Umpires: DP Buultjens (SL) and PJ McConnell
Referee: Tony Mann
Man of the Match: IT Botham

England innings (50 overs maximum)			*R*	*B*
*GA Gooch	c Tendulkar	b Shastri	51	89
IT Botham	c More	b Kapil Dev	9	21
RA Smith	c Azharuddin	b Prabhakar	91	108
GA Hick	c More	b Banerjee	5	6
NH Fairbrother	c Srikkanth	b Srinath	24	34
+AJ Stewart		b Prabhakar	13	15
CC Lewis	c Banerjee	b Kapil Dev	10	6
DR Pringle	c Srikkanth	b Srinath	1	3
DA Reeve	not out		8	8
PAJ DeFreitas	run out		1	5
PCR Tufnell	not out		3	5

Extras: (b 1, lb 6, w 13) 20
Total: (9 wickets, 50 overs) 236

FoW: 1-21 (Botham), 2-131 (Gooch), 3-137 (Hick),
4-197 (Fairbrother), 5-198 (Smith), 6-214 (Lewis),
7-222 (Pringle), 8-223 (Stewart), 9-224 (DeFreitas).

Bowling	O	M	R	W
Kapil Dev	10	0	38	2 (6w)
Prabhakar	10	3	34	2
Srinath	9	1	47	2 (5w)
Banerjee	7	0	45	1
Tendulkar	10	0	37	0 (1w)
Shastri	4	0	28	1 (1w)

India innings (target: 237 runs from 50 overs)			R	B
RJ Shastri	run out		57	112
K Srikkanth	c Botham	b DeFreitas	39	50
*M Azharuddin	c Stewart	b Reeve	0	1
SR Tendulkar	c Stewart	b Botham	35	44
VG Kambli	c Hick	b Botham	3	11
PK Amre	run out		22	31
N Kapil Dev	c DeFreitas	b Reeve	17	18
ST Banerjee	not out		25	16
+KS More	run out		1	4
M Prabhakar		b Reeve	0	2
J Srinath	run out		11	8

Extras: (lb 9, w 7, nb 1) 17
Total: (all out, 49.2 overs) 227

FoW: 1-63 (Srikkanth), 2-63 (Azharuddin), 3-126 (Tendulkar),
4-140 (Kambli), 5-149 (Shastri), 6-187 (Kapil Dev),
7-194 (Amre), 8-200 (More), 9-201 (Prabhakar),
10-227 (Srinath).

Bowling	O	M	R	W
Pringle	10	0	53	0 (1w)
Lewis	9.2	0	36	0 (1nb, 5w)
DeFreitas	10	0	39	1
Reeve	6	0	38	3 (1w)
Botham	10	0	27	2
Tufnell	4	0	25	0

28 February: MacKay (Australia)

An estimated 3000-strong crowd went home disappointed with a
no-result. Start of play was delayed by five hours. Then, when Sri
Lanka won the toss and the teams emerged for a 20-overs-a-side
encounter, only two balls were possible before heavy showers
submerged the ground.

Toss: Sri Lanka
Umpires: ID Robinson (Zim) and DR Shepherd (Eng)
Referee: A Pettigrew
ODI Debuts: A Jadeja (Ind).

India innings (20 overs maximum)		R	B
K Srikkanth	not out	1	2
N Kapil Dev	not out	0	0

Extras: 0
Total: (0 wickets, 0.2 overs) 1

DNB: *M Azharuddin, SR Tendulkar, VG Kambli, PK Amre, A Jadeja,
SLV Raju, M Prabhakar, +KS More, J Srinath.

Bowling	O	M	R	W
Ramanayake	0.2	0	1	0

Sri Lanka team:
RS Mahanama, UC Hathurusingha, AP Gurusinha, *PA de Silva,
A Ranatunga, ST Jayasuriya, +HP Tillakaratne, RS Kalpage,
CPH Ramanayake, KIW Wijegunawardene, GP Wickramasinghe.

1 March: Woolloongabba, Brisbane

In salubrious weather, Australia, electing to bat first, were propped
up by an exquisite essay from Dean Jones after Kapil Dev and Manoj
Prabhakar had pinned down some of the other Australians with
penetrative line and length.

India, too, were subdued at the start, with Shastri hampered by a knee injury. But Azharuddin's artful 93 and Sanjay Manjrekar, son of Vijay and a worthy chip of the old block, with three fours and a six, carried the Indians to within striking distance. The lower order battled on spiritedly. Thirteen runs were required off Tom Moody's final over. Kiran More clipped the first two balls to the fine-leg boundary. The next bowled him. Prabhabhar took a single in the fourth, but was run out off the next. With four needed from the last ball, Javagal Srinath swung at it; Steve Waugh spilled it near the fence, but hurled it back to substitute wicketkeeper, David Boon. Venkatapathy Raju failed to make his ground while attempting a third run, which would have tied the scores. Rain clipped 15 minutes and three overs of play, when India were 45 from 16.2 overs. This reduced their target by two runs, taking into account Australia's three least fruitful overs. The 12,000-odd spectators, therefore, witnessed a nail-biting finish, which, to the delight of the majority, ended in the home side's favour.

Toss: Australia
Umpires: BL Aldridge (NZ) and ID Robinson (Zim)
Referee: MW Johnson
Man of the Match: DM Jones

Australia innings (50 overs maximum)			*R*	*B*
MA Taylor	c More	b Kapil Dev	13	18
GR Marsh		b Kapil Dev	8	28
+DC Boon	c Shastri	b Raju	43	60
DM Jones	c & b Prabhakar		90	108
SR Waugh		b Srinath	29	48
TM Moody		b Prabhakar	25	23
*AR Border	c Jadeja	b Kapil Dev	10	10
CJ McDermott	c Jadeja	b Prabhakar	2	5
PL Taylor	run out		1	1
MG Hughes	not out		0	4

Extras: (lb 7, w 5, nb 4) 16
Total: (9 wickets, 50 overs) 237

DNB: MR Whitney.

FoW: 1-18 (MA Taylor), 2-31 (Marsh), 3-102 (Boon), 4-156 (Waugh), 5-198 (Moody), 6-230 (Jones), 7-235 (Border), 8-236 (McDermott), 9-237 (PL Taylor).

Bowling	O	M	R	W
Kapil Dev	10	2	41	3 (1nb, 1w)
Prabhakar	10	0	41	3 (1nb, 2w)
Srinath	8	0	48	1 (2nb, 1w)
Tendulkar	5	0	29	0 (1w)
Raju	10	0	37	1
Jadeja	7	0	34	0

India innings (target: 236 runs from 47 overs)			R	B
RJ Shastri	c Waugh	b Moody	25	67
K Srikkanth		b McDermott	0	10
*M Azharuddin	run out		93	103
SR Tendulkar	c Waugh	b Moody	11	19
N Kapil Dev	lbw	b Waugh	21	21
SV Manjrekar	run out		47	42
A Jadeja		b Hughes	1	4
+KS More		b Moody	14	8
J Srinath	not out		8	8
M Prabhakar	run out		1	1
SLV Raju	run out		0	0

Extras: (lb 8, w 5) 13
Total: (all out, 47 overs) 234

FoW: 1-6 (Srikkanth), 2-53 (Shastri), 3-86 (Tendulkar), 4-128 (Kapil Dev), 5-194 (Azharuddin), 6-199 (Jadeja), 7-216 (Manjrekar), 8-231 (More), 9-232 (Prabhakar), 10-234 (Raju).

Bowling	O	M	R	W
McDermott	9	1	35	1
Whitney	10	2	36	0
Hughes	9	1	49	1
Moody	9	0	56	3
Waugh	10	0	50	1

4 March: Sydney Cricket Ground (Day/Night)

Before winning the toss, India rested Ravi Shastri and replaced him with youngster Ajay Jadeja to open the innings, who impressed in this slot. But quite the most charming innings came from Sachin Tendulkar, still only 18 and playing in his first World Cup, who contributed an unbeaten 54. Son of a Marathi professor and poet, this prodigious talent added 60 in eight overs with Kapil Dev.

When it came to Pakistan's turn to bat, Aamir Sohail was the dominant partner in an 88-run stand for the third wicket with Javed Miandad, who, uncharacteristically, took 34 overs to compile 40, thus stiffening the task for his teammates. This first World Cup clash between the South Asian rivals was made slightly unsavoury by a conflict between wicketkeeper More and Miandad. The former's enthusiastic shout for a leg-side catch provoked a verbal exchange and then a contemptuous response from Miandad. The umpires reported the matter to the match referee, who asked the respective team managers to resolve the issue. More, however, could look back with satisfaction at the cricketing aspect, having snapped up two catches, pulled off a stumping and run-out Imran Khan. India won quite easily as the last eight Pakistani wickets fell in a clatter for just 68 runs in front of over 10,000 people.

Toss: India
Umpires: PJ McConnell and DR Shepherd (Eng)
Referee: Ted Wykes
Man of the Match: SR Tendulkar

India innings *(49 overs maximum)*			R	B
A Jadeja	c Zahid Fazal	b Wasim Haider	46	81
K Srikkanth	c Moin Khan	b Aaqib Javed	5	40
*M Azharuddin	c Moin Khan	b Mushtaq Ahmed	32	51
VG Kambli	c Inzamam-ul Haq	b Mushtaq Ahmed	24	42
SR Tendulkar	not out		54	62
SV Manjrekar		b Mushtaq Ahmed	0	1
N Kapil Dev	c Imran Khan	b Aaqib Javed	35	26
+KS More	run out		4	4
M Prabhakar	not out		2	1

Extras: (lb 3, w 9, nb 2) 14
Total: (7 wickets, 49 overs) 216

DNB: J Srinath, SLV Raju.

FoW: 1-25 (Srikkanth), 2-86 (Azharuddin), 3-101 (Jadeja),
4-147 (Kambli), 5-148 (Manjrekar), 6-208 (Kapil Dev),
7-213 (More).

Bowling	O	M	R	W
Wasim Akram	10	0	45	0
Aaqib Javed	8	2	28	2
Imran Khan	8	0	25	0
Wasim Haider	10	1	36	1
Mushtaq Ahmed	10	0	59	3
Aamir Sohail	3	0	20	0

Pakistan innings *(target: 217 runs from 49 overs)*			R	B
Aamir Sohail	c Srikkanth	b Tendulkar	62	103
Inzamam-ul Haq	lbw	b Kapil Dev	2	7
Zahid Fazal	c More	b Prabhakar	2	10
Javed Miandad		b Srinath	40	113
Saleem Malik	c More	b Prabhakar	12	9
*Imran Khan	run out		0	5
Wasim Akram	st More	b Raju	4	8
Wasim Haider		b Srinath	13	25
+Moin Khan	c Manjrekar	b Kapil Dev	12	12
Mushtaq Ahmed	run out		3	4
Aaqib Javed	not out		1	12

Extras: (lb 6, w 15, nb 1) 22
Total: (all out, 48.1 overs) 173

FoW: 1-8 (Inzamam-ul Haq), 2-17 (Zahid Fazal), 3-105 (Aamir Sohail),
4-127 (Saleem Malik), 5-130 (Imran Khan), 6-141 (Wasim Akram),
7-141 (Javed Miandad), 8-161 (Moin Khan),
9-166 (Mushtaq Ahmed), 10-173 (Wasim Haider).

Bowling	O	M	R	W
Kapil Dev	10	0	30	2
Prabhakar	10	1	22	2
Srinath	8.1	0	37	2
Tendulkar	10	0	37	1
Raju	10	1	41	1

7 March: Hamilton (New Zealand)

A crowd of about 1500 waited patiently as rain devoured three hours
of play in the morning. Then, India won the toss and Tendulkar,
again Man of the Match, starred in the 32 overs allocated to India.
He hit eight fours and a six in his 81 and put on 99 in 15 overs with
Manjrekar for the fourth wicket. The Indians thus set Zimbabwe a
target of 204 to win. But with another downpour terminating the
match after 19.1 overs, the contest was determined by the
controversial rule on shortened innings. Unfortunate against Australia
on this count, India were, perhaps, a trifle lucky on this occasion.
Zimbabwe had knocked up 104 for one when the fatal showers
ensued; while India had reached 106 for three at the same juncture.
With Andy Flower going well, another 100 from 13 was not
unattainable. There was, thus, some commiseration for Zimbabwe.
India won by 55 runs after their total was revised to 158, as compared
to Zimbabwe's to 103 on the basis of their highest scoring 19 overs.

Toss: India
Umpires: DP Buultjens (SL) and SG Randell (Aus)
Referee: BJ Paterson
Man of the Match: SR Tendulkar

India innings *(32 overs maximum)*			R	B
K Srikkanth		b Burmester	32	32
N Kapil Dev	lbw	b Brandes	10	14
*M Azharuddin	c Flower	b Burmester	12	15
SR Tendulkar	c Campbell	b Burmester	81	77
SV Manjrekar	c Duers	b Traicos	34	34
VG Kambli		b Traicos	1	2
A Jadeja	c Omarshah	b Traicos	6	6
+KS More	not out		15	8
J Srinath	not out		6	4

Extras: (lb 3, w 3) 6
Total: (7 wickets, 32 overs) 203

DNB: M Prabhakar, SLV Raju.

FoW: 1-23 (Kapil Dev), 2-43 (Azharuddin), 3-69 (Srikkanth),
4-168 (Manjrekar), 5-170 (Kambli), 6-182 (Jadeja),
7-184 (Tendulkar).

Bowling	O	M	R	W
Brandes	7	0	43	1
Duers	7	0	48	0
Burmester	6	0	36	3 (3w)
Omarshah	6	1	38	0
Traicos	6	0	35	3

Zimbabwe innings *(target: 159 runs from 19 overs)*			R	B
AH Omarshah		b Tendulkar	31	51
+A Flower	not out		43	56
AC Waller	not out		13	7

Extras: (b 1, lb 11, w 5) 17
Total: (1 wicket, 19.1 overs) 104

DNB: AJ Pycroft, *DL Houghton, ADR Campbell, IP Butchart,
EA Brandes, MG Burmester, AJ Traicos, KG Duers.

FoW: 1-79 (Omarshah).

Bowling	O	M	R	W
Kapil Dev	4	0	6	0 (2w)
Prabhakar	3	0	14	0 (1w)
Srinath	4	0	20	0 (1w)
Tendulkar	6	0	35	1 (1w)
Raju	2.1	0	17	0

10 March: Basin Reserve, Wellington

A gathering of more than 6500 saw India launch themselves encouragingly after winning the toss. Azharuddin was in fine fettle, though the diminutive Tendulkar was tied down by Curtly Ambrose's extra bounce. But it was Anderson Cummins who did the most damage. He took four wickets, the first of these being Azhar caught at long off in the 43rd over, when the Indians were 166. The advantage of having wickets in hand was, thus, completely squandered, by India as seven wickets fell for only 31 runs.

The West Indies flew off the block to reach 50 in six overs, with Brian Lara on 36. They were equally relaxed at 81 from 11 when the 20-minute interruption came. This disruption trimmed four overs and three runs off the innings. When play resumed, Lara left immediately and Simmons followed, victim to a falling catch by Tendulkar. Richie Richardson and Gus Logie didn't last long either. But Keith Arthurton and Carl Hooper steadied the ship and remained unseparated in an 83-run stand. The West Indies won by five wickets, their target having been reduced to 195 off 46 overs. They thus became the first side in the competition to trump a rain-adjusted target.

Toss: India
Umpires: SG Randell (Aus) and SJ Woodward
Referee: AR Isaac
Man of the Match: AC Cummins

India innings (50 overs maximum)			R	B
A Jadeja	c Benjamin	b Simmons	27	61
K Srikkanth	c Logie	b Hooper	40	70
*M Azharuddin	c Ambrose	b Cummins	61	84
SR Tendulkar	c Williams	b Ambrose	4	11
SV Manjrekar	run out		27	40
N Kapil Dev	c Haynes	b Cummins	3	4
PK Amre	c Hooper	b Ambrose	4	8
+KS More	c Hooper	b Cummins	5	5
M Prabhakar	c Richardson	b Cummins	8	10
J Srinath	not out		5	5
SLV Raju	run out		1	1

Extras: (lb 6, w 5, nb 1) 12
Total: (all out, 49.4 overs) 197

FoW: 1-56 (Jadeja), 2-102 (Srikkanth), 3-115 (Tendulkar),
4-166 (Azharuddin), 5-171 (Kapil Dev), 6-173 (Manjrekar),
7-180 (More), 8-186 (Amre), 9-193 (Prabhakar),
10-197 (Raju).

Bowling	O	M	R	W
Ambrose	10	1	24	2
Benjamin	9.4	0	35	0 (4w)
Cummins	10	0	33	4
Simmons	9	0	48	1 (1nb 1w)
Hooper	10	0	46	1
Arthurton	1	0	5	0

West Indies innings (target: 195 runs from 46 overs)			R	B
DL Haynes	c Manjrekar	b Kapil Dev	16	16
BC Lara	c Manjrekar	b Srinath	41	37
PV Simmons	c Tendulkar	b Prabhakar	22	20
*RB Richardson	c Srikkanth	b Srinath	3	8
KLT Arthurton	not out		58	99
AL Logie	c More	b Raju	7	10
CL Hooper	not out		34	57

Extras: (lb 8, w 2, nb 4) 14
Total: (5 wickets, 40.2 overs) 195

DNB: +D Williams, WKM Benjamin, CEL Ambrose, AC Cummins.

FoW: 1-57 (Haynes), 2-81 (Lara), 3-88 (Simmons),
4-98 (Richardson), 5-112 (Logie).

Bowling	O	M	R	W
Kapil Dev	8	0	45	1
Prabhakar	9	0	55	1 (1nb 1w)
Raju	10	2	32	1 (1w)
Srinath	9	2	23	2 (3nb)
Tendulkar	3	0	20	0
Srikkanth	1	0	7	0
Jadeja	0.2	0	5	0

12 March: Dunedin (New Zealand)

Anticipating rain, Azharuddin opted for first strike. Srikkanth holed out on the long-on boundary in the very first over and Jadeja pulled a hamstring, which forced him to retire. These departures conjoined the captain with Tendulkar, who, together, realized 127 in 30 overs. Azhar then welcomed back Patel with a six, but in trying to repeat the stroke was brilliantly caught by Greatbatch. Tendulkar continued with Kapil, and the Indians reached a respectable total of 230. But Greatbatch, who had been batting in the tournament like a gunner on a roll, was not one to respect any score. He powered to 73 before being caught at square-leg mid-way through the venture, which put the New Zealanders ahead of the required rate. Four more wickets fell, including Crowe's, who was run out by More, scooting to gully to whip the ball back and knock down the stumps without even having a good look at them. But Andrew Jones then anchored the Kiwis to victory. New Zealand won by four wickets before nearly 10,000 fans. New Zealand's sixth win equalled West Indies' record run in the 1983 World Cup, and virtually barricaded India from further progress.

Toss: New Zealand
Umpires: PJ McConnell (Aus) and ID Robinson (Zim)
Referee: WJ Henderson
Man of the Match: MJ Greatbatch

India innings (50 overs maximum)			R	B
A Jadeja	retired hurt		13	32
K Srikkanth	c Latham	b Patel	0	3
*M Azharuddin	c Greatbatch	b Patel	55	98
SR Tendulkar	c Smith	b Harris	84	107
SV Manjrekar	c & b Harris		18	25
N Kapil Dev	c Larsen	b Harris	33	16
ST Banerjee	c Greatbatch	b Watson	11	9
+KS More	not out		2	8
J Srinath	not out		4	3

Extras: (b 1, lb 4, w 4, nb 1) 10
Total: (6 wickets, 50 overs) 230

DNB: M Prabhakar, SLV Raju.

FoW: 1-4 (Srikkanth), 2-149 (Azharuddin), 3-166 (Tendulkar),
4-201 (Manjrekar), 5-222 (Kapil Dev), 6-223 (Banerjee).

Bowling	O	M	R	W
Cairns	8	1	40	0 (1nb)
Patel	10	0	29	2
Watson	10	1	34	1
Larsen	9	0	43	0
Harris	9	0	55	3 (2w)
Latham	4	0	24	0 (2w)

New Zealand innings (target: 231 runs from 50 overs)			R	B
MJ Greatbatch	c Banerjee	b Raju	73	77
RT Latham	b Prabhakar		8	22
AH Jones	not out		67	107
*MD Crowe	run out		26	28
+IDS Smith	c sub (PK Amre)	b Prabhakar	9	8
KR Rutherford	lbw	b Raju	21	22
CZ Harris	b Prabhakar		4	17
CL Cairns	not out		4	5

Extras: (b 4, lb 3, w 4, nb 8) 19

Total: (6 wickets, 47.1 overs) 231

DNB: DN Patel, GR Larsen, W Watson.

FoW: 1-36 (Latham), 2-118 (Greatbatch), 3-162 (Crowe),
4-172 (Smith), 5-206 (Rutherford), 6-225 (Harris).

Bowling	O	M	R	W
Kapil Dev	10	0	55	0 (1nb 1w)
Prabhakar	10	0	46	3 (2w)
Banerjee	6	1	40	0 (1nb)
Srinath	9	0	35	0 (3nb 2w)
Raju	10	0	38	2
Tendulkar	1	0	2	0
Srikkanth	1.1	0	8	0 (1nb)

15 March: Adelaide Oval

A cloudburst curtailed the match to 30 overs a side. South Africa
then inserted India. After Srikkanth fell early to a one-handed catch
by Peter Kirsten, Azhar, full of delicate strokes, added 78 with
makeshift opener, Manjrekar, and followed this with 71 in eight overs
with Kapil Dev, who produced a hurricane 42. The net result was a
rapid run rate of six an over.

Yet, asked to open, Kirsten advanced at almost a run a ball, much to the appreciation of the 6000-odd spectators, before he was yorked. He added 128 with Hudson, who registered his third fifty in four innings. Kepler Wessels, then, completed the task of scoring 24 off four overs as South Africa stormed home by six wickets.

With this win, the South Africans were certain of a semi-final place, unless thwarted by political developments back home. The United Cricket Board of South Africa indicated they would feel obliged to withdraw from the tournament if a plebiscite of whites in South Africa two days later rejected constitutional reform to usher in a democratic, multiracial system of government. It would have been a breach of trust if it had, for South Africa's entry in the World Cup had been on an unwritten understanding that their politics would not revert to a *status quo ante*. An overwhelming vote for change, however, made the matter a non-issue.

Toss: South Africa
Umpires: DP Buultjens (SL) and Khizer Hayat (Pak)
Referee: Barry Gibbs
Man of the Match: PN Kirsten

India innings (30 overs maximum)			R	B
K Srikkanth	c Kirsten	b Donald	0	5
SV Manjrekar		b Kuiper	28	53
*M Azharuddin	c Kuiper	b Pringle	79	77
SR Tendulkar	c Wessels	b Kuiper	14	14
N Kapil Dev		b Donald	42	29
VG Kambli	run out		1	3
PK Amre	not out		1	1
J Srinath	not out		0	0

Extras: (lb 7, w 6, nb 2) 15
Total: (6 wickets, 30 overs) 180

DNB: +KS More, M Prabhakar, SLV Raju.

FoW: 1-1 (Srikkanth), 2-79 (Manjrekar), 3-103 (Tendulkar), 4-174 (Kapil Dev), 5-177 (Kambli), 6-179 (Azharuddin).

Bowling	O	M	R	W
Donald	6	0	34	2 (3w)
Pringle	6	0	37	1 (2nb 2w)
Snell	6	1	46	0
McMillan	6	0	28	0
Kuiper	6	0	28	2 (1w)

South Africa innings (target: 181 runs from 30 overs)			R	B
AC Hudson	b Srinath		53	73
PN Kirsten	b Kapil Dev		84	86
AP Kuiper	run out		7	6
JN Rhodes	c Raju	b Prabhakar	7	3
*KC Wessels	not out		9	6
WJ Cronje	not out		8	6

Extras: (lb 10, nb 3) 13
Total: (4 wickets, 29.1 overs) 181

DNB: BM McMillan, +DJ Richardson, RP Snell, MW Pringle, AA Donald.

FoW: 1-128 (Hudson), 2-149 (Kuiper), 3-157 (Kirsten), 4-163 (Rhodes).

Bowling	O	M	R	W
Kapil Dev	6	0	36	1
Prabhakar	5.1	1	33	1
Tendulkar	6	0	20	0
Srinath	6	0	39	1 (3nb)
Raju	6	0	43	0

This match was the last in which the omnipotent Kapil Dev would be seen in the World Cup. He had performed in four such competitions and enjoyed the singular honour of leading India to their 1983 conquest.

After retiring, he carried his buoyancy in cricket to his business activities. But to his chagrin, in 2000, aspersions were cast on him vis-à-vis match fixing during a spell as India's coach. He tearfully dispelled such insinuations in a television interview, but noticeably distanced himself from the game thereafter – his new passion being golf. In September 2006, though, he succeeded Sunil Gavaskar as the chairman of India's National Cricket Academy in Bangalore.

Knowing Kapil, it's hard to believe he indulged in anything crooked in connection with a game he had seized with such refreshing candour and into which he had put his heart and soul.

Semi-final, 21 March: Eden Park Auckland

The day began with Crowe being a bit prematurely – though perhaps not undeservingly – crowned Man of the Series for his batting and captaincy. He then proceeded to win the toss, bat first and demonstrate his pedigree with a quicksilver 91, which was decorated with three sixes. Greatbatch had typically given New Zealand an explosive start, hitting sixes off Wasim Akram and Aaqib Javed. But subsequently, Mushtaq Ahmed's leg-spin applied the brakes, before Crowe went into cruise control, adding 113 in 107 balls with Ken Rutherford. But as the batsmen crossed after the latter had skied a catch to Moin Khan, Crowe unfortunately pulled a hamstring. He continued with Greatbatch as his runner, but, in a comedy of errors, was run out by the latter. Nevertheless, Ian Smith and the tail sword-fenced their way to 262. This was no soft target and looked especially elusive half way through the Pakistani innings.

The Pakistanis needed 123 from 15 overs at 8.2 an over after Imran himself had failed to ignite. But this situation was turned on its head by the precocious Inzamam-ul Haq. He raced to 50 off 31 balls and then to 60, which glittered with seven fours and a six, to fairly forcibly snatch the game from the Kiwis. With Miandad, he added 87 in 10 overs. Indeed, when the rotund young man was run out, the target had eased to 36 in five. This was comfortably negotiated, as Wasim and Moin threw their bats at virtually every delivery and Miandad chugged along at just the right pace to remain undefeated with a half-century.

Pakistan, consequently, qualified for their first World Cup final by getting the better of the hitherto unbeatable New Zealanders twice in four days. The fusillade of shots from Inzamam's bat paralysed the Kiwis. The strategy of opening the bowling in the tournament with Patel paid off again, as this off-spinner returned figures of one for 28 in his first eight overs; but his last two cost 22. Imran Khan rushed to embrace his heroes, as Crowe limped away, as much metaphorically as to physically accompany his colleagues in a lap of thanksgiving to the 32,000-plus capacity crowd. Wright had led the side while he nursed his hamstring.

Toss: New Zealand
Umpires: SA Bucknor (WI) and DR Shepherd (Eng)
Referee: PJP Burge (Aus)
Man of the Match: Inzamam-ul Haq

New Zealand innings (50 overs maximum)			R	B
MJ Greatbatch	b Aaqib Javed		17	22
JG Wright	c Rameez Raja	b Mushtaq Ahmed	13	44
AH Jones	lbw	b Mushtaq Ahmed	21	53
*MD Crowe	run out		91	83
KR Rutherford	c Moin Khan	b Wasim Akram	50	68
CZ Harris	st Moin Khan	b Iqbal Sikander	13	12
+IDS Smith	not out		18	10
DN Patel	lbw	b Wasim Akram	8	6
GR Larsen	not out		8	6

Extras: (lb 11, w 8, nb 4) 23
Total: (7 wickets, 50 overs) 262

DNB: DK Morrison, W Watson.

FoW: 1-35 (Greatbatch), 2-39 (Wright), 3-87 (Jones), 4-194 (Rutherford), 5-214 (Harris), 6-221 (Crowe), 7-244 (Patel).

Bowling	O	M	R	W
Wasim Akram	10	1	40	2 (4nb 2w)
Aaqib Javed	10	2	45	1 (2w)
Mushtaq Ahmed	10	0	40	2
Imran Khan	10	0	59	0 (3w)
Iqbal Sikander	9	0	56	1 (1w)
Aamer Sohail	1	0	11	0

Pakistan innings (target: 263 runs from 50 overs)			R	B
Aamir Sohail	c Jones	b Patel	14	20
Rameez Raja	c Morrison	b Watson	44	55
*Imran Khan	c Larsen	b Harris	44	93
Javed Miandad	not out		57	69
Saleem Malik	c sub	b Larsen	1	2
Inzamam-ul Haq	run out		60	37
Wasim Akram		b Watson	9	8
+Moin Khan	not out		20	11

Extras: (b 4, lb 10, w 1) 15
Total: (6 wickets, 49 overs) 264

DNB: Mushtaq Ahmed, Iqbal Sikander, Aaqib Javed.

FoW: 1-30 (Aamir Sohail), 2-84 (Rameez Raja),
3-134 (Imran Khan), 4-140 (Saleem Malik),
5-227 (Inzamam-ul Haq), 6-238 (Wasim Akram).

Bowling	O	M	R	W
Patel	10	1	50	1
Morrison	9	0	55	0 (1w)
Watson	10	2	39	2 (1nb)
Larsen	10	1	34	1
Harris	10	0	72	1

Semi-final, 22 March: Sydney Cricket Ground

England were unhindered by the morning conditions and, so, kept the scoreboard ticking. But the *pièce de résistance* came from Graeme Hick. This former Zimbabwean, after getting the benefit of the doubt in an lbw appeal and being caught off a no-ball before opening his account, went on to score 83 off 90 balls, adding 71 in 14 overs with Alec Stewart and 73 with Neil Fairbrother. Dermott Reeve then hurtled to 25 off 14 balls, which was helped by 17 of 18 pillaged from Alan Donald's final over.

Thrown down a gauntlet of 5.62 runs an over, South Africa erased 58 from their first 10 overs. Kirsten was handicapped by injury, but Andrew Hudson almost completed his fourth 50 of the tournament. Adrian Kuiper scorched three fours in a row off Gladstone Small, while Jonty Rhodes, hitherto more discernible for his fielding, now clicked with the willow. Such efforts compressed the 'ask' to 47 off five overs. Brian McMillan and David Richardson reduced this by another 25 in 2.5 overs. But this is when rain intervened and sank South Africa.

The requirement of 22 from 13 balls before the shower was first revised to 22 in seven and then to an impossible 21 off one. McMillan could only manage a single off Lewis. The vanquished were shattered and the victors left morally encumbered, while the 35,000 crowd felt a little cheated. The South Africans, though, cheerfully did a round of the ground. They were just so relieved to have been welcomed back to the international fold.

Many trashed the Organizing Committee. Under the rules, a completely new match could be held the next day only if the team batting second did not face at least 25 overs. Others insisted it was nemesis at work: Wessels fielded first fully cognizant of the pitfall, not to mention the weather forecast. Besides, South Africa's over rate was torpid and this provoked a financial penalty.

Toss: South Africa
Umpires: BL Aldridge (NZ) and SG Randell
Referee: FJ Cameron (NZ)
Man of the Match: GA Hick

England innings (45 overs maximum)			R	B
*GA Gooch	c Richardson	b Donald	2	9
IT Botham		b Pringle	21	23
+AJ Stewart	c Richardson	b McMillan	33	54
GA Hick	c Rhodes	b Snell	83	90
NH Fairbrother		b Pringle	28	50
AJ Lamb	c Richardson	b Donald	19	22
CC Lewis	not out		18	16
DA Reeve	not out		25	14

Extras: (b 1, lb 7, w 9, nb 6) 23
Total: (6 wickets, 45 overs) 252

DNB: PAJ DeFreitas, GC Small, RK Illingworth.

FoW: 1-20 (Gooch), 2-39 (Botham), 3-110 (Stewart), 4-183 (Fairbrother), 5-187 (Hick), 6-221 (Lamb).

Bowling	O	M	R	W
Donald	10	0	69	2 (2nb 5w)
Pringle	9	2	36	2 (4nb 1w)
Snell	8	0	52	1 (2w)
McMillan	9	0	47	1
Kuiper	5	0	26	0
Cronje	4	0	14	0

South Africa innings (target: 252 runs from 43 overs)			R	B
*KC Wessels	c Lewis	b Botham	17	21
AC Hudson	lbw	b Illingworth	46	52
PN Kirsten		b DeFreitas	11	26
AP Kuiper		b Illingworth	36	44
WJ Cronje	c Hick	b Small	24	45
JN Rhodes	c Lewis	b Small	43	38
BM McMillan	not out		21	21
+DJ Richardson	not out		13	10

Extras: (lb 17, w 4) 21
Total: (6 wickets, 43 overs) 232

DNB: RP Snell, MW Pringle, AA Donald.

FoW: 1-26 (Wessels), 2-61 (Kirsten), 3-90 (Hudson), 4-131 (Kuiper), 5-176 (Cronje), 6-206 (Rhodes).

Bowling	O	M	R	W
Botham	10	0	52	1 (3w)
Lewis	5	0	38	0
DeFreitas	8	1	28	1 (1w)
Illingworth	10	1	46	2
Small	10	1	51	2

Final, 25 March: Melbourne Cricket Ground

Perhaps recognizing the savage consequences of rain and the fact that no side had won a World Cup final batting second, Imran opted to bat. Initially, this move seemed to be a mistake as Pringle had Pakistan in shaky straits at 24 for two in nine overs. But the veterans, Imran and Miandad, now dug in. Gooch dropped Imran when he was nine, but the duo slowly saw off the shine. Pakistan, though, could only post 70 in 25 overs. Yet, by the 31st over, they had motored to 139. However, Miandad, batting with the aid of a runner, perished to a reverse sweep. And Imran was caught by Richard Illingworth off Botham. The heavy hitters, Inzamam (35 balls) and Wasim (18 balls), then, took over. Their 52 in six overs boosted the runs from the last 20 overs to 153 despite Pringle's last over costing just two runs and ensnaring both their wickets.

England suffered an early setback when Botham was adjudged caught behind. Stewart, however, was not shown the dreaded finger when Moin claimed another catch. Yet, the Surrey cricketer, son of Micky, who had toured India in 1963–64 as Mike Smith's vice-captain, failed to persevere. Mushtaq, thereafter, bamboozled Hick with a googly and also dislodged Gooch. With 181 needed from 29 overs, England faced a monumental task. But the battle-hardened Allan Lamb, selected ahead of Robin Smith, whose fitness was a question mark, put 72 of these on the board from 14 overs in association with Fairbrother, the left-handed Lancastrian nicknamed the 'finisher'. However, Wasim, the latter's county mate, was, now, reintroduced for a final burst. Fairbrother, who had run out of specialist batsmen as accomplices and was himself down to seeking the assistance of a runner, eventually top-edged to the wicketkeeper. The others simply caved in. Pakistan won by 22 runs. As a matter of personal satisfaction, Imran took the wicket of Illingworth.

An attendance of nearly 90,000, thus, witnessed a worthy climax to the tournament. Imran affirmed this was the most fulfilling and satisfying cricketing moment of his life. He described the victory as a triumph of youth over experience. He also attributed the success to the edge his aggressive specialist bowlers provided over Gooch's all-rounders.

Imran had practically hand-picked his squad. The absence of star pace bowler Waqar Younis, who suffered a stress fracture before the team left Pakistan, was a serious setback. They lost four of their first five matches (including their meeting with Zimbabwe), but went on to win the next five. They peaked perfectly, while England seemed to have run out of steam. The English won all their matches in New Zealand, but were less impressive on the faster Australian wickets they encountered in the knockout stage. 'It's not the end of the world', Gooch remarked after the match, 'but it is close to it.' He admitted England had been beaten fair and square. The three-figure stand between Imran and Miandad frustrated the Englishmen, while Wasim shattered their last hope with successive deliveries to dismiss Lamb and Lewis, one swinging in and then straightening and the other cutting in sharply.

So, Pakistan, thrice semi-finalists in the past, won the World Cup for the first time. England had now three times been within a match of a coronation, but never crowned the king. A limited-overs record crowd in Australia paid £880,000 to watch the final. Also, the international television audience – in 29 countries – ran into hundreds of millions.

Toss: Pakistan
Umpires: BL Aldridge (NZ) and SA Bucknor (WI)
Referee: PJP Burge
Man of the Match: Wasim Akram
Man of the Series: MD Crowe (NZ)

Pakistan innings (50 overs maximum)			R	B
Aamir Sohail	c Stewart	b Pringle	4	19
Rameez Raja	lbw	b Pringle	8	26
*Imran Khan	c Illingworth	b Botham	72	110
Javed Miandad	c Botham	b Illingworth	58	98
Inzamam-ul Haq		b Pringle	42	35
Wasim Akram	run out		33	19
Saleem Malik	not out		0	1

Extras: (lb 19, w 6, nb 7) 32
Total: (6 wickets, 50 overs) 249

DNB: Ijaz Ahmed, + Moin Khan, Mushtaq Ahmed, Aaqib Javed.

FoW: 1-20 (Aamir Sohail), 2-24 (Rameez Raja),
3-163 (Javed Miandad), 4-197 (Imran Khan),
5-249 (Inzamam-ul Haq), 6-249 (Wasim Akram).

Bowling	O	M	R	W	
Pringle	10	2	22	3	(5nb 3w)
Lewis	10	2	52	0	(2nb 1w)
Botham	7	0	42	1	
DeFreitas	10	1	42	0	(1w)
Illingworth	10	0	50	1	
Reeve	3	0	22	0	(1w)

England innings (target: 250 runs from 50 overs)			R	B
*GA Gooch	c Aaqib Javed	b Mushtaq Ahmed	29	66
IT Botham	c Moin Khan	b Wasim Akram	0	6
+AJ Stewart	c Moin Khan	b Aaqib Javed	7	16
GA Hick	lbw	b Mushtaq Ahmed	17	36
NH Fairbrother	c Moin Khan	b Aaqib Javed	62	70
AJ Lamb		b Wasim Akram	31	41
CC Lewis		b Wasim Akram	0	1
DA Reeve	c Rameez Raja	b Mushtaq Ahmed	15	32
DR Pringle	not out		18	16
PAJ DeFreitas	run out		10	8
RK Illingworth	c Rameez Raja	b Imran Khan	14	1

Extras: (lb 5, w 13, nb 6) 24

Total: (all out, 49.2 overs) 227

FoW: 1-6 (Botham), 2-21 (Stewart), 3-59 (Hick), 4-69 (Gooch),
5-141 (Lamb), 6-141 (Lewis), 7-180 (Fairbrother),
8-183 (Reeve), 9-208 (DeFreitas), 10-227 (Illingworth).

Bowling	O	M	R	W
Wasim Akram	10	0	49	3 (4nb 6w)
Aaqib Javed	10	2	27	2 (1nb 3w)
Mushtaq Ahmed	10	1	41	3 (1w)
Ijaz Ahmed	3	0	13	0 (2w)
Imran Khan	6.2	0	43	1 (1nb)
Aamir Sohail	10	0	49	0 (1w)

Imran, then 40, and in the twilight of his career, beamed in delight as he held aloft the £7500 Waterford crystal trophy. An iconic all-rounder in his country, he had by personal example inspired his younger colleagues through difficult patches in the competition. In such circumstances, they reacted, he said, like a cornered tiger. Earlier, he had described the championship as the worst organized of all the World Cups. He and Miandad (who became the highest overall run scorer) were the only ones to have played in all five tournaments.

The Australians, disillusioned by the team's poor showing, started rooting for South Africa, led as they were by Bloemfontein-born former Australian batsman, Kepler Wessels. (A sizeable number of white South Africans who had migrated to Australia, supplemented, if not spearheaded, the support.) The South Africans had only three matches in India – one of which they won – as previous experience of ODIs. Now coached by Mike Procter, a distinguished all-rounder for Gloucestershire during South Africa's isolation, with the quite expeditious Alan Donald the lynchpin of their attack, they stepped coolly on to the world stage. Kirsten, who was left out of the original tour squad, was to average over 68 in the preliminary matches.

Defeated by New Zealand and Sri Lanka, the South Africans dramatically turned the tables on the West Indians and complemented this win with another over Pakistan at Brisbane, a match in which rain favoured the Proteas, formerly the Springboks (a change brought about to abandon an animal symbol of the apartheid era for the softer image of a flower). Jonty Rhodes, though, brought spectators to their feet with his gymnastic fielding, which included running out Inzamam-ul Haq while being airborne.

Beyond the boundary, the white minority who had discriminatingly ruled South Africa for decades, probably realized the value of scrapping their repugnant racism, as they saw live pictures from the other side of the Indian Ocean of how warmly their cricketers had been accepted as a result of the promise of a conversion to civilized ways.

Bookmakers had quickly revised odds as the propensities of past winners, India and the West Indies, oscillated uncertainly. A new-look Caribbean side led by a slightly unsure Richie Richardson won their first match by making 221 without losing a wicket against Pakistan. They subsequently seemed to lose their way, though a young left-hander, Brian Lara, announced himself emphatically with four half centuries. He, then, blossomed into an all-time great.

Sri Lanka successfully chased down 313 against Zimbabwe at New Plymouth in New Zealand. But the Zimbabweans upset England by nine runs, thanks to Eddo Brandes, after themselves being bowled out for a mere 134 on a lively pitch at Albury in Australia. England had, by this stage, already qualified for the last four, their previous run having included a comprehensive win over Australia.

Border running out Azhar was noteworthy as were other dismissals such as the stumping of Harris from a Mushtaq wide, the dismantling of Botham's middle stump by McMillan, Healy's catching in general and Mushtaq's googly to flummox Hick.

The pool of umpires from the competing nations injected a flavour of internationalism, with Steve Bucknor and David Shepherd generally the most error free. Bouncers above the shoulder, though, were not no-balled with equal strictness.

As in 1987, neither of the hosts reached the final. But the tournament gave rise to significant profits, struck many a chord and kept the cricketing world on tenterhooks.

However, far too many matches were decided somewhat artificially – by the rules governing stoppages caused by inclement weather. This left a bit of an unsavoury taste in the mouth. While India had only themselves to blame for their elimination in the league phase, their match with Sri Lanka was completely washed out and the ones with Australia, Zimbabwe, West Indies and South Africa settled by the aforesaid controversial method, albeit not always to India's disadvantage. In summary, India suffered from an unsettled opening combination and inadequate bowling and fielding.

THE 1996 WORLD CUP

All things considered, the sixth World Cup, sponsored by Wills, wasn't wholly memorable. The competition was clouded by an extended group stage in India, Pakistan and Sri Lanka and a hasty knockout segment.

The imminence of spectator unrest finally surfaced with the scratching of a semi-final at Kolkata, following bottle throwing into the playing area and lighting of fires in the stands by some unruly elements among the spectators. Such unsportsmanlike behaviour reflected an unrecognizable facet of the Eden Gardens crowd, which had been so knowledgeable in earlier eras.

The Wills World Cup also put commerce before cricket. The local media hype of Indian and Pakistani cricketers created an indomitable image of them among the subcontinental masses. To them, peculiarly, defeat for their respective sides was unthinkable.

The scenario was in sharp contrast to the 1987 World Cup, which was generally acknowledged to be quite a success. Of course, that competition provided negligible profit, whereas the event now panned out to be an accountant's delight. The style of administering the game had altered significantly for the worse. The itineraries were inexplicable and the travel quite wearing.

Such rudimentary defects could have been dealt with by the ICC at source. But the governors of the sport adopted a hands-off policy, transferring all responsibility to the three-nation (India, Pakistan and Sri Lanka) Organizing Committee. Fortunately, the ICC have not repeated this mistake since and have increasingly strengthened their control over the World Cup.

The incorporation of three associate member countries in the draw was laudable. This enlarged the field to 12 teams. However, it also made the outcome of the league stage, divided into two groups of six sides each, a fairly foregone conclusion. The tournament only spluttered to life from the quarter finals. The ICC cannot be absolved of responsibility for such imbalance either. Predictably, the three associate nations and the minnows of test cricket, Zimbabwe, were eliminated. Dispensing with the round of eight – with teams only progressing to the semi-finals from the first phase – would have made the pre-quarter final segment more interesting. Patrons to a certain extent called the bluff, as the group games in Pakistan were poorly attended.

The decision to spread matches to various corners of India to keep associations affiliated to the BCCI in good humour was indefensible as most of the 17 venues lacked the infrastructure to host an international event. Even the opening ceremony in Kolkata was a disaster. The much-touted laser show malfunctioned, the master of ceremonies, the actor Saeed Jaffrey, sounded rather well fortified and the 100,000 attendees wondered what on earth was going on.

It was egg on the face of local chieftain, Jagmohan Dalmiya, later to become president of the ICC and one of the most powerful administrators in world cricket. Such embarrassment coincided with a fracas between, on the one hand, the organizers and, on the other, Australia and West Indies over the refusal of these two teams to play at Colombo, following a bomb blast in the Sri Lankan capital a fortnight earlier. Positions being entrenched, the matches were forfeited, though it was a commentary on the cosiness of the format that Australia and West Indies could make such sacrifices without seriously endangering their progress to the business end of the tournament.

The Sri Lankans had a smirk as well as a disconsolate look on their faces. They obtained four points by default and an automatic passage to the last eight, but had been denied the pleasure of hosting two of the best teams in the competition, especially when this island needed a respite from its gory civil war between the Sinhalese-dominated Central Government and Tamil separatists.

At 4 a.m. after the previous night's opening charade, four bleary eyed squads assembled in the lobby of Kolkata's Oberoi Grand Hotel to catch a 6 a.m. flight to Delhi, where they had to wait several hours before connecting with flights to their first-game destinations. Clearly, either no one cared or had not thought of arranging charter flights at decent hours.

As the world's top cricketers criss-crossed the subcontinent, P. V. Narasimha Rao, whose liberalization had – unwittingly – contributed much to the financial well-being of Indian cricket, was in the the final lap of his remarkable five-year term as India's prime minister. His compatriot from Andhra Pradesh state, Mohammed Azharuddin, was still captain of India.

18 February: Cuttack

While Azharuddin became the seventh cricketer to win 200 ODI caps, all Kenyans were making their international debuts. Their batsmen, though, initially gave a good account of themselves. After being invited to bat, Steve Tikolo impressed with 65, hitting a six and six fours and putting on 96 with his skipper, Maurice Odumbe. But the middle order underestimated the accurate leg-spinner Anil Kumble, who, as a result, benefited with three wickets in four overs. India were, thus, set a target of 200.

Ajay Jadeja and Sachin Tendulkar erased 100 of these runs in 20 overs en route to compiling India's highest partnership for any wicket in the World Cup. But the former began to suffer from cramps and holed out on the boundary in the 33rd over. The special talent of Tendulkar was rewarded in that he scored his fifth ODI hundred, although he was stuck on 99 for nine balls. Neither Navjot Sidhu nor Vinod Kambli quite found his feet. They, too, succumbed in the deep. However, Tendulkar reasserted control as he cruised to 127, with the assistance of 15 fours and a six. It was wicketkeeper Nayan Mongia, though, who hit the winning boundary. India won by seven wickets in this ancient, bustling city in the eastern state of Orissa on the Bay of Bengal.

Toss: India
Umpires: KT Francis (SL) and DR Shepherd (Eng)
TV Umpire: S Toohey (Neth)
Referee: CH Lloyd (WI)
ODI Debuts: RW Ali, DN Chudasama, AY Karim, HS Modi, TM Odoyo, EO Odumbe, MO Odumbe, KO Otieno, MA Suji, LO Tikolo, SO Tikolo (Kenya).
Man of the Match: SR Tendulkar

Kenya innings (50 overs maximum)			*R*	*B*
DN Chudasama	c Mongia	b Prasad	29	51
+KO Otieno	c Mongia	b Raju	27	58
SO Tikolo	c Kumble	b Raju	65	83
*MO Odumbe	st Mongia	b Kumble	26	57
HS Modi	c Jadeja	b Kumble	2	3
TM Odoyo	c Prabhakar	b Kumble	8	18
EO Odumbe	not out		15	21
AY Karim	not out		6	11

Extras: (b 2, lb 11, w 7, nb 1) 21
Total: (6 wickets, 50 overs) 199

DNB: LO Tikolo, MA Suji, RW Ali.

FoW: 1-41 (Chudasama), 2-65 (Otieno), 3-161 (MO Odumbe), 4-161 (SO Tikolo), 5-165 (Modi), 6-184 (Odoyo).

Bowling	O	M	R	W
Prabhakar	5	1	19	0
Srinath	10	0	38	0 (5w)
Prasad	10	0	41	1 (2w)
Kumble	10	0	28	3
Raju	10	2	34	2
Tendulkar	5	0	26	0

India innings (target: 200 runs from 50 overs)			R	B
A Jadeja	c Ali	b Karim	53	85
SR Tendulkar	not out		127	138
NS Sidhu	c Suji	b SO Tikolo	1	11
VG Kambli	c LO Tikolo	b MO Odumbe	2	11
+NR Mongia	not out		8	7

Extras: (lb 5, w 6, nb 1) 12
Total: (3 wickets, 41.5 overs) 203

DNB: *M Azharuddin, M Prabhakar, J Srinath, A Kumble, BKV Prasad, SLV Raju.

FoW: 1-163 (Jadeja), 2-167 (Sidhu), 3-182 (Kambli).

Bowling	O	M	R	W
Ali	5	0	25	0
EO Odumbe	3	0	18	0 (3w)
Suji	5	0	20	0
Odoyo	3	0	22	0 (1nb)
Karim	10	1	27	1
LO Tikolo	3	0	21	0 (3w)
MO Odumbe	9.5	1	39	1
SO Tikolo	3	0	26	1

21 February: Gwalior (Day/Night)

On a perfectly good batting pitch, it was hardly surprising that the West Indies opted for first strike. What was unforeseen was their performance thereafter. They lost two early wickets, but did not incur any further loss up to the half-way mark. At this point, though, captain Richie Richardson's exit prompted a collapse, from which the West Indians never recovered; indeed, later disintegrating a second time. Both times three wickets went down for eight runs in 12 balls. Of course, Brian Lara was rather unlucky to be adjudged caught behind off his fifth ball. But the West Indies were dismissed for 173, which was, in fact, less than what the Kenyans had scored against the Indians.

India, too, lost a couple of wickets at the start of their venture, but remained unfazed. Again the resolute Tendulkar came to the rescue. He stroked his way to 70 off 91 balls to earn his second successive Man of the Match award, but was thereafter run out in a misunderstanding with Kambli, his friend from school days. Tragically for the West Indies, Courtney Browne had dropped a skier when Tendulkar was 22. Courtney Walsh returned for a mean spell, but the match had by this stage virtually slipped out of the West Indians' fingers. Indeed, Kambli made sure he finished the job. India reached their target in 40 overs to win by five wickets. This match was the first real challenge for both teams and India passed the test with flying colours. Some 30,000 spectators celebrated by lighting torches and setting off firecrackers, which smokily diffused the floodlights in this erstwhile seat of the Maharaja of Gwalior (now a part of Madhya Pradesh state), the last of whom, Madhavrao Scindia, became president of the BCCI before he died in an air accident in September 2001.

Toss: West Indies
Umpires: Khizer Hayat (Pak) and ID Robinson (Zim)
TV Umpire: S Toohey (Neth)
Referee: R Subba Row (Eng)
Man of the Match: SR Tendulkar

West Indies innings (50 overs maximum)			R	B
SL Campbell		b Srinath	5	14
*RB Richardson	c Kambli	b Prabhakar	47	70
BC Lara	c Mongia	b Srinath	2	5
S Chanderpaul	c Azharuddin	b Kapoor	38	66
RIC Holder		b Kumble	0	3
RA Harper		b Kumble	23	40
+CO Browne		b Prabhakar	18	45
OD Gibson		b Kumble	6	5
IR Bishop	run out		9	28
CEL Ambrose	c Kumble	b Prabhakar	8	15
CA Walsh	not out		9	11

Extras: (lb 2, w 5, nb 1) 8
Total: (all out, 50 overs) 173

FoW: 1-16 (Campbell), 2-24 (Lara), 3-91 (Richardson),
4-99 (Holder), 5-99 (Chanderpaul), 6-141 (Harper),
7-141 (Browne), 8-149 (Gibson), 9-162 (Ambrose),
10-173 (Bishop).

Bowling	O	M	R	W
Prabhakar	10	0	39	3 (1nb)
Srinath	10	0	22	2
Kumble	10	0	35	3 (5w)
Prasad	10	0	34	0
Kapoor	10	2	41	1

India innings (target: 174 runs from 50 overs)			R	B
A Jadeja		b Ambrose	1	3
SR Tendulkar	run out		70	91
NS Sidhu		b Ambrose	1	5
*M Azharuddin	c Walsh	b Harper	32	59
VG Kambli	not out		33	48
M Prabhakar	c & b Harper		1	2
+NR Mongia	not out		24	33

Extras: (lb 3, w 1, nb 8) 12

Total: (5 wickets, 39.4 overs) 174

DNB: AR Kapoor, A Kumble, J Srinath, BKV Prasad.

FoW: 1-2 (Jadeja), 2-15 (Sidhu), 3-94 (Azharuddin), 4-125 (Tendulkar), 5-127 (Prabhakar).

Bowling	O	M	R	W
Ambrose	8	1	41	2 (2nb, 1w)
Walsh	9	3	18	0 (2nb)
Bishop	5	0	28	0 (3nb)
Gibson	8.4	0	50	0 (1nb)
Harper	9	1	34	2

27 February: Wankhede Stadium, Mumbai (Day/Night)

It was the first-ever floodlit international in India's commercial capital, and the batsmen responded with a correspondingly dazzling display. Mark Taylor sprinted to 59 as Australia posted 103 for the first wicket at five an over after winning the toss. They seemed set to score 300. A bit overshadowed in this partnership, Mark Waugh now blossomed to become the first to score back-to-back centuries in the World Cup. His composition was engraved with three sixes and eight fours. But the spinners, Venkatapathy Raju and Kumble, chipped away and the last seven wickets fell for just 26 – four of them in the final over.

Yet, India failed to transmit this momentum to their batting. In six overs they conceded two wickets to Damien Fleming, while Glenn McGrath sent down three maidens. Then, Tendulkar decided not to entirely disappoint his home crowd. He hit three fours in McGrath's fifth over and hurried from 12 to 56 off 25 balls, planting seven fours and a six. He took a breather after Fleming cleaned up Azhar, but ultimately still managed an explosive 90 off 84 deliveries, with seven more boundaries. India remained in the hunt until he was stumped off a wide from Mark Waugh, toying with off-spin. Shane

Warne was accurate, but Sanjay Manjrekar and Nayan Mongia persevered. India were, however, short of wickets to successfully conclude the assault. Australia won by 16 runs, with two overs to spare. Fleming finished with a five-wicket haul.

Toss: Australia
Umpires: RS Dunne (NZ) and DR Shepherd (Eng)
TV Umpire: TM Samarasinghe (SL)
Referee: CH Lloyd (WI)
Man of the Match: ME Waugh

Australia innings (50 overs maximum)			*R*	*B*
ME Waugh	run out (Prasad)		126	135
*MA Taylor	c Srinath	b Raju	59	73
RT Ponting	c Manjrekar	b Raju	12	21
SR Waugh	run out (Raju)		7	15
SG Law	c & b Kumble		21	31
MG Bevan	run out (Jadeja)		6	5
S Lee	run out (Mongia)		9	10
+IA Healy	c Kumble	b Prasad	6	10
SK Warne	c Azharuddin	b Prasad	0	1
DW Fleming	run out (Mongia/Prasad)		0	1
GD McGrath	not out		0	0

Extras: (lb 8, w 2, nb 2) 12
Total: (all out, 50 overs) 258

FoW: 1-103 (Taylor), 2-140 (Ponting), 3-157 (SR Waugh),
4-232 (ME Waugh), 5-237 (Law), 6-244 (Bevan), 7-258 (Lee),
8-258 (Warne), 9-258 (Healy), 10-258 (Fleming).

Bowling	*O*	*M*	*R*	*W*	
Prabhakar	10	0	55	0	
Srinath	10	1	51	0	
Prasad	10	0	49	2	(2nb, 2w)
Kumble	10	1	47	1	
Raju	10	0	48	2	

India innings (target: 259 runs from 50 overs)			*R*	*B*
A Jadeja	lbw	b Fleming	1	17
SR Tendulkar	st Healy	b ME Waugh	90	84
VG Kambli		b Fleming	0	2
*M Azharuddin		b Fleming	10	17
SV Manjrekar	c Healy	b SR Waugh	62	91
M Prabhakar	run out (Ponting)		3	6
+NR Mongia	c Taylor	b Warne	27	32
A Kumble		b Fleming	17	22
J Srinath	c Lee	b Fleming	7	12
BKV Prasad	c Bevan	b SR Waugh	0	2
SLV Raju	not out		3	4

Extras: (b 5, lb 8, w 8, nb 1) 22
Total: (all out, 48 overs) 242

FoW: 1-7 (Jadeja), 2-7 (Kambli), 3-70 (Azharuddin),
4-143 (Tendulkar), 5-147 (Prabhakar), 6-201 (Mongia),
7-205 (Manjrekar), 8-224 (Srinath), 9-231 (Prasad),
10-242 (Kumble).

Bowling	*O*	*M*	*R*	*W*
McGrath	8	3	48	0 (1nb)
Fleming	9	0	36	5 (2w)
Warne	10	1	28	1 (2w)
Lee	3	0	23	0 (2w)
ME Waugh	10	0	44	1 (1w)
Bevan	5	0	28	0
SR Waugh	3	0	22	2 (1w)

2 March: Feroz Shah Kotla, Delhi

The nerve centre of political power in India for centuries, Delhi, old and new, has many attractions. But the cricket ground controlled by the unfittingly politicized Delhi and District Cricket Association at the otherwise alluring setting of Feroz Shah Kotla (inner citadel of the fourteenth-century settlement of Ferozabad, now in ruins) is not one of them. Its historically substandard facilities for players and the public alike – now slightly improved after the construction of a new stadium – are not exactly endearing.

Here, India seemed to be psychologically smitten after being sent in to bat by their southern neighbour. Play was delayed by a quarter of an hour because of a dew-laden outfield, following which the hosts initiated their innings in light mist and struggled to get their eye in. But 100 in 25 overs represented a considerable recovery. Indeed, after a brief shower, the last 11 overs fetched 105. Tendulkar blasted his way to 137 – his second century of the tournament. Launching into five sixes and eight fours, he realized 175 with Azhar, which improved on India's all-wicket record in the World Cup established in the same tournament in the Kenya match. Ravindra Pushpakumara's last over resulted in a bountiful 23 for India as they coasted to 271 for three.

But Sri Lanka immediately replied in kind. It was a blitzkrieg from Sanath Jayasuriya and Romesh Kaluwitharana as they smashed 42 in the first three overs and Manoj Prabhakar yielded 11 and 22 in his first two. The 50 came up in the fifth, but Kumble now took an excellent catch off Prasad's bowling to dismiss Kalu as he attempted his seventh four, and, then, himself proceeded to capably contain the Sri Lankan middle order. But Jayasuriya galloped on, lashing nine fours and two sixes in his 79, although the latter phase of his effort was leisurely in comparison to the early riot. Indeed, having set off at double the needed pace, Sri Lanka lost three quick wickets – Kumble completed a run-out of Gurusinha and then removed Jayasuriya and Aravinda de Silva. And, consequently, Sri Lanka fell behind the required rate. Another specialist spinner might have served India better. They had instead opted for a four-man seam attack. In essence, Arjuna Ranatunga and Hashan Tillekeratne repaired the damage, adding 131 for the 5th wicket and Sri Lanka won with eight balls to spare. This victory ensured them first place in their group. In the final analysis, it was their unsure start in the morning that cost India the match.

Toss: Sri Lanka
Umpires: CJ Mitchley (SA) and ID Robinson (Zim)
TV Umpire: Ikram Rabbani (Pak)
Referee: JR Reid (NZ)
Man of the Match: ST Jayasuriya

India innings (50 overs maximum)			R	B
M Prabhakar	c Gurusinha	b Pushpakumara	7	36
SR Tendulkar	run out		137	137
SV Manjrekar	c Kaluwitharana	b Dharmasena	32	46
*M Azharuddin	not out		72	80
VG Kambli	not out		1	1

Extras: (b 4, lb 7, w 11) 22
Total: (3 wickets, 50 overs) 271

DNB: A Jadeja, +NR Mongia, J Srinath, A Kumble, SA Ankola, BKV Prasad.

FoW: 1-27 (Prabhakar), 2-93 (Manjrekar), 3-268 (Tendulkar).

Bowling	O	M	R	W
Vaas	9	3	37	0 (2w)
Pushpakumara	8	0	53	1 (7w)
Muralitharan	10	1	42	0 (1w)
Dharmasena	9	0	53	1 (1w)
Jayasuriya	10	0	52	0
Ranatunga	4	0	23	0

Sri Lanka innings (target: 272 runs from 50 overs)			R	B
ST Jayasuriya	c Prabhakar	b Kumble	79	76
+RS Kaluwitharana	c Kumble	b Prasad	26	16
AP Gurusinha	run out		25	27
PA de Silva	st Mongia	b Kumble	8	14
*A Ranatunga	not out		46	63
HP Tillakaratne	not out		70	98

Extras: (b 4, lb 9, w 3, nb 2) 18
Total: (4 wickets, 48.4 overs) 272

DNB: RS Mahanama, HDPK Dharmasena, WPUJC Vaas,
KR Pushpakumara, M Muralitharan.

FoW: 1-53 (Kaluwitharana), 2-129 (Gurusinha), 3-137 (Jayasuriya),
4-141 (de Silva).

Bowling	O	M	R	W
Prabhakar	4	0	47	0
Srinath	9.4	0	51	0
Prasad	10	1	53	1 (1w, 2nb)
Ankola	5	0	28	0
Kumble	10	1	39	2
Tendulkar	10	0	41	0 (2w)

6 March: Kanpur

This industrial city, with its polluted air and scandalous infrastructure, nestling on the banks of the river Ganges, regarded as holy by religious Hindus, clings on as an international cricketing venue after it generated India's first-ever test victory over Australia in 1959. Jasu Patel, an off-spinner with a sharpish action, not much recognized before or since, took 14 wickets in the match, including nine for 69 in one innings, to send Richie Benaud's side headlong to defeat. Until the previous season, tests here had been played on matting wickets. This time, it was held on underprepared turf and Patel exploited this rather better than the Aussie slow bowlers, including Benaud.

Now, there were no apparent devils in the pitch. Quite simply, Zimbabwe preferred to chase rather than set a target. India, however, were seriously jolted when they lost three wickets for only 32 by the 13th over. Heath Streak disfigured Tendulkar's stumps, while Manjrekar and Azharuddin were both caught at mid-wicket. The crisis, though, was an opportunity for Sidhu and Kambli to impress; neither had been in the limelight in previous games. They capably seized this chance by adding 142 in 29 overs. Kambli, a rugged left-hander, was the more aggressive, reaching his 50 a ball ahead of Sidhu, despite giving the Sikh a 22-run start. He was fortunate to be let off twice, but recorded 106, with 11 fours, before being consumed in the deep. Then, Ajay Jadeja plundered 19 off Charles Lock's last over. With this contribution, India reached 247 for five.

For Zimbabwe, Grant Flower and Andrew Waller dashed to 50 in 11 overs, but the introduction of the spinners halted the progress and sharply altered the course of the match. Flower departed in Raju's first over and Waller in Kumble's second. After 25 overs, Zimbabwe had been 92 for two, to India's 85 for three, but three wickets in successive overs thereafter put paid to the Zimbabweans' World Cup campaign. India won by 40 runs.

Toss: Zimbabwe
Umpires: SA Bucknor (WI) and CJ Mitchley (SA)
TV Umpire: TM Samarasinghe (SL).
Referee: JR Reid (NZ)
Man of the Match: A Jadeja

India innings (50 overs maximum)			R	B
SR Tendulkar	b Streak		3	12
NS Sidhu	c Streak	b PA Strang	80	116
SV Manjrekar	c Campbell	b Lock	2	18
*M Azharuddin	c Campbell	b BC Strang	2	10
VG Kambli	c GW Flower	b Lock	106	110
A Jadeja	not out		44	27
+NR Mongia	not out		6	9

Extras: (lb 1, w 3) 4
Total: (5 wickets, 50 overs) 247

DNB: A Kumble, J Srinath, BKV Prasad, SLV Raju.

FoW: 1-5 (Tendulkar), 2-25 (Manjrekar), 3-32 (Azharuddin), 4-174 (Sidhu), 5-219 (Kambli).

Bowling	O	M	R	W
Streak	10	3	29	1 (1nb)
Lock	10	1	57	2 (2w)
BC Strang	5	1	22	1
PA Strang	10	0	55	1
Peall	6	0	35	0 (1w)
Whittall	3	0	19	0
GW Flower	3	0	16	0
Campbell	3	0	13	0

Zimbabwe innings (target: 248 runs from 50 overs)			R	B
AC Waller	c Tendulkar	b Kumble	22	36
GW Flower	c Azharuddin	b Raju	30	42
GJ Whittall	run out		10	29
ADR Campbell	c & b Jadeja		28	55
*+A Flower		b Raju	28	40
CN Evans	c Srinath	b Jadeja	6	5
HH Streak	lbw	b Raju	30	39
PA Strang		b Srinath	14	21
BC Strang	lbw	b Srinath	3	13
SG Peall	c Raju	b Kumble	9	14
ACI Lock	not out		2	4

Extras: (b 4, lb 9, w 11, nb 1) 25
Total: (all out, 49.4 overs) 207

FoW: 1-59 (GW Flower), 2-59 (Waller), 3-96 (Campbell),
4-99 (Whittall), 5-106 (Evans), 6-168 (Streak),
7-173 (A Flower), 8-193 (PA Strang), 9-195 (BC Strang),
10-207 (Peall).

Bowling	O	M	R	W
Srinath	10	1	36	2 (1w)
Prasad	7	0	40	0 (4w)
Kumble	9.4	1	33	2 (1w)
Raju	10	2	30	3
Tendulkar	6	0	23	0
Jadeja	7	0	32	2 (1w)

The quarter final line-up was, therefore, England versus Sri Lanka, South Africa versus West Indies, Australia versus New Zealand and a high-voltage showdown between India and Pakistan.

Quarter final, 9 March: Chinaswamy Stadium, Bangalore

In this city, now the Silicon Valley of the East, India decided to bat; but, in spite of limited venom on the part of the Pakistani bowlers, their top order failed to capitalize. Tendulkar was off-colour in scoring 31, while Sidhu missed his hundred when beaten by a top-spinner from Mushtaq Ahmed, though he charted India to an imposing 168 for two. Vitally, though, the scoring rate was barely 4.5 an over until Jadeja, with the cooperation of the lower order, corrected this trend. He himself raced to 45 (four fours and two sixes). Then with the tail in harness, 51 runs were lambasted off the last three overs. Waqar Younis bore the brunt of this bombardment, costing 40 in just two overs — as opposed to 27 in his first eight. But when he finally smothered Jadeja's explosion, he became only the fourth bowler to capture 200 wickets in ODIs.

A slow over rate reduced Pakistan's allocation to 49 overs, the only instance of such a penalty being imposed in the competition. Their openers were, however, undaunted. Saeed Anwar breezed to 48 in 32 balls, which included a bracelet of two sixes, before he skied a catch to Kumble off Srinath's bowling. Aamir Sohail, standing in as skipper for an injured Wasim Akram, reached 55 with the help of a six, when he cut injudiciously at Venkatesh Prasad. Pakistan took full advantage of the first 15 overs, scoring 113 for two, which put them markedly ahead of India at the same juncture. But Prasad snatched a couple of more wickets and, steadily, the run rate slipped downwards. Rashid Latif, with two towering sixes in his 26, kept the fight alive but Kumble, first, had him stumped and then polished off the tail.

When Javed Miandad, unable to force the pace, was run out, this was journey's end for a long and lustrous career. With typical rebelliousness, he laced the announcement of his retirement with a frontal attack against the Pakistani team management for not treating him with due importance. More significantly, it was curtains for the defending champions' campaign.

This face-off sparked intense emotions, which rather boiled over in Pakistan after India's victory. A fan, reportedly, sprayed his television set with bullets before shooting himself. Others burned Wasim's effigy. Speculation was rife he might have pulled out of the match without cause. He vehemently denied this charge. The previous year's allegations of match fixing against him didn't help. But the truth is, the match was keenly fought and a complete cliffhanger.

Toss: India
Umpires: SA Bucknor (WI) and DR Shepherd (Eng)
TV Umpire: RS Dunne (NZ).
Referee: R Subba Row (Eng)
Man of the Match: NS Sidhu

India innings (50 overs maximum)			*R*	*B*
NS Sidhu		b Mushtaq Ahmed	93	115
SR Tendulkar		b Ata-ur-Rehman	31	59
SV Manjrekar	c Javed Miandad	b Aamir Sohail	20	43
*M Azharuddin	c Rashid Latif	b Waqar Younis	27	22
VG Kambli		b Mushtaq Ahmed	24	26
A Jadeja	c Aamir Sohail	b Waqar Younis	45	25
+NR Mongia	run out		3	3
A Kumble	c Javed Miandad	b Aaqib Javed	10	6
J Srinath	not out		12	4
BKV Prasad	not out		0	0

Extras: (lb 3, w 15, nb 4) 22

Total: (8 wickets, 50 overs) 287

DNB: SLV Raju.

FoW: 1-90 (Tendulkar), 2-138 (Manjrekar), 3-168 (Sidhu),
4-200 (Azharuddin), 5-226 (Kambli), 6-236 (Mongia),
7-260 (Kumble), 8-279 (Jadeja).

Bowling	O	M	R	W
Waqar Younis	10	1	67	2 (1w)
Aaqib Javed	10	0	67	1 (1nb, 4w)
Ata-ur-Rehman	10	0	40	1 (3nb, 1w)
Mushtaq Ahmed	10	0	56	2 (3w)
Aamir Sohail	5	0	29	1 (4w)
Saleem Malik	5	0	25	0 (2w)

Pakistan innings (target: 288 runs from 49 overs)			R	B
*Aamir Sohail		b Prasad	55	46
Saeed Anwar	c Kumble	b Srinath	48	32
Ijaz Ahmed	c Srinath	b Prasad	12	23
Inzamam-ul Haq	c Mongia	b Prasad	12	20
Saleem Malik	lbw	b Kumble	38	50
Javed Miandad	run out		38	64
+Rashid Latif	st Mongia	b Raju	26	25
Mushtaq Ahmed	c & b Kumble		0	2
Waqar Younis	not out		4	21
Ata-ur-Rehman	lbw	b Kumble	0	1
Aaqib Javed	not out		6	10

Extras: (b 1, lb 3, w 5) 9
Total: (9 wickets, 49 overs) 248

FoW: 1-84 (Saeed Anwar), 2-113 (Aamir Sohail),
3-122 (Ijaz Ahmed), 4-132 (Inzamam-ul Haq),
5-184 (Saleem Malik), 6-231 (Rashid Latif),
7-232 (Mushtaq Ahmed), 8-239 (Javed Miandad),
9-239 (Ata-ur-Rehman).

Bowling	O	M	R	W
Srinath	9	0	61	1 (1w)
Prasad	10	0	45	3 (2w)
Kumble	10	0	48	3
Raju	10	0	46	1 (1w)
Tendulkar	5	0	25	0
Jadeja	5	0	19	0 (1w)

Dilip Doshi: The only Indian to win a Man of the Match award in the Gillette Cup.
Photo Credit: Dilip Doshi

Clive Lloyd: Captained the West Indies to victory in the 1975 and 1979 World Cups in England. He also scored a match-winning century in the final of the former event.

Photo Credit: Patrick Eagar

Vivian Richards: Dominated
the 1979 World Cup final with
a decisive hundred.

Photo Credit: Patrick Eagar

The unassuming Albion Sports Complex: Venue of a match that marked the
turning point for India in one-day cricket.

Kapil Dev Nikhanj hooking at Tunbridge Wells in course of his inspiring 175 not out against Zimbabwe, from where India never looked back in the 1983 World Cup. *Photo Credit:* Patrick Eagar

Indian Prime Minister Indira Gandhi shaking hands with Kapil Dev when the Indian team called on her after their triumph in 1983 World Cup.
Photo Credit: The Hindu

Sunil Gavaskar, Indian captain in the 1985 Benson & Hedges 'World Championship of Cricket', was showered with champagne by his teammates after India crushed Pakistan in the final at the Melbourne Cricket Ground.
Photo Credit: Getty Images

Mohammed Azharuddin: A rising star for India in the 1987 World Cup.
India, though, lost in the semi-finals.
Photo Credit: The Hindu

Volatile spectators
rioted at Eden Gardens
as India veered to
defeat against Sri Lanka
in the semi-finals of the
1996 World Cup.
Photo Credit: Patrick Eagar

Sachin Tendulkar: Still only 18, he left no one in doubt about his promise
on his debut in a World Cup in Australia in 1992. *Photo Credit:* The Hindu

Allan Donald is run out and the Australia-South Africa semi-final in the 1999 World Cup ends in a dramatic tie. The Australians qualified for the final on better net run-rate.   *Photo Credit:* Patrick Eagar

Australian captain Ricky Ponting celebrates his century against India in the 2003 World Cup final. Australia won the match easily.
Photo Credit: The Hindu

Rahul Dravid: Top-scored in the 1999 World Cup with an aggregate of 461 - not bad for a batsman considered by some to be too slow for one-day cricket!
Photo Credit: The Hindu

Saurav Ganguly: A success in both the 1999 and 2003 World Cups. He skippered India and scored three hundreds in the latter event.
Photo Credit: The Hindu

Semi-final, 13 March: Eden Gardens, Kolkata (Day/Night)

Conditions, especially in day/night circumstances, arguably dictated batting first. But Azharuddin did otherwise. There was, of course, little criticism when Jayasuriya and Kaluwitharana, Sri Lanka's audacious openers, both holed out at third man in the very first over. Asanka Gurusinha did not last long either; but Aravinda de Silva threw caution to the winds and adhered to the predetermined tactics of going for shots in the early overs, when fielding restrictions applied. Prasad suffered, giving away 22 off his first two overs. Indeed, when de Silva was bowled in the 15th over, he had accumulated 66, studded with 14 fours; and Sri Lanka had 85 on the board. Thereafter, Arjuna Ranatunga and Roshan Mahanama (who was later constrained by cramps) maintained a steady five-an-over run rate.

A target of 252 was by no means beyond India's reach. But Tendulkar was stumped and, seven balls later, Azharuddin was caught and bowled by Kumar Dharmasena. The estimated 100,000 spectators plunged into a shocked silence. Soon, this soundless atmosphere turned into a noisy and then disruptive outburst as seven Indian wickets tumbled for only 22 runs. Indian supporters in an enclosure adjacent to the pavilion hurled glass bottles on to the field and set seats ablaze. Match referee, Clive Lloyd, who probably had nightmares of the 1967 New Year's Day riot at the same ground, when he was a young member of the West Indies side under Sir Garry Sobers, at first ordered the teams off for 15 minutes, then attempted a resumption before declaring Sri Lanka winners by default.

The difference between 1967 and now was that the earlier unrest was caused by blatant overselling of tickets by corrupt elements in the Cricket Association of Bengal, while this time it occurred because the complexion of the crowd at the Eden Gardens had changed drastically in the 1990s as compared to previous decades. Whereas in the past generally people acquainted with cricket attended international matches at the Eden Gardens, following the craze for one-day cricket triggered by India's victory in the 1983 World Cup, the spectators now were mainly those who could muscle their way into the ground with money power. This transformation, unfortunately, translated into little knowledge about the game and, worse, a tendency to illegally gamble on the sport – the centre of this unlicensed activity being a locality in the city called Burrabazar (or big market).

Lloyd's was a fair interpretation, as India required a Herculean 132 runs from 15.5 overs, although the BCCI would have preferred the match to be awarded to Sri Lanka on the basis of their better run rate. He rightly deemed it was impossible for play to continue after Aashish Kapoor's exit to a running catch in the deep by de Silva. Jayasuriya compensated his batting failure by capturing three for 12 in seven overs in addition to taking two catches and executing a run-out.

Bizarrely, the presentation ceremony proceeded amidst smoking stands. Post-match interviews were carried out in the same atmosphere. This was rather in tune with India's stoic response to trouble, but an unnerving sight for folks from outside the subcontinent, whether at the ground or watching on TV.

Sri Lanka had recovered splendidly after an awkward start. But the riot hogged the headlines. Indian cricket officials – and genuine cricket lovers in Kolkata – squirmed in embarrassment. However, others were angry over the failure of their players; and captain Azhar had to be given armed security at his Hyderabad residence.

Toss: India
Umpires: RS Dunne (NZ) and CJ Mitchley (SA)
TV Umpire: Mahboob Shah (Pak)
Referee: CH Lloyd (WI)
Man of the Match: PA de Silva

Sri Lanka innings (50 overs maximum)			*R*	*B*
ST Jayasuriya	c Prasad	b Srinath	1	3
+RS Kaluwitharana	c Manjrekar	b Srinath	0	1
AP Gurusinha	c Kumble	b Srinath	1	16
PA de Silva		b Kumble	66	47
RS Mahanama	retired hurt		58	101
*A Ranatunga	lbw	b Tendulkar	35	42
HP Tillakaratne	c Tendulkar	b Prasad	32	43
HDPK Dharmasena		b Tendulkar	9	20
WPUJC Vaas	run out (Azharuddin)		23	16
GP Wickramasinghe	not out		4	9
M Muralitharan	not out		5	4

Extras: (b 1, lb 10, w 4, nb 2) 17
Total: (8 wickets, 50 overs) 251

FoW: 1-1 (Kaluwitharana), 2-1 (Jayasuriya), 3-35 (Gurusinha),
4-85 (de Silva), 5-168 (Ranatunga), 6-206 (Dharmasena),
7-236 (Tillakaratne), 8-244 (Vaas).

Bowling	O	M	R	W
Srinath	7	1	34	3
Kumble	10	0	51	1 (1w)
Prasad	8	0	50	1 (2nb, 2w)
Kapoor	10	0	40	0
Jadeja	5	0	31	0
Tendulkar	10	1	34	2 (1w)

India innings (target: 252 runs from 50 overs)			R	B
SR Tendulkar	st Kaluwitharana	b Jayasuriya	65	88
NS Sidhu	c Jayasuriya	b Vaas	3	8
SV Manjrekar		b Jayasuriya	25	48
*M Azharuddin	c & b Dharmasena		0	6
VG Kambli	not out		10	29
J Srinath	run out		6	6
A Jadeja		b Jayasuriya	0	1
+NR Mongia	c Jayasuriya	b de Silva	1	8
AR Kapoor	c de Silva	b Muralitharan	0	1
A Kumble	not out		0	0

Extras: (lb 5, w 5) 10
Total: (8 wickets, 34.1 overs) 120

DNB: BKV Prasad.

FoW: 1-8 (Sidhu), 2-98 (Tendulkar), 3-99 (Azharuddin),
4-101 (Manjrekar), 5-110 (Srinath), 6-115 (Jadeja),
7-120 (Mongia), 8-120 (Kapoor).

Bowling	O	M	R	W
Wickramasinghe	5	0	24	0 (2w)
Vaas	6	1	23	1
Muralitharan	7.1	0	29	1 (1w)
Dharmasena	7	0	24	1
Jayasuriya	7	1	12	3 (1w)
de Silva	2	0	3	1 (1w)

This was Siddhu's last World Cup appearance for India. A few months later, he walked out of a tour of England, reportedly, as a result of leg pulling by Azharuddin, and went into retirement. Said to be a loner as a cricketer, he recoined himself as a talkative TV personality and wit. His comic yet creative use of language, including English, was a concealed talent he has now revealed. He has also remained in the limelight by getting elected to the Indian Parliament from the city of the Sikhs' Golden Temple, Amritsar. In November 2006, though, he was convicted of manslaughter relating to an incident in 1989, which could irreparably damage his reputation.

Semi-final, 14 March: Punjab Cricket Association Stadium, Mohali

At this splendid facility on the outskirts of Chandigarh, Punjab and Haryana's common capital and a city planned by a French architect, Le Corbusier, the match appeared to be over when Australia after 40 minutes were 15 for four on a pitch with a lining of grass on it. It seemed like the worst decision in the tournament by a captain after winning the toss. Ambrose and Bishop had blasted out both Waughs, Ricky Ponting and Taylor for a total of four runs. But hereafter it was runs not ruins, as Stuart Law and Michael Bevan at first defended steadfastly and then ventured into shots to realize 138 in 32 overs. This endeavour boosted the score past 200, which seemed unreachable after the initial rout.

But even after Warne removed Courtney Browne with his first ball, the target looked well within the West Indies' grasp. Indeed, they were 165 for two, requiring a mere 41 from the last nine. Lara had departed but Shivnarine Chanderpaul appeared to be closing in on a century and Richie Richardson on a-happier-than-envisaged ending to his captaincy. However, as soon as the Guyanese left-hander – hamstrung by cramps – left, amazing panic set in. Stroke players Roger Harper and Ottis Gibson were sent in to finish the job, but their short-lived stays only augmented the pressure. Jimmy Adams and Keith Arthurton soon fell. Australia were now in the reckoning for the first time, and they strengthened their hold when Warne took three for six off his next three overs. Richardson, though, was still unbeaten and the one to face Fleming as he started the final over. He despatched the first ball for four, so West Indies needed six from five deliveries, with two wickets in hand. But he then set off for a thoughtless single, which not only ran out Ambrose, but also gave the strike to Walsh, who attempting a cross-batted heave was bowled. The last eight wickets, thus, subsided for a motley 29 runs, and the West Indies snatched an exceptional defeat from the jaws of victory. In contrast, Taylor had marvellously kept his cool. He later generously admitted West Indies had won 95 per cent of the match.

Toss: Australia
Umpires: BC Cooray (SL) and S Venkataraghavan (Ind)
TV Umpire: Khizer Hayat (Pak).
Referee: JR Reid (NZ)
Man of the Match: SK Warne

Australia innings (50 overs maximum)			R	B
ME Waugh	lbw	b Ambrose	0	2
*MA Taylor		b Bishop	1	11
RT Ponting	lbw	b Ambrose	0	15
SR Waugh		b Bishop	3	18
SG Law	run out		72	105
MG Bevan	c Richardson	b Harper	69	110
+IA Healy	run out		31	28
PR Reiffel	run out		7	11
SK Warne	not out		6	6

Extras: (lb 11, w 5, nb 2) 18
Total: (8 wickets, 50 overs) 207

DNB: DW Fleming, GD McGrath.

FoW: 1-0 (ME Waugh), 2-7 (Taylor), 3-8 (Ponting),
4-15 (SR Waugh), 5-153 (Law), 6-171 (Bevan),
7-186 (Reiffel), 8-207 (Healy).

Bowling	O	M	R	W
Ambrose	10	1	26	2 (3w)
Bishop	10	1	35	2 (3nb, 1w)
Walsh	10	1	33	0 (1nb)
Gibson	2	0	13	0 (1nb)
Harper	9	0	47	1
Adams	9	0	42	0 (1w)

West Indies innings (target: 208 runs from 50 overs)			R	B
S Chanderpaul	c Fleming	b McGrath	80	126
+CO Browne	c & b Warne		10	18
BC Lara		b SR Waugh	45	45
*RB Richardson	not out		49	83
RA Harper	lbw	b McGrath	2	5
OD Gibson	c Healy	b Warne	1	2
JC Adams	lbw	b Warne	2	11
KLT Arthurton	c Healy	b Fleming	0	4
IR Bishop	lbw	b Warne	3	3
CEL Ambrose	run out		2	2
CA Walsh	b Fleming		0	1

Extras: (lb 4, w 2, nb 2) 8
Total: (all out, 49.3 overs) 202

FoW: 1-25 (Browne), 2-93 (Lara), 3-165 (Chanderpaul),
4-173 (Harper), 5-178 (Gibson), 6-183 (Adams),
7-187 (Arthurton), 8-194 (Bishop), 9-202 (Ambrose),
10-202 (Walsh).

Bowling	O	M	R	W
McGrath	10	2	30	2 (1nb)
Fleming	8.3	0	48	2 (1w)
Warne	9	0	36	4 (1w)
ME Waugh	4	0	16	0
SR Waugh	7	0	30	1
Reiffel	5	0	13	0 (2nb)
Bevan	4	1	12	0
Law	2	0	13	0

Final, 17 March: Gaddafi Stadium, Lahore (Day/Night)

The province of Punjab was vivisected at the time of the partition of British-ruled India into today's India and Pakistan. The state, therefore, falls on both sides of the border between the two countries, with the bigger slice and the capital of the pre-demarcated region – Lahore, the pride of Punjabis – falling under Pakistani jurisdiction.

It was the first day/night international to be played in Pakistan. Conditions in this northern part of the country were cool and there was hardly any sunlight, following overnight storms. The dampness notwithstanding, the Australians would have batted first. But Ranatunga's decision to field was made in quest of some early wickets from his seamers. He also backed his batsmen to chase down a target rather than set one.

But the show didn't quite go according to plan. The hitherto accurate Chaminda Vaas pitched too short, although the Sri Lankan quicks did succeed in removing the dangerous Mark Waugh, who flicked a half-volley to square-leg. Not that this made a vast difference, for Taylor and Ponting carried the score to 137 by the 27th over, before the captain mistimed a sweep and his partner missed a cut. De Silva, the successful bowler, in fact, produced five overs of off-spin for two wickets, conceding only 19 runs.

This paved the way for newcomers to the crease to be exposed to a quartet of spinners, who increasingly made the ball bite off the track. Such bowling discomfited the incoming batsmen to the extent of making them struggle. They were hard put to pierce the in-field, let alone sound the boundary boards. Where Taylor had struck eight fours and a six, his colleagues managed only five fours between them and not one such stroke materialized from the 24th to the 49th over, other than Law pulling a six. The balance, therefore, shifted quite dramatically and only 178 runs were registered by the 40th over, not to mention the loss of five wickets. The wily Ranatunga had, thus, implacably tightened his grip over the match.

The gritty Australians fought back, though, by taking two early wickets. By the sixth over, Jayasuriya had been run out and Kaluwitharana had spooned a pull to square-leg. Law, then, spilled Gurusinha at deep mid-wicket when he was 53 and three half-chances also went down. The evening dew also made it harder for the spinners, Warne and Mark Waugh, to grip the ball.

Gurusinha rubbed salt into the wound by hitting Warne for four to long-on and six over long-off from successive deliveries. Such activity engineered acceleration at both ends, as de Silva settled in with characteristic elan. After Gurusinha departed to an indiscreet slog, the portly right-hander retreated to taking singles and only punishing the bad ball so as to enable the new man, Ranatunga, to get his eye in. Once this was accomplished, they took a dozen off a Mark Waugh over. Sri Lanka needed 51 from the last ten overs, after the required rate had risen to almost a run a ball. This figure became a mere ten off five as de Silva completed a masterly hundred – only the third three-figure knock in a World Cup final (after Clive Lloyd in 1975 and Viv Richards in 1979) – and signed off with 107, which included 13 meticulous fours.

Australia had run out of answers in their third searching encounter in a week. And a side batting second had won for the first time in six World Cup finals. Sri Lanka had controlled the match almost throughout. Their batting was more adept at handling spin; their spinners froze the opposition after the medium pacers had conceded 72 runs in the first 13 overs; and their catching and fielding were faultless. Only in the pace department did the Aussies have an edge.

Toss: Sri Lanka
Umpires: SA Bucknor (WI) and DR Shepherd (Eng)
TV Umpire: CJ Mitchley (SA).
Referee: CH Lloyd (WI)
Man of the Match: PA de Silva
Man of the Series: ST Jayasuriya

Australia innings (50 overs maximum)			R	B
*MA Taylor	c Jayasuriya	b de Silva	74	83
ME Waugh	c Jayasuriya	b Vaas	12	15
RT Ponting		b de Silva	45	73
SR Waugh	c de Silva	b Dharmasena	13	25
SK Warne	st Kaluwitharana	b Muralitharan	2	5
SG Law	c de Silva	b Jayasuriya	22	30
MG Bevan	not out		36	49
+IA Healy		b de Silva	2	3
PR Reiffel	not out		13	18

Extras: (lb 10, w 11, nb 1) 22
Total: (7 wickets, 50 overs) 241

DNB: DW Fleming, GD McGrath.

FoW: 1-36 (ME Waugh), 2-137 (Taylor), 3-152 (Ponting),
4-156 (Warne), 5-170 (SR Waugh), 6-202 (Law),
7-205 (Healy).

Bowling	O	M	R	W
Wickramasinghe	7	0	38	0 (2w)
Vaas	6	1	30	1
Muralitharan	10	0	31	1 (1w)
Dharmasena	10	0	47	1 (1nb)
Jayasuriya	8	0	43	1 (5w)
de Silva	9	0	42	3 (3w)

Sri Lanka innings (target: 242 runs from 50 overs)			R	B
ST Jayasuriya	run out		9	7
+RS Kaluwitharana	c Bevan	b Fleming	6	13
AP Gurusinha		b Reiffel	65	99
PA de Silva	not out		107	124
*A Ranatunga	not out		47	37

Extras: (b 1, lb 4, w 5, nb 1) 11
Total: (3 wickets, 46.2 overs) 245

DNB: HP Tillakaratne, RS Mahanama, HDPK Dharmasena, WPUJC Vaas, GP Wickramasinghe, M Muralitharan.

FoW: 1-12 (Jayasuriya), 2-23 (Kaluwitharana), 3-148 (Gurusinha).

Bowling	O	M	R	W
McGrath	8.2	1	28	0
Fleming	6	0	43	1 (4w)
Warne	10	0	58	0 (1nb, 1w)
Reiffel	10	0	49	1
ME Waugh	6	0	35	0
SR Waugh	3	0	15	0 (1nb)
Bevan	3	0	12	0

The rain returned as soon as Prime Minister Benazir Bhutto presented the Wills World Cup to Ranatunga, playing his fourth World Cup. The crowd sympathy lay with Sri Lanka; but there were no hard feelings towards the Australians over their reservations about Saleem Malik, earlier suspected of taking bribes. A well-organized climax was watched by a stadium bursting at the seams, although the official capacity was no more than 23,826.

Earlier, England's outdated strategies and comparative neglect of the only limited-overs event of consequence were caught out instantly. They won only two games in the competition, both against non-test-playing opposition, and one of those, against Holland, by an uncomfortably narrow margin. The damage caused by manager Raymond Illingworth's stubbornness became obvious as their disastrous campaign continued. England had pioneered one-day cricket; now, others had noticeably left them straggling, developing creative ways of combating the defensive options of fielding sides.

The adoption of pinch-hitters to take advantage of the first 15 overs, when fielding restrictions applied, was one such. The better batting wickets of the subcontinent lent themselves to such innovation. Sri Lanka, through their bombardiers, Jayasuriya – later to be heralded the Most Valued Player of the Tournament – and Kaluwitharana, took over from where Mark Greatbatch of New Zealand had left off in 1992. As the outcome proved, none other did it better.

As a sidelight, Taylor's sportsmanship, in refusing to claim a slip catch at a pivotal stage against the West Indies, was laudatory. The brilliant batting of Mark Waugh and Tendulkar also made a big impression. Besides, the catch by Kenya's beefy, bespectacled and none-too-nimble wicket-keeper, Tariq Iqbal, to dismiss Lara testified a spirit that took Kenya to victory by 73 runs; here was one of the greatest upsets the World Cup has known and, perhaps, a bad portent for West Indian cricket. For their part, Kenyans played their cricket without inhibition.

Toss: West Indies
Umpires: Khizer Hayat (Pak) and VK Ramaswamy
TV Umpire: SK Bansal
Referee: MAK Pataudi
Man of the Match: MO Odumbe

Kenya innings (50 overs maximum)			*R*	*B*
DN Chudasama	c Lara	b Walsh	8	7
+IT Iqbal	c Cuffy	b Walsh	16	32
KO Otieno	c Adams	b Walsh	2	5
SO Tikolo	c Adams	b Harper	29	50
*MO Odumbe	hit wicket	b Bishop	6	30
HS Modi	c Adams	b Ambrose	26	74
MA Suji	c Lara	b Harper	0	4
TM Odoyo	st Adams	b Harper	24	59
EO Odumbe		b Cuffy	1	4
AY Karim	c Adams	b Ambrose	11	27
RW Ali	not out		6	19

Extras: (lb 10, w 14, nb 13) 37
Total: (all out, 49.3 overs) 166

FoW: 1-15 (Chudasama), 2-19 (Otieno), 3-45 (Iqbal),
4-72 (MO Odumbe), 5-77 (Tikolo), 6-81 (Suji),
7-125 (Odoyo), 8-126 (EO Odumbe), 9-155 (Modi),
10-166 (Karim).

Bowling	O	M	R	W
Ambrose	8.3	1	21	2 (5w)
Walsh	9	0	46	3 (6nb, 3w)
Bishop	10	2	30	1 (2nb, 1w)
Cuffy	8	0	31	1 (7nb, 5w)
Harper	10	4	15	3
Arthurton	4	0	13	0

West Indies innings (target: 167 runs from 50 overs)			R	B
SL Campbell		b Suji	4	12
*RB Richardson		b Ali	5	11
BC Lara	c Iqbal	b Ali	8	11
S Chanderpaul	c Tikolo	b MO Odumbe	19	48
KLT Arthurton	run out		0	6
+JC Adams	c Modi	b MO Odumbe	9	37
RA Harper	c Iqbal	b MO Odumbe	17	18
IR Bishop	not out		6	42
CEL Ambrose	run out		3	13
CA Walsh	c Chudasama	b Karim	4	8
CE Cuffy		b Ali	1	8

Extras: (b 5, lb 6, w 4, nb 2) 17
Total: (all out, 35.2 overs) 93

FoW: 1-18 (Richardson), 2-22 (Campbell), 3-33 (Lara),
4-35 (Arthurton), 5-55 (Chanderpaul), 6-65 (Adams),
7-78 (Harper), 8-81 (Ambrose), 9-89 (Walsh), 10-93 (Cuffy).

Bowling	O	M	R	W
Suji	7	2	16	1
Ali	7.2	2	17	3
Karim	8	1	19	1
MO Odumbe	10	3	15	3
Odoyo	3	0	15	0

Defeat, however, acted as a tonic and the West Indies rallied to reach the last eight – lifted by 93 not out from their beleaguered captain, Richie Richardson, against Australia at the league stage and then proceeded to get the better of South Africa in the quarter final. The South Africans had, in fact, played impressive cricket prior to this fixture.

The tournament achieved one aim, that of increasing the profile of cricket through television coverage on a technically impressive but slightly uncritical scale. It also generated unprecedented income, much to the satisfaction of the organizers and the participating boards. But, perhaps, the most lingering memory of this World Cup was the unbridled joy of its unsuspected winners, Sri Lanka.

THE 1999 WORLD CUP

In the intervening period between the 1996 and 1999 World Cups, India's capital, New Delhi, had turned into a terminus, with governments arriving and departing with an unsettling frequency. A fourth such administration since the one headed by Narasimha Rao lost the general elections in 1996, a disparate coalition with Atal Bihari Vajpayee of the pro-Hindu Bharatiya Janata Party as prime minister, was now in charge. But reiterating India's diversity and pluralism, a Muslim, Mohammed Azharuddin, continued at the helm of the Indian cricket team.

The aberration created by the 1992 World Cup in Australia being held five and not four years after the previous competition was corrected in 1999, when the event, returning to England after 16 years, took place three, not four years after the previous one and, thereby, the tournament was restored to a quadrennial framework based on its inception in 1975.

For this latest edition, the England and Wales Cricket Board (ECB) divided the 12 participants into two groups, with the top three in each group qualifying for the Super Six and retaining the points they had obtained from the two teams that had also gone through from their group. They then met the qualifying teams from the other group, with the top four on points entering the semi-finals.

The format was complicated, and it backfired. On the face of it, ties on points were to be resolved by the result of the match between the teams involved. However, there were three-way ties in both qualifying groups; and New Zealand and Zimbabwe, fourth and fifth in the Super Six, had shared the one washed-out game of the entire tournament. To resolve dead heats one had to fall back on net run rate, which meant a reliance on calculators rather than cricket.

So, the tournament revolved around technical knockouts; and even a semi-final, which ended in a tie, was decided on net run rate in the Super Six stage. Earlier, Zimbabwe had topped their group to make it to the Super Six, having beaten the teams that went through with them, but lost to the two that were eliminated. Such complexities rather befuddled followers of the tournament and converted a potentially exciting encounter – Australia versus the West Indies – into a ludicrous affair, as both teams attempted to manipulate the system to their advantage.

The net run rate clause denied the West Indies a place in the last six. The West Indians would have gone through if they had won more quickly against Bangladesh, whereas England's demise was due to a lack of vigilance about the pitfalls their own officials had created. The England dream was that the World Cup would reignite affection for cricket in the hearts of their youngsters, who had got disillusioned as a result of losing the Ashes series – still incongruously (because what matters today is the ICC Test Championship and not any specific bilateral contest) all-important in the English psyche – six times running.

Administratively, the 1999 World Cup looked doomed from the start. The ECB had rejected the hitherto accepted concept of a sole sponsor and wanted eight commercial partners, who would be entitled to utilizing all prime advertising space. To their dismay, they got commitments from only four, two of whom (NatWest and Vodafone) were already firm sponsors of English cricket; the others were Pepsi and Emirates Airlines, the latter paying half in the form of air passages rather than cash.

The tournament got underway in mid-May, generally too early for international cricket in England. Indeed, a drizzle spoilt the opening ceremony. As it is, a grand, Olympic-style unveiling was eschewed; only a modest fireworks display was in evidence.

15 May: Hove

The setting and the 6000 spectators created a fairground atmosphere at the dwelling of Sussex County Cricket Club. But this ambience and a fitting finish were darkened by the unethical conduct – certainly against the spirit of the game – of the South Africans. Hansie Cronje and Allan Donald were wired up with earphones in a three-way live radio link with coach, Bob Woolmer, who, sitting in the dressing room with the benefit of TV close-ups and without the pressure of having to think on his feet, was happily rendering advice. With sticking plaster over the earpieces, the captain and premier pace bowler had even attempted to camouflage the instruments (and perhaps also to prevent them from falling off). Such subterfuge prevailed for an hour before referee, Talat Ali, scrutinizing the TV pictures, put a stop to the nonsense. It was baffling that India did not lodge a serious protest. It was also pathetic that the ICC took no meaningful action against South Africa. They merely meekly proscribed the practice for the rest of the tournament.

While much has strenuously been argued to the contrary, the incident bespoke a lacuna in Cronje, not that the other two were any less innocent. It was, therefore, unsurprising he got involved in match fixing. Credit for identifying such involvement goes to Delhi's police. As K. K. Paul, the detective (and later police commissioner) who unearthed the conspiracy, revealed to me, this was by accident, as they were intercepting phone calls for a different purpose when they stumbled on a clinching conversation between Cronje and an illegal bookmaker.

Where others may have escaped the net in a murky phase in world cricket, thanks to strict officers like Paul, Cronje did not. Other countries pontificated aplenty on the subject of corruption, but most of them failed to deliver up to expectations.

India, batting first, lost Sachin Tendulkar during the remote conferencing – not that this element was necessarily to blame for the exit. The little master had promised much only to disappoint. But Saurav Ganguly and Rahul Dravid persevered to realize 130 between them. The former, playing in his 100th one-day international, was in good touch. The duo, however, failed to drive home their dominance in the face of a characteristically confining Donald. The Kolkata left-hander took the high risk of testing Jonty Rhodes' arm.

Mysorean Javagal Srinath, genuinely fast, removed Gary Kirsten and Herschelle Gibbs early. But an unruffled Jacques Kallis steered his side to within 27 runs of victory, with 26 balls to come. After he was run out by Venkatesh Prasad, Lance Klusener bludgeoned his first three deliveries for four. The rest was easy. As the fielders headed back to the pavilion, a spectator got too close to Azhar and Dravid for comfort. This prompted the Indian captain to call for greater security.

Toss: India
Umpires: SA Bucknor (WI) and DR Shepherd
TV Umpire: ID Robinson (Zim)
Referee: Talat Ali (Pak)
Man of the Match: JH Kallis

India innings (50 overs maximum)			R	B
SC Ganguly	run out (Rhodes/Kallis)		97	142
SR Tendulkar	c Boucher	b Klusener	28	46
R Dravid		b Klusener	54	75
*M Azharuddin	c Boje	b Klusener	24	24
A Jadeja	c Kirsten	b Donald	16	14
RR Singh	not out		4	3
+NR Mongia	not out		5	2

Extras: (b 6, lb 2, w 11, nb 6) 25
Total: (5 wickets, 50 overs) 253

DNB: AB Agarkar, J Srinath, A Kumble, BKV Prasad.

FoW: 1-67 (Tendulkar, 15.3 ov), 2-197 (Dravid, 41.4 ov), 3-204 (Ganguly, 43.4 ov), 4-235 (Jadeja, 48.2 ov), 5-247 (Azharuddin, 49.3 ov).

Bowling	O	M	R	W
Pollock	10	0	47	0 (4nb)
Kallis	10	1	43	0 (2w)
Donald	10	0	34	1 (2w)
Klusener	10	0	66	3 (2nb, 2w)
Boje	5	0	31	0 (1w)
Cronje	5	0	24	0

South Africa innings (target: 254 runs from 50 overs)			R	B
G Kirsten		b Srinath	3	22
HH Gibbs	lbw	b Srinath	7	8
+MV Boucher		b Kumble	34	36
JH Kallis	run out (Prasad/Srinath)		96	128
DJ Cullinan	c Singh	b Ganguly	19	35
*WJ Cronje	c Jadeja	b Agarkar	27	30
JN Rhodes	not out		39	31
L Klusener	not out		12	4

Extras: (lb 4, w 3, nb 10) 17
Total: (6 wickets, 47.2 overs) 254

DNB: SM Pollock, N Boje, AA Donald.

FoW: 1-13 (Gibbs, 2.4 ov), 2-22 (Kirsten, 6.5 ov),
3-68 (Boucher, 13.6 ov), 4-116 (Cullinan, 25.4 ov),
5-180 (Cronje, 38.4 ov), 6-227 (Kallis, 45.4 ov).

Bowling	O	M	R	W
Srinath	10	0	69	2 (4nb, 1w)
Prasad	8.2	0	32	0 (1w)
Kumble	10	0	44	1 (1w)
Agarkar	9	0	57	1 (5nb)
Singh	2	0	10	0
Ganguly	4	0	16	1 (1nb)
Tendulkar	4	0	22	0

19 May: Leicester

Four thousand excited fans watched the closest contest of the tournament up to this point. India won the toss and invited Zimbabwe to bat. But other than when Andy Flower and Alistair Campbell were at the crease, the Zimbabweans failed to make sufficiently brisk progress. Undisciplined Indian bowling, though, gifted 51 extras, a fifth of the total. Consequently, the over rate was also so badly affected that four overs were deducted when India batted. Zimbabwe were no great shakes either on this front: they permitted 39 sundries, which created a World Cup record for a match, but one which was to survive only for a day. Nayan Mongia, though, with five dismissals, equalled the ODI record for a wicketkeeper, held by among others his compatriot Syed Kirmani.

India started smoothly, rattling up 44 in the seventh over before Dravid departed. Left-handed Sadagopan Ramesh, replacing Tendulkar who had flown back to Mumbai to attend his father's funeral, and Ajay Jadeja added 99 before Ramesh skied to mid-on. The middle order kept up the pace. Srinath, then, produced two massive sixes, and India needed only nine runs from two overs. Henry Olonga was reintroduced. He had been quite wayward in his previous spell, which cost 17 runs in three overs. Now, Robin Singh holed out to cover off his second ball, Srinath was yorked by his fifth and Prasad was lbw to the last. Zimbabwe had triumphed by three runs. They had played two matches and won as many; whereas India had lost both their outings.

Toss: India
Umpires: DL Orchard (SA) and P Willey
TV Umpire: DB Hair (Aus)
Referee: CW Smith (WI)
Man of the Match: GW Flower

Zimbabwe innings (50 overs maximum)			R	B
NC Johnson	c Mongia	b Srinath	7	10
GW Flower	c Mongia	b Jadeja	45	89
PA Strang		b Agarkar	18	26
MW Goodwin	c Singh	b Ganguly	17	40
+A Flower	not out		68	85
*ADR Campbell	st Mongia	b Kumble	24	29
GJ Whittall		b Kumble	4	8
SV Carlisle		b Srinath	1	2
HH Streak	c Mongia	b Prasad	14	18
EA Brandes	c Mongia	b Prasad	2	5
HK Olonga	not out		1	4

Extras: (lb 14, w 21, nb 16) 51
Total: (9 wickets, 50 overs) 252

FoW: 1-12 (Johnson, 2.4 ov), 2-45 (Strang, 9.5 ov),
3-87 (Goodwin, 21.2 ov), 4-144 (GW Flower, 31.1 ov),
5-204 (Campbell, 40.3 ov), 6-211 (Whittall, 42.4 ov),
7-214 (Carlisle, 43.2 ov), 8-244 (Streak, 47.6 ov),
9-250 (Brandes, 49.2 ov).

Bowling	O	M	R	W
Srinath	10	1	35	2 (5nb, 1w)
Prasad	10	1	37	2 (1nb, 4w)
Agarkar	9	0	70	1 (5nb, 4w)
Ganguly	5	0	22	1 (3nb, 1w)
Singh	2	0	11	0
Kumble	10	0	41	2 (1nb, 2w)
Jadeja	4	0	22	1 (3w)

India innings (target: 253 runs from 46 overs)			R	B
SC Ganguly	c Brandes	b Johnson	9	8
S Ramesh	c Goodwin	b GW Flower	55	77
R Dravid	c GW Flower	b Streak	13	14
*M Azharuddin	c Campbell	b Streak	7	11
A Jadeja	lbw	b Streak	43	76
RR Singh	c Campbell	b Olonga	35	47
AB Agarkar	run out (Goodwin)		1	5
+NR Mongia		b Whittall	28	24
J Srinath		b Olonga	18	12
A Kumble	not out		1	1
BKV Prasad	lbw	b Olonga	0	1

Extras: (b 1, lb 4, w 24, nb 10) 39
Total: (all out, 45 overs) 249

FoW: 1-13 (Ganguly, 1.5 ov), 2-44 (Dravid, 6.4 ov),
3-56 (Azharuddin, 8.6 ov), 4-155 (Ramesh, 27.5 ov),
5-174 (Jadeja, 32.2 ov), 6-175 (Agarkar, 33.2 ov),
7-219 (Mongia, 40.5 ov), 8-246 (Singh, 44.2 ov),
9-249 (Srinath, 44.5 ov), 10-249 (Prasad, 44.6 ov).

Bowling	O	M	R	W
Brandes	3	0	27	0 (3w)
Johnson	7	0	51	1 (5nb, 1w)
Streak	9	0	36	3 (1nb, 7w)
Olonga	4	0	22	3 (6w)
Whittall	4	0	26	1 (2w)
Strang	8	0	49	0
GW Flower	10	0	33	1 (1w)

23 May: Bristol

Kenya sought to improve their chances by putting India in. Indeed, the game was still in the balance with India on 92 for two. But at this point, Tendulkar, back from his father's cremation the day before, entered the fray. An 8500 crowd at this headquarters of Gloucestershire County Cricket Club thunderously greeted his advent. In an emotionally charged ambience, he responded with a resounding display. He began cautiously, but soon stepped on the pedal to acquire 50 off 54 balls and then 100 in 84. He went on to clip the last ball of the innings for six over mid-wicket – his third over-boundary in addition to 16 fours. Ultimately, his 140 came off only 101 balls. It was the first of his 22 ODI hundreds not as an opener, and a fairytale return after his personal tragedy. It went unnoticed that at the other end, Dravid, too, produced a sublime century and the pair added a World Cup record-breaking 237 in 29 overs. This partnership surpassed the 207 by the Waugh brothers, also against Kenya in 1996.

Kenya were possibly shell-shocked by the Tendulkar-led assault. Their first boundary did not materialize until the 10th over. Still, Steve Tikolo and Kennedy Otieno stitched together 118. Anil Kumble and Venkatesh Prasad were injured and missing from the Indian attack, but Debasis Mohanty, from Orissa, pronouncedly bending the ball both ways, compensated for their absence. The lasting memory, though, was of Tendulkar's ton. He dedicated his highest World Cup score to his late father. After two defeats, it revived India's hopes of making the cut for the Super Six. India won by 94 runs.

Toss: Kenya
Umpires: DB Cowie (NZ) and ID Robinson (Zim)
TV Umpire: JW Holder
Referee: PJP Burge (Aus)
Man of the Match: SR Tendulkar

India innings (50 overs maximum)			*R*	*B*
S Ramesh	run out (Tikolo)		44	66
SC Ganguly	lbw	b Suji	13	26
R Dravid	not out		104	109
SR Tendulkar	not out		140	101

Extras: (lb 5, w 21, nb 2) 28
Total: (2 wickets, 50 overs) 329

DNB: *M Azharuddin, A Jadeja, +NR Mongia, N Chopra, AB Agarkar, J Srinath, DS Mohanty.

FoW: 1-50 (Ganguly, 10.4 ov), 2-92 (Ramesh, 20.5 ov).

Bowling	O	M	R	W
Suji	10	2	26	1 (3w)
Angara	7	0	66	0 (1nb, 6w)
Odoyo	9	0	59	0 (1nb, 2w)
Tikolo	9	1	62	0 (2w)
Karim	7	0	52	0 (5w)
Odumbe	8	0	59	0

Kenya innings (target: 330 runs from 50 overs)			R	B
+KO Otieno	c Agarkar	b Chopra	56	82
RD Shah	c sub (RR Singh)	b Mohanty	9	29
SK Gupta	lbw	b Mohanty	0	1
SO Tikolo	lbw	b Mohanty	58	75
MO Odumbe	c sub (RR Singh)	b Mohanty	14	28
TM Odoyo		b Agarkar	39	55
*AY Karim		b Srinath	8	15
AV Vadher	not out		6	13
MA Suji	not out		1	4

Extras: (lb 10, w 31, nb 3) 44
Total: (7 wickets, 50 overs) 235

DNB: HS Modi, JO Angara.

FoW: 1-29 (Shah, 11.1 ov), 2-29 (Gupta, 11.2 ov), 3-147 (Otieno, 27.6 ov), 4-165 (Tikolo, 32.3 ov), 5-193 (Odumbe, 40.2 ov), 6-209 (Karim, 44.4 ov), 7-233 (Odoyo, 49.1 ov).

Bowling	O	M	R	W
Srinath	10	3	31	1 (4w)
Agarkar	10	0	35	1 (1nb, 7w)
Mohanty	10	0	56	4 (1nb)
Ganguly	9	0	47	0 (1nb, 3w)
Chopra	10	2	33	1 (2w)
Tendulkar	1	0	23	0 (2w)

26 May: Taunton

Nearly 7000 assembled at this old-fashioned west country ground (made famous by Ian Botham, Vivian Richards and Joel Garner), home of Somerset County Cricket Club. Arjuna Ranatunga won the toss and sent India in, possibly anticipating some assistance for his quicker bowlers. When Chaminda Vaas cut one back to dislodge Ramesh's off-stump, it seemed he may have got it right. But the wicket was of consistent bounce and the straight boundaries relatively short. Consequently, Ganguly and Dravid dished out an exotic exhibition to establish a clutch of ODI records. Their staggering stand of 318 in 45 overs was the highest in any ODI, eclipsing the previous record of 275 notched up by Azharuddin and Jadeja against Zimbabwe in 1997–98. Ganguly clobbered 183 off 158 balls, then the fourth-highest ODI score, with seven sixes and 16 fours, and second only to Gary Kirsten's 188 not out against the United Arab Emirates in the 1996 World Cup. India's 373 for six was the highest versus test opposition in the World Cup, although behind Sri Lanka's 398 for five against Kenya also in 1996. The left-hander–right-hander combination complemented each other perfectly. Ganguly, reminiscent of another Bengal left-hander, Ambar Roy, timed the ball beautifully; his century came off 119 deliveries. He then demonstrated what a good striker of the ball he was by collecting the rest of his runs in 39 balls. (Presumptuously nicknamed 'Maharaj', he has, by a section of his fellow Bengalis, been adoringly tagged with the epaulette of 'Prince' of his city of Kolkata after the respected former England opener, now commentator, Geoffrey Boycott referred to him as such. In an environment where his state of

West Bengal has produced few regular incumbents in the Indian side, his success has been a dizzying experience for such Bengalis, including much of Kolkata's overwhelmed media.) Dravid was business-like and completed practically a run-a-ball hundred – his second in successive matches. Even Muttiah Muralitharan was at his wits' end.

Sri Lanka reinstated Romesh Kaluwitharana as opener. But both he and Sanath Jayasuriya, great successes in 1996, were back in the dressing room within five overs. The game then petered out into an inevitable defeat for the Sri Lankans. And with it, dissipated their hopes of retaining the title.

Toss: Sri Lanka
Umpires: RS Dunne (NZ) and DR Shepherd
TV Umpire: R Julian
Referee: CW Smith (WI)
Man of the Match: SC Ganguly

India innings (50 overs maximum)		*R*	*B*
S Ramesh	b Vaas	5	4
SC Ganguly	c sub (UDU Chandana) b Wickramasinghe	183	158
+R Dravid	run out (Muralitharan)	145	129
SR Tendulkar	b Jayasuriya	2	3
A Jadeja	c & b Wickramasinghe	5	4
RR Singh	c de Silva b Wickramasinghe	0	1
*M Azharuddin	not out	12	7
J Srinath	not out	0	0

Extras: (lb 3, w 12, nb 6) 21
Total: (6 wickets, 50 overs) 373

DNB: A Kumble, BKV Prasad, DS Mohanty.

FoW: 1-6 (Ramesh, 0.5 ov), 2-324 (Dravid, 45.4 ov),
3-344 (Tendulkar, 46.5 ov), 4-349 (Jadeja, 47.3 ov),
5-349 (Singh, 47.4 ov), 6-372 (Ganguly, 49.5 ov).

Bowling	O	M	R	W
Vaas	10	0	84	1 (3nb, 1w)
Upashantha	10	0	80	0 (3nb, 3w)
Wickramasinghe	10	0	65	3 (1w)
Muralitharan	10	0	60	0 (2w)
Jayawardene	3	0	21	0
Jayasuriya	3	0	37	1 (2w)
de Silva	4	0	23	0 (1w)

Sri Lanka innings (target: 374 runs from 50 overs)

			R	B
ST Jayasuriya	run out (Srinath)		3	7
+RS Kaluwitharana	lbw	b Srinath	7	15
MS Atapattu	lbw	b Mohanty	29	29
PA de Silva	lbw	b Singh	56	74
DPMD Jayawardene	lbw	b Kumble	4	5
*A Ranatunga		b Singh	42	57
RS Mahanama	run out (Tendulkar)		32	45
WPUJC Vaas	c Ramesh	b Singh	1	4
KEA Upashantha	c Azharuddin	b Singh	5	17
GP Wickramasinghe	not out		2	6
M Muralitharan	c Tendulkar	b Singh	4	3

Extras: (b 4, lb 12, w 8, nb 7) 31
Total: (all out, 42.3 overs) 216

FoW: 1-5 (Jayasuriya, 2.1 ov), 2-23 (Kaluwitharana, 4.3 ov),
3-74 (Atapattu, 14.2 ov), 4-79 (Jayawardene, 15.3 ov),
5-147 (de Silva, 28.1 ov), 6-181 (Ranatunga, 34.3 ov),
7-187 (Vaas, 36.4 ov), 8-203 (Upashantha, 40.6 ov),
9-204 (Mahanama, 41.3 ov), 10-216 (Muralitharan, 42.3 ov).

Bowling	O	M	R	W
Srinath	7	0	33	1 (1nb, 2w)
Prasad	8	0	41	0
Mohanty	5	0	31	1
Kumble	8	0	27	1 (2w)
Ganguly	5	0	37	0 (2nb, 1w)
Singh	9.3	0	31	5 (4nb, 2w)

29–30 May: Edgbaston, Birmingham

On a lovely, sunny morning, before a capacity 20,000 crowd, Alec Stewart won his fifth toss of the tournament and elected to field. The pitch was a slow seamer, and the English bowlers exploited it well by not allowing any liberties to the Indian batsmen. Ganguly was unfortunate to be run out when Dravid's straight drive touched bowler Mark Ealham's fingertips before hitting the non-striker's stumps. But this setback was offset by Tendulkar escaping a run-out and a catch before he eventually hit Ealham down mid-wicket's throat. In the circumstances, Dravid's 82-ball 53 was the highest score for the Indians.

An ominous cloud cover had come to preside over play when it was England's turn to bat. Such conditions were ideal for Mohanty's swing bowling. Stewart and Graeme Hick were both out to him off consecutive legal deliveries (as the one in between was a wide). Nasser Hussain then succumbed in deteriorating light, just before a torrential downpour halted play. England were 73 for three in 20.3 overs, with Graham Thorpe, quite the most skilful of the English batsmen, unbeaten on 36. The match resumed the next morning – the only group tie in the tournament to spill over into the reserve day. To England's disappointment – and English media unduly fretted over this decision – Thorpe was ruled leg before wicket by umpire Javed Akhtar. Neil Fairbrother tried to keep the score ticking, but without much support. England were, thus, eliminated in the preliminary stage of a World Cup for the first time; and, calamitously, this debacle had occurred at home.

England had arrived at Birmingham reasonably certain of a Super Six place. But Zimbabwe's giant killing of South Africa meant they had no alternative to beating India. When the weather was no longer a factor – on the second day – their batsmen crumbled to pressure. Also, contributing to the exit was their defeat at the hands of South Africa and the lackadaisical approach in their three victories. For young Andrew Flintoff, a conspicuous failure in the tournament, the final insult was having his bat nicked from the dressing room.

Toss: England
Umpires: DB Hair (Aus) and Javed Akhtar (Pak)
TV Umpire: DB Cowie (NZ)
Referee: PJP Burge (Aus)
Man of the Match: SC Ganguly
Close of play:
Day 1: India 232/8, England 73/3 (Thorpe 31*, Fairbrother 1*; 20.3 ov)

India innings (50 overs maximum)			R	B
SC Ganguly	run out (Ealham)		40	59
S Ramesh	c Hick	b Mullally	20	41
R Dravid	c Ealham	b Flintoff	53	82
SR Tendulkar	c Hick	b Ealham	22	40
*M Azharuddin	c Hussain	b Ealham	26	35
A Jadeja	c Fraser	b Gough	39	30
+NR Mongia		b Mullally	2	5
J Srinath		b Gough	1	2
A Kumble	not out		6	8
BKV Prasad	not out		2	3

Extras: (lb 7, w 10, nb 4) 21
Total: (8 wickets, 50 overs) 232

DNB: DS Mohanty.

FoW: 1-49 (Ramesh, 12.5 ov), 2-93 (Ganguly, 21.2 ov),
3-139 (Tendulkar, 33.3 ov), 4-174 (Dravid, 39.5 ov),
5-188 (Azharuddin, 43.5 ov), 6-209 (Mongia, 46.4 ov),
7-210 (Srinath, 47.1 ov), 8-228 (Jadeja, 49.1 ov).

Bowling	O	M	R	W
Gough	10	0	51	2 (2nb, 3w)
Fraser	10	2	30	0 (2w)
Mullally	10	0	54	2 (1nb, 4w)
Ealham	10	2	28	2 (1nb, 1w)
Flintoff	5	0	28	1
Hollioake	5	0	34	0

England innings (target: 233 runs from 50 overs)			R	B
N Hussain	b Ganguly		33	63
*+AJ Stewart	c Azharuddin	b Mohanty	2	9
GA Hick		b Mohanty	0	1
GP Thorpe	lbw	b Srinath	36	57
NH Fairbrother	c Mongia	b Ganguly	29	62
A Flintoff	lbw	b Kumble	15	21
AJ Hollioake	lbw	b Kumble	6	13
MA Ealham	c Azharuddin	b Ganguly	0	3
D Gough	c Kumble	b Prasad	19	25
ARC Fraser	not out		15	17
AD Mullally		b Srinath	0	2

Extras: (b 4, lb 4, w 5, nb 1) 14
Total: (all out, 45.2 overs) 169

FoW: 1-12 (Stewart, 3.1 ov), 2-13 (Hick, 3.2 ov),
3-72 (Hussain, 19.1 ov), 4-81 (Thorpe, 23.4 ov),
5-118 (Flintoff, 31.3 ov), 6-130 (Hollioake, 35.5 ov),
7-131 (Ealham, 36.5 ov), 8-132 (Fairbrother, 38.4 ov),
9-161 (Gough, 44.1 ov), 10-169 (Mullally, 45.2 ov).

Bowling	O	M	R	W
Srinath	8.2	3	25	2
Mohanty	10	0	54	2 (1nb, 5w)
Prasad	9	1	25	1
Ganguly	8	0	27	3
Kumble	10	1	30	2

Super Six, 4 June: The Oval, London

India invited Australia to bat, but an excellent team effort, spearheaded by Mark Waugh – who got 83 – set the Indians 283 to win, a target never achieved in a 50-over ODI in England.

Then, in four impeccable overs, McGrath emphatically ensured history would not be created. With remarkable accuracy and movement off the wicket, he constricted India to an unenviable 17 for four. He removed Tendulkar for a duck – a prized wicket since this Mumbai maestro had scored hundreds in his last three appearances against the Aussies – and the others just caved in. Jadeja and Robin Singh rallied to realize 141 for the fifth wicket, with the former posting three figures – so far the fifth in the competition, all by Indians. It was a brave but fruitless endeavour, for the result was never in doubt once McGrath had sliced through the top order. Twenty-one runs in Warne's 6th over, though, brought a cheer from the sizeable Indian supporters among the 18,000 attendees. Australia eventually won by 77 runs.

Both teams had made it to the Super Six without any points, or wins against other qualifiers, from their respective groups. The reverse for India, therefore, reduced their chances of advancing to the semi-finals. Interestingly, speculation about the suitability of the white ball in English conditions (used for one-day cricket, as opposed to the traditional red leather in test matches) increased after this match. The debate was generated by a proliferation of wides in the tournament, which insinuated difficulty on the part of bowlers to control the ball. Now, it was suggested that it was hard to keep track of in gloomy light.

Toss: India
Umpires: SA Bucknor (WI) and P Willey
TV Umpire: ID Robinson (Zim)
Referee: RS Madugalle (SL)
Man of the Match: GD McGrath

Australia innings (50 overs maximum)			R	B
ME Waugh	c Prasad	b Singh	83	99
+AC Gilchrist	c Mohanty	b Ganguly	31	52
RT Ponting		b Singh	23	36
DS Lehmann	run out (Jadeja)		26	33
*SR Waugh	c Kumble	b Mohanty	36	40
MG Bevan	c Mongia	b Prasad	22	27
TM Moody	not out		26	20
SK Warne	not out		0	0

Extras: (lb 14, w 10, nb 11) 35
Total: (6 wickets, 50 overs) 282

DNB: PR Reiffel, DW Fleming, GD McGrath.

FoW: 1-97 (Gilchrist, 20.1 ov), 2-157 (ME Waugh, 30.1 ov),
3-158 (Ponting, 30.4 ov), 4-218 (SR Waugh, 41.5 ov),
5-231 (Lehmann, 43.6 ov), 6-275 (Bevan, 49.3 ov).

Bowling	O	M	R	W
Srinath	10	2	34	0 (2nb, 4w)
Mohanty	7	0	47	1 (1nb, 1w)
Prasad	10	0	60	1 (1nb, 1w)
Kumble	10	0	49	0
Ganguly	5	0	31	1 (1nb, 1w)
Singh	7	0	43	2 (2nb, 3w)
Tendulkar	1	0	4	0

India innings (target: 283 runs from 50 overs)			R	B
SC Ganguly		b Fleming	8	12
SR Tendulkar	c Gilchrist	b McGrath	0	4
R Dravid	c Gilchrist	b McGrath	2	6
A Jadeja	not out		100	138
*M Azharuddin	c SR Waugh	b McGrath	3	9
RR Singh	c Reiffel	b Moody	75	94
+NR Mongia	run out (Bevan)		2	9
J Srinath	c Gilchrist	b SR Waugh	0	2
A Kumble	c Gilchrist	b SR Waugh	3	6
BKV Prasad	lbw	b Fleming	2	9
DS Mohanty	run out (Warne/Gilchrist)		0	3

Extras: (lb 3, w 4, nb 3) 10
Total: (all out, 48.2 overs) 205

FoW: 1-1 (Tendulkar, 0.6 ov), 2-10 (Dravid, 2.5 ov),
3-12 (Ganguly, 3.4 ov), 4-17 (Azharuddin, 6.2 ov),
5-158 (Singh, 37.3 ov), 6-181 (Mongia, 42.2 ov),
7-186 (Srinath, 42.6 ov), 8-192 (Kumble, 44.4 ov),
9-204 (Prasad, 47.4 ov), 10-205 (Mohanty, 48.2 ov).

Bowling	O	M	R	W
McGrath	10	1	34	3 (2nb, 1w)
Fleming	9	1	33	2 (1w)
Reiffel	10	1	30	0
Moody	10	0	41	1 (1w)
ME Waugh	1	0	7	0
Warne	6.2	0	49	0 (1w)
SR Waugh	2	0	8	2

Super Six, 8 June: Old Trafford, Manchester

With 22,000 animated spectators made up of Indians, Pakistanis and indigenous folks packing the stands on a sparkling day, India won the toss, but made heavy weather with the bat. Tendulkar touched off momentarily, and held the stage initially to cross 8000 ODI runs. But Dravid struggled to penetrate the gaps in the field and, therefore, got rather bogged down. However, skipper Azharuddin proficiently farmed the strike and, as the overs started to run out, rose to a crescendo. In the course of his innings, he added 60 in nine overs with Robin Singh.

The destination for Pakistan was 228; and the classy Saeed Anwar made light of this journey with a barrage of half-a-dozen fours. But the pacy Srinath started the rot before transferring the baton to Prasad, his Karnataka teammate. The latter, cutting the ball off the wicket as he was wont to, scalped Saleem Malik, Anwar himself, Moin Khan, who briefly threatened to take the game away from the Indians with his 34, Inzamam, uncharacteristically out of touch during his 30-over stay, and Wasim Akram, playing at his adopted home of Lancashire, caught on the square-leg boundary trying to force the pace. Prasad's figures of five for 27 were an authentic reflection of his incisiveness. He had rendered yeoman service to Indian cricket as a seamer; his leg-cutters being particularly effective. His compatriots on and off the field were ecstatic.

While widely acknowledged to be the better one-day side in the 1990s, Pakistan had, now, lost all three encounters with their arch-rivals in the World Cup – in 1992, 1996 and now. And Azhar and Tendulkar had been members of the Indian team in all such successes.

The clash between India and Pakistan, whose armies were then locked in combat in the freezing Himalayan heights of Kargil in Jammu and Kashmir state, had caused concern about the resulting tension spilling over to England. Security in and around the ground and in sensitive South Asian neighbourhoods elsewhere was, therefore, especially tight. But in the end, three arrests, nine ejections and one flag-burning (of the Indian tricolour) incident during a fracas between rival groups were less alarming than apprehended. Indeed, the lively behaviour of the fans – flag waving, whistle blowing and drum beating – introduced an almost unprecedented spectacle at a cricket match in England.

Toss: India
Umpires: SA Bucknor (WI) and DR Shepherd
TV Umpire: DB Hair (Aus)
Referee: R Subba Row
Man of the Match: BKV Prasad

India innings (50 overs maximum)			R	B
SR Tendulkar	c Saqlain Mushtaq	b Azhar Mahmood	45	65
S Ramesh		b Abdul Razzaq	20	31
R Dravid	c Shahid Afridi	b Wasim Akram	61	89
A Jadeja	c Inzamam-ul Haq	b Azhar Mahmood	6	14
*M Azharuddin	c Ijaz Ahmed	b Wasim Akram	59	77
RR Singh	c Wasim Akram	b Shoaib Akhtar	16	21
+NR Mongia	not out		6	4

Extras: (b 1, lb 3, w 8, nb 2) 14
Total: (6 wickets, 50 overs) 227

DNB: J Srinath, A Kumble, BKV Prasad, DS Mohanty.

FoW: 1-37 (Ramesh, 11.2 ov), 2-95 (Tendulkar, 20.5 ov),
3-107 (Jadeja, 24.3 ov), 4-158 (Dravid, 39.5 ov),
5-218 (Azharuddin, 48.5 ov), 6-227 (Singh, 49.6 ov).

Bowling	O	M	R	W
Wasim Akram	10	0	27	2 (1nb)
Shoaib Akhtar	10	0	54	1 (2w)
Abdul Razzaq	10	0	40	1 (4w)
Azhar Mahmood	10	0	35	2
Saqlain Mushtaq	10	0	67	0 (2w)

Pakistan innings *(target: 228 runs from 50 overs)*			R	B
Saeed Anwar	c Azharuddin	b Prasad	36	44
Shahid Afridi	c Kumble	b Srinath	6	5
Ijaz Ahmed	c Azharuddin	b Srinath	11	24
Saleem Malik	lbw	b Prasad	6	19
Inzamam-ul Haq	lbw	b Prasad	41	93
Azhar Mahmood	c Mongia	b Kumble	10	17
+Moin Khan	c Tendulkar	b Prasad	34	37
Abdul Razzaq		b Srinath	11	12
*Wasim Akram	c Kumble	b Prasad	12	16
Saqlain Mushtaq	lbw	b Kumble	0	4
Shoaib Akhtar	not out		0	3

Extras: (lb 11, w 2) 13
Total: (all out, 45.3 overs) 180

FoW: 1-19 (Shahid Afridi, 2.3 ov), 2-44 (Ijaz Ahmed, 9.4 ov),
3-52 (Saleem Malik, 13.5 ov), 4-65 (Saeed Anwar, 17.4 ov),
5-78 (Azhar Mahmood, 24.2 ov), 6-124 (Moin Khan, 34.2 ov),
7-146 (Abdul Razzaq, 39.1 ov), 8-175 (Inzamam-ul Haq, 43.4 ov),
9-176 (Saqlain Mushtaq, 44.3 ov), 10-180 (Wasim Akram, 45.3 ov).

Bowling	O	M	R	W
Srinath	8	1	37	3
Mohanty	10	2	31	0 (2w)
Prasad	9.3	2	27	5
Kumble	10	0	43	2
Singh	8	1	31	0

Super Six, 12 June: Trent Bridge, Nottingham

India were fortunate with the coin, but the pitch proved to be less dependable than envisaged. Their batsmen misjudged the track by being flamboyant where a little watchfulness might have paid dividends. They looked stylish, but their stay in the middle was temporary. The only one who seemed to understand the trick was Jadeja. He showed patience, particularly during the middle overs, before cashing in later. Circumspection was demanded against Geoff Allott, who was constantly threatening and became the first bowler to bag 20 wickets in a solitary World Cup. But the other New Zealand bowlers could have been treated with less caution.

The Kiwi openers set off at close to five an over and the runs always hovered around this rate. Mathew Horne was asked to anchor the innings and did so dutifully. In the context of the match, this performance was priceless, though his 74 was nothing special in terms of batsmanship. Roger Twose, on the other hand, was demonstrating the hardiness of an Antipodean from the outreaches of the southern hemisphere. With 58 runs required off as many balls, rain stopped play for over an hour. This interruption could have played havoc with a batsman's concentration. It didn't in his case. New Zealand won by five wickets. It was a victory of temperament over talent.

Even a win would not have elevated India to the semi-final. Only once in 12 matches prior to this one had a target of 250 proved inadequate – that was when India lost to South Africa in the opening game. It emphasized the point that India's bowling was quite harmless in less-than-helpful situations. In the run-up to the tournament, this event had been marketed as a carnival. But when Azhar and Steve Waugh strongly objected to the post-match field invasions, the organizers clamped down to the extent of even scolding Indian supporters among the over 14,000 spectators at this match for being too noisy. Not surprisingly, they were not amused.

Toss: India
Umpires: DB Hair (Aus) and DR Shepherd
TV Umpire: RE Koertzen (SA)
Referee: Talat Ali (Pak)
Man of the Match: RG Twose

India innings *(50 overs maximum)*			R	B
SR Tendulkar		b Nash	16	22
SC Ganguly		b Allott	29	62
R Dravid	c Fleming	b Cairns	29	35
A Jadeja	c Parore	b Cairns	76	103
*M Azharuddin	c Parore	b Larsen	30	43
RR Singh	run out (Fleming/Cairns)		27	29
J Srinath	not out		6	7
+NR Mongia	not out		3	6

Extras: (b 4, lb 8, w 13, nb 10) 35
Total: (6 wickets, 50 overs) 251

DNB: A Kumble, BKV Prasad, DS Mohanty.

FoW: 1-26 (Tendulkar, 5.1 ov), 2-71 (Dravid, 14.6 ov),
3-97 (Ganguly, 22.6 ov), 4-187 (Azharuddin, 40.4 ov),
5-241 (Jadeja, 47.3 ov), 6-243 (Singh, 47.6 ov).

Bowling	O	M	R	W
Allott	10	1	33	1 (2w)
Nash	10	1	57	1 (3nb, 5w)
Cairns	10	0	44	2 (2nb)
Larsen	10	0	40	1 (1nb, 1w)
Astle	7	0	49	0
Harris	3	0	16	0

New Zealand innings *(target: 252 runs from 50 overs)*			R	B
MJ Horne	run out (sub [N Chopra])		74	116
NJ Astle	c Dravid	b Mohanty	26	27
CD McMillan	c Dravid	b Srinath	6	7
*SP Fleming	c Mongia	b Mohanty	15	23
RG Twose	not out		60	77
CL Cairns	c Kumble	b Singh	11	30
+AC Parore	not out		26	14

Extras: (b 4, lb 11, w 16, nb 4) 35
Total: (5 wickets, 48.2 overs) 253

DNB: CZ Harris, DJ Nash, GR Larsen, GI Allott.

FoW: 1-45 (Astle, 9.3 ov), 2-60 (McMillan, 13.1 ov),
3-90 (Fleming, 21.5 ov), 4-173 (Horne, 34.4 ov),
5-218 (Cairns, 45.1 ov).

Bowling	O	M	R	W
Srinath	10	1	49	1 (2nb, 1w)
Mohanty	10	0	41	2 (1w)
Prasad	10	0	44	0 (2w)
Singh	4	0	27	1
Ganguly	2	0	15	0 (2nb)
Kumble	9.2	0	48	0 (2w)
Tendulkar	3	0	14	0 (2w)

This proved to be Azharuddin's last hooray in the World Cup. He continued to turn out for India in ODIs as well as tests until 2000, when the BCCI, quite sensationally, found him guilty of match fixing and banned him for life from all cricket under their auspices for life. Uniquely, he blazed hundreds in his first and last tests; but was denied further distinction – he was left stranded one short of 100 appearances.

Jadeja, too, followed Azhar into oblivion for the same reason, but his suspension was revoked by a court order in 2005 and he has, therefore, returned to playing first-class cricket.

More mysteriously, Mongia also got the chop.

Semi-final, 16 June: Old Trafford, Manchester

The most valuable partnership in New Zealand's innings against Pakistan, after they won the toss, stemmed from Stephen Fleming and Twose, who put on 94. But Shoaib Akhtar was at his fastest and he, then, sent Fleming's stump cartwheeling with a spectacular yorker. Indeed, in his allotted overs, spread over three spells, he made a stunning impact. As his captain commented after the match, pace does matter in one-day cricket. All the same, the Kiwis compiled a fighting total of 241, albeit helped by 47 extras carelessly contributed by the Pakistanis.

The New Zealand effort was, however, made to look ridiculous by an opening gambit of 194 runs between Anwar and Wajahatullah Wasti – a World Cup record for the first wicket. Indeed, they looked like completing the assignment on their own when the latter made his exit in the 41st over. Anwar continued to record a hundred in consecutive matches – his 17th in ODIs, which brought him level with Desmond Haynes, with only Tendulkar ahead of him. Ijaz Ahmed joined the party to crack 28 off 21 balls. Some overexcited Pakistani supporters among the 22,000 spectators ran on to the field when their side were still six runs short of victory. This intrusion held up play for 10 minutes. Even when play resumed, Twose could not attempt to catch what was awarded as Anwar's match-winning stroke – a lofted off-drive – as the crowd streamed on to the green. The two runs needed were never actually completed as the players raced to the pavilion for safety. Pakistan, thus, explosively entered the final, with their fans setting off firecrackers in the manner people rejoice in this country's North West Frontier Province. Security was lax; Fleming appealed for stricter measures, fanning the demand for the hitherto unthinkable in England – fencing in of spectators.

Toss: New Zealand
Umpires: DB Hair (Aus) and P Willey
TV Umpire: DL Orchard (SA)
Referee: CW Smith (WI)
Man of the Match: Shoaib Akhtar

New Zealand innings (50 overs maximum)			R	B
MJ Horne		b Abdul Razzaq	35	48
NJ Astle		b Shoaib Akhtar	3	18
CD McMillan	c Moin Khan	b Wasim Akram	3	19
*SP Fleming		b Shoaib Akhtar	41	57
RG Twose	c Ijaz Ahmed	b Abdul Razzaq	46	83
CL Cairns	not out		44	48
CZ Harris		b Shoaib Akhtar	16	21
+AC Parore		b Wasim Akram	0	4
DJ Nash	not out		6	10

Extras: (b 4, lb 14, w 17, nb 12) 47
Total: (7 wickets, 50 overs) 241

DNB: GR Larsen, GI Allott.

FoW: 1-20 (Astle, 5.3 ov), 2-38 (McMillan, 10.3 ov),
3-58 (Horne, 15.1 ov), 4-152 (Fleming, 33.5 ov),
5-176 (Twose, 39.3 ov), 6-209 (Harris, 45.4 ov),
7-211 (Parore, 46.4 ov).

Bowling	O	M	R	W
Wasim Akram	10	0	45	2 (4nb, 7w)
Shoaib Akhtar	10	0	55	3 (2nb, 1w)
Abdul Razzaq	8	0	28	2 (1w)
Saqlain Mushtaq	8	0	36	0 (1w)
Azhar Mahmood	9	0	32	0 (3w)
Shahid Afridi	5	0	27	0 (2nb, 2w)

Pakistan innings (target: 242 runs from 50 overs)			R	B
Saeed Anwar	not out		113	148
Wajahatullah Wasti	c Fleming	b Cairns	84	123
Ijaz Ahmed	not out		28	21

Extras: (lb 3, w 7, nb 7) 17
Total: (1 wicket, 47.3 overs) 242

DNB: Inzamam-ul Haq, Abdul Razzaq, Shahid Afridi, +Moin Khan,
*Wasim Akram, Azhar Mahmood, Saqlain Mushtaq, Shoaib Akhtar.

FoW: 1-194 (Wajahatullah, 40.3 ov).

Bowling	O	M	R	W
Allott	9	0	41	0 (1nb, 1w)
Nash	5	0	34	0 (2nb, 2w)
Larsen	10	0	40	0 (1nb)
Cairns	8	0	33	1 (3nb)
Harris	6	0	31	0
Astle	7.3	0	41	0 (1w)
McMillan	2	0	19	0 (1w)

Semi-final, 17 June: Edgbaston, Birmingham

The match glittered with shining performances. South Africa sent Australia in. Shaun Pollock, striking form, which had eluded him earlier in the tournament, was marvellously penetrative. His comrade-in-arms, the fast and furious Donald, picked up a pair of wickets in two separate overs. Kallis, despite nursing an injury on his waist, bowled with speed and accuracy. But Steve Waugh and Bevan crafted a recovery, which initially indicated restraint, then scientific hitting.

Kallis led the chase with an unruffled 50. Then, Shane Warne skittled Herschelle Gibbs' stumps with a prodigiously turning leg-break. His first eight overs cost only 12 runs. He grabbed three more wickets. However, Man of the Tournament, Klusener's hefty hitting motored South Africa to the brink of victory. He had been unstoppable in the tournament; now he pummelled 31 runs off 14 balls, converting a tough target into a cakewalk. Only one was required off four balls, with the brawny left-hander facing the bowling. At the non-striker's end was Donald, if not anything else, a seasoned campaigner. It was a rerun for Damien Fleming, who had bowled the last over in the semi-final against the West Indies four years before, which Australia won. This time, though, Klusener had despatched the first two balls of the over for fours. It was a daunting task. But Steve Waugh held his breath; tightened the ring of fielders saving the single. Klusener drove the next ball straight; and Donald, taking too much of a start, would have been run out if Darren Lehman's throw been more unerring. The following delivery, Klusener drove to mid-on and dashed off for a single. Donald, who had stayed put inside his crease, dropped his bat and set off in response. Mark Waugh returned the ball to Fleming, who in a piece of quick thinking, rolled it to Gilchrist, who whipped off the bails. Donald was run out. South Africa had choked. The match had dramatically ended in a tie.

This was not just *the* match of the tournament, but one of the most memorable ODIs ever played. The outcome meant South Africa were ousted because of the critical fact that Australia finished higher than them in the Super Six table by virtue of a better net run rate. Many among the 20,000 odd spectators, though, were left bewildered.

Toss: South Africa
Umpires: DR Shepherd and S Venkataraghavan (Ind)
TV Umpire: SA Bucknor (WI)
Referee: R Subba Row
Man of the Match: SK Warne

Australia innings (50 overs maximum)			R	B
+AC Gilchrist	c Donald	b Kallis	20	39
ME Waugh	c Boucher	b Pollock	0	4
RT Ponting	c Kirsten	b Donald	37	48
DS Lehmann	c Boucher	b Donald	1	4
*SR Waugh	c Boucher	b Pollock	56	76
MG Bevan	c Boucher	b Pollock	65	101
TM Moody	lbw	b Pollock	0	3
SK Warne	c Cronje	b Pollock	18	24
PR Reiffel		b Donald	0	1
DW Fleming		b Donald	0	2
GD McGrath	not out		0	1

Extras: (b 1, lb 6, w 3, nb 6) 16
Total: (all out, 49.2 overs) 213

FoW: 1-3 (ME Waugh, 0.5 ov), 2-54 (Ponting, 13.1 ov),
3-58 (Lehmann, 13.6 ov), 4-68 (Gilchrist, 16.6 ov),
5-158 (SR Waugh, 39.3 ov), 6-158 (Moody, 39.6 ov),
7-207 (Warne, 47.6 ov), 8-207 (Reiffel, 48.1 ov),
9-207 (Fleming, 48.3 ov), 10-213 (Bevan, 49.2 ov).

Bowling	O	M	R	W
Pollock	9.2	1	36	5
Elworthy	10	0	59	0 (2nb, 1w)
Kallis	10	2	27	1 (1nb, 1w)
Donald	10	1	32	4 (1w)
Klusener	9	1	50	0 (3nb)
Cronje	1	0	2	0

South Africa innings (target: 214 runs from 50 overs)			R	B
G Kirsten		b Warne	18	42
HH Gibbs		b Warne	30	36
DJ Cullinan	run out (Bevan)		6	30
*WJ Cronje	c ME Waugh	b Warne	0	2
JH Kallis	c SR Waugh	b Warne	53	92
JN Rhodes	c Bevan	b Reiffel	43	55
SM Pollock	b Fleming		20	14
L Klusener	not out		31	16
+MV Boucher		b McGrath	5	10
S Elworthy	run out (Reiffel/McGrath)		1	1
AA Donald	run out (ME Waugh/Fleming/Gilchrist)		0	0

Extras: (lb 1, w 5) 6
Total: (all out, 49.4 overs) 213

FoW: 1-48 (Gibbs, 12.2 ov), 2-53 (Kirsten, 14.1 ov),
3-53 (Cronje, 14.3 ov), 4-61 (Cullinan, 21.2 ov),
5-145 (Rhodes, 40.3 ov), 6-175 (Kallis, 44.5 ov),
7-183 (Pollock, 45.5 ov), 8-196 (Boucher, 48.2 ov),
9-198 (Elworthy, 48.4 ov), 10-213 (Donald, 49.4 ov).

Bowling	O	M	R	W
McGrath	10	0	51	1 (1w)
Fleming	8.4	1	40	1 (3w)
Reiffel	8	0	28	1
Warne	10	4	29	4 (1w)
ME Waugh	8	0	37	0
Moody	5	0	27	0

Final, 20 June: Lord's, London

Wasim Akram chose to bat and this was probably the right decision, for the wicket looked amenable to a decent total. Anwar struck three fours at the expense of Fleming, who rather sprayed it around. But that was the end of the purple patch for Pakistan. Wasti flirted with a ball from McGrath that deviated and jumped and Mark Waugh flung himself to his right to bring off a classic slip catch with both hands. For Australia, the wheels were now in motion.

Anwar played on. For a while, Abdul Razzaq and Ijaz Ahmed looked comfortable, although the former got a reprieve when he was spilled at long-off. The escape, though, was short-lived as soon afterwards Steve Waugh made no mistake at extra cover. With the Pakistanis wobbling at 69 for three after 21 overs, Waugh introduced Warne. This move virtually settled the issue. The leg-spinner conjured amazing turn to get rid of Ijaz, who had been resisting tenaciously. The ball pitched around leg and hit off. It veritably unnerved the rest of the Pakistani batting. They counterattacked, but for every boundary hit, a stroke was clipped into the safe hands of an Australian fielder. To add insult to injury, Inzamam was given out caught behind by umpire David Shepherd off the batsman's pad. The Sultan of Multan stared in disbelief and walked off rather reluctantly. When Wasim skied a catch, Warne pocketed four wickets, which boosted his tally for the tournament to 20, a joint record for the World Cup with Allott of New Zealand. McGrath wrapped up the innings when Ponting maintained his team's dizzy standard of catching with a take at third slip. Pakistan were bundled out for 132 in the 39th over.

Adam Gilchrist set off like the French TGV. Shoaib was a bit unfortunate when his first delivery was snicked by Gilchrist and fell perilously close to long-leg. Thereafter, the ball thudded into the boundary boards with a rapidity that dashed all hope of any twist or turn relieving Pakistan. Gilchrist's 50 transpired off 33 balls. He was, in fact, back in the dressing room by the 11th over. It, of course, took 10 more for Australia to accomplish their task, in course of which Mark Waugh crossed 1000 World Cup runs. Australia had expended only 121 balls when Lehman unleashed the winning stroke.

The victory paired the Aussies with the West Indies in winning the World Cup a second time. This, the 200th World Cup match, had been decided in less than 60 overs. The first World Cup final, at Lord's 24 years earlier almost to the day, had lasted nearly ten hours.

Those who, reportedly, paid touts £2500 for a ticket may have felt cheated, unless they were rich Australians. Pakistan, who had earlier seemed promising, had been thoroughly exposed. It was always a question of which Pakistani side would turn up. In the event, the wrong one did. Uniquely for Lord's, to control a secton of the crowd, announcements were made in Urdu, Pakistan's national language. This precaution, though, did not deter overrunning of the outfield. Akram later remarked Pakistan could have defended 180. Such a claim seemed unrealistic.

The crowd of 28,000 was, however, was replete with bored bystanders, while the involvement and exuberance appeared to be greater outside the perimeter of the premises. Dozens of Pakistani fans stood atop a building site with a bird's eye view of proceedings. But the police soon evacuated the vantage point and expelled the enthusiasts from that area.

So, Australia regained the World Cup after 12 years and, thereby, the best test team in the world also became the world one-day champions. In short, they emerged as the undisputed champions of cricket, an honour held by the West Indies in the 1970s and early 1980s. The West Indies had surrendered their unqualified dominance – when India beat them – at this very ground 16 years earlier.

Toss: Pakistan
Umpires: SA Bucknor (WI) and DR Shepherd
TV Umpire: S Venkataraghavan (Ind)
Referee: RS Madugalle (SL)
Man of the Match: SK Warne
Player of the Tournament: L Klusener (SA)

Pakistan innings (50 overs maximum)			*R*	*B*
Saeed Anwar		b Fleming	15	17
Wajahatullah Wasti	c ME Waugh	b McGrath	1	14
Abdul Razzaq	c SR Waugh	b Moody	17	51
Ijaz Ahmed		b Warne	22	46
Inzamam-ul Haq	c Gilchrist	b Reiffel	15	33
+Moin Khan	c Gilchrist	b Warne	6	12
Shahid Afridi	lbw	b Warne	13	16
Azhar Mahmood	c & b Moody		8	17
*Wasim Akram	c SR Waugh	b Warne	8	20
Saqlain Mushtaq	c Ponting	b McGrath	0	4
Shoaib Akhtar	not out		2	6

Extras: (lb 10, w 13, nb 2) 25
Total: (all out, 39 overs) 132

FoW: 1-21 (Wajahatullah, 4.4 ov), 2-21 (Saeed Anwar, 5.1 ov),
3-68 (Abdul Razzaq, 19.4 ov), 4-77 (Ijaz Ahmed, 23.4 ov),
5-91 (Moin Khan, 27.1 ov), 6-104 (Inzamam-ul Haq, 30.1 ov),
7-113 (Shahid Afridi, 31.6 ov), 8-129 (Azhar Mahmood, 36.6 ov),
9-129 (Wasim Akram, 37.2 ov), 10-132 (Saqlain Mushtaq, 38.6 ov).

Bowling	O	M	R	W
McGrath	9	3	13	2
Fleming	6	0	30	1 (2nb, 4w)
Reiffel	10	1	29	1 (2w)
Moody	5	0	17	2 (1w)
Warne	9	1	33	4 (2w)

Australia innings (target: 133 runs from 50 overs)			R	B
ME Waugh	not out		37	52
+AC Gilchrist	c Inzamam-ul Haq	b Saqlain Mushtaq	54	36
RT Ponting	c Moin Khan	b Wasim Akram	24	27
DS Lehmann	not out		13	9

Extras: (lb 1, w 1, nb 3) 5
Total: (2 wickets, 20.1 overs) 133

DNB: *SR Waugh, MG Bevan, TM Moody, SK Warne, PR Reiffel,
DW Fleming, GD McGrath.

FoW: 1-75 (Gilchrist, 10.1 ov), 2-112 (Ponting, 17.4 ov).

Bowling	O	M	R	W
Wasim Akram	8	1	41	1 (2nb, 1w)
Shoaib Akhtar	4	0	37	0 (1nb)
Abdul Razzaq	2	0	13	0
Azhar Mahmood	2	0	20	0
Saqlain Mushtaq	4.1	0	21	1

When Australia embarked on their final group match, they were in serious danger of early elimination. It was an equally close call during their last Super Six match. But having made it to the final by the skin of their teeth, they redeemed themselves when it mattered the most.

A section of the British press were confident England would make it through to the Super Six stage. For this not to happen, Zimbabwe had to beat South Africa and England had to lose to India very badly. Both occurred and the Englishmen were out 16 days into the championship, with another 21 to come. As Wisden put it, the hosts were reduced to serving cucumber sandwiches at the tea party. But the English public, partly because of the enthusiasm of Britons of South Asian descent (though most of them failed the Tebbit test of loyalty to the United Kingdom – advocated by a former British cabinet minister Norman Tebbit – by supporting countries of their origin), did not lose interest.

All 18 English county headquarters staged at least one match. The other three were outside the beaten track – Edinburgh, Dublin and Amstelveen in Holland.

Fortunately, the unpopular Duckworth/Lewis (devised by Frank Duckworth and Tony Lewis, the latter a Welshman and former captain of England) system was never utilized. It was generally believed that the team batting second had an advantage because of morning moisture. But among the teams batting first, 19 won and 21 lost, thus throwing up a hung jury. Of course, captains more frequently opted to field after winning the toss in May than June, when it was warmer.

The lacquered white ball was reckoned to be harder than its red counterpart. It seemed to swing more, including in reverse, which the bowlers couldn't always control, thus conceding 979 wides. But bowlers, reduced to cannon fodder in the 1996 World Cup, competed on equal terms with batsmen. Often, the 15th over passed with little change in the close-in cordon.

Jayasuriya, pinch-hitter par excellence in 1996, scored only 82 in five matches this time. The defending champions were a shadow of their former selves. Their captain Arjuna Ranatunga was duly sacked, as was his English counterpart Stewart.

The great shock was Bangladesh's defeat of Pakistan, who had already qualified for the Super Six, in the final fixture of the preliminary stage at Northampton. English bookmakers had offered 33–1 on Pakistan to win. Inevitably, such prior odds led to an assumption that the match was fixed. Wasim did not help contradict this impression by being beside himself with laughter on the pavilion balcony every time a Pakistani wicket fell and remarking after the match his side had only lost to their Muslim 'brothers'. However, there was no evidence to establish any wrongdoing. It was just a major upset. Bangladesh, who had dispensed with their coach Gordon Greenidge the previous evening, were, in fact, without his services in the second half of the match after he left the ground prematurely. There were joyful celebrations in London's East End, where tens of thousands of British Bangladeshis reside.

Bangladesh also beat Scotland, and so finished a respectable fifth in the Group B table. But the other associate members of the ICC or the non-test-playing sides taking part in the tournament only made up the numbers.

Rahul Dravid, once considered to be too slow for one-day cricket, was the leading scorer of the tournament, amassing 461 runs. His parents were downcast when the demands of cricket compelled him to discontinue his pursuit of a Masters degree in business administration. They have had no regrets since.

Australian politicians jostled with each other to jump into the spotlight to fete their players. In Pakistan, postmortems began. Quite unjustifiably, talk of bribery returned to haunt Pakistani cricket, instead of an acceptance that they had been beaten fair and square.

7

Extras

THE 1998 ICC KNOCKOUT

IN 1997, UNDER JAGMOHAN DALMIYA'S STEWARDSHIP, THE ICC initiated its Development Programme with the aim of nurturing cricket into a genuinely international sport. They sought to achieve this objective by popularizing it in the associate and affiliate member countries. The game's governing body had moved into new offices overlooking the nursery at Lord's with a modest bank balance. With the enterprising Indian businessman, nominated by the BCCI, at the ICC's helm, the ICC immediately set about exploring ways and means of enhancing their revenue (and thereby their fiscal independence) and their clout among members, not to mention meaningfully administering the game, including focusing on its development in non-full-member countries with a genuine aptitude for the sport.

To achieve this objective they conceived of, and launched, a one-day competition, envisaged to be second only in importance to the World Cup, the first of which was held in Bangladesh in 1998 and was called the 'ICC Knockout Tournament', later to become the Champions Trophy. While the hosting of this event would rotate among members, it would be entirely under the control of the ICC.

Also, profits from the biennial tournaments would be wholly retained by the governing body and set aside for progression of the game in associate and affiliate countries. This programme was, in fact, allocated US $6.5 million per annum until 2008.

There was, and still is, some confusion as to what the first precursor to the Champions Trophy was called. The ICC referred to it as the ICC Knockout Tournament; officially, it was called the 'Wills International Cup', while popularly it was known as the 'Mini World Cup'. Irrespective of the appellation, the tournament, reportedly, contributed about £10 million to the Development Programme.

Some officials at the ICC were more enthusiastic about Disney World in Florida, USA, or Sharjah as the venue. But the organization finally settled on Dhaka, Bangladesh, then an associate member. After one of the worst floods devastated India's eastern neighbour only weeks before the competition, it was nearly shifted to Kolkata, only a few hundred miles from the Bangladeshi capital. Yet, despite the hosts not taking part, cricket fans in the country responded with great fervour to the most important sporting occasion in its blood-stained history.

It was mandatory for all nine test-playing ICC members to partake. England, though, sent a second-string side. While the locals did not think so, the pitches were slow and low at the Bangabandhu (or 'Friend of Bengal', as Sheikh Mujibur Rahman, the founder of the country was fondly revered before he was assassinated in August 1975) Stadium and the cricket not extraordinary. But it was a short and sharp affair, with eight matches squeezed into nine days. The schedule was strenuous for the players, but it instilled a definite momentum to the matches.

India's Sachin Tendulkar unfurled the essay of the tournament with 141 against Australia. But South Africa's Jacques Kallis stole the thunder in the semi-final and final, with the explosive West Indian, Philo Wallace, not far behind as a batsman. Hansie Cronje, perhaps, advanced the most as both leader and player. Two years later, he was caught by the Delhi Police for taking bribes to throw matches.

Reflecting prevailing ICC rankings, New Zealand and Zimbabwe featured in the pre-quarter finals; and with the former winning by five wickets, this result determined the line-up for the last eight.

In the quarter finals, South Africa beat England by six wickets, Sri Lanka got the better of New Zealand by five wickets, West Indies defeated Pakistan by 30 runs and India subdued Australia by 44 runs.

28 October: Dhaka

Toss: Australia
Umpires: SA Bucknor (WI) and RS Dunne (NZ)
TV Umpire: DL Orchard (SA)
Referee: RS Madugalle (SL)
Man of the Match: SR Tendulkar

India innings (50 overs maximum)			R	B
SC Ganguly	c Gilchrist	b Kasprowicz	1	6
SR Tendulkar	run out (Kasprowicz)		141	128
*M Azharuddin	lbw	b Fleming	0	3
R Dravid	run out (Gilchrist)		48	80
A Jadeja	run out (Kasprowicz)		71	65
RR Singh	c Gilchrist	b Kasprowicz	3	2
AB Agarkar		b Kasprowicz	10	12
SB Joshi	run out (Julian)		3	7
J Srinath		not out	5	4
+NR Mongia		not out	0	0

Extras: (lb 8, w 10, nb 7) 25
Total: (8 wickets, 50 overs) 307

DNB: A Kumble.

FoW: 1-7 (Ganguly, 1.6 ov), 2-8 (Azharuddin, 2.5 ov),
3-148 (Dravid, 26.1 ov), 4-280 (Tendulkar, 45.1 ov),
5-286 (Jadeja, 45.5 ov), 6-292 (Singh, 46.4 ov),
7-301 (Agarkar, 48.6 ov), 8-305 (Joshi, 49.5 ov).

Bowling	O	M	R	W
Fleming	10	1	45	1
Kasprowicz	9	0	71	3 (5nb, 4w)
Julian	10	0	39	0 (2nb, 3w)
SR Waugh	3	0	23	0
Young	8	0	64	0 (3w)
ME Waugh	6	0	27	0
Lehmann	4	0	30	0

Australia innings (target: 308 runs from 50 overs)			R	B
ME Waugh	c Mongia	b Joshi	74	79
+AC Gilchrist		b Srinath	25	26
RT Ponting		b Joshi	41	53
BP Julian	c Dravid	b Srinath	20	16
DS Lehmann	lbw	b Agarkar	27	37
*SR Waugh	c & b Tendulkar		7	13
MG Bevan		b Tendulkar	8	14
DR Martyn	c Jadeja	b Tendulkar	24	17
BE Young	c Dravid	b Tendulkar	18	24
MS Kasprowicz	run out (Dravid)		7	8
DW Fleming	not out		2	4

Extras: (lb 3, w 5, nb 2) 10
Total: (all out, 48.1 overs) 263

FoW: 1-51 (Gilchrist, 8.3 ov), 2-145 (Ponting, 25.2 ov),
3-167 (ME Waugh, 27.5 ov), 4-172 (Julian, 29.2 ov),
5-194 (SR Waugh, 34.2 ov), 6-210 (Bevan, 38.5 ov),
7-217 (Lehmann, 39.6 ov), 8-247 (Martyn, 44.3 ov),
9-257 (Kasprowicz, 46.1 ov), 10-263 (Young, 48.1 ov).

Bowling	O	M	R	W
Srinath	9	0	36	2 (1nb, 1w)
Agarkar	10	0	61	1 (2w)
Kumble	9	0	44	0
Joshi	8	0	57	2
Singh	3	0	24	0 (1nb)
Tendulkar	9.1	0	38	4 (2w)

Semi-final, 30 October: Dhaka

In the first semi-final, South Africa thrashed Sri Lanka by 92 runs...

Toss: Sri Lanka
Umpires: SA Bucknor (WI) and S Venkataraghavan (Ind)
TV Umpire: DR Shepherd (Eng)
Referee: R Subba Row (Eng)
Man of the Match: JH Kallis

South Africa innings (39 overs maximum)			R	B
MJR Rindel	c Jayasuriya	b Vaas	8	12
DJ Cullinan	lbw	b Dharmasena	30	43
N Boje	c de Silva	b Zoysa	28	23
+MV Boucher	c Mahanama	b Zoysa	0	1
JH Kallis	not out		113	100
*WJ Cronje	c Atapattu	b Chandana	20	30
JN Rhodes	c Atapattu	b Muralitharan	0	1
PL Symcox	c Atapattu	b Chandana	11	9
DM Benkenstein	not out		18	17

Extras: (b 1, lb 6, w 3, nb 2) 12
Total: (7 wickets, 39 overs) 240

DNB: DN Crookes, S Elworthy.

FoW: 1-12 (Rindel, 2.4 ov), 2-55 (Boje, 9.2 ov),
3-57 (Boucher, 9.5 ov), 4-87 (Cullinan, 16.2 ov),
5-168 (Cronje, 29.5 ov), 6-181 (Rhodes, 30.6 ov),
7-196 (Symcox, 33.1 ov).

Bowling	O	M	R	W
Vaas	6	0	33	1
Zoysa	6	0	34	2 (1nb)
Dharmasena	7	0	37	1 (2w)
Muralitharan	6	0	48	1 (1nb)
Jayasuriya	6	0	42	0 (1w)
Chandana	8	0	39	2

Sri Lanka innings (target: 224 runs from 34 overs)			R	B
ST Jayasuriya		b Elworthy	22	17
+RS Kaluwitharana	c Cronje	b Elworthy	9	13
WPUJC Vaas	c Rhodes	b Cronje	18	16
PA de Silva	c Boje	b Elworthy	5	9
MS Atapattu	c Cullinan	b Symcox	19	23
*A Ranatunga	c Boucher	b Cronje	4	8
RS Mahanama	c Crookes	b Symcox	10	12
UDU Chandana	lbw	b Symcox	20	23
HDPK Dharmasena	c Cullinan	b Crookes	6	15
DNT Zoysa		not out	2	8
M Muralitharan	absent hurt	-		

Extras: (lb 4, w 10, nb 3) 17
Total: (all out, 23.4 overs) 132

FoW: 1-19 (Kaluwitharana, 3.2 ov), 2-40 (Jayasuriya, 5.2 ov),
3-48 (de Silva, 7.3 ov), 4-74 (Vaas, 9.3 ov),
5-80 (Ranatunga, 11.3 ov), 6-96 (Mahanama, 14.5 ov),
7-113 (Atapattu, 18.2 ov), 8-125 (Chandana, 20.5 ov),
9-132 (Dharmasena, 23.4 ov).

Bowling	O	M	R	W
Kallis	4	0	34	0 (1nb, 2w)
Elworthy	4	0	21	3 (1nb, 2w)
Rindel	1	0	13	0 (1nb, 2w)
Cronje	5	1	26	2 (2w)
Symcox	7	0	27	3 (1w)
Crookes	2.4	0	7	1 (1w)

...and West Indies trounced India by six wickets.

Semi-final, 31 October: Dhaka

Toss: India
Umpires: DL Orchard (SA) and P Willey (Eng)
TV Umpire: RS Dunne (NZ)
Referee: RS Madugalle (SL)
ODI Debut: RD King (WI).
Man of the Match: M Dillon

India innings (50 overs maximum)			R	B
SC Ganguly	st Jacobs	b Lewis	83	116
SR Tendulkar	c Hooper	b Dillon	8	14
*M Azharuddin	lbw	b Dillon	1	4
R Dravid	c Williams	b Hooper	20	54
A Jadeja	run out (Lara)		13	18
RR Singh	not out		73	63
+NR Mongia		b Dillon	25	28
J Srinath	not out		6	3

Extras: (lb 5, w 8) 13
Total: (6 wickets, 50 overs) 242

DNB: AB Agarkar, A Kumble, SB Joshi.
FoW: 1-14 (Tendulkar, 3.6 ov), 2-21 (Azharuddin, 5.6 ov),
3-91 (Dravid, 25.6 ov), 4-125 (Jadeja, 31.1 ov),
5-153 (Ganguly, 39.0 ov), 6-236 (Mongia, 49.3 ov).

Bowling	O	M	R	W
King	10	2	26	0 (2w)
Dillon	8	1	38	3 (1w)
Hooper	10	0	42	1
Simmons	10	0	47	0 (3w)
Arthurton	3	0	26	0
Lewis	9	0	58	1 (2w)

West Indies innings (target: 243 runs from 50 overs)			R	B
PA Wallace	c & b Tendulkar		39	45
SC Williams	c Mongia	b Srinath	5	7
S Chanderpaul		b Tendulkar	74	74
*BC Lara	not out		60	89
CL Hooper	c Agarkar	b Kumble	8	5
KLT Arthurton	not out		40	67

Extras: (b 4, lb 8, w 2, nb 5) 19
Total: (4 wickets, 47 overs) 245

DNB: PV Simmons, +RD Jacobs, RN Lewis, RD King, M Dillon.

FoW: 1-27 (Williams, 2.1 ov), 2-108 (Wallace, 16.2 ov),
3-143 (Chanderpaul, 24.2 ov), 4-156 (Hooper, 25.5 ov).

Bowling	O	M	R	W
Srinath	7	0	56	1 (5nb)
Agarkar	4	0	25	0 (1w)
Kumble	10	0	52	1
Joshi	10	0	35	0
Tendulkar	10	1	29	2 (1w)
Dravid	6	0	36	0

Final, 1 November: Dhaka

In the final, South Africa triumphed over the West Indies by four wickets to entrench themselves as a force to be reckoned with. Lamentably, not a single mediaperson from either part of the world was present at this match.

Toss: South Africa
Umpires: RS Dunne (NZ) and DR Shepherd (Eng)
TV Umpire: P Willey (Eng)
Referee: RS Madugalle (SL)
Man of the Match: JH Kallis
Man of the Series: JH Kallis

West Indies innings (50 overs maximum)			R	B
PA Wallace	st Boucher	b Cronje	103	102
CB Lambert	c Symcox	b Elworthy	7	12
S Chanderpaul	lbw	b Boje	27	54
*BC Lara		b Crookes	11	9
CL Hooper	c Rhodes	b Kallis	49	56
KLT Arthurton	lbw	b Kallis	8	14
PV Simmons	c Rhodes	b Kallis	8	13
+RD Jacobs	c Rhodes	b Cronje	14	21
RN Lewis	lbw	b Kallis	0	1
RD King	lbw	b Kallis	7	15
M Dillon	not out		0	0

Extras: Total (all out, 49.3 overs) 245

FoW: 1-18 (Lambert, 5.1 ov), 2-94 (Chanderpaul, 23.4 ov),
3-125 (Lara, 26.5 ov), 4-180 (Wallace, 34.4 ov),
5-193 (Arthurton, 37.6 ov), 6-213 (Simmons, 41.5 ov),
7-232 (Hooper, 45.4 ov), 8-232 (Lewis, 45.5 ov),
9-243 (Jacobs, 48.6 ov), 10-245 (King, 49.3 ov).

Bowling	O	M	R	W
Symcox	10	0	29	0
Elworthy	7	0	48	1 (1w)
Boje	10	1	44	1 (1w)
Rindel	2	0	13	0
Crookes	3	0	33	1 (2w)
Cronje	10	0	44	2 (1w)
Kallis	7.3	0	30	5 (1w)

South Africa innings (target: 246 runs from 50 overs)			R	B
DJ Cullinan	run out (Arthurton)		21	25
MJR Rindel	run out (Arthurton)		49	56
+MV Boucher	st Jacobs	b Hooper	4	6
JH Kallis	c & b Simmons		37	51
*WJ Cronje	not out		61	77
JN Rhodes	c Jacobs	b Simmons	3	9
DM Benkenstein	c Hooper	b Dillon	27	40
DN Crookes	not out		24	21

Extras: (b 3, lb 3, w 13, nb 3) 22
Total: (6 wickets, 47 overs) 248

DNB: N Boje, PL Symcox, S Elworthy.

FoW: 1-54 (Cullinan, 7.3 ov), 2-60 (Boucher, 9.2 ov),
3-118 (Kallis, 20.4 ov), 4-134 (Rindel, 25.1 ov),
5-137 (Rhodes, 26.5 ov), 6-211 (Benkenstein, 41.2 ov).

Bowling	O	M	R	W
Dillon	10	0	53	1 (4w)
King	10	0	42	0 (2w)
Hooper	10	1	45	1 (2w)
Simmons	8	0	45	2 (1nb, 2w)
Lewis	9	0	57	0 (2nb)

THE 2000 ICC KNOCKOUT

The second edition of what was to become the Champions Trophy – still the ICC Knockout – was hosted in Kenya, the idea being to give the game a fillip in associate member countries with a promise of becoming full members in future.

Andy Atkinson, the former Warwickshire groundsman, transformed Nairobi's Gymkhana Club's pitches, infamous for being lifeless, into tracks suitable for strokeplay. This restructuring, entwined with the Kenyan capital's slightly rarified atmosphere – it being at an altitude of 5440 feet – and not so distant boundaries, helped produce a blend of ballistic batting performances. The Indian skipper, Saurav Ganguly, in particular, was majestic in his driving over the top – he hit 12 sixes in three innings.

The downside was a lack of public enthusiasm and an allusion of match fixing that featured in the Anti-Corruption Unit's submission to the ICC. While India's matches were reasonably well attended by people of Indian origin, Afro-Kenyans gave the event a wide berth. Ticket prices were thought to be too expensive for local pockets, not to mention the allegedly prohibitive attitude of administrators. Therefore, how much the event achieved in terms of widening interest for cricket among blacks – the backbone of the population – was a matter for conjecture. However, the tournament made a healthy profit of US $13 million.

Since the previous ICC Knockout in Dhaka two years earlier, Bangladesh and Kenya had joined the list of invitees. They, however, made their exits in the first round, along with the declining West Indies, with Kenya losing to India.

Pre-quarter finals, 3 October: Nairobi

Toss: India
Umpires: SA Bucknor (WI) and DL Orchard (SA)
TV Umpire: DB Hair (Aus)
Referee: RS Madugalle (SL)
ODI Debuts: V Dahiya, Z Khan, Yuvraj Singh (Ind).
Man of the Match: A Kumble

Kenya innings (50 overs maximum)			R	B
+KO Otieno	c Ganguly	b Agarkar	6	8
RD Shah	c Dahiya	b Prasad	60	93
JK Kamande	c Dravid	b Kumble	18	40
SO Tikolo	lbw	b Kumble	5	11
*MO Odumbe	lbw	b Prasad	51	87
TM Odoyo	not out		35	34
M Sheikh		b Khan	0	3
HS Modi		b Khan	0	2
AO Suji	c Dahiya	b Agarkar	2	7
MA Suji	c Ganguly	b Khan	14	17
LN Onyango	not out		0	1

Extras: (lb 10, w 4, nb 3) 17
Total: (9 wickets, 50 overs) 208

FoW: 1-16 (Otieno, 1.6 ov), 2-54 (Kamande, 14.4 ov),
3-64 (Tikolo, 18.1 ov), 4-145 (Shah, 37.6 ov),
5-158 (Odumbe, 41.5 ov), 6-159 (Sheikh, 42.3 ov),
7-159 (Modi, 42.5 ov), 8-174 (AO Suji, 45.2 ov),
9-206 (MA Suji, 49.4 ov).

Bowling	O	M	R	W
Khan	10	0	48	3 (1nb, 1w)
Agarkar	10	1	40	2 (1nb)
Prasad	10	0	47	2 (1w)
Kumble	10	1	22	2
Tendulkar	6	0	25	0
Yuvraj Singh	4	1	16	0 (1nb)

India innings (target: 209 runs from 50 overs)			R	B
*SC Ganguly	st Otieno	b Odumbe	66	101
SR Tendulkar	lbw	b AO Suji	25	35
R Dravid	not out		68	87
VG Kambli	not out		39	33

Extras: (b 1, lb 2, w 7, nb 1) 11
Total: (2 wickets, 42.3 overs) 209

DNB: Yuvraj Singh, RR Singh, AB Agarkar, A Kumble, +V Dahiya, BKV Prasad, Z Khan.

FoW: 1-47 (Tendulkar, 11.6 ov), 2-135 (Ganguly, 30.6 ov).

Bowling	O	M	R	W
MA Suji	10	2	30	0 (1nb)
Odoyo	6	1	18	0 (1w)
AO Suji	10	0	56	1 (5w)
Onyango	4.3	0	34	0
Sheikh	4	0	27	0 (1w)
Tikolo	2	0	13	0
Odumbe	4	0	18	1
Shah	2	0	10	0

In other pre-quarter final matches, Sri Lanka beat the West Indies by 108 runs. The Sri Lankans scored 287–6 in their 50 overs; the West Indies were then bowled out for 179 in 46.4 overs. And England defeated Bangladesh by eight wickets. Bangladesh mustered 232–8 in their 50 overs, which England surpassed by posting 236–2 in 43.5 overs.

Sri Lanka's success over the West Indians didn't last long, though, as they bowed out to Pakistan, who, in turn, were outplayed by New Zealand in the semi-final, notwithstanding a second successive century from Saeed Anwar. New Zealand had emerged from their side of the draw by taming Zimbabwe, who had just recorded a home victory in a one-day series against the Kiwis, but were outgunned here in the quarter final. England, having made heavy weather of Bangladesh, went down tamely to South Africa.

India made a significant impact. They beat both Australia and South Africa, the two fancied sides. The Kangaroos were the reigning World Cup winners, while the Proteas were defending their ICC Knockout title. Ganguly enjoyed an exceptional tournament, scoring 348 runs at an average of 116.00. But what buttressed India's presence was the arrival on the scene of two promising youngsters: teenager Yuvraj Singh, a talented left-handed batsman from Punjab with a good temperament, and a 21-year-old Maharashtra-born left arm quick in Zaheer Khan, who later moved to Baroda in Gujarat.

Quarter final, 7 October: Nairobi

In the first of the eliminations in the round of eight, India got the better of Australia.

Toss: Australia
Umpires: SA Bucknor (WI) and DR Shepherd
TV Umpire: P Willey
Referee: RS Madugalle (SL)
Man of the Match: Yuvraj Singh

India innings (50 overs maximum)			R	B
*SC Ganguly	c Gilchrist	b Gillespie	24	42
SR Tendulkar	c Martyn	b B Lee	38	37
R Dravid	c S Lee	b Gillespie	9	18
VG Kambli	c Gilchrist	b SR Waugh	29	40
Yuvraj Singh	c & b S Lee		84	80
RR Singh		b Harvey	19	30
+V Dahiya	c ME Waugh	b B Lee	5	11
AB Agarkar	c McGrath	b S Lee	3	9
A Kumble	run out (Ponting)		12	21
Z Khan	not out		13	13
BKV Prasad	not out		6	1

Extras: (b 1, lb 12, w 8, nb 2) 23
Total: (9 wickets, 50 overs, 234 mins) 265

FoW: 1-66 (Tendulkar, 11.4 ov), 2-76 (Ganguly, 14.1 ov), 3-90 (Dravid, 18.4 ov), 4-130 (Kambli, 24.5 ov), 5-194 (R R Singh, 36.1 ov), 6-215 (Dahiya, 39.5 ov), 7-222 (Agarkar, 42.1 ov), 8-239 (Yuvraj Singh, 46.4 ov), 9-258 (Kumble, 49.3 ov).

Bowling	O	M	R	W
McGrath	9	0	61	0 (1nb)
B Lee	10	0	39	2 (1nb, 2w)
Gillespie	8	0	39	2
Harvey	9	1	54	1 (2w)
S Lee	10	0	31	2 (4w)
SR Waugh	4	0	28	1

Australia innings (target: 266 runs from 48 overs)			R	B
ME Waugh	c Kumble	b Agarkar	7	24
+AC Gilchrist	c Ganguly	b Khan	33	23
IJ Harvey	c Yuvraj Singh	b Prasad	25	24
RT Ponting	c Singh	b Tendulkar	46	59
MG Bevan	run out (Yuvraj Singh)		42	52
*SR Waugh		b Khan	23	34
DR Martyn		b Singh	1	8
S Lee	run out (Ganguly)		4	6
B Lee	c Ganguly	b Agarkar	31	28
JN Gillespie	c Singh	b Prasad	14	16
GD McGrath	not out		6	8

Extras: (lb 4, w 7, nb 2) 13
Total: (all out, 46.4 overs, 219 mins) 245

FoW: 1-43 (ME Waugh, 7.1 ov), 2-51 (Gilchrist, 8.5 ov), 3-86 (Harvey, 15.6 ov), 4-159 (Ponting, 28.5 ov), 5-163 (Bevan, 31.2 ov), 6-169 (Martyn, 33.6 ov), 7-189 (S Lee, 36.5 ov), 8-224 (SR Waugh, 42.1 ov), 9-226 (B Lee, 43.3 ov), 10-245 (Gillespie, 46.4 ov).

Bowling	O	M	R	W
Khan	10	0	40	2 (1nb, 3w)
Agarkar	8	1	59	2 (2w)
Prasad	7.4	0	43	2 (1w)
Kumble	8	0	42	0
Tendulkar	7	0	31	1 (1w)
Singh	6	0	26	1 (1nb)

In the other quarter finals, Pakistan drubbed Sri Lanka by nine wickets; New Zealand defeated Zimbabwe by 64 runs; and South Africa packed off England by eight wickets.

Then, in the first of the semi-finals, Pakistan failed to defend their score against New Zealand.

Semi-final, 11 October: Nairobi

Toss: Pakistan
Umpires: DL Orchard (SA) and DR Shepherd
TV Umpire: S Venkataraghavan (Ind)
Referee: R Subba Row
Man of the Match: SB O'Connor

Pakistan innings (50 overs maximum)			R	B
Saeed Anwar	c Parore	b Allott	104	115
Imran Nazir	c Spearman	b O'Connor	21	27
Yousuf Youhana	c Fleming	b Astle	24	43
Inzamam-ul Haq	st Parore	b Astle	1	6
Ijaz Ahmed	c & b Harris		3	6
*+Moin Khan	run out (Fleming/Wiseman)		2	4
Abdul Razzaq	c Astle	b O'Connor	48	49
Wasim Akram	c Fleming	b O'Connor	34	35
Azhar Mahmood	c Styris	b O'Connor	4	4
Saqlain Mushtaq	c & b O'Connor		2	4
Arshad Khan	not out		2	5

Extras: (lb 3, w 2, nb 2) 7
Total: (all out, 49.2 overs, 203 mins) 252

FoW: 1-59 (Imran Nazir, 9.6 ov), 2-111 (Yousuf Youhana, 23.2 ov), 3-120 (Inzamam-ul Haq, 25.2 ov), 4-133 (Ijaz Ahmed, 28.1 ov), 5-143 (Moin Khan, 29.4 ov), 6-178 (Saeed Anwar, 36.1 ov), 7-237 (Abdul Razzaq, 45.6 ov), 8-243 (Azhar Mahmood, 47.1 ov), 9-249 (Wasim Akram, 47.6 ov), 10-252 (Saqlain Mushtaq, 49.2 ov).

Bowling	O	M	R	W
Allott	10	0	57	1 (1nb)
O'Connor	9.2	0	46	5 (1w)
Styris	10	1	41	0 (1w)
Astle	10	0	50	2
Harris	7	0	36	1 (1nb)
Wiseman	3	0	19	0

New Zealand innings (target: 253 runs from 50 overs)			R	B
CM Spearman		b Azhar Mahmood	1	5
NJ Astle	c Moin Khan	b Azhar Mahmood	49	81
*SP Fleming	c Inzamam-ul Haq	b Azhar Mahmood	12	1
RG Twose	c Wasim Akram	b Saqlain Mushtaq	87	101
CD McMillan	not out		51	56
+AC Parore		b Azhar Mahmood	10	12
CZ Harris	run out (Imran Nazir)		0	1
SB Styris	not out		28	31

Extras: (b 4, lb 3, w 5, nb 5) 17
Total: (6 wickets, 49 overs, 225 mins) 255

DNB: PJ Wiseman, SB O'Connor, GI Allott.

FoW: 1-3 (Spearman, 1.2 ov), 2-15 (Fleming, 3.5 ov), 3-150 (Astle, 30.1 ov), 4-169 (Twose, 34.2 ov), 5-187 (Parore, 37.4 ov), 6-187 (Harris, 37.5 ov).

Bowling	O	M	R	W
Wasim Akram	10	0	47	0 (4w)
Azhar Mahmood	10	0	65	4 (3nb, 1w)
Abdul Razzaq	10	0	41	0 (1nb)
Saqlain Mushtaq	10	0	40	1
Arshad Khan	9	0	55	0

Semi-final, 13 October: Nairobi

In the other play-off in the last four, India continued to carve out a niche by swerving past the South Africans.

Toss: India
Umpires: SA Bucknor (WI) and P Willey
TV Umpire: DR Shepherd
Referee: CW Smith (WI)
Man of the Match: SC Ganguly

India innings (50 overs maximum)			R	B
*SC Ganguly	not out		141	142
SR Tendulkar	c Klusener	b Kallis	39	50
R Dravid	c Boucher	b Klusener	58	71
Yuvraj Singh	c Rhodes	b Kallis	41	35
RR Singh	run out (Donald)		0	1
VG Kambli	lbw	b Donald	0	1
+V Dahiya	c Hall	b Donald	1	3

Extras: (b 1, lb 6, w 5, nb 3) 15
Total: (6 wickets, 50 overs) 295

DNB: AB Agarkar, A Kumble, Z Khan, BKV Prasad.

FoW: 1-66 (Tendulkar, 14.1 ov), 2-211 (Dravid, 39.1 ov),
3-293 (Yuvraj Singh, 48.6 ov), 4-293 (RR Singh, 49.1 ov),
5-293 (Kambli, 49.2 ov), 6-295 (Dahiya, 49.6 ov).

Bowling	O	M	R	W
Pollock	10	1	43	0 (1w)
Telemachus	9	0	62	0
Donald	10	1	34	2 (1w)
Kallis	10	0	71	2 (1w)
Klusener	6	0	29	1 (2nb)
Boje	2	0	26	0
Hall	3	0	23	0 (1nb, 2w)

South Africa innings (target: 296 runs from 50 overs)			R	B
G Kirsten	run out (Ganguly)		12	13
AJ Hall		b Khan	1	4
JH Kallis	c Ganguly	b Prasad	15	18
HH Dippenaar	c Dahiya	b Khan	5	6
JN Rhodes	c Prasad	b Yuvraj Singh	32	55
+MV Boucher	c Tendulkar	b Ganguly	60	77
L Klusener	c Dahiya	b Kumble	29	37
*SM Pollock	st Dahiya	b Kumble	4	10
N Boje		b Tendulkar	10	16
R Telemachus	c Prasad	b Tendulkar	13	13
AA Donald	not out		1	1

Extras: (b 3, lb 4, w 7, nb 4) 18
Total: (all out, 41 overs) 200

FoW: 1-13 (Hall, 2.1 ov), 2-23 (Kirsten, 3.5 ov),
3-28 (Dippenaar, 4.5 ov), 4-50 (Kallis, 7.5 ov),
5-106 (Rhodes, 22.1 ov), 6-161 (Boucher, 32.1 ov),
7-171 (Pollock, 35.3 ov), 8-179 (Klusener, 37.1 ov),
9-199 (Telemachus, 40.4 ov), 10-200 (Boje, 40.6 ov).

Bowling	O	M	R	W
Khan	5	0	27	2 (3nb, 3w)
Prasad	8	0	54	1 (1nb, 1w)
Kumble	9	1	28	2 (2w)
Agarkar	7	1	21	0
Yuvraj Singh	4	1	15	1 (1w)
Tendulkar	5	0	32	2
Singh	2	0	11	0
Ganguly	1	0	5	1

Final, 15 October: Nairobi

The Indians lost the final to New Zealand. As Chris Cairns gushed:
'New Zealand's never got to a final before, let alone win it.' This all-
rounder, a mainstay of the Kiwi line-up, ignored a knee injury to

score a match-winning hundred. This windfall, though, did not prove to be a watershed for the Black Caps, as they went on to lose 11 of their next 13 one-dayers.

Toss: New Zealand
Umpires: SA Bucknor (WI) and DR Shepherd
TV Umpire: DB Hair (Aus)
Referee: RS Madugalle (SL)
Man of the Match: CL Cairns

India innings (50 overs maximum)			*R*	*B*
*SC Ganguly	c Harris	b Astle	117	130
SR Tendulkar	run out (Styris/Astle)		69	83
R Dravid	run out (Styris/Allott)		22	35
Yuvraj Singh	c Twose	b Styris	18	19
VG Kambli	c O'Connor	b Styris	1	5
RR Singh	c Spearman	b Allott	13	11
AB Agarkar	not out		15	17
+V Dahiya	not out		1	2

Extras: (lb 2, w 4, nb 2) 8
Total: (6 wickets, 50 overs, 217 mins) 264

DNB: A Kumble, Z Khan, BKV Prasad.

FoW: 1-141 (Tendulkar, 26.3 ov), 2-202 (Dravid, 38.6 ov),
3-220 (Ganguly, 42.3 ov), 4-229 (Kambli, 43.4 ov),
5-237 (Yuvraj Singh, 45.3 ov), 6-256 (R R Singh, 48.4 ov).

Bowling	*O*	*M*	*R*	*W*
Allott	10	0	54	1 (1nb, 2w)
O'Connor	5	0	37	0 (1w)
Cairns	10	2	40	0 (1w)
Styris	10	0	53	2 (1nb)
Astle	10	0	46	1
Harris	5	0	32	0

New Zealand innings (target: 265 runs from 50 overs)			R	B
CM Spearman	c Yuvraj Singh	b Prasad	3	8
NJ Astle	c Singh	b Kumble	37	48
*SP Fleming	lbw	b Prasad	5	11
RG Twose	st Dahiya	b Kumble	31	35
CL Cairns	not out		102	113
CD McMillan	c Ganguly	b Tendulkar	15	14
CZ Harris	c Singh	b Prasad	46	72
+AC Parore	not out		3	4

Extras: (lb 15, w 1, nb 7) 23
Total: (6 wickets, 49.4 overs, 220 mins) 265

DNB: SB Styris, SB O'Connor, GI Allott.

FoW: 1-6 (Spearman, 1.5 ov), 2-37 (Fleming, 5.4 ov),
3-82 (Astle, 14.6 ov), 4-109 (Twose, 18.5 ov),
5-132 (McMillan, 23.2 ov), 6-254 (Harris, 48.3 ov).

Bowling	O	M	R	W
Khan	7	0	54	0 (6nb)
Prasad	7	0	27	3 (1w)
Agarkar	6.4	0	44	0
Kumble	9	0	55	2
Tendulkar	10	1	38	1
Yuvraj Singh	10	0	32	0 (1nb)

THE 2002 NATWEST SERIES FINAL

This triangular one-day series featuring England, India and Sri Lanka was made memorable by an extraordinary finale. India had acquired the reputation of chokers in one-day finals – they hadn't won one since beating Zimbabwe in the Coca-Cola Champions Trophy at Sharjah in 1998. But the obvious depth and flair in their batting this time made them serious challengers.

However, as the Sri Lankans fell by the wayside and England and India confronted each other for the title fight, the English batsmen virtually repeated the hammering meted out to India in the 1975 World Cup at the same ground with a total of 325. Marcus Trescothick, in good nick in the tournament, bludgeoned a more than a run-a-ball hundred and Nasser Hussain, too, got a century, albeit under a bit of strain.

Chasing 326 in any circumstamces is a distant dream; and at 146 for five, with the cream of their batting, including Sachin Tendulkar and Rahul Dravid, cooling their heels, defeat for India seemed inescapable. But this was when 21-year-old Mohammad Kaif, a specialist batsman sent in at number seven, joined 20-year-old Yuvraj Singh to snatch the trophy from England's grasp with two innings of remarkable composure combined with cut and thrust.

It was later revealed that in Kaif's home town of Allahabad in India's Uttar Pradesh state, his parents, resigned to an Indian defeat, switched off their TV set to, instead, go to the cinema. Yuvraj Singh, son of Yograj Singh, a medium pacer who played a solitary test for India in New Zealand in 1981, was generally a major success. This was the third time he calmly and crisply extricated Indian from a crisis.

The sight of Andrew Flintoff peeling off his shirt to whirl it like a ceiling fan at Mumbai's Wankhede Stadium after England won an ODI there earlier the same year was fresh in Indian memory. Saurav Ganguly, now, returned the disagreeable compliment from the dressing room balcony of Lord's, before running on to the pitch to hug his heroes, especially Kaif, who steered the ship to safety with an unbeaten hundred. It was a riposte a captain of India could have done without.

13 July, Lord's: London

Toss: England
Umpires: SA Bucknor (WI) and DR Shepherd
TV Umpire: P Willey
Referee: MJ Procter (SA)
Man of the Match: M Kaif
Player of the Series: ME Trescothick

England innings (50 overs maximum)			R	B
ME Trescothick		b Kumble	109	100
NV Knight		b Khan	14	29
*N Hussain		b Nehra	115	128
A Flintoff		b Khan	40	32
MP Vaughan	c Mongia	b Khan	3	5
PD Collingwood	not out		3	4
RC Irani	not out		10	7

Extras: (b 2, lb 16, w 7, nb 6) 31

Total: (5 wickets, 50 overs, 206 mins) 325

DNB: +AJ Stewart, AJ Tudor, D Gough, AF Giles.

FoW: 1-42 (Knight, 7.4 ov), 2-227 (Trescothick, 36.5 ov), 3-307 (Flintoff, 46.5 ov), 4-312 (Hussain, 47.6 ov), 5-312 (Vaughan, 48.1 ov).

Bowling	O	M	R	W
Nehra	10	0	66	1 (2nb, 1w)
Khan	10	1	62	3 (1nb, 2w)
Kumble	10	0	54	1
Harbhajan Singh	10	0	53	0 (2w)
Ganguly	3	0	28	0 (2nb)
Sehwag	4	0	26	0
Yuvraj Singh	3	0	18	0

India innings (target: 326 runs from 50 overs)			R	B
V Sehwag		b Giles	45	49
*SC Ganguly		b Tudor	60	43
D Mongia	c Stewart	b Irani	9	15
SR Tendulkar		b Giles	14	19
+R Dravid	c Knight	b Irani	5	12
Yuvraj Singh	c Tudor	b Collingwood	69	63
M Kaif	not out		87	75
Harbhajan Singh		b Flintoff	15	13
A Kumble	c Stewart	b Flintoff	0	2
Z Khan	not out		4	7

Extras: (b 3, lb 8, w 6, nb 1) 18
Total: (8 wickets, 49.3 overs, 219 mins) 326

DNB: A Nehra.

FoW: 1-106 (Ganguly, 14.3 ov), 2-114 (Sehwag, 15.6 ov),
3-126 (Mongia, 18.3 ov), 4-132 (Dravid, 20.6 ov),
5-146 (Tendulkar, 23.6 ov), 6-267 (Yuvraj Singh, 41.4 ov),
7-314 (Harbhajan Singh, 47.3 ov), 8-314 (Kumble, 47.5 ov).

Bowling	O	M	R	W
Gough	10	1	63	0 (3w)
Tudor	9	0	62	1 (1nb, 1w)
Flintoff	7.3	0	55	2 (2w)
Irani	10	0	64	2
Giles	10	0	47	2
Collingwood	3	0	24	1

THE 2002 ICC CHAMPIONS TROPHY

Controversy over player contracts preceded the tournament. But
the increased use of technology on an experimental basis added some
spice. The trial added greater efficiency to lbw decisions, but was
ineffectual regarding doubtful catches. The benefit, therefore, went
in favour of batsmen. The ICC later ruled that such aid from cameras
would not become common practice. The legitimacy of a catch,
though, could still be checked with the third or TV umpire. The
weather was hot and humid – it's only marginally better in the neo-
equatorial climate of Sri Lanka at the best of times. But cricket fans
in Sri Lanka had reason to reflect on the tournament – the third in
the series and now officially christened ICC Champions Trophy –
with nostalgia.

The planning of the tournament left much to be desired. The
pitches were, predictably, pensive – right up Sri Lanka's street. The
list of entries rose to 12 from 11 in Nairobi; and the teams were
divided into four pools of three each. Australia, New Zealand and
Bangladesh were in Pool 1; India, England and Zimbabwe in Pool 2;
South Africa, the West Indies and Kenya in Pool 3; and Pakistan, Sri
Lanka and the Netherlands in Pool 4.

Apart from Kenya, who gave the West Indies a run for their money, the small fishes were unceremoniously washed aside. The public response was poor, except for Sri Lanka and India matches, despite it being the most important cricketing event on Sri Lankan soil after the ceasefire in the country's civil war. The format and allocation of the league matches came in for some criticism. The nearest thing to an upset came early when the West Indies pushed South Africa all the way in a last-ball thriller.

13 September: Colombo

Toss: South Africa
Umpires: DR Shepherd and S Venkataraghavan (Ind)
TV Umpire: DJ Harper (Aus)
Referee: RS Madugalle
Man of the Match: JN Rhodes

West Indies innings (50 overs maximum)			R	B
CH Gayle	c Boucher	b Donald	49	55
S Chanderpaul	c Dippenaar	b Dawson	45	98
BC Lara	c Donald	b Boje	21	33
*CL Hooper	lbw	b Pollock	26	32
RR Sarwan		b Kallis	36	34
WW Hinds	c Kallis	b Donald	12	17
+RD Jacobs	c Pollock	b Kallis	25	21
MV Nagamootoo	run out (sub [JL Ontong])		10	10
VC Drakes	not out		0	0
M Dillon	not out		1	1

Extras: (lb 5, w 7, nb 1) 13
Total: (8 wickets, 50 overs, 222 mins) 238

DNB: PT Collins.

FoW: 1-63 (Gayle, 14.5 ov), 2-107 (Lara, 26.2 ov),
3-153 (Chanderpaul, 35.5 ov), 4-153 (Hooper, 36.2 ov),
5-191 (Hinds, 42.5 ov), 6-220 (Sarwan, 47.1 ov),
7-230 (Jacobs, 49.1 ov), 8-237 (Nagamootoo, 49.5 ov).

Bowling	O	M	R	W
Pollock	10	1	34	1 (1nb)
Dawson	10	1	51	1 (4w)
Donald	8	0	44	2 (1w)
Kallis	9	0	41	2 (2w)
Boje	7	0	34	1
Klusener	6	0	29	0

South Africa innings (target: 239 runs from 49 overs)			R	B
GC Smith	c Jacobs	b Hooper	33	55
HH Gibbs		b Dillon	8	10
JH Kallis	c Jacobs	b Drakes	10	25
HH Dippenaar	c Nagamootoo	b Hooper	53	84
JN Rhodes		b Hooper	61	70
+MV Boucher		b Dillon	23	21
L Klusener	c Chanderpaul	b Dillon	23	28
*SM Pollock	c Chanderpaul	b Dillon	10	6
N Boje	not out		0	0
AC Dawson	not out		4	1

Extras: (b 1, lb 3, w 7, nb 6) 17
Total: (8 wickets, 49 overs, 221 mins) 242

DNB: AA Donald.

FoW: 1-13 (Gibbs, 2.2 ov), 2-50 (Kallis, 11.6 ov),
3-61 (Smith, 16.3 ov), 4-178 (Dippenaar, 39.4 ov),
5-179 (Rhodes, 39.6 ov), 6-220 (Boucher, 46.6 ov),
7-234 (Pollock, 48.3 ov), 8-236 (Klusener, 48.5 ov).

Bowling	O	M	R	W
Dillon	10	1	60	4 (2nb, 3w)
Collins	9	0	38	0 (3nb, 1w)
Hooper	10	1	42	3 (1w)
Drakes	8	1	36	1 (1w)
Nagamootoo	9	0	41	0 (1nb)
Gayle	3	0	21	0

In other matches in Pool 3, the West Indies beat Kenya by 29 runs, and the Kenyans also lost to South Africa by 176 runs.

India, who flew straight from England (where they had dramatically won the NatWest one-day series and drawn the tests 1–1 after a stirring victory at Headingley) to Sri Lanka for the tournament, adjusted admirably to the completely different conditions.

14 September: Colombo

Toss: India
Umpires: EAR de Silva and RE Koertzen (SA)
TV Umpire: SA Bucknor (WI)
Referee: Wasim Raja (Pak)
ODI Debut: RW Price (Zim).
Man of the Match: M Kaif

India innings (50 overs maximum)			R	B
*SC Ganguly	c Campbell	b Hondo	13	12
V Sehwag	c A Flower	b Ervine	48	36
D Mongia	c Campbell	b Hondo	0	4
SR Tendulkar	c Campbell	b Hondo	7	16
+R Dravid	run out (Carlisle)		71	81
Yuvraj Singh	c Ervine	b Hondo	3	7
M Kaif	not out		111	112
A Kumble	not out		18	36

Extras: (b 1, lb 2, w 10, nb 4) 17
Total: (6 wickets, 50 overs, 209 mins) 288

DNB: Harbhajan Singh, Z Khan, A Nehra.

FoW: 1-25 (Ganguly, 3.2 ov), 2-25 (Mongia, 3.6 ov), 3-67 (Tendulkar, 9.5 ov), 4-84 (Sehwag, 12.1 ov), 5-87 (Yuvraj Singh, 13.2 ov), 6-204 (Dravid, 37.3 ov).

Bowling	O	M	R	W
Streak	7	0	48	0 (2nb)
Hondo	9	1	62	4 (2nb, 1w)
Ervine	8	0	60	1 (3w)
Whittall	8	0	39	0 (2w)
Price	10	0	38	0
Marillier	5	0	23	0
GW Flower	3	0	15	0 (1w)

Zimbabwe innings (target: 289 runs from 50 overs)			R	B
ADR Campbell	c Yuvraj Singh	b Khan	8	26
DD Ebrahim	lbw	b Khan	0	3
+A Flower	c Ganguly	b Tendulkar	145	164
GW Flower	run out (Yuvraj Singh/Dravid)		33	41
SV Carlisle		b Tendulkar	2	4
GJ Whittall	c Dravid	b Khan	29	30
DA Marillier	c Ganguly	b Kumble	14	19
SM Ervine		b Khan	7	14
*HH Streak	not out		4	3

Extras: (b 6, lb 16, w 6, nb 4) 32
Total: (8 wickets, 50 overs, 228 mins) 274

DNB: DT Hondo, RW Price.

FoW: 1-1 (Ebrahim, 0.4 ov), 2-43 (Campbell, 10.1 ov),
3-127 (GW Flower, 26.4 ov), 4-130 (Carlisle, 27.3 ov),
5-201 (Whittall, 39.1 ov), 6-240 (Marillier, 44.6 ov),
7-263 (A Flower, 48.4 ov), 8-274 (Ervine, 49.6 ov).

Bowling	O	M	R	W
Khan	10	2	45	4 (1nb, 1w)
Nehra	8	0	37	0 (2nb, 2w)
Kumble	10	0	48	1 (1nb, 1w)
Harbhajan Singh	10	0	44	0 (1w)
Yuvraj Singh	3	0	24	0
Tendulkar	7	0	41	2 (1w)
Ganguly	2	0	13	0

In the next match in Pool 2, England, too, defeated Zimbabwe – by 108 runs. This result enticingly set up a clash to decide who would go forward to the semi-finals. In the event, India won convincingly.

22 September: Colombo

Toss: England
Umpires: SA Bucknor (WI) and RB Tiffin (Zim)
TV Umpire: RE Koertzen (SA)
Referee: Wasim Raja (Pak)
Man of the Match: V Sehwag

England innings (50 overs maximum)			R	B
ME Trescothick	c Laxman	b Nehra	0	8
NV Knight	c Harbhajan Singh	b Yuvraj Singh	50	70
*N Hussain	c Dravid	b Nehra	1	11
RC Irani	lbw	b Kumble	37	47
OA Shah	c Dravid	b Kumble	34	47
ID Blackwell	run out (Sehwag/Dravid)		82	68
+AJ Stewart	c Ganguly	b Tendulkar	35	44
DG Cork	not out		6	5
AF Giles	not out		2	3

Extras: (b 5, lb 9, w 5, nb 3) 22
Total: (7 wickets, 50 overs, 219 mins) 269

DNB: AR Caddick, MJ Hoggard.

FoW: 1-2 (Trescothick, 3.1 ov), 2-7 (Hussain, 5.2 ov),
3-80 (Irani, 18.4 ov), 4-127 (Knight, 27.5 ov),
5-153 (Shah, 33.1 ov), 6-257 (Stewart, 48.1 ov),
7-264 (Blackwell, 49.2 ov).

Bowling	O	M	R	W
Khan	10	2	40	0 (2nb)
Nehra	10	0	49	2 (1nb, 1w)
Kumble	9	0	58	2
Harbhajan Singh	10	0	42	0 (2w)
Ganguly	1	0	10	0
Tendulkar	2	0	13	1
Yuvraj Singh	3	0	18	1
Sehwag	5	0	25	0 (1w)

India innings (target: 270 runs from 50 overs)		R	B
V Sehwag	c & b Blackwell	126	104
*SC Ganguly	not out	117	109
VVS Laxman	run out (Shah/Stewart)	4	8
SR Tendulkar	not out	9	20

Extras: (b 1, lb 1, w 9, nb 4) 15

Total: (2 wickets, 39.3 overs, 183 mins) 271

DNB: +R Dravid, Yuvraj Singh, M Kaif, A Kumble,

Harbhajan Singh, Z Khan, A Nehra.

FoW: 1-192 (Sehwag, 28.4 ov), 2-200 (Laxman, 31.2 ov).

Bowling	O	M	R	W
Caddick	7	0	59	0 (2w)
Hoggard	10	0	54	0 (1nb, 1w)
Cork	5.3	0	45	0 (3nb, 4w)
Irani	5	0	34	0
Giles	4	0	31	0
Blackwell	8	0	46	1 (2w)

In the last four, figuring in the same half of the draw, India edged out South Africa by 10 runs in a closely fought encounter.

Semi-final, 25 September: Colombo

Toss: India
Umpires: DR Shepherd and RB Tiffin (Zim)
TV Umpire: DJ Harper (Aus)
Referee: RS Madugalle
ODI Debut: RJ Peterson (SA).
Man of the Match: V Sehwag

India innings (50 overs maximum)			R	B
V Sehwag	c Klusener	b Kallis	59	58
*SC Ganguly	c Dippenaar	b Ntini	13	13
VVS Laxman	c Boucher	b Donald	22	33
SR Tendulkar	run out (Boucher/Rhodes)		16	29
+R Dravid	lbw	b Klusener	49	67
Yuvraj Singh	c Gibbs	b Pollock	62	72
M Kaif	c Rhodes	b Pollock	19	21
Harbhajan Singh		b Donald	4	4
Z Khan	c Smith	b Pollock	0	3
A Kumble	not out		2	2
A Nehra	not out		1	1

Extras: (b 2, lb 1, w 8, nb 3) 14
Total: (9 wickets, 50 overs, 215 mins) 261

FoW: 1-42 (Ganguly, 5.4 ov), 2-102 (Laxman, 16.1 ov),
3-108 (Sehwag, 17.5 ov), 4-135 (Tendulkar, 25.2 ov),
5-207 (Dravid, 40.5 ov), 6-254 (Yuvraj Singh, 48.1 ov),
7-254 (Kaif, 48.2 ov), 8-255 (Khan, 48.6 ov),
9-260 (Harbhajan Singh, 49.5 ov).

Bowling	O	M	R	W
Pollock	9	0	43	3 (1nb)
Ntini	5	0	37	1 (2nb, 1w)
Donald	8	0	41	2 (1w)
Kallis	8	1	50	1 (2w)
Klusener	10	0	40	1
Peterson	10	0	47	0

South Africa innings (target: 262 runs from 50 overs)			R	B
HH Gibbs	retired hurt		116	119
GC Smith	c Yuvraj Singh	b Khan	4	5
JH Kallis	c Dravid	b Sehwag	97	133
JN Rhodes	c Yuvraj Singh	b Harbhajan Singh	1	3
HH Dippenaar	c Kumble	b Harbhajan Singh	0	3
+MV Boucher	c Yuvraj Singh	b Sehwag	10	16
L Klusener	c Kaif	b Sehwag	14	21
*SM Pollock	not out		0	0

Extras: (b 1, lb 3, w 5) 9
Total: (6 wickets, 50 overs, 225 mins) 251

DNB: RJ Peterson, AA Donald, M Ntini.

FoW: 1-14 (Smith, 2.6 ov), 2-194 (Rhodes, 38.2 ov),
3-194 (Dippenaar, 38.5 ov), 4-213 (Boucher, 43.3 ov),
5-247 (Kallis, 49.2 ov), 6-251 (Klusener, 49.6 ov).

Bowling	O	M	R	W
Khan	9	2	27	1 (4w)
Nehra	7.3	0	41	0 (1w)
Kumble	10	0	53	0
Harbhajan Singh	10	0	37	2
Yuvraj Singh	3	0	17	0
Ganguly	1.3	0	15	0
Tendulkar	4	0	32	0
Sehwag	5	0	25	3

Australia, the favourites, were rampant. They overwhelmed New Zealand by 164 runs and Bangladesh by nine wickets in Pool 1. But they were stopped in their tracks by Sri Lanka, who had hastened to the semi-final by subjugating Pakistan by eight wickets and then swamping the Dutch by 206 runs in Pool 4. The Sri Lankan spinners now cut the Aussies to size. It was a popular win – by seven wickets – as the Australians have been rather unloved in Sri Lanka since Muttiah Muralitharan was no-balled for chucking by Australian umpire Darrell Hair in the mid-1990s.

Semi-final, 27 September: Colombo

Toss: Australia
Umpires: SA Bucknor (WI) and DL Orchard (SA)
TV Umpire: RE Koertzen (SA)
Referee: Wasim Raja (Pak)
Man of the Match: PA de Silva

Australia innings (50 overs maximum)			R	B
+AC Gilchrist	c Atapattu	b Dharmasena	31	24
ML Hayden		b de Silva	13	18
*RT Ponting	lbw	b Vaas	3	22
DR Martyn	run out (Arnold)		28	47
DS Lehmann	run out (Jayasuriya)		0	7
MG Bevan	c Arnold	b Dharmasena	12	37
SR Watson	c Jayasuriya	b Muralitharan	7	26
SK Warne	st Sangakkara	b Muralitharan	36	69
B Lee		b Jayasuriya	18	38
JN Gillespie	not out		2	3
GD McGrath	b Muralitharan		0	1

Extras: (b 10, lb 1, w 1) 12
Total: (all out, 48.4 overs, 195 mins) 162

FoW: 1-49 (Hayden, 6.5 ov), 2-49 (Gilchrist, 7.1 ov),
3-56 (Ponting, 11.2 ov), 4-57 (Lehmann, 12.6 ov),
5-96 (Martyn, 24.5 ov), 6-97 (Bevan, 25.5 ov),
7-107 (Watson, 32.4 ov), 8-153 (Lee, 46.3 ov),
9-162 (Warne, 48.3 ov), 10-162 (McGrath, 48.4 ov).

Bowling	O	M	R	W
Vaas	7	2	31	1 (1w)
Gunaratne	2	0	15	0
Dharmasena	10	1	30	2
de Silva	10	2	16	1
Muralitharan	9.4	0	26	3
Chandana	7	0	22	0
Jayasuriya	3	0	11	1

Sri Lanka innings (target: 163 runs from 50 overs)			R	B
*ST Jayasuriya		b Warne	42	51
MS Atapattu	lbw	b McGrath	51	113
+KC Sangakkara	c Gilchrist	b McGrath	48	63
PA de Silva	not out		2	16
DPMD Jayawardene	not out		1	3

Extras: (b 4, lb 2, w 7, nb 6) 19
Total: (3 wickets, 40 overs, 191 mins) 163

DNB: RP Arnold, WPUJC Vaas, M Muralitharan, HDPK Dharmasena, UDU Chandana, PW Gunaratne.

FoW: 1-67 (Jayasuriya, 14.6 ov), 2-142 (Sangakkara, 33.6 ov), 3-160 (Atapattu, 39.2 ov).

Bowling	O	M	R	W
McGrath	10	1	41	2 (1w)
Gillespie	8	1	28	0 (2w)
Warne	10	2	25	1 (3nb)
Lee	7	1	39	0 (3nb, 2w)
Lehmann	5	0	24	0 (1w)

The 5000 Indian fans, who had hopped across from the South Asian mainland, augmented the passion at the final. But the event proved to be an out-and-out damp squib, as two separate attempts to stage it were crushed by torrential rain. If the rules had permitted continuance of the first match to a reserve day, the issue could have been resolved satisfactorily. In the event, the climax was a farce.

First Final, 29 September: Colombo

Toss: Sri Lanka
Umpires: SA Bucknor (WI) and DR Shepherd
TV Umpire: DJ Harper (Aus)
Referee: CH Lloyd (WI)
Man of the Match: No award

Sri Lanka innings (50 overs maximum)			R	B
*ST Jayasuriya	c Harbhajan Singh	b Agarkar	74	89
MS Atapattu	c Agarkar	b Harbhajan Singh	34	46
+KC Sangakkara	c Sehwag	b Harbhajan Singh	54	89
PA de Silva	c Dravid	b Harbhajan Singh	18	25
DPMD Jayawardene	c & b Tendulkar		13	20
RP Arnold	not out		18	18
WPUJC Vaas	not out		11	13

Extras: (b 6, lb 8, w 8) 22
Total: (5 wickets, 50 overs, 210 mins) 244

DNB: M Muralitharan, HDPK Dharmasena, CRD Fernando, PW Gunaratne.

FoW: 1-65 (Atapattu, 12.5 ov), 2-155 (Jayasuriya, 30.4 ov), 3-185 (de Silva, 38.4 ov), 4-207 (Sangakkara, 44.2 ov), 5-212 (Jayawardene, 45.4 ov).

Bowling	O	M	R	W
Khan	10	0	43	0 (2w)
Srinath	8	0	55	0 (4w)
Agarkar	6	0	37	1 (1w)
Harbhajan Singh	10	1	27	3
Sehwag	10	0	32	0
Tendulkar	6	0	36	1 (1w)

India innings (target: 245 runs from 50 overs)		R	B
D Mongia	not out	1	7
V Sehwag	not out	13	5

Extras: 0
Total: (0 wickets, 2 overs, 8 mins) 14

DNB: *SC Ganguly, SR Tendulkar, +R Dravid, Yuvraj Singh, M Kaif, Harbhajan Singh, Z Khan, AB Agarkar, J Srinath.

Bowling	O	M	R	W
Vaas	1	1	0	0
Gunaratne	1	0	14	0

Second Final, 30 September: Colombo

Toss: Sri Lanka
Umpires: SA Bucknor (WI) and DR Shepherd
TV Umpire: DJ Harper (Aus)
Referee: CH Lloyd (WI)
Man of the Match: No Award

Sri Lanka innings (50 overs maximum)			R	B
*ST Jayasuriya		b Khan	0	1
+KC Sangakkara	run out (Mongia/ Harbhajan Singh)		26	46
MS Atapattu	c Mongia	b Agarkar	10	17
PA de Silva	c Kaif	b Kumble	27	24
DPMD Jayawardene	c Ganguly	b Khan	77	99
RP Arnold	not out		56	101
UDU Chandana	c Kaif	b Harbhajan Singh	1	3
WPUJC Vaas	c Kumble	b Khan	17	10
M Muralitharan	not out		0	0

Extras: (w 7, nb 1) 8
Total: (7 wickets, 50 overs, 211 mins) 222

DNB: CRD Fernando, HDPK Dharmasena.

FoW: 1-0 (Jayasuriya, 0.1 ov), 2-24 (Atapattu, 7.1 ov), 3-63 (de Silva, 13.1 ov), 4-71 (Sangakkara, 16.3 ov), 5-189 (Jayawardene, 45.2 ov), 6-193 (Chandana, 46.4 ov), 7-215 (Vaas, 49.2 ov).

Bowling	O	M	R	W
Khan	9	1	44	3 (1nb, 1w)
Agarkar	5	1	36	1 (1w)
Harbhajan Singh	10	0	34	1
Kumble	10	1	41	1 (1w)
Sehwag	8	0	31	0
Tendulkar	8	0	36	0 (1w)

India innings (target: 223 runs from 50 overs)			R	B
D Mongia	c Jayawardene	b Vaas	0	9
V Sehwag	not out		25	22
SR Tendulkar	not out		7	22

Extras: (b 1, w 4, nb 1) 6
Total: (1 wicket, 8.4 overs, 48 mins) 38

DNB: *SC Ganguly, +R Dravid, Yuvraj Singh, M Kaif, Harbhajan Singh, Z Khan, AB Agarkar, A Kumble.

FoW: 1-6 (Mongia, 2.3 ov).

Bowling	O	M	R	W
Vaas	4.4	1	24	1
Fernando	4	0	13	0 (1nb, 4w)

8

The Rainbow Cup

IN 1994, SOUTH AFRICA HELD ITS FIRST ELECTIONS ON THE BASIS of universal suffrage. As a process of reconciliation from the deeply divisive system that had existed earlier, its new rulers, led by the charismatic Nelson Mandela, hailed the new nation as the 'rainbow' republic or as a beautiful integration of the different colours of its people. This, multiracial South Africa, making its presence felt after decades of seclusion, spearheaded the staging of the 2003 World Cup, with Zimbabwe and Kenya as its partners.

The three African host countries were keen to promote themselves as desirable destinations for tourists; hence an extravagant opening ceremony in Cape Town that smelt of a not-so-subtle travel commercial. In financial terms, with profits of US $194 million representing a huge increase on the $51million made in 1999, the 8th World Cup was the most successful yet.

On the eve of Australia's opening encounter, Shane Warne, their Man of the Match in the 1999 World Cup semi-final and final, was sent home after reports confirmed he had taken performance-enhancing drugs during the Victoria Bitter (VB) Series in Australia the previous month. He was, thereafter, banned for a year, quite a light sentence considering the seriousness of the offence. Warne admitted wrongdoing, but gave a story that suggested he had committed this offence unknowingly. To accept this explanation was either naivety or not in the spirit of sport. Previously, Australian authorities had taken a lenient view of Mark Waugh and Warne's confession that they had accepted money from a bookmaker in Sri Lanka to offer their views on matches!

However, all-rounder Andy Bichel reflected Australia's depth of talent and paceman Brett Lee their incisiveness. The latter finished with 22 wickets to Chaminda Vaas' 23 – a World Cup record. 'Lee is not a match winner,' taunted Shoaib Akhtar. The Pakistani bowled the fastest ball of the tournament: a 100-mph delivery against England. But despite the needling, Lee proved to be more of a match winner.

Conflicts between the World Cup's sponsors and existing contracts of players, particularly when it came to the Indians, provoked the ICC to threaten member boards with damages. In turn, the BCCI issued warnings to their players over endorsement of rival products. In the end, the ICC withheld the BCCI's share of revenue until the issue was resolved.

Meanwhile, matters extraneous to cricket, such as whether it was safe to play in Kenya and morally right to do so in Zimbabwe, given the violent and repressive nature of President Robert Mugabe's regime, afflicted the event.

The 14 teams were sectioned off into two groups in the first stage. In one group, New Zealand refused to play in Nairobi; in the other, England desisted from visiting Harare. The ICC awarded the matches to the hosts, which threw the tournament out of gear. Had England gone to Harare and avoided defeat, they, rather than Zimbabwe, would have reached the second phase. By winning four of the five pool matches they actually played, New Zealand reached the Super Six anyway, but the forfeiture enabled Kenya to go through at the expense of the improving West Indies and eventually qualify for the semi-final.

The ICC withheld $3.5 million from England's share of revenue and $2.5 million from New Zealand's.

Two prominent Zimbabwean players, Andy Flower and Henry Olonga, one white, the other black, took the field against Namibia in Harare wearing black armbands after issuing a statement 'mourning

the death of democracy in our beloved Zimbabwe'. The ICC asked
them to abstain from making political gestures. Flower said he was
not making a political statement but a humanitarian plea. For what
turned out to be Zimbabwe's next match – against India nine days
later – the pair wore black wristbands, Olonga in his capacity as
twelfth man, having been dropped in what looked like an act of
retaliation.

As the tournament continued, it appeared that the selection of
Zimbabwe's team had become highly politicized, with preference
given to those not critical of Mugabe's regime. Andy Pycroft, a
selector, resigned after being told the team was 'non-negotiable'. It
was also clear that Flower and Olonga's days as Zimbabwe players
were numbered. For Flower, at 34, this prospect posed little hardship;
indeed, he had already arranged to play professionally for Essex and
South Australia in domestic competition in England and Australia,
respectively. But Olonga, only 26, lost much more.

Public expectations of a home victory were sky high long before
South Africa's opening encounter with the West Indies – graced by
an accomplished hundred from Brian Lara – South Africa lost by
three runs. The outcome for the hosts could hardly have been worse.
They failed to beat any major opposition and stumbled at the first
hurdle. They were trounced by New Zealand in a rain-affected match
in Johannesburg, and the elements also had a say in their do-or-die
affair with Sri Lanka in Durban. With South Africa needing 269 under
lights, the contest was on a knife-edge when it started to rain. The
dressing room sent word to the batsmen, Mark Boucher and Lance
Klusener, that the Duckworth/Lewis target at the end of the next
over – the 45th – was 229, provided they lost no more wickets.
Boucher attained this target by hitting the fifth ball from Muttiah
Muralitharan for six and then blocking the last.

But the rain had intensified and the umpires took the players
off, never to return. A score of 229 would tie the match, as
Duckworth/Lewis clearly stated. While a tie was fine for Sri Lanka,
it wasn't for South Africa. So, for the second World Cup in a row,
South Africa lost a bit synthetically. But while the South African
camp were justly criticized for misreading the Duckworth/Lewis

charts, the fact remains that had the electronic scoreboard at Kingsmead carried the par score (as commonly happens in England), the mistake might not have occurred.

However, an African team, Kenya, did make it to the semi-final. They enjoyed the greatest giant-killing run in international cricket. Yet, had they played and lost to New Zealand, they would not have made the second phase. The enthusiasm of their players, coached by Sandeep Patil, a member of the 1983 World Cup-winning Indian squad in 1983, and of their red-white-and-green-painted supporters, were a delightful sight.

Though they later lost to South Africa by ten wickets, Kenya defended a score of 210 to beat Sri Lanka in Nairobi. Collins Obuya, who was inspired to bowl leg-spin by watching Mushtaq Ahmed on television in the 1996 World Cup, took five for 24 against a team normally accomplished at playing slow bowling. Next, the Kenyans confirmed a Super Six place with an altogether less surprising victory over Bangladesh. The points from the New Zealand 'win' were carried forward to the second stage, meaning that Kenya began the Super Sixes second only to Australia, and they sealed a semi-final spot with victory over Zimbabwe, their third over test opposition.

12 February: Paarl

It was a dream day for Holland's Tim de Leede, who had previously frequented several English county 'second XIs', but collected Sachin Tendulkar as his first World Cup wicket and proceeded to take three more. During his knock of 52, Tendulkar surpassed Javed Miandad as the highest run-getter in World Cups. (This was the Indian's fourth World Cup as compared to the Pakistani having partaken in six.) Yuvraj Singh and Dinesh Mongia, then, prevented an embarrassing total after the Indians, considered to be a dazzling batting line-up, had opted to bat first.

Subsequently, early wickets bagged during the Dutch reply averted any Indian awkwardness. However, Holland's tail wagged, and it was not until the second-last over that India wrapped up their opponent's innings. Daan van Bunge, a student from The Hague, scored 62. Anil Kumble, a wildlife conservationist, technically, boasted the best bowling figures – also his career best in the World Cup. A wrist spinner of a faster variety, who bowls more googlies and top-spinners than leg-breaks, his wicket taking in one-day cricket in general had not up to this point had not been as abundant as in tests. India won by 68 runs.

Toss: India
Umpires: DJ Harper (Aus) and P Willey (Eng)
TV Umpire: Nadeem Ghauri (Pak)
Referee: DT Lindsay
ODI Debut: J Smits (NL).
Man of the Match: TBM de Leede

India innings (50 overs maximum)			*R*	*B*
*SC Ganguly	c Smits	b Lefebvre	8	32
SR Tendulkar	c Smits	b de Leede	52	72
V Sehwag	c Zuiderent	b Kloppenburg	6	9
+R Dravid		b de Leede	17	38
Yuvraj Singh	c & b Adeel Raja		37	56
M Kaif	c Lefebvre	b Adeel Raja	9	21
D Mongia	run out (Kloppenburg/ de Leede)		42	49
Harbhajan Singh		b de Leede	13	8
A Kumble	run out (Scholte/ de Leede)		9	7
Z Khan	lbw	b de Leede	0	2
J Srinath	not out		0	0

Extras: (lb 2, w 8, nb 1) 11
Total: (all out, 48.5 overs, 206 mins) 204

FoW: 1-30 (Ganguly, 11.5 ov), 2-56 (Sehwag, 14.6 ov),
3-81 (Tendulkar, 23.3 ov), 4-91 (Dravid, 25.6 ov),
5-114 (Kaif, 31.5 ov), 6-169 (Yuvraj Singh, 43.5 ov),
7-186 (Harbhajan Singh, 46.2 ov), 8-203 (Kumble, 48.2 ov),
9-204 (Mongia, 48.4 ov), 10-204 (Khan, 48.5 ov).

Bowling	O	M	R	W
Schiferli	10	2	49	0
Lefebvre	9	1	27	1 (2w)
de Leede	9.5	0	35	4 (2w)
Kloppenburg	10	0	40	1 (1nb, 3w)
Adeel Raja	9	0	47	2
van Troost	1	0	4	0

Netherlands innings (target: 205 runs from 50 overs)			R	B
JF Kloppenburg	c Sehwag	b Srinath	0	4
DLS van Bunge		b Srinath	62	116
HJC Mol	c Dravid	b Srinath	2	30
B Zuiderent	c Sehwag	b Khan	0	6
TBM de Leede	c Dravid	b Harbhajan Singh	0	9
LP van Troost	c Dravid	b Kumble	1	10
RH Scholte	lbw	b Kumble	1	5
*RP Lefebvre	lbw	b Kumble	3	14
E Schiferli	c Mongia	b Kumble	13	21
+J Smits	c Sehwag	b Srinath	26	66
Adeel Raja	not out		0	10

Extras: (b 2, lb 6, w 18, nb 2) 28
Total: (all out, 48.1 overs, 204 mins) 136

FoW: 1-0 (Kloppenburg, 0.4 ov), 2-29 (Mol, 8.2 ov),
3-31 (Zuiderent, 9.4 ov), 4-38 (de Leede, 12.6 ov),
5-42 (van Troost, 15.5 ov), 6-44 (Scholte, 17.1 ov),
7-54 (Lefebvre, 21.3 ov), 8-82 (Schiferli, 27.5 ov),
9-131 (van Bunge, 44.4 ov), 10-136 (Smits, 48.1 ov).

Bowling	O	M	R	W
Srinath	9.1	1	30	4 (1nb, 1w)
Khan	8	1	17	1 (9w)
Harbhajan Singh	10	1	20	1
Kumble	10	1	32	4 (1nb, 1w)
Ganguly	4	0	14	0 (2w)
Tendulkar	4	0	9	0
Sehwag	3	0	6	0

15 February: SuperSport Park, Centurion

India's decision to bat first was jettisoned by a swinging ball. Their batsmen simply failed to cope; the top six in their order scoring just 51 among them. There was no colourful strokeplay so characteristic of the Indians. That is, not until Harbhajan Singh briefly fluttered in the pressureless situation of a lost cause. Glenn McGrath's nagging line and Lee's whiplash pace created considerable uncertainty. But it was Jason Gillespie who broke the Indian backbone. Introduced as first change, he operated with unerring accuracy. Indeed, he sent down his entire quota of 10 overs without a break, finishing with three for 13. He removed Tendulkar with a mesmerizing slower off-cutter. This dismissal smothered India's last chance of erecting a respectable total.

Australia expended a mere 22.2 overs to overhaul this lowest-ever Indian total in the World Cup. Adam Gilchrist and Mathew Hayden briefly delighted the 18,000-odd crowd, which clearly didn't get its money's worth from a match hyped as one of the most alluring early encounters of the tournament. Australia trotted to victory by nine wickets.

Toss: India
Umpires: EAR de Silva (SL) and DR Shepherd (Eng)
TV Umpire: BG Jerling
Referee: CH Lloyd (WI)
Man of the Match: JN Gillespie

India innings (50 overs maximum)			R	B
*SC Ganguly	c Gilchrist	b Lee	9	21
SR Tendulkar	lbw	b Gillespie	36	59
V Sehwag	c Gilchrist	b Lee	4	4
+R Dravid		b Gillespie	1	23
Yuvraj Singh	lbw	b McGrath	0	8
M Kaif	c Symonds	b Gillespie	1	16
D Mongia	c Symonds	b Lee	13	39
A Kumble	not out		16	38
Harbhajan Singh	lbw	b Hogg	28	32
Z Khan	lbw	b Lehmann	1	9
J Srinath	run out (Lehmann)		0	2

Extras: (lb 5, w 10, nb 1) 16
Total (all out, 41.4 overs, 176 mins) 125

FoW: 1-22 (Ganguly, 5.4 ov), 2-41 (Sehwag, 7.2 ov),
3-44 (Dravid, 13.1 ov), 4-45 (Yuvraj Singh, 14.6 ov),
5-50 (Kaif, 17.6 ov), 6-78 (Tendulkar, 27.3 ov),
7-80 (Mongia, 28.3 ov), 8-120 (Harbhajan Singh, 37.2 ov),
9-125 (Khan, 40.4 ov), 10-125 (Srinath, 41.4 ov).

Bowling	O	M	R	W
McGrath	8	3	23	1
Lee	9	1	36	3 (1nb, 3w)
Gillespie	10	2	13	3 (1w)
Symonds	6	0	25	0 (4w)
Hogg	4.4	0	16	1
Lehmann	4	0	7	1

Australia innings (target: 126 runs from 50 overs)			R	B
+AC Gilchrist	st Dravid	b Kumble	48	61
ML Hayden	not out		45	49
*RT Ponting	not out		24	24

Extras: (lb 3, w 8) 11
Total: (1 wicket, 22.2 overs, 91 mins) 128

DNB: DR Martyn, DS Lehmann, MG Bevan, A Symonds, GB Hogg,
B Lee,
GD McGrath, JN Gillespie.

FoW: 1-100 (Gilchrist, 17.3 ov).

Bowling	O	M	R	W
Srinath	4	0	26	0 (1w)
Khan	4	0	26	0 (1w)
Harbhajan Singh	7.2	0	49	0 (1w)
Kumble	7	0	24	1 (1w)

19 February: Harare

Saurav Ganguly's side's rather flat start to the tournament had provoked angry public protests back in India, and among Mumbai lobbyists – keen to see Tendulkar back at the helm – a desire for the sacking of the skipper. But the Mumbaikar and Delhi's Virender Sehwag, after India were sent in, responded with a thumping opening stand of 99; though the later order was restricted by Grant Flower's steady left-arm spin. First, he tied Dinesh Mongia in knots before having him caught in the deep. Then, he deceived Tendulkar with one that came in with the arm and then straightened. He was thereafter withdrawn from the attack because of a finger injury, and India reached 255, which was more than what had been earlier expected.

In any case, Zimbabwe soon found themselves in the woods. Javagal Srinath swiftly removed the openers, and the best endeavour of Andy Flower to disturb the bowlers had little effect. Indeed, a captain's bowling effort thereafter virtually emasculated the Zimbaweans. Ganguly ensnared three wickets for two runs in six balls. In fact, at 87 for six, Zimbabwe's primary objective was to save face before their 6000-odd supporters and not suffer too much in terms of their net run rate. As India won by 83 runs, it was later revealed that a sporadic check by the ICC had discovered that bats belonging to players on both sides were marginally wider than permitted by the laws of cricket.

Toss: Zimbabwe
Umpires: EAR de Silva (SL) and RE Koertzen (SA)
TV Umpire: DB Hair (Aus)
Referee: CH Lloyd (WI)
Man of the Match: SR Tendulkar

India innings *(50 overs maximum)*			R	B
V Sehwag	c Taibu	b Whittall	36	38
SR Tendulkar		b GW Flower	81	91
D Mongia	c Hondo	b GW Flower	12	37

*SC Ganguly	c Streak	b Blignaut	24	36
+R Dravid	not out		43	55
Yuvraj Singh	c Taibu	b Murphy	1	5
M Kaif	lbw	b Hondo	25	24
Harbhajan Singh	c Murphy	b Streak	3	5
Z Khan	not out		13	8

Extras: (b 4, lb 4, w 9) 17
Total: (7 wickets, 50 overs) 255

DNB: A Nehra, J Srinath.

FoW: 1-99 (Sehwag, 16.4 ov), 2-142 (Mongia, 27.3 ov),
3-142 (Tendulkar, 27.5 ov), 4-182 (Ganguly, 37.6 ov),
5-184 (Yuvraj Singh, 38.6 ov), 6-227 (Kaif, 46.3 ov),
7-234 (Harbhajan Singh, 47.6 ov).

Bowling	O	M	R	W
Streak	9	0	46	1 (1w)
Blignaut	10	0	54	1 (5w)
Hondo	9	1	56	1
Whittall	6	0	37	1
GW Flower	6	0	14	2 (1w)
Murphy	10	0	40	1 (2w)

Zimbabwe innings (target: 256 runs from 50 overs)		R	B
CB Wishart	b Srinath	12	19
MA Vermeulen	c Dravid	b Srinath	0	5
A Flower	b Harbhajan Singh	22	54
GW Flower	c Harbhajan Singh	b Ganguly	23	39
DD Ebrahim	c sub (AB Agarkar)	b Ganguly	19	27
AM Blignaut	c Mongia	b Ganguly	2	5
+T Taibu	not out	29	44
GJ Whittall	c Khan	b Sehwag	28	26
*HH Streak	c Kaif	b Harbhajan Singh	20	33
BA Murphy	b Khan	2	9
DT Hondo	b Khan	2	9

Extras: (b 4, lb 2, w 5, nb 2) 13
Total: (all out, 44.4 overs) 172

FoW: 1-1 (Vermeulen, 0.6 ov), 2-23 (Wishart, 8.1 ov),
3-48 (A Flower, 16.3 ov), 4-83 (GW Flower, 23.4 ov),
5-83 (Ebrahim, 23.5 ov), 6-87 (Blignaut, 25.3 ov),
7-124 (Whittall, 31.6 ov), 8-160 (Streak, 39.5 ov),
9-165 (Murphy, 42.1 ov), 10-172 (Hondo, 44.4 ov).

Bowling	O	M	R	W
Srinath	8	1	14	2
Khan	7.4	0	23	2 (1nb, 3w)
Nehra	7	0	35	0 (1nb)
Harbhajan Singh	10	0	42	2 (2w)
Ganguly	5	1	22	3
Sehwag	3	0	14	1
Mongia	4	0	16	0

23 February: Pietermaritzburg

It was a comparatively minor engagement, but on momentous soil, for it was at the railroad junction here in 1893 that an Indian barrister, Mohandas Karamchand, later 'Mahatma' (Great Soul), Gandhi, was ejected from a first-class compartment of a train (although he held a perfectly valid ticket) for the colour of his skin by a white conductor. This one, supercharged incident probably changed the course of world history, starting with the liberation of India and decolonization in the rest of the world. Before the match, the Indian cricketers had, appropriately, participated in the unveiling of a plaque to the memory of the apostle of non-violence at the aforementioned railway station.

On the field, Tendulkar paid his tribute with his 34th ODI hundred and picked up his second successive Man of the Match award. As the ground reverberated to chants of 'Sachin, Sachin' from the 5000-strong crowd, he effortlessly posted 152, after Namibia, who had opted to field first, had the mortification of grassing him on 32. Ganguly was, perhaps, in even better form, as he smote

sixes and fours with superb timing. In tandem, they realized 244 –
their third partnership of over 200 in ODIs. India's batting had at
last clicked, albeit against a non-test-playing team.

Jan-Berrie Burger then embarked on an adventurous reply, hitting
four fours and a six; and Namibia batted out 42 of their 50 overs.
India's 181-run win was their biggest in the World Cup; but there
was a casualty in Ashish Nehra – who was more in rhythm than any
other Indian bowler – retiring after damaging his ankle early in his
spell.

Toss: Namibia
Umpires: Aleem Dar (Pak) and DR Shepherd (Eng)
TV Umpire: KC Barbour (Zim)
Referee: Wasim Raja (Pak)
ODI Debut: BO van Rooi (Namibia).
Man of the Match: SR Tendulkar

India innings (50 overs maximum)			R	B
V Sehwag	c Keulder	b van Vuuren	24	24
SR Tendulkar		b van Vuuren	152	151
*SC Ganguly	not out		112	119
Yuvraj Singh	not out		7	7

Extras: (lb 2, w 13, nb 1) 16
Total: (2 wickets, 50 overs, 207 mins) 311

DNB: +R Dravid, D Mongia, M Kaif, Harbhajan Singh, Z Khan,
A Nehra, J Srinath.

FoW: 1-46 (Sehwag, 7.5 ov), 2-290 (Tendulkar, 47.4 ov).

Bowling	O	M	R	W
Snyman	10	0	57	0 (1nb, 3w)
van Vuuren	10	1	53	2 (1w)
LJ Burger	6	0	49	0 (1w)
van Rooi	6	0	36	0 (1w)
BL Kotze	10	0	64	0
DB Kotze	8	0	50	0 (3w)

Namibia innings (target: 312 runs from 50 overs)			R	B
SJ Swanepoel	lbw	b Khan	9	21
AJ Burger		b Mongia	29	30
LJ Burger	lbw	b Khan	0	2
D Keulder	c Mongia	b Harbhajan Singh	4	19
BG Murgatroyd	lbw	b Harbhajan Singh	0	6
*DB Kotze		c & b Mongia	27	50
+M van Schoor	c Dravid	b Yuvraj Singh	24	61
BO van Rooi	c Mongia	b Yuvraj Singh	17	31
BL Kotze	c Dravid	b Yuvraj Singh	3	18
G Snyman	c Srinath	b Yuvraj Singh	5	6
RJ van Vuuren	not out		0	4

Extras: (lb 1, w 8, nb 3) 12
Total: (all out, 42.3 overs, 163 mins) 130

FoW: 1-19 (Swanepoel, 5.2 ov), 2-21 (LJ Burger, 7.4 ov),
3-43 (Keulder, 12.5 ov), 4-47 (AJ Burger, 13.3 ov),
5-47 (Murgatroyd, 14.6 ov), 6-98 (DB Kotze, 31.6 ov),
7-99 (van Schoor, 33.2 ov), 8-124 (van Rooi, 40.3 ov),
9-124 (BL Kotze, 40.6 ov), 10-130 (Snyman, 42.3 ov).

Bowling	O	M	R	W
Srinath	6	0	25	0 (1w)
Nehra	0.1	0	0	0
Khan	7.5	0	24	2 (2nb, 1w)
Harbhajan Singh	10	1	34	2 (1w)
Mongia	10	1	24	2 (1w)
Sehwag	4	0	16	0 (1nb)
Yuvraj Singh	4.3	2	6	4

26 February: Kingsmead, Durban (Day/Night)

Justifying their decision to bat first, India treated the 18,000-plus attendance to a riotous start, with 75 emanating from 11 overs. But Andrew Flintoff now applied the brakes. Sehwag, the new swashbuckler in the Indian squad, was caught off a front edge and Tendulkar, continuing his crimson touch, holed out at point. Rocked back, India only managed 21 in the next 10. The Lancastrian all-rounder, accurate and of extra bounce, conceded just nine in his first eight overs. But Rahul Dravid and Yuvraj Singh could not be silenced. They compensated with a run-a-ball stand of 62 although England, thereafter, resurrected themselves with four wickets from the last four balls.

Nick Knight paid the penalty for underestimating Mohammed Kaif's athleticism and was run out in the second over of the Englishmen's reply; Marcus Trescothick mishooked to make his exit. Both openers were thus back in the hut in quick time. With the ball wobbling in the clamminess of a South African summer evening, Michael Vaughan was lucky to survive a hypnotic spell from Zaheer Khan. But it was Nehra, his ankle strapped after hurting it in the previous match, who made the inroads. In his third and fourth overs, he extracted a bottom edge from Nasser Hussain, had Alec Stewart plumb in front with an in-swinger and Vaughan caught behind with a virtually unplayable delivery. The top six had flopped for 62; only Flintoff, in pristine form in this match, averted utter disgrace. To be fair, England probably fell foul of the toss; but they also had an inspired Nehra to contend with, as India won by 82 runs. Bowling at around 90 miles per hour and with admirable control, this left-armer from Delhi grabbed six for 23. His career record before this fixture was 30 wickets in 32 ODIs. His two most flattering World Cup figures were both posted at the bowling paradise of Headingley, Leeds. This effort was his third-best.

Toss: India
Umpires: RE Koertzen and SJA Taufel (Aus)
TV Umpire: EAR de Silva (SL)
Referee: RS Madugalle (SL)
Man of the Match: A Nehra

India innings (50 overs maximum)			R	B
V Sehwag	c & b Flintoff		23	29
SR Tendulkar	c Collingwood	b Flintoff	50	52
*SC Ganguly	c Trescothick	b White	19	38
D Mongia	lbw	b Collingwood	32	66
+R Dravid	c Collingwood	b Caddick	62	72
Yuvraj Singh	c Hussain	b Anderson	42	38
M Kaif	c Flintoff	b Caddick	5	6
Harbhajan Singh	not out		0	1
Z Khan	run out (Stewart)		0	0
J Srinath	c Trescothick	b Caddick	0	1

Extras: (b 1, lb 4, w 9, nb 3) 17
Total: (9 wickets, 50 overs, 223 mins) 250

DNB: A Nehra.

FoW: 1-60 (Sehwag, 9.5 ov), 2-91 (Tendulkar, 15.2 ov),
3-107 (Ganguly, 22.1 ov), 4-155 (Mongia, 36.2 ov),
5-217 (Yuvraj Singh, 46.2 ov), 6-250 (Kaif, 49.3 ov),
7-250 (Dravid, 49.4 ov), 8-250 (Khan, 49.5 ov),
9-250 (Srinath, 49.6 ov).

Bowling	O	M	R	W
Caddick	10	0	69	3 (2nb, 2w)
Anderson	10	0	61	1 (5w)
Flintoff	10	2	15	2 (1w)
White	10	0	57	1 (1nb)
Irani	6	0	28	0
Collingwood	4	0	15	1

England innings (target: 251 runs from 50 overs)			R	B
ME Trescothick	c Tendulkar	b Khan	8	23
NV Knight	run out (Kaif)		1	3
MP Vaughan	c Dravid	b Nehra	20	47
*N Hussain	c Dravid	b Nehra	15	30

+AJ Stewart	lbw	b Nehra	0	1
PD Collingwood	c Sehwag	b Nehra	18	38
A Flintoff	c Sehwag	b Srinath	64	73
C White	c Dravid	b Nehra	13	9
RC Irani	c Sehwag	b Nehra	0	2
AR Caddick	not out		13	41
JM Anderson	lbw	b Khan	2	8

Extras: (lb 5, w 7, nb 2) 14
Total: (all out, 45.3 overs, 211 mins) 168

FoW: 1-6 (Knight, 1.1 ov), 2-18 (Trescothick, 6.4 ov),
3-52 (Hussain, 16.2 ov), 4-52 (Stewart, 16.3 ov),
5-62 (Vaughan, 18.6 ov), 6-93 (Collingwood, 26.1 ov),
7-107 (White, 30.1 ov), 8-107 (Irani, 30.3 ov),
9-162 (Flintoff, 42.5 ov), 10-168 (Anderson, 45.3 ov).

Bowling	O	M	R	W
Khan	9.3	1	29	2 (3w)
Srinath	10	0	37	1 (1w)
Nehra	10	2	23	6
Ganguly	6	0	34	0 (2nb)
Harbhajan Singh	10	0	40	0 (2w)

1 March: SuperSport Park, Centurion

The much awaited, frenetically discussed clash – between India and Pakistan – now took place. Large segments of the cricketing world, including millions (not the grossly exaggerated figure of one billion, for less than 10 per cent of homes in India had TV sets at the time) in the subcontinent, were transfixed to this face-off. The arch-rivals were meeting for the first time in three years. In boiling weather and with virtually all the 20,000 seats in the stadium taken up, the cricket – as can often be the case – was not an anti-climax.

Pakistan won the toss and made good use of a flat wicket. Saeed Anwar, all wrist and placement, led the way with a hundred. His contribution was invaluable despite there being only seven fours in it. Indeed, it took a golden yorker from Nehra, continuing to impress in the tournament, to uproot him. Younis Khan, later in the innings, exhibited a puckish flurry of strokes.

However, it was Tendulkar who really emblazoned the occasion by dishing out a riveting display – perhaps the innings of the tournament. Targeting 274 against a star-studded pace attack, with Shoaib Akhtar at his fastest, he was three musketeers rolled into one. His cut for six, a highly unorthodox stroke, as much silenced as thrilled the audience; he swirled one into the leg side, pushed another down the ground; all in Akhtar's first over. India's 100 came up in the 12th over. Tendulkar, granted a life on 32 and suffering from cramps, finished on 98 off 75 balls. It was enough to elicit a third Man of the Match award in the tournament. Kaif's contribution after two quick wickets fell went almost unnoticed. But after the thunder and lightning, Dravid and Yuvraj guided the ship safely to shore. Pakistan conceded 28 extras. But this was no indictment of Taufeeq Umar, substituting for Rashid Latif, who was struck on the helmet and could not keep wickets. It was a case of the Pakistani bowlers trying too hard and thereby erring in line.

Thus, India's 100 per cent record against their neighbours in the World Cup remained intact, with four wins in as many outings. The six-wicket victory also ensured India's advance into the Super Six.

Toss: Pakistan
Umpires: RE Koertzen (SA) and DR Shepherd (Eng)
TV Umpire: BF Bowden (NZ)
Referee: MJ Procter
Man of the Match: SR Tendulkar

Pakistan innings (50 overs maximum)			R	B
Saeed Anwar		b Nehra	101	126
Taufeeq Umar		b Khan	22	32
Abdul Razzaq	c Dravid	b Nehra	12	29
Inzamam-ul Haq	run out (Sehwag/			
	Kumble)		6	3
Yousuf Youhana	c Khan	b Srinath	25	42
Younis Khan	c Mongia	b Khan	32	36
Shahid Afridi	c Kumble	b Mongia	9	7
+Rashid Latif	not out		29	25
Wasim Akram	not out		10	6

Extras: (b 2, lb 7, w 11, nb 7) 27
Total: (7 wickets, 50 overs, 215 mins) 273

DNB: *Waqar Younis, Shoaib Akhtar.

FoW: 1-58 (Taufeeq Umar, 10.5 ov), 2-90 (Abdul Razzaq, 20.6 ov), 3-98 (Inzamam-ul Haq, 21.6 ov), 4-171 (Yousuf Youhana, 36.1 ov), 5-195 (Saeed Anwar, 40.1 ov), 6-208 (Shahid Afridi, 41.3 ov), 7-256 (Younis Khan, 48.1 ov).

Bowling	O	M	R	W
Khan	10	0	46	2 (5nb, 5w)
Srinath	10	0	41	1 (1nb, 1w)
Nehra	10	0	74	2 (2w)
Kumble	10	0	51	0 (1w)
Ganguly	3	0	14	0
Sehwag	4	0	19	0 (1w)
Mongia	3	0	19	1

India innings (target: 274 runs from 50 overs)			R	B
SR Tendulkar	c Younis Khan	b Shoaib Akhtar	98	75
V Sehwag	c Shahid Afridi	b Waqar Younis	21	14
*SC Ganguly	lbw	b Waqar Younis	0	1
M Kaif		b Shahid Afridi	35	60
+R Dravid	not out		44	76
Yuvraj Singh	not out		50	53

Extras: (b 1, lb 3, w 19, nb 5) 28
Total: (4 wickets, 45.4 overs, 238 mins) 276

DNB: D Mongia, A Kumble, Z Khan, J Srinath, A Nehra.

FoW: 1-53 (Sehwag, 5.4 ov), 2-53 (Ganguly, 5.5 ov), 3-155 (Kaif, 21.4 ov), 4-177 (Tendulkar, 27.4 ov).

Bowling	O	M	R	W
Wasim Akram	10	0	48	0 (3nb, 1w)
Shoaib Akhtar	10	0	72	1 (7w)
Waqar Younis	8.4	0	71	2 (2w)
Shahid Afridi	9	0	45	1
Abdul Razzaq	8	0	36	0 (2nb, 1w)

Super Six, 7 March: Newlands, Cape Town (Day/Night)

Kenya played to their carefully cultivated strengths – good fielding, paceless bowling and the will to bat through 50 overs.

It was a liberally disposed crowd of around 18,000. Success with the coin gave Kenya an opportunity to bat in dry, afternoon conditions, when the wicket was at its best. Besides, they were assisted by some abysmal Indian catching as three simple chances were floored in the first hour – all off the persistent, yet hapless, Nehra. Kennedy Otieno escaped in two such instances to post a patient 70 – the top score for his side.

Then, sustained swing bowling in a helpful environment air and a brilliant catch by Tony Suji off a well-timed clip from Tendulkar depressed India to 24 for three in the 10th over. But Ganguly found an ally in Dravid and, more tangibly, in Yuvraj. The lastmentioned, by swinging with the spin, stepped up the run rate, while his captain made sure he stayed till the end. With this 21st ODI hundred, Ganguly swept past Saeed Anwar to reach the second spot in the all-time list, which was, as one would expect, headed by Tendulkar with 34 centuries. The skipper's contribution helped India cross another barrier – by six wickets. It was only the second time in eight day/nighters in the tournament that a team had won chasing in the dewy circumstances under lights; it was a hard-earned victory by a side considered on paper to be much superior. After the match, Ganguly was asked if India had considered throwing the game in order to devise meeting the Kenyans in the semi-finals. The answer was emphatically in the negative. As South Africa's experience had demonstrated, it's a folly to complicate matters with calculators.

Toss: Kenya
Umpires: DJ Harper (Aus) and P Willey (Eng)
TV Umpire: SJA Taufel (Aus)
Referee: Wasim Raja (Pak)
Man of the Match: SC Ganguly

Kenya innings *(50 overs maximum)*			R	B
+KO Otieno		b Harbhajan Singh	79	134
RD Shah	run out (Khan)		34	52
*SO Tikolo	c Khan	b Harbhajan Singh	3	11
TM Odoyo	lbw	b Mongia	32	55
MO Odumbe	not out		34	24
CO Obuya	c Mongia	b Srinath	8	11
PJ Ongondo	c Tendulkar	b Srinath	8	7
MA Suji	not out		11	6

Extras: (b 4, lb 8, w 4) 16
Total: (6 wickets, 50 overs, 210 mins) 225

DNB: AO Suji, BJ Patel, HS Modi.

FoW: 1-75 (Shah, 20.6 ov), 2-81 (Tikolo, 23.2 ov),
3-157 (Otieno, 39.6 ov), 4-165 (Odoyo, 42.4 ov),
5-191 (Obuya, 46.1 ov), 6-206 (Ongondo, 48.1 ov).

Bowling	O	M	R	W
Khan	10	1	53	0 (2w)
Srinath	10	0	43	2 (1w)
Nehra	10	2	30	0 (1w)
Harbhajan Singh	10	0	41	2
Mongia	8	0	37	1
Yuvraj Singh	2	0	9	0

India innings *(target: 226 runs from 50 overs)*			R	B
V Sehwag	c Tikolo	b Odoyo	3	8
SR Tendulkar	c AO Suji	b MA Suji	5	12
*SC Ganguly	not out		107	120
M Kaif	lbw	b Odoyo	5	13
+R Dravid	c & b Obuya		32	73
Yuvraj Singh	not out		58	64

Extras: (lb 5, w 8, nb 3) 16
Total: (4 wickets, 47.5 overs, 205 mins) 226

DNB: D Mongia, Harbhajan Singh, Z Khan, A Nehra, J Srinath.

FoW: 1-5 (Sehwag, 1.5 ov), 2-11 (Tendulkar, 4.3 ov),
3-24 (Kaif, 9.2 ov), 4-108 (Dravid, 29.3 ov).

Bowling	O	M	R	W
MA Suji	10	3	27	1
Odoyo	7	0	27	2 (1nb)
Ongondo	5	0	31	0 (1w)
AO Suji	7	0	25	0 (1nb)
Obuya	9.5	2	50	1 (1nb, 3w)
Odumbe	3	0	25	0
Tikolo	6	0	36	0

Super Six, 10 March: Wanderers, Johannesburg

To the 23,000 spectators, Sanath Jayasuriya, with a dodgy thumb
and an injured forearm, represented a soldier just back from a
battlefront. After he inserted India on a decent pitch, he was also
tormented by a huge headache. With the exception of Chaminda
Vaas, Sri Lanka's faster bowlers were all over the place. Tendulkar
and Sehwag pounced on such aberrance to pile up 153 for the
opening wicket. It was their best effort in 10 innings together and
their third three-figure partnership. Tendulkar treated Vaas with due
respect and peered at Muttiah Muralitharan probingly, but brushed
aside the rest imperiously. He, unfortunately, missed a second
hundred in 10 days, but crossed 500 runs for the second World Cup
in a row. Sehwag, the destroyer from Delhi, displayed a more sensible
approach than he was reputed to have, before a crescendo of shots
concluded at long-on.

From a Sri Lankan standpoint, 293 was a demoralizing target.
By the fourth over during their pursuit, this had become even more
distant, as Marvan Atapattu, Jehan Mubarak, Mahela Jayawardene

and Aravinda de Silva all departed without troubling the scorers. Mubarak seemed a misfit at number three and Jayawardene looked desperately out of nick. Then, a handicapped Jayasuriya hoisted Srinath to cover, which resulted in one of the agile Kaif's four catches – a World Cup fielding record. Srinath, Kapil's successor as India's primary pace bowler, had justified the faith reposed in him by captain Ganguly, who had coaxed him out of retirement for the event. India won by a record margin of 183 runs, and their mounting dash and dexterity clinched them a place in the last four. Sri Lanka could at this juncture also have got there, but the road had become more labyrinthine.

Toss: Sri Lanka
Umpires: DR Shepherd (Eng) and SJA Taufel (Aus)
TV Umpire: DJ Harper (Aus)
Referee: CH Lloyd (WI)
Man of the Match: J Srinath

India innings (50 overs maximum)			R	B
SR Tendulkar	c Sangakkara	b de Silva	97	120
V Sehwag	c de Silva	b Muralitharan	66	76
*SC Ganguly		b Vaas	48	53
M Kaif		b Muralitharan	19	24
Yuvraj Singh		b Vaas	5	6
+R Dravid	not out		18	12
D Mongia	c de Silva	b Muralitharan	9	7
Harbhajan Singh	not out		7	5

Extras: (b 4, lb 9, w 7, nb 3) 23
Total: (6 wickets, 50 overs, 210 mins) 292

DNB: Z Khan, A Nehra, J Srinath.

FoW: 1-153 (Sehwag, 26.2 ov), 2-214 (Tendulkar, 38.5 ov), 3-243 (Ganguly, 43.4 ov), 4-251 (Yuvraj Singh, 45.2 ov), 5-265 (Kaif, 46.5 ov), 6-277 (Mongia, 48.3 ov).

Bowling	O	M	R	W
Vaas	10	2	34	2 (1nb)
Nissanka	6	0	49	0 (5w)
Fernando	10	1	61	0 (1nb, 1w)
Muralitharan	10	0	46	3
Jayasuriya	3	0	27	0
de Silva	6	0	32	1 (1w)
Arnold	5	0	30	0 (1nb)

Sri Lanka innings (target: 293 runs from 50 overs)			R	B
MS Atapattu	c Kaif	b Srinath	0	7
*ST Jayasuriya	c Kaif	b Srinath	12	19
J Mubarak	c Dravid	b Srinath	0	2
DPMD Jayawardene	lbw	b Khan	0	4
PA de Silva	lbw	b Srinath	0	3
+KC Sangakkara	c Yuvraj Singh	b Nehra	30	33
RP Arnold	lbw	b Khan	8	28
WPUJC Vaas	c Tendulkar	b Nehra	9	15
RAP Nissanka	c Kaif	b Nehra	0	4
CRD Fernando	not out		13	10
M Muralitharan	c Kaif	b Nehra	16	14

Extras: (b 1, lb 5, w 14, nb 1) 21
Total: (all out, 23 overs, 123 mins) 109

FoW: 1-2 (Atapattu, 1.3 ov), 2-2 (Mubarak, 1.5 ov),
3-3 (Jayawardene, 2.4 ov), 4-15 (de Silva, 3.4 ov),
5-40 (Jayasuriya, 7.6 ov), 6-59 (Sangakkara, 14.5 ov),
7-75 (Arnold, 17.2 ov), 8-78 (Vaas, 18.4 ov),
9-78 (Nissanka, 18.6 ov), 10-109 (Muralitharan, 22.6 ov).

Bowling	O	M	R	W
Khan	7	0	33	2 (1nb, 5w)
Srinath	9	1	35	4 (2w)
Nehra	7	1	35	4 (1w)

Super Six, 14 March: SuperSport Park, Centurion

New Zealand were in difficulty no sooner had the crowd of 16,000 settled into their seats. After India won the toss, Zaheer Khan, left-arm, fast-medium from the western Indian city of Baroda in Gujarat state, zeroed in to send Craig McMillan and Nathan Astle packing in the very first over. At the non-striker's end, Stephen Fleming looked like a trainer whose lightweight ward had been punched by a heavyweight. Every move Ganguly made thereafter was richly rewarded. Only the lower half of the Kiwi batting provided any resistance.

India's main worry had been the express pace of Shane Bond. Predictably, Sehwag snicked his sixth ball to slip and Ganguly was yorked by sheer speed. Tendulkar, then, skied Daryl Tuffey after lashing him for three successive fours. There, thus, arose a glimmer of hope for New Zealand, and a murmur of a match in hand among the 16,000 in the galleries. But Dravid was let off by the keeper and this proved too costly a mistake. He and Kaif then showed the New Zealanders a clean pair of heels to complete a seven-wicket victory with nine overs to spare. The latter wrapped up proceedings with two fours off Scott Styris. India — already guaranteed a place in the semi-final — won their seventh game in a row in a show of increasing confidence. It was also a mentally restorative result after their drubbing in New Zealand only a few weeks earlier. The Kiwis now could only hope Zimbabwe would get the better of Sri Lanka.

Toss: India
Umpires: DJ Harper (Aus) and P Willey (Eng)
TV Umpire: DB Hair (Aus)
Referee: RS Madugalle (SL)
Man of the Match: Z Khan

New Zealand innings (50 overs maximum)			R	B
CD McMillan	c Harbhajan Singh	b Khan	0	2
*SP Fleming	c Tendulkar	b Srinath	30	59
NJ Astle	lbw	b Khan	0	1
SB Styris	c Dravid	b Nehra	15	21
+BB McCullum		b Khan	4	16
CL Cairns	c Khan	b Harbhajan Singh	20	26
CZ Harris	lbw	b Khan	17	37
JDP Oram		b Sehwag	23	54
DL Vettori	c Ganguly	b Harbhajan Singh	13	40
DR Tuffey	c & b Mongia		11	13
SE Bond	not out		0	6

Extras: (lb 5, w 4, nb 4) 13
Total: (all out, 45.1 overs, 187 mins) 146

FoW: 1-0 (McMillan, 0.2 ov), 2-0 (Astle, 0.3 ov),
3-38 (Styris, 8.1 ov), 4-47 (McCullum, 13.4 ov),
5-60 (Fleming, 17.3 ov), 6-88 (Cairns, 25.3 ov),
7-96 (Harris, 28.2 ov), 8-129 (Vettori, 39.6 ov),
9-144 (Oram, 43.2 ov), 10-146 (Tuffey, 45.1 ov).

Bowling	O	M	R	W
Khan	8	0	42	4 (2nb, 1w)
Srinath	8	0	20	1 (3w)
Nehra	10	3	24	1 (1nb)
Harbhajan Singh	10	2	28	2
Ganguly	2	0	4	0
Tendulkar	5	0	20	0 (1nb)
Sehwag	2	1	3	1
Mongia	0.1	0	0	1

India innings (target: 147 runs from 50 overs)			R	B
V Sehwag	c Styris	b Bond	1	6
SR Tendulkar	c Oram	b Tuffey	15	16
*SC Ganguly		b Bond	3	6
M Kaif	not out		68	129
+R Dravid	not out		53	89

Extras: (w 8, nb 2) 10
Total: (3 wickets, 40.4 overs, 168 mins) 150

DNB: Yuvraj Singh, D Mongia, J Srinath, A Nehra, Z Khan,
Harbhajan Singh.

FoW: 1-4 (Sehwag, 1.6 ov), 2-9 (Ganguly, 3.5 ov),
3-21 (Tendulkar, 4.5 ov).

Bowling	O	M	R	W
Tuffey	10	1	41	1 (1nb, 4w)
Bond	8	2	23	2 (1nb, 2w)
Oram	5	0	20	0
Vettori	5	0	18	0
McMillan	2	1	4	0
Styris	6.4	0	29	0 (1w)
Harris	4	1	15	0

Semi-final, 18 March: St George's Park, Port Elizabeth

In an era in which sportsmanship has been overtaken by career
compulsions, Adam Gilchrist, rather refreshingly, walked even after
umpire Rudi Koertzen's decision had gone in his favour. He had got
a faint touch in attempting a sweep that ricocheted off his pads. (As
he later so eloquently emphasized with his demeanour in India in
2004, when captaining Australia in the absence of Ricky Ponting,
this is the estimable way he plays his cricket.) His nobility, though,
led to a crisis as Ponting's was only a brief stay. This opened the
shutter for Sri Lanka after they had lost the toss, but they squandered
the ray of light. Kumar Sangakkara muffed an easy stumping chance
off Jayasuriya when Symonds was on 33; the Australian didn't look
back, adjusting well to another slightly awkward pitch at this coastal
venue. Jayasuriya later dismissed Lehmann and Bevan off consecutive
deliveries; but Symonds stayed put in a watchful rather than a forceful
manner.

Sri Lanka required just 213 to win. The in-touch Atapattu was
floored by Brad Hogg at cover when he was 14, but his off stump

was knocked back by the very next delivery from Brett Lee, timed at 99.4 mph. Jayasuriya replied with a six off this speedster only to be soon consumed at square leg off McGrath. Then Bichel got into the act. He fielded a defensive push from Sangakkara on his follow-through, swivelled and broke the stumps at the batsman's end to beat a doddering de Silva. It was an unfitting end to a fine career as this stocky Sri Lankan artiste faded into the sunset.

A late-afternoon downpour interrupted Sri Lanka's first healthy partnership – 47 for the eighth wicket between Sangakkara and Vaas. So, the match was decided on the Duckworth/Lewis rule – Australia winning by 48 runs, without any protests from the 14,500 onlookers. With this win, the Australians qualified for their fifth World Cup final and their third sequentially.

Toss: Australia
Umpires: RE Koertzen and DR Shepherd (Eng)
TV Umpire: BF Bowden (NZ)
Referee: CH Lloyd (WI)
Man of the Match: A Symonds

Australia innings (50 overs maximum)			R	B
+AC Gilchrist	c Sangakkara	b de Silva	22	20
ML Hayden	c Tillakaratne	b Vaas	20	38
*RT Ponting	c Jayasuriya	b Vaas	2	8
DS Lehmann		b Jayasuriya	36	66
A Symonds	not out		91	118
MG Bevan	c Sangakkara	b Jayasuriya	0	1
GB Hogg	st Sangakkara	b de Silva	8	19
IJ Harvey	c Sangakkara	b Vaas	7	10
AJ Bichel	not out		19	21

Extras: (lb 3, w 3, nb 1) 7
Total: (7 wickets, 50 overs, 199 mins) 212

DNB: B Lee, GD McGrath.
FoW: 1-34 (Gilchrist, 5.2 ov), 2-37 (Ponting, 6.5 ov),
3-51 (Hayden, 12.2 ov), 4-144 (Lehmann, 34.6 ov),
5-144 (Bevan, 36.1 ov), 6-158 (Hogg, 40.3 ov),
7-175 (Harvey, 43.5 ov).

Bowling	O	M	R	W
Vaas	10	1	34	3 (1nb, 1w)
Gunaratne	8	0	60	0 (1w)
de Silva	10	0	36	2 (1w)
Muralitharan	10	0	29	0
Jayasuriya	10	0	42	2
Arnold	2	0	8	0

Sri Lanka innings (target: 172 runs from 38.1 overs)		R	B
MS Atapattu		b Lee	14	17
*ST Jayasuriya	c Symonds	b McGrath	17	24
HP Tillakaratne	c Gilchrist	b Lee	3	15
DA Gunawardene	c Ponting	b Lee	1	4
PA de Silva	run out (Bichel)		11	16
+KC Sangakkara	not out		39	70
DPMD Jayawardene	c Gilchrist	b Hogg	5	8
RP Arnold	c Lee	b Hogg	3	27
WPUJC Vaas	not out		21	50

Extras: (b 4, lb 1, w 2, nb 2) 9
Total: (7 wickets, 38.1 overs, 167 mins) 123

DNB: M Muralitharan, PW Gunaratne.

FoW: 1-21 (Atapattu, 3.6 ov), 2-37 (Jayasuriya, 8.5 ov),
3-37 (Tillakaratne, 9.3 ov), 4-43 (Gunawardene, 11.2 ov),
5-51 (de Silva, 13.1 ov), 6-60 (Jayawardene, 16.1 ov),
7-76 (Arnold, 24.2 ov).

Bowling	O	M	R	W
McGrath	7	1	20	1
Lee	8	0	35	3 (2nb, 2w)
Bichel	10	4	18	0
Hogg	10	1	30	2
Harvey	2.1	0	11	0
Lehmann	1	0	4	0

Semi-final, 20 March: Kingsmead, Durban (Day/Night)

Captaining India for the 99th time in a one-day international, Ganguly took charge himself after deciding to bat. With a contemptuously played innings, he laid the foundation of an august if not unassailable total. Leg-spinner Obuya bowled two economical overs. Ganguly then danced down the track to hit the first ball of the next for six and repeated the stroke before the end of the over. Obuya was taken off after six overs lest he became too expensive. A century from Tendulkar appeared to be on the cards before he pulled Steve Tikolo to deep midwicket. Ganguly, however, pressed on to equal Mark Waugh's 1996 record of three hundreds in a World Cup, heralding the landmark with his fifth over-boundary, which had laziness written all over it. Bat and helmet raised, he soaked in the applause.

Ganguly's counterpart, Tikolo, was also the highest scorer in course of the Kenyan response. But all Ganguly had to do was to unleash his fast-medium trio to record a 91-run victory. With this eighth win on the trot, India matched their record of consecutive successes, established in 1985. They had become professional enough not to be complacent against unfancied opposition. As for the Kenyans, though there was no fairytale ending, they happily acknowledged the cheers from an 18,000 plus attendance, their spot in the history books secured.

Kenya's romantic journey brought huge benefits. The ICC earmarked more than £1 million for their development. Moreover, the players, who had threatened strike action over pay before the tournament began, picked up $530,000 in prize money, having at one stage anticipated a mere fraction of this sum.

Toss: India
Umpires: SA Bucknor (WI) and DJ Harper (Aus)
TV Umpire: SJA Taufel (Aus)
Referee: MJ Procter
Man of the Match: SC Ganguly

India innings *(50 overs maximum)*			R	B
V Sehwag	c Odumbe	b Ongondo	33	56
SR Tendulkar	c DO Obuya	b Tikolo	83	101
*SC Ganguly	not out		111	114
M Kaif	run out (CO Obuya)		15	20
Yuvraj Singh	c DO Obuya	b Odoyo	16	10
+R Dravid	not out		1	1

Extras: (w 9, nb 2) 11
Total: (4 wickets, 50 overs, 222 mins) 270

DNB: D Mongia, J Srinath, A Nehra, Z Khan, Harbhajan Singh.

FoW: 1-74 (Sehwag, 18.3 ov), 2-177 (Tendulkar, 37.5 ov),
3-233 (Kaif, 45.5 ov), 4-267 (Yuvraj Singh, 49.3 ov).

Bowling	O	M	R	W	
Suji	10	1	62	0	
Odoyo	10	1	45	1	(2nb, 1w)
Ongondo	10	1	38	1	
Karim	4	0	25	0	(1w)
Tikolo	10	0	60	1	(2w)
CO Obuya	6	0	40	0	(1w)

Kenya innings *(target: 271 runs from 50 overs)*			R	B
+KO Otieno	c Dravid	b Srinath	15	43
RD Shah	lbw	b Khan	1	17
PJ Ongondo	c Khan	b Nehra	0	5
TM Odoyo	c Sehwag	b Nehra	7	15
*SO Tikolo		b Tendulkar	56	83
MO Odumbe	c Khan	b Yuvraj Singh	19	16
HS Modi	c Dravid	b Khan	9	25
DO Obuya	run out (Kaif/			
	Harbhajan Singh)		3	23
CO Obuya	lbw	b Tendulkar	29	42
MA Suji		b Khan	1	8
AY Karim	not out		0	1

Extras: (b 16, lb 8, w 15) 39
Total: (all out, 46.2 overs, 190 mins) 179

FoW: 1-20 (Shah, 8.2 ov), 2-21 (Ongondo, 10.1 ov),
3-30 (Otieno, 13.1 ov), 4-36 (Odoyo, 14.3 ov),
5-63 (Odumbe, 18.4 ov), 6-92 (Modi, 26.4 ov),
7-104 (DO Obuya, 33.1 ov), 8-161 (Tikolo, 43.4 ov),
9-179 (CO Obuya, 45.4 ov), 10-179 (Suji, 46.2 ov).

Bowling	O	M	R	W
Khan	9.2	2	14	3 (3w)
Srinath	7	1	11	1 (1w)
Nehra	5	1	11	2 (2w)
Harbhajan Singh	10	1	32	0
Yuvraj Singh	6	0	43	1
Sehwag	3	1	16	0 (1w)
Tendulkar	6	0	28	2 (3w)

Final, 23 March: Wanderers, Johannesburg

Ganguly amazed many by inserting Australia. It had, obviously, been a collective decision, but he as captain was the final arbiter. His critics immediately attributed this decision to his fear of facing Australia's fast bowlers. But there was some life in the pitch for India's quicker bowlers, though the seamers, hitherto promising, now crumpled under pressure.

Zaheer took 10 balls to complete his first over, conceding 15 runs; and that set a trend. Gilchrist and Hayden took full advantage, albeit a little chancily, and after nine overs, Australia were 74 without loss. Ganguly switched to spin in the next over and Harbhajan, who had terminated the Kangaroos' unbeaten run in tests in 2001 to be dubbed 'turbanator' by Australian media, succeeded in repatriating both openers back to the pavilion.

But now history didn't deter the Aussies. Ponting and Damien Martyn proceeded to raise a partnership of 234, which was a record for Australia in ODIs for any wicket. So was their total. Martyn's showing was the more noteworthy, since he had skipped the semi-final with a finger injury and was not thought to have recovered. His batting was cerebral; he read the circumstances to precision and was unselfish. He gave a six over handicap to Ponting, but reached his fifty first.

Ponting was just into starters, though. His 50 took 74 balls to Martyn's 46 and contained a solitary four. But his next 47 balls gave rise to 90 runs, with eight leg-side sixes (the highest number of over-boundaries in any World Cup innings, beating the seven by Viv Richards and Ganguly) and three more fours.

The shift in strategy was signalled by Harbhajan's reintroduction in the 39th over. Ponting blasted him out of the attack with two consecutive sixes over midwicket. Nehra had a go; but he, too, was greeted by a spectacular one-handed slog-sweep off a low full toss, which also sailed over midwicket. Off the second-last ball of the innings, he lofted Srinath for a towering six over long-on. His 140 was the highest personal contribution by any player in a World Cup final. Tendulkar, though, was declared the Man of the Tournament. Australia's change of gear had been awe-inspiring: 109 came off the last ten overs, and 64 off the last five. Srinath haemorrhaged 87 runs, the most profuse in a World Cup final.

The phalanx of Indian supporters in a capacity crowd of 32,000 had lost their verve, and their spirits were irreversibly deflated when Tendulkar made his exit, top-edging McGrath to be caught and bowled off the fifth ball. Sehwag survived a catch on account of a no-ball, and bravely kept India ticking with a run-a-ball innings, which was embroidered with ten fours and three sixes. But he was caught napping by a direct throw from Lehmann at deep midoff, which terminated a blossoming partnership of 88 with Dravid.

Showers briefly promised Indian fans the prospect of a replay. Sensing Australia had to bowl a minimum of 25 overs to secure a result, Ponting employed his spinners, Hogg and Darren Lehman, at both ends. India cashed in by flaying them to all parts of the ground. Bichel and McGrath were brought back as the lights were switched on, but the rain became so intense that the players were compelled to leave the field, with India on 103 for three. When they returned, 25 minutes later – without any reduction in overs – Australia consummated a 125-run victory, their third triumph in a World Cup and their 17th successive one-day win. It came under threatening skies and to the accompaniment of thunderclaps. The Australians took home US $2 million as winnings.

Toss: India
Umpires: SA Bucknor (WI) and DR Shepherd (Eng)
TV Umpire: RE Koertzen (SA)
Referee: RS Madugalle (SL)
Man of the Match: RT Ponting
Player of the Series: SR Tendulkar

Australia innings (50 overs maximum)			R	B
+AC Gilchrist	c Sehwag	b Harbhajan Singh	57	48
ML Hayden	c Dravid	b Harbhajan Singh	37	54
*RT Ponting	not out		140	121
DR Martyn	not out		88	84

Extras: (b 2, lb 12, w 16, nb 7) 37
Total: (2 wickets, 50 overs, 205 mins) 359

DNB: DS Lehmann, MG Bevan, A Symonds, GB Hogg, AJ Bichel, B Lee, GD McGrath.

FoW: 1-105 (Gilchrist, 13.6 ov), 2-125 (Hayden, 19.5 ov).

Bowling	O	M	R	W
Khan	7	0	67	0 (2nb, 6w)
Srinath	10	0	87	0 (3nb, 2w)
Nehra	10	0	57	0 (3w)
Harbhajan Singh	8	0	49	2
Sehwag	3	0	14	0
Tendulkar	3	0	20	0 (1w)
Mongia	7	0	39	0 (2nb)
Yuvraj Singh	2	0	12	0

India innings (target: 360 runs from 50 overs)			R	B
SR Tendulkar	c & b McGrath		4	5
V Sehwag	run out (Lehmann)		82	81
*SC Ganguly	c Lehmann	b Lee	24	25
M Kaif	c Gilchrist	b McGrath	0	3
+R Dravid		b Bichel	47	57
Yuvraj Singh	c Lee	b Hogg	24	34
D Mongia	c Martyn	b Symonds	12	11
Harbhajan Singh	c McGrath	b Symonds	7	8
Z Khan	c Lehmann	b McGrath	4	8
J Srinath		b Lee	1	4
A Nehra	not out		8	4

Extras: (b 4, lb 4, w 9, nb 4) 21
Total: (all out, 39.2 overs, 180 mins) 234

FoW: 1-4 (Tendulkar, 0.5 ov), 2-58 (Ganguly, 9.5 ov),
3-59 (Kaif, 10.3 ov), 4-147 (Sehwag, 23.5 ov),
5-187 (Dravid, 31.5 ov), 6-208 (Yuvraj Singh, 34.5 ov),
7-209 (Mongia, 35.2 ov), 8-223 (Harbhajan Singh, 37.1 ov),
9-226 (Srinath, 38.2 ov), 10-234 (Khan, 39.2 ov).

Bowling	O	M	R	W
McGrath	8.2	0	52	3
Lee	7	1	31	2 (4nb, 2w)
Hogg	10	0	61	1 (2w)
Lehmann	2	0	18	0
Bichel	10	0	57	1 (4w)
Symonds	2	0	7	2 (1w)

South Africa's early exit contributed to the event failing to capture the imagination of the country's majority. A broadening of cricket's appeal had been one of the aims of the Organizing Committee. To this end, sponsor companies were required to have a black empowerment element and a total of 50,000 tickets were reserved for black children to attend every game. However, a survey revealed that only a small minority of black South Africans expressed interest in the World Cup.

The event was criticized in some circles for being too elaborate and too long. Participants were increased from 12 in 1999 to 14, the number of games to 54 and the duration to over six weeks.

There were no reserve days at the pool stage, which cost the West Indies dear. Their game with Bangladesh was rained off when they were in a dominant position; had it been completed, West Indies, and not Kenya, would have gone through to the Super Six. The staging of day/night matches in the seaside cities of Durban and Cape Town was also questioned. The ball certainly seemed to swing more for the sides bowling second, though the results were not unduly skewed.

The umpiring was generally good. And the biggest security operation mounted by the ICC led by the former police commissioner of London, Lord Paul Condon, head of the ICC's Anti-Corruption Unit, declared the tournament – the first World Cup since the Cronje scandal – clean.

Two days after England's game against Australia, Nasser Hussain, exhausted by an arduous winter, was making his resignation speech as one-day captain. He and Pollock were not the only leaders to jump or fall. In the, now-customary post-World Cup captaincy clearance, so too did Sanath Jayasuriya of Sri Lanka, Carl Hooper of the West Indies, Waqar Younis of Pakistan and Khaled Masud of Bangladesh.

The Pakistanis were the biggest disappointment. They won no match of consequence. Against Australia, Waqar was ordered out of the attack for bowling two beamers; Gilchrist subsequently launched a racial abuse charge against Rashid Latif, which was, however, turned down by match referee Clive Lloyd. Shahid Afridi was suspended and fined by his own board for sledging during the politically sensitive match against India.

On the other hand, John Davison, Canada's 32-year-old Australian recruit, smashed the fastest century in World Cup history against the West Indies only four days after his team had been dismissed for 36. Then, there was Namibia's Jan-Berrie Burger applying his beefy blade to England's attack in Port Elizabeth and the exemplary glove work of Jeroen Smits, the Dutch keeper who conceded only five byes in six matches.

Shoaib Akhtar of Pakistan swung his way to the highest score by a number 11 batsman in one-day internationals; the West Indian Ramnaresh Sarwan returned from hospital after being felled by a bouncer to take the field to a standing ovation; and Aasif Karim, a 39-year-old from Kenya, bowled maiden after maiden to Australia.

But the pièce de résistance was when the Canadians, made up of amateurs, beat the game's newest test nation, Bangladesh, by 60 runs. Until the warm-up games, the Canadians had not played together for five months.

9

More Extras

THE 2004 ICC CHAMPIONS TROPHY

THE MOST IMPORTANT ONE-DAY TOURNAMENT IN WORLD CRICKET after the World Cup, namely, the Champions Trophy, had notched up financial successes in its first three editions. However, other than in the inaugural episode in Bangladesh, it had not attracted consistent crowd support, while media interest, including television distribution, had been lukewarm and general public enthusiasm, with the exception of the subcontinent, nothing to write home about either.

Nevertheless, there was heightened hope and expectation that holding of the championship at the spiritual depository of the game, namely, England, would provide this event with just the right impetus to establish it firmly in the hearts and minds of cricket lovers. As it transpired, this endeavour was a mixed success.

Only in the current elongated English season is cricket, under the auspices of the ECB, still played beyond the first week of September. Climatically, it is supposed to be too cold and the advantage of summer – when the weather is not only more welcoming, but when people are in a cricket-going frame of mind (what with schools and universities closed and government as well as the private sector on a relative slowdown) – has virtually vanished.

If the ECB were passionate about hosting the contest, it ought to have excavated 16 days' space in June or July for it. One can understand they had already committed themselves for this period, in which case, they could have passed for 2004 and instead bid for 2006. It would have been better for the reputation of both the ICC and the ECB, had the organization of the tournament occurred wholeheartedly rather than in a half-hearted manner.

September is not ideal for an international cricketing jamboree in most places. If it's too late for England, it's too early for south-eastern Australia and New Zealand and parts of South Africa, while the West Indies is still in the grip of hurricane threats and the eastern and southern segments of the subcontinent are experiencing the receding monsoon. Only north-western India and Pakistan are sufficiently dry and stable for a relatively low-risk venture.

Relations between the ICC and the English cricket establishment were said to be frosty. Whether this or any other reason caused it, the non-cooperation of the MCC in lending Lord's as a venue for the tourney was unfortunate. It reiterated the long-held suspicion that this club is still not reconciled to cricket having slipped out of its grasp. Southampton, which boasted a futuristic, new stadium in the Rose Bowl, Edgbaston in Birmingham, a hospitable site, and The Oval in London — historically significant and as distinguished a cricketing arena as any — comprised the three theatres of competition.

In sharp contrast to the packed stands that normally greet an international cricket fixture in England, attendance at all matches, other than India's two games, the Australia–New Zealand engagement and the final, or in 11 of the 15 matches, was noticeably sparse, although only Sachin Tendulkar and Muttiah Muralitharan (both nursing injuries) among top players were missing from the eligible or preferred list. The marketing effort left a lot to be desired. But this time the Champions Trophy at least produced winners, which the previous one in Sri Lanka did not.

Most games were held in freezing conditions, which made the toss unfairly important. In all but two instances, the side winning the toss inserted the opposition. Pakistan bucked this trend in the semi-final and paid the penalty. In the seven actually competitive fixtures, only once did a team batting first win.

Zimbabwe, denuded of their better cricketers, did not disgrace themselves; they gave Sri Lanka something to think about. But Bangladesh and Kenya were unequal to their tasks. The United States of America, a combination of Caribbean settlers, were beaten by Australia in less than three hours, while New Zealand's batsmen plundered 110 off the Americans in the last five overs. Inciting interest in cricket in the US has long been an ICC dream, but they have failed to wheedle tangible media attention there.

As for India, the executor – as finance minister under Narasimha Rao – of its dynamic economic reforms in 1991, Dr Manmohan Singh, had, in May 2004, himself become prime minister, after his Congress party emerged as the single largest in the country's 'house of the people' (the Lok Sabha), defeating the right-wing, Bharatiya Janata Party-led National Democratic Alliance and formed a coalition government with like-minded regional parties, with parliamentary support from leftist groups.

For India's cricketers, their first outing – against Kenya – was more in the nature of a warm-up.

11 September: Southampton

Toss: Kenya
Umpires: DJ Harper (Aus) and RE Koertzen (SA)
TV Umpire: Aleem Dar (Pak)
Referee: CH Lloyd (WI)
ODI Debuts: RG Aga, MA Ouma (Kenya).
Man of the Match: SC Ganguly

India innings (50 overs maximum)			R	B
*SC Ganguly		b MA Suji	90	124
V Sehwag		b Odoyo	17	27
VVS Laxman	st Otieno	b Tikolo	79	99
Yuvraj Singh	c Otieno	b Odoyo	9	9
M Kaif	not out		49	29
R Dravid	not out		30	16

Extras: (b 4, lb 5, w 3, nb 4) 16
Total: (4 wickets, 50 overs) 290

DNB: +KD Karthik, Harbhajan Singh, IK Pathan, AB Agarkar, A Nehra.

FoW: 1-30 (Sehwag, 9.1 ov), 2-191 (Ganguly, 38.3 ov), 3-204 (Yuvraj Singh, 41.4 ov), 4-213 (Laxman, 43.1 ov).

Bowling	O	M	R	W
MA Suji	10	2	42	1
Odoyo	10	1	43	2
Ongondo	5	0	27	0 (1w)
Aga	9	0	70	0 (2nb, 2w)
Tikolo	10	0	53	1
Patel	3	0	21	0
AO Suji	3	0	25	0 (2nb)

Kenya innings (target: 291 runs from 50 overs)			R	B
+KO Otieno	run out (Kaif)		0	9
RD Shah	c Karthik	b Harbhajan Singh	33	53
*SO Tikolo	lbw	b Pathan	2	10
HS Modi	c Ganguly	b Pathan	5	0
TM Odoyo	c Karthik	b Harbhajan Singh	15	42
RG Aga	c Ganguly	b Harbhajan Singh	0	3
MA Ouma	c Karthik	b Agarkar	49	93
BJ Patel	not out		40	77
MA Suji	not out		6	7

Extras: (b 10, lb 9, w 19, nb 4) 42
Total: (7 wickets, 50 overs) 192

DNB: PJ Ongondo, AO Suji.

FoW: 1-9 (Otieno, 4.1 ov), 2-13 (Tikolo, 6.5 ov), 3-21 (Modi, 8.6 ov), 4-58 (Shah, 17.4 ov), 5-62 (Aga, 19.1 ov), 6-74 (Odoyo, 23.4 ov), 7-166 (Ouma, 44.6 ov).

Bowling	O	M	R	W
Pathan	6	1	11	2 (1w)
Nehra	7	1	17	0 (2nb, 4w)
Agarkar	10	0	42	1 (1nb, 2w)
Harbhajan Singh	10	2	33	3 (2w)
Ganguly	5	0	21	0
Yuvraj Singh	4	0	17	0 (2w)
Sehwag	8	1	32	0 (1nb)

19 September: Edgbaston, Birmingham

India's next appearance – versus Pakistan – was the real test, as only the winners here would progress to the semi-finals. A desultory competition awoke at last with a full house at this Mecca of the English Midlands; and a 20,000-strong crowd got their money's worth.

The match was low scoring, but gripping. Fortunes fluctuated teasingly. Inserted on a fresh pitch, India soon crashed to 28 for three. They then slumped to 106 for six in the 34th over. But the ever-reliable Rahul Dravid was still there. At first, he defended against the danger man, Shoaib Akhtar, then trimmed this fiery fast bowler to size. Ajit Agarkar (who scored an attacking test hundred at Lord's in 2002) later joined in the frolic. Such enterprise lifted the despondency that had shrouded the Indians for much of the morning. A total of 200 was not uncompetitive.

The highly promising Irfan Pathan swung the ball curvaceously and at greater pace than usual. He diminished Pakistan to 27 for three. But Anil Kumble had been mistakenly ignored for this match; and India failed to break through the defences of the seasoned and skilful Inzamam-ul Haq and Yousuf Youhana, who steadily rebuilt the Pakistani innings with a partnership of 75. At 152 for six, though, the match could still have gone either way. But Shahid Afridi, entering at number eight and often a thorn in the side for India, broke the shackles with two sky-scraping sixes, which conclusively swung the game Pakistan's way. Youhana, unruffled and untroubled, then carried

Pakistan to a three-wicket win with four balls to spare. This was a significant victory for Pakistan, for they had lost to India every time the two crossed swords in the World Cup.

Toss: Pakistan
Umpires: RE Koertzen (SA) and SJA Taufel (Aus)
TV Umpire: SA Bucknor (WI)
Referee: CH Lloyd (WI)
Man of the Match: Yousuf Youhana

India innings (50 overs maximum)			R	B
*SC Ganguly	c Moin Khan	b Mohammad Sami	0	5
V Sehwag	c Shoaib Malik	b Naved-ul Hasan	10	20
VVS Laxman	c Shoaib Malik	b Naved-ul Hasan	3	9
M Kaif	c Moin Khan	b Shoaib Akhtar	27	59
+R Dravid	c & b Naved-ul Hasan		67	108
Yuvraj Singh	c Moin Khan	b Shoaib Akhtar	0	3
RS Gavaskar	c Moin Khan	b Abdul Razzaq	13	43
AB Agarkar	c Yousuf Youhana	b Naved-ul Hasan	47	50
IK Pathan	c Yousuf Youhana	b Shoaib Akhtar	6	8
Harbhajan Singh	not out		3	3
A Nehra	c Shahid Afridi	b Shoaib Akhtar	0	2

Extras: (lb 10, w 3, nb 11) 24
Total: (all out, 49.5 overs) 200

FoW: 1-1 (Ganguly, 0.5 ov), 2-10 (Laxman, 3.2 ov),
3-28 (Sehwag, 9.2 ov), 4-73 (Kaif, 19.2 ov),
5-73 (Yuvraj Singh, 19.5 ov), 6-106 (Gavaskar, 33.5 ov),
7-188 (Dravid, 46.6 ov), 8-193 (Agarkar, 48.2 ov),
9-199 (Pathan, 49.2 ov), 10-200 (Nehra, 49.5 ov).

Bowling	O	M	R	W	
Mohammad Sami	9	1	50	1	(3nb, 2w)
Naved-ul Hasan	9	1	25	4	(3nb)
Abdul Razzaq	10	0	27	1	(1nb)
Shoaib Akhtar	9.5	1	36	4	(4nb, 1w)
Shahid Afridi	2	0	23	0	
Shoaib Malik	10	0	29	0	

Pakistan innings (target: 201 runs from 50 overs)			R	B
Yasir Hameed	c Nehra	b Pathan	15	29
Imran Farhat	c Dravid	b Pathan	0	4
Shoaib Malik	c Dravid	b Pathan	5	7
*Inzamam-ul Haq	c Dravid	b Agarkar	41	79
Yousuf Youhana	not out		81	114
Abdul Razzaq		b Sehwag	9	21
+Moin Khan	c Yuvraj Singh	b Nehra	10	13
Shahid Afridi	c Sehwag	b Yuvraj Singh	25	12
Naved-ul Hasan	not out		5	17

Extras: (b 2, lb 5, w 3) 10
Total: (7 wickets, 49.2 overs) 201

DNB: Mohammad Sami, Shoaib Akhtar.

FoW: 1-1 (Imran Farhat, 0.6 ov), 2-10 (Shoaib Malik, 2.6 ov),
3-27 (Yasir Hameed, 10.3 ov), 4-102 (Inzamam-ul Haq, 28.4 ov),
5-127 (Abdul Razzaq, 35.4 ov), 6-152 (Moin Khan, 40.2 ov),
7-187 (Shahid Afridi, 45.2 ov).

Bowling	O	M	R	W
Pathan	9	1	34	3
Nehra	10	0	45	1 (1w)
Agarkar	10	2	33	1 (2w)
Harbhajan Singh	10	1	37	0
Ganguly	4	0	17	0
Sehwag	4	0	22	1
Yuvraj Singh	2.2	0	6	1

Even in India, interest in the Champions Trophy crashed after India's elimination. According to reports, advertising rates connected with the TV transmission of the event tumbled from Rs 300,000 (£3600) for 10 seconds to Rs 50,000.

Semi-final, 21 September: Edgbaston, Birmingham

Meanwhile, England, lined up against Australia in the last four, had the satisfaction of recording a rare win over their arch-rivals.

Toss: England
Umpires: BF Bowden (NZ) and RE Koertzen (SA)
TV Umpire: Aleem Dar (Pak)
Referee: MJ Procter (SA)
Man of the Match: MP Vaughan

Australia innings (50 overs maximum)			R	B
+AC Gilchrist	c Trescothick	b Gough	37	50
ML Hayden	c Trescothick	b Harmison	17	21
*RT Ponting	c Gough	b Giles	29	41
DR Martyn	c Trescothick	b Vaughan	65	91
DS Lehmann		b Vaughan	38	42
A Symonds	run out (Vaughan)		0	2
MJ Clarke		b Flintoff	42	34
B Lee		b Gough	15	17
JN Gillespie		b Gough	0	1
MS Kasprowicz	not out		0	2
GD McGrath	not out		0	1

Extras: (b 3, lb 4, w 7, nb 2) 16
Total: (9 wickets, 50 overs) 259

FoW: 1-44 (Hayden, 7.6 ov), 2-69 (Gilchrist, 13.6 ov),
3-114 (Ponting, 25.1 ov), 4-189 (Lehmann, 38.5 ov),
5-190 (Symonds, 39.4 ov), 6-210 (Martyn, 42.4 ov),
7-249 (Lee, 48.4 ov), 8-249 (Gillespie, 48.5 ov),
9-258 (Clarke, 49.5 ov).

Bowling	O	M	R	W
Gough	7	1	48	3
Harmison	10	0	53	1 (2nb, 1w)
Flintoff	10	0	56	1 (1w)
Giles	10	0	40	1 (3w)
Wharf	3	0	13	0
Vaughan	10	0	42	2 (1w)

England innings (target: 260 runs from 50 overs)			R	B
ME Trescothick		b Symonds	81	88
VS Solanki	lbw	b Gillespie	7	18
*MP Vaughan	c Hayden	b Lee	86	122
AJ Strauss	not out		52	42
A Flintoff	c Hayden	b Lee	16	9
PD Collingwood	not out		6	4

Extras: (lb 5, w 5, nb 4) 14
Total: (4 wickets, 46.3 overs) 262

DNB: +GO Jones, AG Wharf, AF Giles, D Gough, SJ Harmison.

FoW: 1-21 (Solanki, 5.2 ov), 2-161 (Trescothick, 31.3 ov), 3-227 (Vaughan, 42.4 ov), 4-249 (Flintoff, 44.6 ov).

Bowling	O	M	R	W
McGrath	8	0	46	0 (1w)
Gillespie	8	0	32	1 (1nb, 1w)
Kasprowicz	10	0	52	0 (1w)
Lee	8.3	0	65	2 (3nb, 2w)
Lehmann	6	0	28	0
Symonds	6	1	34	1

Semi-final, 22 September: Southampton

In the other meeting at the penultimate stage, the West Indies faced Pakistan and caused an upset.

Toss: Pakistan
Umpires: DB Hair (Aus) and SJA Taufel (Aus)
TV Umpire: DR Shepherd
Referee: RS Madugalle (SL)
ODI Debut: Salman Butt (Pak).
Man of the Match: RR Sarwan

Pakistan innings *(50 overs maximum)*			R	B
Yasir Hameed	run out (Bravo/Browne)		39	56
Salman Butt	c Sarwan	b Bradshaw	0	2
Shoaib Malik	c Browne	b Bravo	17	58
*Inzamam-ul Haq	c Browne	b WW Hinds	21	44
Yousuf Youhana	c Browne	b Bravo	12	28
Abdul Razzaq	run out (Bravo/Browne)		6	17
+Moin Khan	lbw	b WW Hinds	0	2
Shahid Afridi	st Browne	b Gayle	17	13
Naved-ul Hasan		b Collymore	0	4
Mohammad Sami		b Collymore	0	4
Shoaib Akhtar	not out		0	2

Extras: (lb 4, w 15) 19
Total: (all out, 38.2 overs) 131

FoW: 1-1 (Salman Butt, 0.3 ov), 2-65 (Yasir Hameed, 18.1 ov),
3-71 (Shoaib Malik, 21.3 ov), 4-100 (Yousuf Youhana, 29.2 ov),
5-109 (Abdul Razzaq, 32.6 ov), 6-111 (Inzamam-ul Haq, 34.1 ov),
7-112 (Moin Khan, 34.4 ov), 8-116 (Naved-ul-Hasan, 35.6 ov),
9-125 (Mohammad Sami, 37.4 ov), 10-131 (Shahid Afridi, 38.2 ov).

Bowling	O	M	R	W
Bradshaw	8	0	23	1
Collymore	9	2	24	2 (4w)
Bravo	9	0	41	2 (7w)
WW Hinds	10	0	27	2 (2w)
RO Hinds	1	0	1	0 (1w)
Gayle	1.2	0	11	1

West Indies innings *(target: 132 runs from 50 overs)*			R	B
CH Gayle	lbw	b Shoaib Akhtar	1	8
WW Hinds	c & b Shoaib Akhtar		5	12
RR Sarwan	not out		56	85
*BC Lara	retired hurt		31	30
S Chanderpaul	c Salman Butt	b Shoaib Malik	11	24
RL Powell	not out		6	11

Extras: (b 2, lb 10, w 9, nb 1) 22
Total: (3 wickets, 28.1 overs) 132

DNB: DJ Bravo, RO Hinds, +CO Browne, IDR Bradshaw, CD Collymore.

FoW: 1-8 (Gayle, 2.2 ov), 2-20 (WW Hinds, 4.2 ov),
3-102 (Chanderpaul, 23.6 ov).

Bowling	O	M	R	W
Shoaib Akhtar	7	1	18	2 (4w)
Mohammad Sami	3	0	23	0
Naved-ul Hasan	7	2	24	0 (1w)
Abdul Razzaq	6	0	39	0 (3w)
Shoaib Malik	5	0	15	1 (1nb, 1w)
Yousuf Youhana	0.1	0	1	0

Final, 25 September: The Oval, London

On a wintry September day, with light conditions not as favourable
as mid-summer, England were confident of getting the better of the
West Indies, having battered them in test matches only a few weeks
earlier. But it all went rather pear-shaped.

The West Indies still needed 71 runs to win when their eighth
wicket fell. But an hour later, in fading light, the number 10 batsman,
Ian Bradshaw, cracked a ball from Alex Wharf to the square third-
man boundary to secure the fourth Champions Trophy. Keeping him
company with an almost equal contribution was Courtney Browne.
It was a personal triumph for Brian Lara. Three days earlier, he had
been stung on the neck by a Shoaib Akhtar delivery and was doubtful
for the final. But not only did he take the field, but also his canny use
of a limited attack, including throwing up a surprise packet in Wavell
Hinds' medium–paced swingers, overcame the Englishmen's
challenge.

Toss: West Indies
Umpires: RE Koertzen (SA) and SJA Taufel (Aus)
TV Umpire: DB Hair (Aus)
Referee: RS Madugalle (SL)
Man of the Match: IDR Bradshaw
Player of the Tournament: RR Sarwan

England innings *(50 overs maximum)*			R	B
ME Trescothick	run out (Lara/Gayle)		104	124
VS Solanki	c Browne	b Bradshaw	4	13
*MP Vaughan		b Bradshaw	7	18
AJ Strauss	run out (Bravo)		18	33
A Flintoff	c Lara	b WW Hinds	3	6
PD Collingwood	c Chanderpaul	b WW Hinds	16	40
+GO Jones	c Lara	b WW Hinds	6	18
AF Giles	c Lara	b Bravo	31	37
AG Wharf	not out		3	6
D Gough	st Browne	b Gayle	0	1
SJ Harmison	run out		2	2

Extras: (b 1, lb 7, w 15) 23
Total: (all out, 49.4 overs) 217

FoW: 1-12 (Solanki, 4.2 ov), 2-43 (Vaughan, 10.3 ov),
3-84 (Strauss, 19.6 ov), 4-93 (Flintoff, 22.1 ov),
5-123 (Collingwood, 32.3 ov), 6-148 (Jones, 38.2 ov),
7-211 (Trescothick, 47.4 ov), 8-212 (Giles, 48.3 ov),
9-214 (Gough, 49.1 ov), 10-217 (Harmison, 49.4 ov).

Bowling	O	M	R	W
Bradshaw	10	1	54	2 (3w)
Collymore	10	1	38	0 (3w)
Gayle	9.4	0	52	1
Bravo	10	0	41	1 (9w)
WW Hinds	10	3	24	3

West Indies innings *(target: 218 runs from 50 overs)*			R	B
CH Gayle	c & b Harmison		23	33
WW Hinds	c Solanki	b Harmison	3	16
RR Sarwan	c Strauss	b Flintoff	5	7
*BC Lara	c Jones	b Flintoff	14	28
S Chanderpaul	c Vaughan	b Collingwood	47	66
DJ Bravo	c Jones	b Flintoff	0	7

RO Hinds	c Jones	b Trescothick	8	19
RL Powell	c Trescothick	b Collingwood	14	16
+CO Browne	not out		35	55
IDR Bradshaw	not out		34	51

Extras :(lb 11, w 19, nb 5) 35
Total : (8 wickets, 48.5 overs) 218

DNB: CD Collymore.

FoW: 1-19 (WW Hinds, 3.5 ov), 2-35 (Sarwan, 8.1 ov),
3-49 (Gayle, 9.4 ov), 4-72 (Lara, 16.3 ov),
5-80 (Bravo, 18.3 ov), 6-114 (RO Hinds, 24.5 ov),
7-135 (Powell, 29.2 ov), 8-147 (Chanderpaul, 33.4 ov).

Bowling	O	M	R	W
Gough	10	1	58	0 (5w)
Harmison	10	1	34	2 (3w)
Flintoff	10	0	38	3 (4nb, 2w)
Wharf	9.5	0	38	0 (1nb)
Trescothick	3	0	17	1 (2w)
Collingwood	6	0	22	2 (1w)

It may have all ended well for England, if they had lifted their first major international trophy (and by that I mean the World Cup, Champions Trophy or the one-off Benson & Hedges World Championship). This elusive honour they were fancied to attain. One of the English bookmakers had offered odds of 100 to one on them. But as the glorious uncertainties of cricket have oft revealed, there can be many a slip between the cup and the lip!

THE 2006 CHAMPIONS TROPHY

Drama, quite unprecedented in the annals of cricket, preceded the fifth Champions Trophy. Towards the end of August 2006, for the first time in 129 years, a side – Pakistan – forfeited a test match after failing to reappear in the field on time in the fourth and final test against England at The Oval. The umpires who imposed this penalty were Darrell Hair of Australia and Billy Doctrove of the West Indies. Inzamam-ul-Haq, Pakistan's captain, was, under the ICC's Code of Conduct, accused of ball tampering and bringing the game into disrepute.

The matter was referred to Sri Lanka's Ranjan Madugalle, the ICC's chief referee, for adjudication. He presided over a hearing and reached the conclusion that Inzamam was innocent of the first charge, but guilty of the second, for which he was levied the most lenient sentence of a four-match one-day international ban.

Hair, the senior umpire, was convinced that the condition of the ball had changed 'markedly'. His colleague, Doctrove concurred. Inzamam remonstrated over the double jeopardy of a replacement ball and a five-run penalty at the time, but play continued until the next tea break.

After the interval, though, Pakistan refused to resume playing. Hair warned them of the consequences. He, thereafter, re-entered the ground, waited a while, before dramatically taking off the bails to signal the end of the match and a victory by default to England.

While there was a history of suspicion relating to Pakistani players scuffing up or picking the seam of a ball, it was still a most serious charge and unambiguously translated to cheating.

The Laws of Cricket render an umpire's decision to be final, regardless of whether he is right or wrong. He is not required to provide any evidence to substantiate his ruling. However, Madugalle ignored this regulation and instead opted to uphold the principle of natural justice.

He summarized: 'Having regard to the seriousness of the allegation of ball tampering (it is an allegation of cheating), I am not satisfied on the balance of probabilities that there is sufficiently cogent evidence that the fielding team had taken action likely to interfere with the condition of the ball. In my judgment, the marks are as consistent with normal wear and tear of a match ball after 56 overs as they are with deliberate human intervention.'

More upheaval besieged Pakistan. Younis Khan, appointed as captain in place of Inzamam for the Champions Trophy, at first, refused this invitation, before altering his mind. Then, on the eve of the tournament, fast bowlers Shoaib Akhtar and Mohammed Asif were sent home after failing dope tests ordered by the Pakistan Cricket Board (PCB). The former was, initially, debarred from playing for two years and the latter for one year by the PCB, but let off by the same body after cricketers appealed against these rulings. The ICC, backed by the World Anti-Doping Agency, were not amused. In the midst of such turmoil, Shahryar Khan, the urbane chairman of the PCB and a cousin of India's former captain, Tiger Pataudi, resigned from his post.

Khan was replaced by Nasim Ashraf, another appointee of General Pervez Musharraf, the president of Pakistan. In one of his first steps, the new incumbent called on his players to stop displaying their religious beliefs in public. Allegedly, at Inzamam's insistence, the Pakistani team habitually engaged in communal worship. In a clear caution to Inzamam, who belongs to a Muslim sect, one of whose objectives is to convert people to Islam, Ashraf said: 'There should be no pressure on players who don't pray regularly or any compulsion on them to do it.' In an age when every move or utterance of cricketers is telecast nationally and transnationally to wide audiences, there should be no abuse of this medium. One's faith must remain a private matter.

But what preoccupied those concentrating on cricket was not Pakistan's predicament, but whether the Champions Trophy would at last make an universal impact and, if Australia, the undisputed world champions, would correct the aberration of never having won the tourney.

Contrary to the 2004 competition, wherein 12 sides participated, the 2006 format reverted to restricting entries to test-playing teams only. However, based on rankings at a cut off point in the spring of 2006, the bottom four, namely, Sri Lanka, the West Indies, Zimbabwe and Bangladesh, were obliged to participate in a qualifying phase, from which, predictably, the first two made the grade. Indeed, the

Sri Lankans, because of their purple patch in one-dayers in the run-up to the championship, which included a clean sweep of a series in England, were seamlessly catapulted from qualifiers to favourites by a segment of subcontinental opinion.

Sri Lanka joined South Africa, New Zealand and Pakistan in Group B, while the foursome in Group A consisted of the West Indies, Australia, India and England.

The staging of the 2006 Champions Trophy in India was a *fait accompli* –this having been agreed to by the BCCI during the Jagmohan Dalmiya-controlled regime. Yet, the new dispensation under Sharad Pawar, India's food and agriculture minister, had to be dragged kicking and screaming to fulfil their obligations. They sulked about the lack of financial benefit to them, while officials of their member associations involved in hosting matches quibbled over share of gate receipts and even, immaturely, accused the ICC of behaving like colonialists.

None of the fixtures could be held in eastern or southern India as these parts of the country were subject to the vagaries of the retreating monsoon. Indeed, even the selected regions had suffered from an extended rainy season, which had affected wicket preparation in the concerned venues, including the magnificent Cricket Club of India's Brabourne Stadium, where superior cricket was returning for the first time since 1989. It's a sad commentary on the internecine squabbles of Indian cricket that this 'Lord's of India' has not hosted a test match since 1972, as the Mumbai Cricket Association, in a fit of pique, built the less distinguished Wankhede Stadium a stone's throw away to deny Brabourne Stadium the privilege.

The unreliability of pitches in the second innings in the initial matches at the Brabourne Stadium catalysed Andy Atkinson, the ICC's ground consultant, to apply a polyvinyl acetate adhesive, mixed with water in a 1:2 ratio, to bind the surface. Such a measure had in the past been adopted in New Zealand and at Old Trafford, Manchester, with good results.

A first for any major one-day tournament was the fact that all matches were day/night affairs. While this consistency was only to be applauded, the subcontinental autumn, particularly in Jaipur and

Mohali, both in northern India, gave rise to dew in the evening session. Thus, ground staff had to resort to treating the outfield with a chemical spray to combat the moisture, as had previously been tried in South Africa.

The unpredictability of outcomes, indeed upsets, lent a tension and a thrill to the tournament. In the group stage, Australia were beaten by the West Indies in a match that produced a hat-trick by the Jamaican fast bowler, Jerome Taylor. South Africa were trounced by New Zealand, who, in turn, were defeated by Sri Lanka. But the Sri Lankans lost to Pakistan and South Africa, before the Pakistanis succumbed to both the Kiwis and the Proteas. All very topsy-turvy, but it was this uncertainty that kept devotees on tenterhooks.

Besides, it was delightful to see decent attendances in several matches not featuring the home side. The only drawback was the slightly disconcerting wickets. But a generally even contest between bat and ball and an efficiently run event blended with a public celebration of it contributed to, as Percy Sonn, the ICC's president, put it, an 'outstanding' Champions Trophy.

15 October: Jaipur

This city of palaces plastered with pink stone has been the seat of the maharajas of Jaipur, belonging to one of India's most prominent princely families. Gayatri Devi, the once gorgeously good-looking last maharani of this state (now an elderly, derecognized dowager in republican India), was a daughter of the maharaja of Coochbehar in West Bengal state, who happened to be one of the early patrons of cricket in India. She, herself, was an avid follower of the game and generous with her hospitality to cricketers.

This time, though, the generosity was extended by the English. On what appeared to be a 200-run pitch, they could only muster 125 in 37 overs, after being put in to bat by Rahul Dravid. Irfan Pathan recaptured his ability to swing the ball with some accuracy and Munaf Patel was characteristically economical to have Andrew Flintoff's side reeling at 27 for four and then at 55 for five. Kevin Pietersen, lynchpin of the England middle order, briefly counterattacked and Paul Collingwood and Jamie Dalrymple – for the sixth wicket – mounted a slight resistance. But the off-spinners Harbhajan Singh and Ramesh Powar soon terminated any thoughts of a serious fight-back.

India, however, rather huffed and puffed to victory. As 16 wickets fell for a modest 251 runs in the match, only Sachin Tendulkar and Yuvraj Singh came to terms with a wicket of uneven bounce – the former eventually having the mortification of receiving a three-quarter length delivery which bounced just shin high. India won by four wickets with 20.3 overs to spare amidst a cacophony of firecrackers in anticipation of Diwali, the biggest Hindu festival.

Toss: India
Umpires: DJ Harper (Aus) and SJA Taufel (Aus)
TV Umpire: BF Bowden (NZ)
Referee: JJ Crowe (NZ)
Man of the Match: MM Patel (Ind)

England innings (50 overs maximum)			*R*	*B*
AJ Strauss	c Dravid	b Pathan	10	32
IR Bell	lbw	b Patel	4	7
A Flintoff	lbw	b Pathan	0	7
MH Yardy	lbw	b Patel	4	9
KP Pietersen	c Tendulkar	b Patel	27	39
PD Collingwood	c Dhoni	b Powar	38	54
JWM Dalrymple	c Dravid	b Powar	24	46
CMW Read	c Pathan	b Harbhajan Singh	2	7
SI Mahmood	c Harbhajan Singh	b Powar	8	13
SJ Harmison	not out		2	8
JM Anderson	run out (Powar)		1	1

Extras: (lb 2, w 2, nb 1) **5**
Total: (all out; 37 overs; 160 mins) **125**

FoW: 1-10 (Bell, 3.2 ov), 2-11 (Flintoff, 4.5 ov), 3-17 (Yardy, 7.3 ov), 4-27 (Strauss, 12.1 ov), 5-55 (Pietersen, 18.5 ov), 6-104 (Collingwood, 30.2 ov), 7-107 (Read, 31.5 ov), 8-119 (Mahmood, 34.3 ov), 9-124 (Dalrymple, 36.3 ov), 10-125 (Anderson, 36.6 ov).

Bowling	O	M	R	W
IK Pathan	8	3	20	2
MM Patel	8	2	18	3
AB Agarkar	5	0	34	0
Harbhajan Singh	8	0	27	1
RR Powar	8	1	24	3

India innings (target: 126 runs from 50 overs)			R	B
V Sehwag	c Strauss	b Harmison	9	4
SR Tendulkar	lbw	b Harmison	35	41
IK Pathan	c Pietersen	b Anderson	19	34
R Dravid	c Strauss	b Anderson	4	3
Yuvraj Singh	not out		27	61
MS Dhoni	c Collingwood	b Dalrymple	7	22
SK Raina		b Dalrymple	0	2
Harbhajan Singh	not out		6	11

Extras: (lb 7, w 11, nb 1) **19**
Total: (6 wickets; 29.3 overs; 142 mins) **126**

DNB: AB Agarkar, RR Powar, MM Patel.

FoW: 1-18 (Sehwag, 1.3 ov), 2-68 (Pathan, 10.1 ov), 3-72 (Dravid, 10.4 ov), 4-98 (Tendulkar, 18.1 ov), 5-119 (Dhoni, 26.3 ov), 6-119 (Raina, 26.5 ov).

Bowling	O	M	R	W
JM Anderson	7	1	40	2
SJ Harmison	6	0	34	2
SI Mahmood	8.3	0	30	0
MH Yardy	4	0	10	0
JWM Dalrymple	4	0	5	2

26 October: Ahmedabad

Tendulkar and Pathan (the futile pinch-hitter) dragging deliveries on to the stumps was proof of a slow pitch and low bounce. With left-armer Ian Bradshaw pegging away in the right areas and Taylor generating hot pace, not to mention Marlon Samuels spearing his fastish off-breaks on to the block hole, the Indians found shot making difficult after being sent in to bat. The promise of Dravid taking charge was nipped in the bud by a bull's-eye from square leg, while Dhoni's uncharacteristic caution as he meandered to 12 off his first 40 balls, despite this being subsequently corrected, cost the hosts critical runs. Indeed, it was left to Harbhajan Singh to inject some urgency to the Indian effort, from which Dhoni took the cue.

With Pathan back to his erratic ways, Chris Gayle briefly took advantage before top-edging Munaf Patel. Therefore, his opening partner, Shivnarine Chanderpaul, silkily pierced the gaps to lay a foundation for Ramnaresh Sarwan and Runako Morton, with a 92-run partnership between them, to put the West Indies in control, although their departures together with the exits of Brian Lara and Dwayne Smith in quick succession seemed to put the cat among the pigeons and postponed the three-wicket victory to the third-last ball of the innings.

Toss: West Indies
Umpires: Aleem Dar (Pak) and DJ Harper (Aus)
TV Umpire: SJA Taufel
Referee: MJ Procter
Man of the Match: S Chanderpaul

India innings (50 overs maximum)		*R*	*B*
V Sehwag	lbw b Taylor	17	20
SR Tendulkar	b Bradshaw	29	45
IK Pathan	b Bradshaw	0	6
R Dravid	run out (Smith)	49	67
Yuvraj Singh	c Bravo b Bradshaw	27	43
MS Dhoni	run out (Baugh/Chanderpaul)	51	65
SK Raina	st Baugh b Samuels	19	37
Harbhajan Singh	b Taylor	15	15
AB Agarkar	run out (Baugh)	1	2
RP Singh	not out	0	1

Extras: (lb 3, w 11, nb 1) **15**
Total: (9 wickets; 50 overs; 222 mins) **223**

DNB: MM Patel.

FoW: 1-22 (Sehwag, 4.3 ov), 2-27 (Pathan, 5.6 ov), 3-69 (Tendulkar, 16.5 ov), 4-130 (Yuvraj Singh, 30.1 ov), 5-131 (Dravid, 30.6 ov), 6-164 (Raina, 41.6 ov), 7-213 (Harbhajan Singh, 48.3 ov), 8-223 (Dhoni, 49.5 ov), 9-223 (Agarkar, 49.6 ov).

Bowling	O	M	R	W
JE Taylor	10	2	33	2
IDR Bradshaw	10	0	30	3
DR Smith	10	1	37	0
DJ Bravo	7	0	51	0
MN Samuels	9	0	35	1
CH Gayle	4	0	34	0

West Indies innings (target: 224 runs from 50 overs)		R	B
CH Gayle	c Singh b Patel	34	37
S Chanderpaul	c Dravid b Sehwag	51	72
DJ Bravo	lbw b Harbhajan Singh	16	33
RR Sarwan	run out (Dravid/Pathan)		53
81			
RS Morton	lbw b Agarkar	45	64
BC Lara	b Pathan	5	5
MN Samuels	not out	5	3
DR Smith	b Agarkar	0	1
CS Baugh	not out	1	2

Extras: (lb 2, w 12) 14
Total: (7 wickets; 49.4 overs; 228 mins) 224

DNB: IDR Bradshaw, JE Taylor

FoW: 1-43 (Gayle, 9.3 ov), 2-100 (Bravo, 21.6 ov),
3-120 (Chanderpaul, 26.6 ov), 4-212 (Morton, 47.5 ov), 5-218 (Lara, 48.4 ov),
6-219 (Sarwan, 48.6 ov), 7-219 (Smith, 49.1 ov).

Bowling	O	M	R	W
IK Pathan	5	0	34	1
MM Patel	8	2	29	1
AB Agarkar	9.4	1	52	2
RP Singh	4	0	29	0
Harbhajan Singh	10	1	27	1
V Sehwag	10	0	36	1
Yuvraj Singh	3	0	15	0

29 October: Mohali, Chandigarh

Here was a virtual quarter final, a must-win match for both Australia and India, if they were to progress to the semi-finals. The Aussies, after being capsized by the West Indies, had recovered to eclipse England.

India won a good toss; and Virender Sehwag rediscovered runs, hitting nine fours. But the Australians gradually contained him by bowling to his body, and Dravid failed to convert his dominance into a more substantial innings. Mohammed Kaif was fluent and Dhoni unsuicidal, despite being frustrated by a stream of yorkers. Essentially, there was no decisive partnership and the visitors were mostly in control.

All the same, a target of 250 under lights, with the likelihood of some life in the pitch for bowlers, was not elementary. Yet, an awful exhibition by the Indian quicks, including the otherwise reliable Munaf Patel, gifted 108 runs in the first 15 overs. Shane Watson posted a personal strike rate of 108.69 and paved the way for Ricky Ponting and Damien Martyn to adopt a relatively risk-free approach against Harbhajan Singh, although the latter was lucky to survive an lbw appeal from Dinesh Mongia at least once. With 23 balls remaining, Australia sailed to shore by six wickets.

Toss: India
Umpires: BF Bowden (N Z) and SA Bucknor (WI)
TV Umpire: MR Benson (Eng)
Referee: RS Madugalle
Man of the Match: DR Martyn

India innings (50 overs maximum)			R	B
V Sehwag	lbw	b Johnson	65	90
SR Tendulkar	c Gilchrist	b McGrath	10	26
D Mongia	c Hussey	b Watson	18	30
R Dravid	c Clarke	b Lee	52	63
M Kaif		b Lee	30	43
MS Dhoni	lbw	b Bracken	28	23
SK Raina	c Watson	b Bracken	13	19
IK Pathan	c Martyn	b McGrath	10	7
Harbhajan Singh	not out		5	3

Extras: (lb 5, w 9, nb 4) **18**
Total: (8 wickets; 50 overs; 232 mins) **249**

DNB: MM Patel, S Sreesanth

FoW: 1-46 (Tendulkar, 9.5 ov), 2-89 (Mongia, 19.4 ov),
3-126 (Sehwag, 28.2 ov), 4-186 (Dravid, 40.2 ov), 5-197 (Kaif, 42.1 ov),
6-224 (Raina, 47.1 ov), 7-239 (Pathan, 48.6 ov), 8-249 (Dhoni, 49.6 ov).

Bowling	O	M	R	W
B Lee	10	1	54	2
GD McGrath	10	1	34	2
NW Bracken	10	2	56	2
MG Johnson	8	0	33	1
SR Watson	9	0	48	1
A Symonds	3	0	19	0

Australia innings (target: 250 runs from 50 overs)			R	B
AC Gilchrist	c Raina	b Sreesanth	23	24
SR Watson	lbw	b Mongia	50	46
RT Ponting	c Tendulkar	b Sreesanth	58	69
DR Martyn	not out		73	104
A Symonds		b Pathan	20	24
MJ Clarke	not out		2	7

Extras: (lb 8, w 18) **26**
Total: (4 wickets; 45.4 overs; 201 mins) **252**

DNJB: MEK Hussey, B Lee, MG Johnson, NW Bracken, GD McGrath

FoW: 1-61 (Gilchrist, 8.5 ov), 2-111 (Watson, 15.5 ov),
3-185 (Ponting, 33.5 ov), 4-230 (Symonds, 42.6 ov).

Bowling	O	M	R	W
IK Pathan	7	0	42	1
MM Patel	8.4	0	61	0
S Sreesanth	8	1	43	2
Harbhajan Singh	10	0	49	0
D Mongia	9	0	36	1
V Sehwag	3	0	13	0

India's omission of both Kaif and Mongia in the first two matches and the persistence with Suresh Raina, his promise notwithstanding, were tactical errors, as was the preference in the squad for Rudra Pratap Singh at the expense of Sreesanth.

With India's elimination, all subcontinental sides for the first time failed to qualify for the last four in a major tournament since the inaugural World Cup in 1975. Indeed, this was a wake-up call for cricket administrations in this region, especially for the nouveau riche BCCI, a reminder that hefty bank balances were useless if they were not properly utilized.

Semi-final, 1 November: Mohali, Chandigarh

It was testimony to the state of the game that both Oceanic teams had eased themselves into the last four; indeed, a compliment to New Zealand, which has a population equal to a medium-sized Indian city and limited resources as far as cricket is concerned. The Kiwis, even after losing their first six wickets for a paltry 35 runs, were no pushovers as Jacob Oram and Daniel Vettori realized 103 runs for the seventh wicket, before the better equipped Aussies prevailed by 34 runs.

Toss: New Zealand
Umpires: SA Bucknor (WI) and RE Koertzen (SA)
TV Umpire: MR Benson
Referee: MJ Procter (SA)
Man of the Match: GD McGrath

Australia innings (50 overs maximum)			R	B
AC Gilchrist	c Oram	b Mills	3	11
SR Watson	c Fulton	b Mills	0	4
RT Ponting	c Vettori	b Mills	58	80
DR Martyn	lbw	b Vettori	26	54
MEK Hussey	c Marshall	b Franklin	35	52
A Symonds		b Bond	58	58
MJ Clarke	c Vettori	b Mills	14	22
B Lee		b Bond	5	5
MG Johnson	run out (Bond)		3	9
NW Bracken	not out		15	8
GD McGrath	not out		0	0

Extras: (lb 6, w 14, nb 3) 23
Total: (9 wickets, 50 overs, 220 mins) **240**

FoW: 1-3 (Watson, 2.2 ov), 2-4 (Gilchrist, 2.5 ov),
3-70 (Martyn, 19.3 ov), 4-123 (Ponting, 28.6 ov), 5-188 (Hussey, 40.1 ov),
6-211 (Symonds, 45.4 ov), 7-220 (Clarke, 46.5 ov), 8-223 (Lee, 47.2 ov),
9-236 (Johnson, 49.5 ov).

Bowling	O	M	R	W
KD Mills	10	1	38	4
SE Bond	10	0	55	2
JEC Franklin	8	1	48	1
JDP Oram	10	1	43	0
DL Vettori	10	0	41	1
NJ Astle	2	0	9	0

New Zealand innings (target: 241 runs from 50 overs)			R	B
L Vincent	c Ponting	b McGrath	1	15
SP Fleming	c Ponting	b Bracken	15	28
NJ Astle		b Lee	0	4
HJH Marshall	c Gilchrist	b McGrath	5	13
PG Fulton		b McGrath	2	13
JDP Oram	St Gilchrist	b Symonds	43	59
BB McCullum	c Martyn	b Bracken	1	4
DL Vettori		b Johnson	79	103
JEC Franklin	c Gilchrist	b Watson	8	11
KD Mills	c Gilchrist	b Lee	21	17
SE Bond	not out		9	11

Extras: (lb 7, w 13, nb 2) 22
Total: (all out, 46 overs, 200 mins) **206**

FoW: 1-16 (Vincent, 5.3 ov), 2-20 (Astle, 6.2 ov), 3-30 (Marshall, 9.2 ov), 4-30
(Fleming, 10.4 ov), 5-34 (Fulton, 13.4 ov), 6-35 (McCullum, 14.2 ov),
7-138 (Oram, 35.1 ov), 8-159 (Franklin, 38.6 ov), 9-180 (Vettori, 42.4 ov),
10-206 (Mills, 45.6 ov).

Bowling	O	M	R	W
B Lee	8	0	31	2
GD McGrath	10	2	22	3
NW Bracken	7	1	36	2
MG Johnson	7	0	38	1
SR Watson	7	0	27	1
A Symonds	7	0	45	1

Semi-final, 2 November: Jaipur

Herschelle Gibbs, visiting India for the first time since admitting his involvement in match fixing during South Africa's 2000 tour of India, was interviewed by the Delhi police on his arrival in India. Form-wise, somewhat in the cooler thereafter, he at last joined the party, only to be overshadowed by a bludgeoning hundred by Chris Gayle, which boasted 17 fours and three sixes and emanated at a strike rate of 98.51. It was his third century of the tournament – the last two back-to-back.

Toss: South Africa
Umpires: Aleem Dar (Pak) and SJA Taufel
TV Umpire: DJ Harper
Referee: JJ Crowe
Man of the Match: CH Gayle

South Africa innings (50 overs maximum)			R	B
GC Smith		b Taylor	19	23
LL Bosman	c Gayle	b Samuels	39	58
JH Kallis	c Sarwan	b Bravo	16	38
HH Gibbs	c Lara	b Bravo	77	90
AB de Villiers	run out (Lara)		46	57
JM Kemp		b Bradshaw	3	7
MV Boucher	c Sarwan	b Samuels	16	11
SM Pollock		b Taylor	4	4
RJ Peterson	not out		15	12
A Nel	not out		0	1

Extras: (b 1, lb 6, w 15, nb 1) **23**

Total: (8 wickets, 50 overs) **258**

DNB: M Ntini

FoW: 1-27 (Smith, 5.1 ov), 2-65 (Kallis, 16.4 ov), 3-96 (Bosman, 22.3 ov), 4-188 (de Villiers, 40.3 ov), 5-195 (Kemp, 42.2 ov), 6-219 (Boucher, 45.2 ov), 7-227 (Pollock, 46.4 ov), 8-256 (Gibbs, 49.4 ov).

Bowling		*O*	*M*	*R*	*W*
IDR Bradshaw		10	0	58	1
JE Taylor		10	1	48	2
DJ Bravo		7	0	41	2
DR Smith		4	1	12	0
CH Gayle		10	0	48	0
MN Samuels		9	0	44	2

West Indies innings (target: 259 runs from 50 overs)			*R*	*B*
CH Gayle	not out		133	135
S Chanderpaul	retired hurt		57	70
RR Sarwan	lbw	b Ntini	27	27
DJ Bravo	run out (Smith)		15	11
BC Lara	c & b Smith		9	10
RS Morton	c de Villiers	b Peterson	0	5
MN Samuels	not out		5	8

Extras: (lb 7, w 6, nb 3) **16**

Total: (4 wickets; 44 overs; 197 mins) **262**

DNB: DR Smith, CS Baugh, IDR Bradshaw, JE Taylor

FoW: 0-154* (Chanderpaul, retired not out), 1-196 (Sarwan, 33.6 ov), 2-226 (Bravo, 37.3 ov), 3-243 (Lara, 40.4 ov), 4-244 (Morton, 41.4 ov)

Bowling	O	M	R	W
SM Pollock	5	0	34	0
M Ntini	7	0	49	1
A Nel	10	1	60	0
GC Smith	10	0	43	0
JH Kallis	5	0	33	0
RJ Peterson	7	0	36	1

Final, 5 November: Brabourne Stadium, Mumbai

Gayle, the Player of the Tournament with 474 runs, and Shivnarine Chanderpaul threatened another blitzkrieg as the West Indians raced past 50 in the sixth over. Brett Lee was brutalized for 36 runs in three overs. Glen McGrath, who replaced him, went for 22 in his first two overs. But at the other end, the unpretentious Nathan Bracken was curling the ball awkwardly in the air. On a slow wicket, Chanderpaul played on, Ramnaresh Sarwan, front-edged and then Gayle was bowled by an almost unplayable outswinger. Typically, the Australians now pounced on their opponents. McGrath returned to his metronomic ways, sending down five overs for two runs and two wickets, including the vital one of Brian Lara, who was induced into an outside edge.

The crowd rallied behind the West Indies. Deafening roars greeted the dismissal of Adam Gilchrist and Ponting. But an unseasonal shower only delayed the inevitable as Watson and Martyn comfortably reached the revised target of 116 with 6.5 overs to spare. The oddity of Australia never having laid hands on the Champions Trophy was, thus, obliterated.

Toss: West Indies
Umpires: Aleem Dar (Pak) and RE Koertzen (SA)
TV Umpire: BF Bowden
Referee: RS Madugalle
Man of the Match: SR Watson

West Indies innings *(50 overs maximum)*			R	B
S Chanderpaul		b Bracken	27	18
CH Gayle		b Bracken	37	27
RR Sarwan	c Hogg	b Bracken	7	9
DJ Bravo	lbw	b Hogg	21	47
BC Lara	c Gilchrist	b McGrath	2	18
RS Morton	c Gilchrist	b McGrath	2	9
MN Samuels	c Ponting	b Watson	7	12
CS Baugh	lbw	b Watson	9	13
IDR Bradshaw		b Lee	7	15
JE Taylor	not out		5	13
CD Collymore	run out (Symonds)		0	5

Extras: (lb 5, w 7, nb 2) **14**
Total: (all out, 30.4 overs, 152 mins) **138**

FoW: 1-49 (Chanderpaul, 5.1 ov), 2-65 (Sarwan, 7.3 ov), 3-80 (Gayle, 9.4 ov), 4-88 (Lara, 14.5 ov), 5-94 (Morton, 18.2 ov), 6-113 (Samuels, 22.4 ov), 7-125 (Baugh, 24.6 ov), 8-125 (Bravo, 25.1 ov), 9-136 (Bradshaw, 28.6 ov), 10-138 (Collymore, 30.4 ov).

Bowling	O	M	R	W
B Lee	7.4	0	49	1
NW Bracken	6	0	22	3
GD McGrath	7	3	24	2
A Symonds	3	0	16	0
SR Watson	3	0	11	2
GB Hogg	4	1	11	1

Australia innings *(target: 116 runs from 35 overs)*			R	B
AC Gilchrist	c Gayle	b Bradshaw	2	9
SR Watson	not out		57	88
RT Ponting	lbw	b Taylor	0	2
DR Martyn	not out		47	71

Extras: (lb 4, w 5, nb 1) **10**
Total: (2 wickets, 28.1 overs, 121 mins) **116**

DNB: MEK Hussey, A Symonds, MJ Clarke, B Lee, GB Hogg, NW Bracken, GD McGrath

FoW: 1-12 (Gilchrist, 2.6 ov), 2-13 (Ponting, 3.6 ov)

Bowling	O	M	R	W
CH Gayle	1	0	5	0
JE Taylor	7	0	42	1
IDR Bradshaw	6	0	21	1
CD Collymore	6	1	19	0
MN Samuels	5	0	9	0
RR Sarwan	3.1	0	16	0

In between the semi-finals and the final of the Champions Trophy, the ICC Board (which comprised chairmen or presidents of national or regional federations) met at Mumbai. They resolved that umpire Darrell Hair 'should not be appointed to international matches involving ICC Full Members', having earlier been withdrawn from the panel of umpires for the tournament. The West Indies, South Africa, India, Sri Lanka, Zimbabwe and Bangladesh, reportedly, supported Pakistan's motion. Hair's sympathizers immediately blamed the BCCI's money power for the sacking. It would be surprising if the last has been heard about this vexed saga.

The ICC Board also referred the law concerning ball tampering to the body's Cricket Committee, while the organization's management was entrusted to prepare a paper evaluating and reviewing the role of the match referee for the Chief Executives' Committee. It is imperative that such reflections negate the fiasco of The Oval in future, as well as maintain the authority of the umpire. Indeed, it's desirable to strike a delicate balance.

10

The Calypso Cup

IN 1998, THE WEST INDIES CRICKET BOARD (WICB), HITHERTO
lacking in confidence as far as resources were concerned, finally
gathered enough courage to bid for the 2007 World Cup. Their
proposal was accepted by the ICC along with allotting the 2003
event to Africa. This completed rotation of the cardinal one-day
competition around all major cricketing regions, indeed corrected
the lacuna of this tournament not having been hosted in a part of
the world which, for significant parts of the 1960s, 1970s and 1980s,
dominated world cricket.

A perennial concern for the WICB was the meagre population
of the Caribbean, resulting, even when fully subscribed, in modest
attendances at grounds and, therefore, yielding insubstantial gate
receipts. But the fiscal framework of world cricket had massively
mutated since India won the 1983 World Cup; therefore,
circumstances from the 1990s onwards were rather different from
earlier decades. Now, it was a television-driven event, which, in turn,
because of the significantly increased audiences everywhere,
especially in India, magnetically attracted stratospheric levels of
sponsorship as compared to the past.

The task of the ICC Cricket World Cup 2007 Incorporated
(CWC), the organizing arm created by the WICB, was made easier,
when in 2001, the ICC, under President Malcolm Grey and Chief

Executive David Richards, sold ground space, sponsorship and television rights for the 2003 and 2007 World Cups and the Champions Trophy tournaments from 2002 to 2006 for US $550 million. This licence was somewhat controversially assigned to Global Cricket Corporation (GCC), a special vehicle created for the purpose, but a subsidiary of News Corporation, controlled by the media magnate, Rupert Murdoch. But importantly, the deal made the ICC solvent and has served the game of cricket in good stead.

The contract, during its term, virtually gave GCC veto rights against the ICC holding any championship other than the World Cup and Champions Trophy for the top teams and provided a significant profit margin. It also granted flexibility to sublicense television coverage to News Corp platforms, such as Sky in the UK and New Zealand and Fox in Australia, if they wanted to. In India, though, Sony Entertainment Television outbid ESPN Star Sports, a 50: 50 joint venture between News Corp and ESPN, to secure the TV rights.

CWC's share of the mop-ups was US $101 million. After meeting all costs, they expect of make a profit of US $60–70 million, which would be a boon for a cash-strapped WICB, who were at the last count at least US $16 million in debt. As long as the surplus from the World Cup is not wasted, this is adequate to redevelop West Indian cricket and instigate its revival.

But obtaining funds to host the World Cup was not the WICB's only headache. Caribbean cricket is a divided house, with territorial rivalries having resurfaced. Gone are the days when Frank Worrell, later knighted, united the different nationalities and ethnic groups in the early 1960s. Sheer talent and consequent triumphs sustained the cohesion thereafter. The mistrust between, say, Jamaicans and Trinidadians in the current West Indies squad is unhelpful. Cricket fans in the Caribbean are also endemically nationalistic.

However, there are exceptions to the trend. Those who are committed to a pan-West Indian cause continue to keep the torch alight at the WICB. One such person is Chris Dehring, whose calling card is professional management rather than mundane politics. He first met me some years ago, when he had come to London to market

West Indies cricket rights. He has since been seconded to oversee the operations pertaining to the World Cup as CWC's chief executive. His endeavours appear to enjoy the support of the Caribbean Community and Common Market (CARICOM). Indeed, the CWC's objective suitably fulfils CARICOM's goal of greater cooperation and integration between member countries on the lines of the European Union.

With the ICC gradually becoming a more credible and efficient body, and following criticism of the running of tournaments in the 1990s, they have asserted greater control over the World Cup. This started with the 2003 event, but has been strengthened further in respect of 2007. So, the stamp of the World Cup being intrinsically an ICC occasion will, in the West Indies, be unmistakeable.

Playing conditions and other ground and stadium facilities, while varying in dimension, would be standardized to the extent possible. In a dry run-cum-sneak preview when India toured the West Indies in 2006, some of the forthcoming amenities were exposed to the players, media and spectators.

For example, on the morning of the first ODI at Kingston, it poured ferociously for about three hours. In most places in the world, there would have been no play whatsoever after such a downpour; at best a truncated match, if the best of sunshine had followed.

At breakfast, with the rain bucketing down, I asked Steve Bucknor what he thought of the prospects. He, a Jamaican, was not very optimistic. Jeff Crowe, the former New Zealand cricketer and match referee, seemed to concur as he advised both teams and media to stay put in their hotels until further instructions.

The sun had, of course, made its appearance by then, but even local experts surmised the outfield was bound to be waterlogged and, consequently, unfit for play. What most people had ignored was a new drainage system, which had been installed at Sabina Park, venue of the match, in preparation for the World Cup. This device performed a miracle. Play started only an hour late; the game was reduced to 45 overs a side, but with the rest of the day being warm and sunny, the match was completed without any difficulty.

But if stereotyping is the aspiration, the grounds at St Lucia and St Kitts did not recover as rapidly as Sabina Park after similar drenching during the test matches there. It will be interesting to see if this inconsistency can be rectified in time for the World Cup.

Twelve stadiums, either brand new or having undergone a massive makeover, will be at the disposal of the 2007 World Cup. Eight of these will actually host competitive matches. The others will be for warm-up games or other purposes, such as the Trelawny Stadium in Jamaica, which will also stage the opening ceremony. The other practice venues will be the Arnos Vale Sports Complex in St Vincent, the 3 Ws Oval (named after Clyde Walcott, Everton Weekes and Worrell) at the University of West Indies (UWI) campus in Barbados and the UWI ground at St Augustine in Trinidad, which replaced the Brian Lara Stadium, in south Trinidad, as this failed to meet the rigorous construction deadline set by the organizers.

The field has been enlarged to 16 from 14 in 2003 and the teams have been grouped on the basis of ICC ODI rankings (given in parentheses) as in April 2005:

Group A St Kitts & Nevis	GroupB Trinidad	Group C Saint Lucia	Group D Jamaica
Australia (1)	Sri Lanka (2)	New Zealand (3)	Pakistan (4)
South Africa (5)	India (8)	England (7)	West Indies (6)
Scotland (12)	Bangladesh (11)	Kenya (10)	Zimbabwe (9)
The Netherlands (16)	Bermuda (15)	Canada (14)	Ireland (13)

For the warm-up matches too, the participants have been divided into clusters of four each. India, West Indies, Kenya and The Netherlands will partake in their practice engagements at Trelawny; Australia, England, Zimbabwe and Bermuda at St Vincent; South Africa, Pakistan, Canada and Ireland at the UWI ground in St. Augustine; and New Zealand, Sri Lanka, Bangladesh and Scotland at the 3 Ws Oval.

In all cases, teams will acclimatize and fine tune at venues different from the ones in which they will be playing their group matches. This trend could be misleading if pitches at the latter turn out to be dissimilar to the former, as has historically been the case between conditions in Jamaica – where wickets are generally much faster – and Trinidad. Batsmen, having limbered up in Jamaica, are liable to end up playing too early in Trinidad; also, fast bowlers might extract less pace and bounce. While identical surfaces can never be guaranteed anywhere – and are not desirable either – a sharp contrast between warm-up and tournament conditions could throw a side off balance.

Date	Group WA Trelawny, Jamaica	Group WB St Vincent	Group WC Trinidad & Tobago	Group WD Barbados
Mon. 05 March	West Indies vs Kenya	England vs Bermuda	England vs Canada	Sri Lanka vs Scotland
Tue. 06 March	India vs The Netherlands	Australia vs Zimbabwe	Pakistan vs Ireland	New Zealand vs Bangaldesh
Thu. 08 March	Kenya vs The Netherlands	Zimbabwe vs Bermuda	Ireland vs Canada	Scotland vs Bangladesh
Fri. 09 March	India vs West Indies	Australia vs England	Pakistan vs South Africa	New Zealand vs Sri Lanka

The opening ceremony is scheduled for 11 March, following which the Group Stage will get underway, with matches taking place at Warner Park, in St Kitts' capital of Basseterre; the Queen's Park Oval, in the Trinidadian capital of Port of Spain; the Beausejour Stadium, near the St Lucian capital of Castries; and Sabina Park, in the Jamaican capital of Kingston. The last two will double as venues for the semi-finals.

Date	Group A St Kitts & Nevis	Group B Trinidad & Tobago	Group C Saint Lucia	Group D Jamaica
Tue. 13 March	Rest	Rest	Rest	West Indies vs Pakistan
Wed. 14 March	Australia vs Scotland	Rest	Kenya vs Canada	Rest
Thu. 15 March	Rest	Sri Lanka vs Bermuda	Rest	Zimbabwe vs Ireland
Fri. 16 March	South Africa vs The Netherlands	Rest	England vs New Zealand	Rest
Sat. 17 March	Rest	India vs Bangladesh	Rest	Pakistan vs Ireland
Sun. 18 March	Australia vs The Netherlands	Rest	England vs Canada	Rest
Mon. 19 March	Rest	India vs Bermuda	Rest	West Indies vs Zimbabwe
Tue. 20 March	South Africa vs Scotland	New Zealand vs Kenya	Rest	Rest
Wed 21 March	Rest	Sri Lanka vs Bangladesh	Rest	Zimbabwe vs Pakistan
Thu. 22 March	Scotland vs The Netherlands	Rest	New Zealand vs Canada	Rest

Fri.	India		West Indies
	vs		vs
23 March Rest	Sri Lanka	Rest	Ireland

Sat.	Australia		England	
	vs		vs	
24 March South Africa	Rest	Kenya	Rest

Sun.	Bermuda		
	vs		
25 March Rest	Bangladesh	Rest	Rest

The Super 8 matches will take place at the Sir Vivian Richards Stadium, north of the Antiguan capital of St Johns, the Providence Stadium, located on the East Bank of the Demerara river near the Guyanese capital of Georgetown, the Queen's Park Stadium, in the Grenadan capital of St Georges and the Kensington Oval, in the Barbadian capital of Bridgetown, with the latter also staging the final.

Date	Antigua & Barbuda	Grenada	Guyana	Barbados
Tue. 27 March	D2* vs A1*		Rest	
Wed. 28 March	Rest		A2 vs B1	
Thu. 29 March	D2 vs C1		Rest	
Fri. 30 March	Rest		D1 vs C2	
Sat. 31 March	A1 vs B2		Rest	
Sun. 01 April	Rest		D2 vs B1	
Mon. 02 April	B2 vs C1		Rest	
Tue. 03 April	Rest		D1 vs A2	
Wed. 04 April	C2 vs B1		Rest	
Sat. 07 April	Rest		B2 vs A2	
Sun. 08 April	A1 vs C2		Rest	
Mon. 09 April	Rest		D1 vs C1	
Tue. 10 April		D2 vs A2		
Wed. 11 April		Rest		C2 vs B2
Thu. 12 April		B1 vs C1		Rest
Fri. 13 April		Rest		A1 vs D1

Sat. 14 April	A2 vs C1	Rest
Sun. 15 April	Rest	B2 vs D1
Mon. 16 April	A1 vs B1	Rest
Tue. 17 April	Rest	A2 vs C2
Wed. 18 April	D1 vs B1	Rest
Thu. 19 April	Rest	D2 vs B2
Fri. 20 April	A1 vs C1	Rest
Sat. 21 April	Rest	D2 vs C2

*This refers to the ranking within the group.

The semi-final between the second and third placed sides at the end of the Super 8 round robin is slated for 24 April at Jamaica and the showdown between the teams finishing first and fourth the following day at St Lucia, with both matches as well as the final allocated a reserve day in case they are affected by the weather. The climax is scheduled for 28 April.

The extended duration of the tournament is a drawback. Where the football World Cup finals, which engulf global interest and has 32 teams involved, consume only a month, for its corresponding competition in cricket to drag for seven weeks is, arguably, a little tedious. It will, of course, be a bonanza for those who want to skip work – and many in India probably will, after staying awake overnight. The expanded starting line-up is also likely to make the first phase less competitive.

The stadiums at Antigua and Grenada were built with the assistance of China and by Chinese workers; the one in Guyana was underwritten by India. The outfields sloping down like upturned saucers will all be sand based so as to facilitate better drainage both away from the middle and below the surface. An underground system of pipes meshed with a foundation of stones will help water seeping down to be drawn off. The squares will be 12 inches deep, with 4 inches of compacted sand and 8 inches of local clay.

Nazeer Ahmed, a Trinidadian professor of soil science, identified the most suitable earth in each territory, except that the ingredient for St Kitts was brought from its twin island of Nevis. The nature of clay tends to differ. Barbadian clay, for instance, hardens more than the others; thus the chronically greater pace and bounce at Bridgetown.

The ICC appear to have kept an eagle eye on every aspect of the preparations. Andy Atkinson, their burly pitch consultant, who rendered excellent service in the Champions Trophy in Nairobi in 2000 and was instrumental in producing near-perfect pitches in Pakistan for India's tour in 2003–04, has been entrusted to ensure 'good one-day wickets with consistent bounce'. He has worked with local ground staff and Andy Roberts, the former West Indian fast bowler and until lately the curator at the Antigua Recreation Ground (ARG), who is overall in charge of pitch preparation.

Given favourable weather conditions and cooperation of the groundsmen, Atkinson is capable of delivering what the doctor ordered. Roberts, too, has crafted some fine surfaces at the ARG. The pitches for the World Cup, though, are mostly in their infancy. The square at St Lucia would be less than four years old, the ones at St Kitts, Sabina Park and the Queen's Park Oval barely a year old, and the rest even younger. They all need to be well rolled to be conducive for their purpose. In recent years, wickets in the West Indies have been spongy yet slow paced.

No previous World Cup has seen the massive scale of investment that has been inoculated into the 2007 World Cup. Dehring estimated that at least US $350 million would have been spent by the various governments to provide new infrastructure, which has covered not only the construction of the stadiums, but also airport terminals and thoroughfares. Besides, the new grounds will not only be multipurpose – and, therefore, have non-cricketing applications – and the upgradation of airports and roads will benefit transportation and tourism, which is central to the economy of most, if not all, the host nations. In short, the World Cup has accelerated development in the Caribbean, and could leave behind a planned legacy for the future.

Including St Vincent (for warm-up games only), nine countries are involved in hosting the event. The CWC devised a bidding process for the states interested in staging matches. Applications were approved or rejected by Dehring's team and the ICC in consultation with an independent body comprising the International Media Group, Rushmans (a well-known event management company) and Sinclair-Knight-Merz Engineering. No World Cup has pursued such a systematic route in selecting venues. Successful governments were required to sign a 'Host Venue Agreement', which obligates them to deliver on several aspects of holding their package of matches as well as commits them and their concerned agencies to cooperate with the Local Organizing Committee (LOC). To facilitate these procedures and to ensure coordination, the Jamaican administration has, for instance,appointed a cabinet minister as a special envoy to the LOC.

Furthermore, given the multinational nature of the enterprise, a 'Sunset Legislation' was enacted by the nine sovereign states hosting the World Cup, which enjoins them with collective laws for a fixed period before and after the event. The nine states have also waived visa requirements for anyone legitimately entering any one of the other territories during, and for a stipulated span either side of, the World Cup.

The 2007 'Bid Book' has now been adopted by the ICC for future tournaments under their auspices. This means that the choice of match sites for the 2011 World Cup may not be the preserve of Indian, Pakistani, Sri Lankan and Bangladeshi authorities and could, emerge from competition between various state associations, city administrations and state governments. Infrastructure and congestion in the Indian subcontinent being what they are, a commensurate commitment would, I imagine, be demanded from interested parties to match international standards in such areas.

There has, however, been criticism in certain political circles in the West Indies about the quantum of expenditure that has been earmarked by the involved governments for the World Cup. Opponents of this exercise have voiced that the money could have been better spent on more pressing economic needs. Such reservations are unlikely to recede, but a successful event, including one that does not witness a premature West Indian exit, might marginalize such sentiments. Otherwise, the resentment could persist.

There is one aspect, though, to which the organizers would do well to pay particular attention. It may be wise to calibrate the entry of fans in accordance with the ability to absorb them. Needless to mention, the West Indies are comprised of limited land masses, and it could become unmanageable for the host countries if an influx well in excess of the hospitality potential were to occur. Arrivals without room reservations could be chaotic for the tiny islands.

The downside is that it's going to be an expensive World Cup for media and touring spectators. March–April marks the peak holiday season in the Caribbean and neither airfares nor hotel rooms are going to be reasonably priced. Therefore, people's wallets are likely to empty quite rapidly.

But all said and done, the centrepiece will be *the cricket*. Here, the outcome of the Group Stage is fairly predictable. While an upset or two would spice the flavour, it is hard to visualize Australia and South Africa being disturbed by either The Netherlands or Scotland in Group A. The other clusters are more intriguing. Bangladesh, on recent form, could conceivably test both India and Sri Lanka in Group B. England, at current potential, and New Zealand cannot underestimate Kenya, giant killers in 2003, in Group C. And Zimbabwe may not be a walkover for Pakistan and West Indies in Group D.

But matters could become really exciting at the Super 8 level – as opposed to the Super 6 in 1999 and 2003. No side will carry forward any points from the previous round nor meet the other qualifier from their group. In effect, if, say, India and Sri Lanka advance from their foursome, they will not meet again in the Super 8, but encounter the six who have moved up from other groups.

The first four on the basis of points acquired in the Super 8 will ascend to the semi-finals. It would be startling if Australia were not one of them, while the rest is a bit of a lottery, though one would expect the West Indies to be in the running on the basis of home advantage.

The four main sponsors of the tournament, or 'official global partners', as they are being called – LG, Pepsi, Hutch and Hero Honda – are all Indian companies or subsidiaries. Of the four secondary supporters or 'official sponsors' as they are being defined – Indian Oil, Cable & Wireless, Visa and Scotiabank, the first mentioned is an Indian public sector undertaking. With Indian firms (not to mention Sony Entertainment Television) bankrolling the event to such an extent, it would be a major mischance if India were precipitately eliminated. Certainly, advertising rates on telecasts of the competition in India could plummet if this were to happen.

The fact is, India have not qualified for the semi-finals in four of the six World Cups outside the subcontinent. At the same time, they compensated for their shortcomings in 1992 and 1999 by impressively entering the final in 2003. Arguably, a trained coach in John Wright made a difference.

But India are, now, under new leadership and management. Saurav Ganguly, captain in 2003, was rather unceremoniously unhinged. His long-servng deputy, Rahul Dravid, is now in the hot seat. Wright has been succeeded by the former Australian captain and master batsman, Greg Chappell. Dravid is a likeable person, uncontroversial, unselfish and the side's most dependable batsman. Chappell is a razor-sharp cricketing brain, ruthless and technologically savvy.

The Ganguly Affair

While his critics say he was asking for it, the BCCI's treatment of Ganguly is indefensible. Any cricketer deserves courtesy if he is to be omitted, especially if he's been the country's most successful skipper ever. The Indian selectors failed to observe basics in dealing with Ganguly, who had, additionally, scored in excess of 5000 runs and averaged above 40 in tests and more than 10,000 runs with an average of over 40 in ODIs. He also had to his name 22 ODI hundreds – second only to Tendulkar.

The East Zone have historically been one of the backwaters of Indian cricket. Indeed, Bengal, the leading Ranji Trophy side in this region, have since India's maiden appearance in tests in 1932, produced only two regular test players – Pankaj Roy, an opener in the 1950s and early 1960s, and Dilip Doshi, a left-arm spinner, in the late 1970s and early 1980s. Ganguly became the third. Saurav, a student of St Xavier's, a premier Jesuit school in Kolkata, got his first break when he was picked as a 19-year-old for India's tour of Australia in 1991–92. Some who watched him at close quarters on that trip concluded he was bereft of physical courage.

To his credit, though, he fought back and perhaps with the tutelage of Jagmohan Dalmiya, the influential Indian cricket official from Kolkata, was not only selected for the 1996 visit to England, but exploded on the international scene with centuries in his first two tests at Lord's and Trent Bridge. Thereafter, with Sachin Tendulkar stepping down from the captaincy in February 2000, the top job all but fell into Ganguly's lap. Many perceived this appointment to be an interim measure until either Tendulkar wanted to return or Dravid was ready to take over. The Bengal cricketer, however, surprised such cynics by registering steady success for India.

To his advantage, the BCCI almost simultaneously hired Wright, who introduced new systems and sensibilities in the management and instruction of the Indian team. The New Zealander's gentle touch as much shaped Ganguly as skipper as it did the others as cricketers. They stunned the cricketing world by vanquishing the hitherto unconquerable Australians under Steve Waugh in a test series in March 2001.

Ganguly stood out as being apolitical and without bias for his state or zone. Practically none of the players successfully drafted in or recalled during his tenure was from his part of the country. He had a hunch that Harbhajan Singh would serve him well. The Sikh responded by capturing 28 wickets in two tests against Australia as India stormed to victory in both. Only Mahendra Singh Dhoni hailed from Ganguly's zone, but not from his state. Few will argue against this choice, for this Jharkhand batsman-wicketkeeper's eruptive strokeplay has added a new dimension to India's batting. If at all Ganguly erred, it was in sometimes overlooking Anil Kumble's claims.

However, personal failures in home tests and ODIs against Pakistan in the spring of 2005 signalled the beginning of his troubles. In the past, even if he experienced some discomfort against fast bowlers pitching it short, he could tackle spinners with his eyes closed. The fact that Pakistan's Danish Kaneria – his class notwithstanding – beat him in the air so easily in these engagements was interpreted as a decrease in the sharpness of his eyes. This can happen all of a sudden to any cricketer after 30; and generally, only a watertight technique can overcome this affliction.

Tiger Pataudi agreed with this assessment. He should know better than anybody else about the handicap of a batsman lacking a 20:20 vision. No one has played international cricket with a greater eye impediment than he.

So, it was widely surmised that the writing was on the wall for Ganguly; and that it was, perhaps, time for him to step aside gracefully. This is, of course, easier said than done, for the enormous income earned by an Indian cricketer of his prominence is not easy to forsake. But regardless of a test hundred against Zimbabwe, a side no longer fit to play at this level, he was having to attritionally score runs in international cricket, which had previously flowed quite effortlessly. More seriously, he was accused by Chappell of manipulating team selection to protect his increasingly insecure place in the side.

The following was, reportedly, the full text of the Indian coach's quite copious email to the then BCCI president, Ranbir Mahendra:

Due to comments made by Mr Sourav Ganguly during the press conference following his innings in the recently completed Test match in Bulawayo [in Zimbabwe] and the subsequent media speculation I would like to make my position clear on two points.

1. *At no stage did I ask Mr Ganguly to step down from the captaincy of the Indian team and;*
2. *At no stage have I threatened to resign my position as Indian team coach.*

Mr Ganguly came to me following the recently completed tri-series of one-day matches here in Zimbabwe and asked me to tell him honestly where he stood as a player in my view. I told him that I thought he was struggling as a player and that it was affecting his ability to lead the team effectively and that the pressure of captaincy was affecting his ability to play to his potential. I also told him that his state of mind was fragile and it showed in the way that he made decisions on and off the field in relation to the team, especially team selection. A number of times during the tri-series the tour selectors had chosen a team and announced it to the group only for Sourav to change his mind on the morning of the game and want to change the team.

On at least one occasion he did change the team and on the morning of the final I had to talk him out of making another last-minute change that I believe would have destroyed team morale and damaged the mental state of the individuals concerned. I also told Sourav that his nervous state was affecting the team in other ways as he was prone to panic during pressure situations in games and that his nervous demeanour was putting undue pressure on the rest of the team. His nervous pacing of the rooms during our batting in the final plus his desire to change the batting order during our innings in the final had also contributed to nervousness in the players waiting to go in to bat. His reluctance to bat first in games I suggested was also giving wrong signals to the team and the opposition and his nervousness at the crease facing bowlers like Shane Bond from NZ was also affecting morale in the dressing room.

On the basis of this and other observations and comments from players in the squad about the unsettling effect Sourav was having on the group I suggested to Sourav that he should consider stepping down from the captaincy at the end of the tour in the interests of the team and in his own best interests if he wanted to prolong his playing career. I told him of my own experiences toward the end of my career and cited other players such as [Allan] Border, [Mark] Taylor and Steve Waugh, all of whom struggled with batting form toward the end of their tenure as Australian captain.

We discussed other issues in relation to captaincy and the time and effort it took that was eating into his mental reserves and making it difficult to prepare properly for batting in games. He commented that he had enjoyed being free of those responsibilities in the time that he was in Sri Lanka following his ban from international cricket and that he would consider my suggestion.

I also raised the matter of selection for the first Test with Sourav and asked him where he thought he should bat. He said "number 5". I told him that *he might like to consider opening in the Test as the middle order was going to be a tight battle with [Mohammed] Kaif and Yuvraj [Singh] demanding selection. Sourav asked me if I was serious. I said it was something to be considered, but it had to be his decision.*

The following day Sourav batted in the match against Zimbabwe "A" team in the game in Mutare. I am not sure of the exact timing of events because I was in the nets with other players when Sourav went in to bat, but the new ball had either just been taken or was imminent when I saw Sourav walking from the field holding his right arm. I assumed he had been hit and made my way to the players' area where Sourav was receiving treatment from the team physiotherapist, John Gloster.

When I enquired as to what had happened Sourav said he had felt a click in his elbow as he played a ball through the leg side and that he thought he should have it investigated. Sourav had complained of pain to his elbow at various stages of the one-day series, but he had resisted having any comprehensive investigation done and, from my observation, had been spasmodic in his treatment habits, often not using ice-packs for the arm that had been prepared for him by John Gloster. I suggested, as had John Gloster, that we get some further tests done immediately. Sourav rejected these suggestions and said he would be "fine". When I queried what he meant by "fine" he said he would be fit for the Test match. I then queried why then was it necessary to be off the field now. He said that he was just taking "precautions".

Rather than make a scene with other players and officials in the vicinity I decided to leave the matter and observe what Sourav would do from that point on. After the loss of Kaif, Yuvraj and [Dinesh] Karthik to the new ball, Sourav returned to the crease with the ball now around 20 overs old. He struggled for runs against a modest attack and eventually threw his wicket away trying to hit one of the spinners over the leg side.

The next day I enquired with a number of the players as to what they had thought of Sourav's retirement. The universal response was that it was "just Sourav" as they recounted a list of times when Sourav had suffered from mystery injuries that usually disappeared as quickly as they had come. This disturbed me because it confirmed for me that he was in a fragile state of mind and it was affecting the mental state of other members of the squad. When we arrived in Bulawayo I decided I needed to ask Sourav if he had overplayed the injury to avoid the danger period of the new ball as it had appeared to me and others within the touring party that he had protected himself at the expense of others. He denied the suggestion and asked why he would do that against such a modest attack. I said that he was the only one who could answer that question.

I was so concerned about the affect that Sourav's actions were having on the team that I decided I could not wait until selection meeting that evening to inform him that I had serious doubts about picking him for the first Test.

I explained that, in my view, I felt we had to pick Kaif and Yuvraj following their good form in the one-day series and that [Virender] Sehwag, [Gautam] Gambhir, [V.V.S.]Laxman and [Rahul] Dravid had to play. He said that his record was better than Kaif and Yuvraj and that they had not proved themselves in Test cricket. I countered with the argument that they had to be given a chance to prove themselves on a consistent basis or we would never know. I also said that their form demanded that they be selected now.

Sourav asked me whether I thought he should be captain of the team. I said that I had serious doubts that he was in the right frame of mind to do it. He asked me if I thought he should step down. I said that it was not my decision to make, that only he could make that decision, but if he did make that decision he had to do it in the right manner or it would have even more detrimental effects than if he didn't stand down. I said that now was not the time to make the decision but that we should discuss it at the selection meeting to be held later in the day.

Sourav then said that if I didn't want him to be captain then he would inform Rahul Dravid that he was going to stand down. I reiterated that it was not my decision to make but he should give it due consideration under the circumstances but not to do it hastily. At that point Sourav went to Rahul and the two of them conferred briefly and then Sourav left the field and entered the dressing room. At that stage I joined the start of the training session.

A short time later Mr [Amitav] Chowdhary [the team manager] came on to the field and informed me that Sourav had told him that I did not want him as captain and that Sourav wanted to leave Zimbabwe immediately if he wasn't playing. I then joined Mr Chowdhary and Rahul Dravid in the *dressing room where we agreed that this was not the outcome that any of us wanted and that the ramifications would not be in the best interests of the team.*

We then spent some time with Sourav and eventually convinced him that he should stay on as captain for the two Tests and then consider his future. In my view it was not an ideal solution but it was better than the alternative of him leaving on a bad note. I believe he has earned the right to leave in a fitting manner. We all agreed that this was a matter that should stay between us and should not, under any circumstances, be discussed with the media.

The matter remained quiet until the press conference after the game when a journalist asked Sourav if he had been asked to step down before the Test. Sourav replied that he had but he did not want to elaborate and make an issue of it. I was then called to the press conference where I was asked if I knew anything of Sourav being asked to step down before the game. I replied that a number of issues had been raised regarding selection but as they were selection matters I did not wish to make any further comment.

Apart from a brief interview on ESPN before which I emphasized that I did not wish to discuss the issue because it was a selection matter I have resisted all other media approaches on the matter.

Since then various reports have surfaced that I had threatened to resign. I do not know where that rumour has come from because I have spoken to no one in regard to this because I have no intention of resigning. I assume that some sections of the media, being starved of information, have made up their own stories.

At the completion of the Test match I was approached by V.V.S. Laxman with a complaint that Sourav had approached him on the eve of the Test saying that I had told Sourav that I did not want Laxman in the team for Test matches. I denied that I had made such a remark to Sourav, or anybody else for that matter, as, on the contrary, I saw Laxman as an integral part of the team. He asked how Sourav could have said what he did. I said that the only way we could go to the bottom of the matter was to speak to Sourav and have him repeat the allegation in front of me.

I arranged for a meeting with the two of them that afternoon. The meeting took place just after 6 p.m. in my room at the Rainbow Hotel in Bulawayo. I told Sourav that Laxman had come to me complaining that Sourav had made some comments to Laxman prior to the Test. I asked Sourav if he would care to repeat the comment in my presence. Sourav then rambled on about how I had told him that I did not see a place for Laxman in one-day cricket, something that I had discussed with Sourav and the selection panel and about which I had spoken to Laxman at the end of the Sri Lankan tour.

Sourav mentioned nothing about the alleged conversation regarding Laxman and Test cricket even when I pushed him on it later in the discussion. As we had to leave for a team function we ended the conversation without Sourav adequately explaining his comments to Laxman.

Again, this is not an isolated incident because I have had other players come to me regarding comments that Sourav had made to them that purport to be comments from me to Sourav about the particular player. In each case the comments that Sourav has passed on to the individual are figments of Sourav's imagination. One can only assume that he does it to unnerve the individual who, in each case, has been a middle order batsman.

Sourav has missed the point of my discussions with him on this matter. It has less to do with his form than it does with his attitude toward the team. Everything he does is designed to maximize his chance of success and is usually detrimental to someone else's chances.

Despite meeting with him in Mumbai after his appointment as captain and speaking with him about these matters and his reluctance to do the preparation and training that is expected of everyone else in the squad he continues to set a bad example.

Greg King's [the team's physical trainer] training reports continue to show Sourav as the person who does the least fitness and training work based on the criterion that has been developed by the support staff to monitor the work load of all the players.

We have also developed parameters of batting, bowling, fielding and captaincy that we believe embodies the "Commitment to Excellence" theme that I espoused at my interview and Sourav falls well below the acceptable level in all areas. I will be pleased to present this documentation when I meet with the special committee in Mumbai later this month.

I can assure you sir that all my actions in this matter, and all others since my appointment, have been with the aim of improving the team performance toward developing a team that will represent India with distinction in Test match and one-day cricket.

As I said to you during our meeting in Colombo, I have serious reservations about the attitude of some players and about Sourav and his ability to take this team to a new high, and none of the things he has done since his reappointment has caused me to change my view. In fact, it has only served to confirm that it is time for him to move on and let someone else build their [sic] team toward the 2007 World Cup.

This team has been made to be fearful and distrusting by the rumour mongering and deceit that is Sourav's modus operandi of divide and rule. Certain players have been treated with favour, all of them bowlers, while others have been shunted up and down the order or left out of the team to suit Sourav's whims.

John Wright obviously allowed this to go on to the detriment of the team. I am not prepared to sit back and allow this to continue or we will get the same results we have been seeing for some time now.

It is time that all players were treated with fairness and equity and that good behaviours [sic] and attitudes are rewarded at the selection table rather than punished.

I can assure you of my very best intentions.

Yours sincerely,
Greg Chappell MBE

Since the email was leaked to a leading Bengali daily in Kolkata and was, thereafter, carried by a number of other Indian newspapers and the issue became rather a public affair, the BCCI summoned Chappell and Ganguly before, among others, Sunil Gavaskar, Srinivas Venkataraghavan and Ravi Shastri, to present their respective versions of events. Following this, the panel recommended that both should forget and forgive and move on. But the Indian selectors, headed by Kiran More, came down heavily in Chappell's favour.

Even though Ganguly stood somewhat exposed on the basis of Chappell's message to Mahendra, the selection committee could have, in a civilized manner, conveyed to him that he no longer figured in their plans. This would have given him an opportunity to announce his retirement, if he wanted to take this route. He had, by this stage, already lost the captaincy. But far from More and company handling the matter with finesse, they recalled Ganguly for two test matches against Sri Lanka before dropping him for the third. Ganguly failed in the first, but scored 40 and 39 in the second, featuring in useful partnerships of 121 and 92.

It is suspected in some quarters that relations between More and Ganguly were a bit strained. The latter, enjoying the patronage of the powerful Dalmiya, may have at times given short shrift to the head selector. Besides, when More and another selector, Pranab Roy, were accused by Abhijit Kale, a Maharashtra Ranji Trophy player, of seeking bribes to pick him in an Indian squad, Ganguly, in a statement, seemed to sympathize with this cricketer.

Ganguly's exclusion created a furore in political circles in India. His state of West Bengal was on the verge of elections. Its Marxist chief minister, Buddhadeb Bhattacharyya, astoundingly, twisted this to be an injustice against Bengal and Bengalis by India's central cricketing establishment. The provincial president of his rival Congress party, Pranab Mukherjee (also then Union defence minister), too, demanded Ganguly's reinstatement. Both have little knowledge about the game; and therefore, shamelessly indulged in naked populism. Street demonstrations rocked Kolkata, protestors burnt effigies of Chappell and More and there was widespread talk of conspiracy against Bengal's favourite son. The politicians were only too happy to fan such flames.

The president of the BCCI, Sharad Pawar, a former chief minister of Maharashtra and later the food and agriculture minister at the Centre, is also only remotely familiar with cricket. His closest link to the sport is the fact that his father-in-law, Sadashiv Shinde, a leg-spinner, appeared in seven tests for India and once captured eight wickets in a match against England at Delhi in 1951, including six for 91 in the first innings.

In the BCCI's quixotic constitution, their president has the final say in the selection of a party for an overseas tour. From all indications, Pawar, a shrewd public figure, subtly but patently invoked such powers to reinduct Ganguly in the squad for Pakistan in

2005–06. Pawar meaningfully dined with the selectors on the eve of their meeting to select the side. Again, Ganguly battled to notch up 34 and 37 in a losing cause at Karachi, but was, thereafter, peremptorily exiled.

Dravid and Chappell managed to arrest India's slump in one-dayers since 2003 by thrashing higher ranked Sri Lanka and Pakistan and drawing with South Africa (they also beat lower placed England). But the Indians met their match in the unfancied West Indians, who beat them 4–1 in the Caribbean, and also held the wooden spoon in a triangular series with the Windies and Australia at Kuala Lumpur. The Indian juggernaut was, thus, brought to a juddering halt.

Having recorded their success on flat, unseaming wickets in the subcontinent, India's batsmen were beguiled by the tennis-ball type bounce in the Caribbean. Accustomed to hitting on the 'up', they either mistimed or played too early. It was a shambles. Dravid crafted a match-winning hundred in the first match, Virender Sehwag two 90s and Mohammed Kaif and Yuvraj Singh three and two fifties, respectively. But as a unit, they went progressively downhill after narrowly losing the second and third encounters.

In bowling, their rising star of recent years, Irfan Pathan demonstrated a fade-out. Only the medium pacer, Ajit Agarkar, and to a certain extent, Harbhajan Singh, the off-spinner, both previously experienced in West Indian conditions, seemed to appreciate the ropes. The others were either expensive or inconsistent.

Perhaps the lesson was timely and a blessing in disguise. There was nothing in the problem that cannot be fixed. Tendulkar is a worry, but a genuine return to form by him could correct the fragility in the batting. At the same time, Sehwag needs to perform. The chances are, the ball will come on to the bat a bit more in the World Cup, thus curtailing the confusion created by a contradictory pace and bounce. Even if this doesn't happen, the Indians would have had the benefit of knowing what to expect and can devise a strategy accordingly.

In bowling, India can only hope that Pathan's loss of form was temporary and not something more serious. His promise as an all-rounder, though, keeps him in the frame. In the interim, though, Munaf Patel has emerged as a disciplined right-arm fast bowler, Sreesanth has enhanced his pace and wicket-taking ability and Zaheer Khan, though slower than before, has made a stirring comeback. Movement in the air is generally not such a critical factor in the West Indies.

The Queen's Park Oval at Port of Spain, where all of India's Group Stage matches will be held, has, over the years, been its happiest hunting ground in the West Indies. This is where they have won three tests and two ODIs, except that they lost both their limited-overs outings here in 2006. The tracks at this venue have traditionally been spinner friendly. But judging by recent evidence, this may not be the character of wickets in the 2007 World Cup.

Assuming Dravid's squad advance to the Super Eight, their first two matches will be at Antigua, the next at Georgetown and the last three at Bridgetown. Then, if India finish either first or fourth, their semi-final will be at St Lucia, or at Kingston, if they stand second or third.

In the past, one of the perquisites of hosting the World Cup has been, within reasonable bounds, to have a say in the preparation of pitches. It would be unfair if such a privilege were withdrawn by the ICC, for the West Indies have previously always endured away conditions. Bitten by visiting pacemen in recent years, though, the West Indians are, now, understandably shy of offering fast tracks to opposition, who might exploit them better. If historical data is any guide, Sabina Park would have greater 'carry', while venues in the Eastern Caribbean, other than Bridgetown, are likely to be more melancholic. However, with the West Indies based at Kingston – and after Brian Lara's outburst against the wicket at Sabina Park for the India test in July 2006 – it would be a brave official who would defy his diktat.

In summary, though, it's hard to be convinced that Australia will not be a serious contender for the crown. But the West Indies have provided enough indication of late, including their performance in the Champions Trophy in the autumn of 2006, to suggest they will be a hard nut to crack in their natural habitat. South Africa reached the semi-final in 1992 and 1999, and, thereby, demonstrated promise of better things to come. Having disappointed at home in 2003, they could this time around be doubly determined. Besides, New Zealand have depth in their batting and an awkward attack, spearheaded by Shane Bond.

Pakistan's prospects depend on whether they are at full strength and in the right frame of mind. Their major concern apart from uncertainty in the pace department, could be an opening combination. It is, naturally, ideal to capitalize with the bat when fielding restrictions apply.

Sri Lanka, after receiving a battering from India, have bounced back remarkably under their new Australian coach, Tom Moody. Indeed, their performance in England and New Zealand in 2006 validated they can also be a threat outside their home comfort zone. They may not enjoy extra bounce, but could relish any lack of pace.

As for India, a middle order drawn from, Dravid, Yuvraj Singh (if available and back at his best), Mohammed Kaif, Ganguly and Laxman (assuming that the last two re-establish their (one-day credentials), with Dhoni to follow, may serve the purpose, but also weaken the fielding potential. The Indian selectors are, now headed by Dilip Vengsarkar.

Kumble and Harbhajan, though, are capable of containing all but the most skilful players of spin. Indeed, on even remotely turning surfaces, they could be match-winners. But the dilemma for the Indians might be: do they play their five best bowlers or adopt horses for courses?

At present, the problem of Indian cricket is one of disproportionately high returns for players. While a handsome remuneration can be an incentive, this can also be a deterrent to determination and diligence. It may be, unviable to reverse the clock, but a system of bonus linked to productivity could be beneficial for Indian cricket.

For India, with such vast resources and a high-profile coach, but an inferiority complex vis-a-vis sport in general, the riddle could be as much in the mind. They have, thus, employed the West Indian sports psychologist, Rudi Webster, to assist their effort. Chappell considers him to be among the best he has ever interacted with. Can Webster, who briefly worked with the Indians in the Caribbean in 2006, inject them with a killer instinct and a mental resilience to bridge the gap between potential and performance? If he succeeds, it will only prove the Indians were innately instilled with mettle, for the caress of the whip only works on thoroughbreds!

Index